RAGGED
DICKS

RAGGED
DICKS

Masculinity, Steel, and the
Rhetoric of the Self-Made Man

JAMES V. CATANO

Southern Illinois University Press
Carbondale and Edwardsville

Epigraph to chapter 5, excerpt from "Cumberland Blues" by Robert
Hunter, © 1970, 1996, 1997, 1998, 1999 by Robert Hunter.

A previous version of chapter 7 entitled "Entrepreneurial
Masculinity: Re-tooling the Self-Made Man," *Journal of American
Culture* 23.2 (2001), was published by Bowling Green State
University Popular Press.

Library of Congress Cataloging-in-Publication Data
Catano, James, V., 1950–
    Ragged dicks : masculinity, steel, and the rhetoric of the self-made man /
James V. Catano.
        p. cm.
    Includes bibliographical references and index.
    1. Men—United States—Psychology. 2. Masculinity—United States.
    3. Self-reliance—United States. 4. Success—United States. 5. Iron and steel
    workers—United States. 6. American literature—History and criticism.
    7. Masculinity in literature. 8. Rhetoric and psychology. 9. Men in litera-
    ture. I. Title.

    HQ1090.3 .C4 2001
    305.31'0973—dc21
                                                            00-053830
    ISBN 0-8093-2395-8 (pbk. : alk. paper)

For Frances and Albert Westbrook,
Margaret and Dominic Catano,
and Annette and Lucien Massé.
Their labor made this work possible.

Contents

Acknowledgments

AS A SCHOLARLY PROJECT, THIS WORK HAS GONE ON a bit longer than I'd like to admit. I have no such qualms in admitting that its endurance and ultimate appearance are a testament to the work of innumerable people who have contributed much to the book's production and, equally important, the experiences and ensuing complex motives that helped generate it. As for the book itself, I especially thank Anna Nardo, whom I trusted as a close, critical, and blessedly creative reader at a moment when I was not putting much trust in the writer. Michelle Massé provided the same kind of reading for the whole project and for its bits and pieces, which I blithely offered—mosaic-like—and which she read as if there were a unity she could see that I could not. I thank Robert Scholes as well, who never blinked when I presented him with that cliché of the business: a partial manuscript offered at MLA and a request that he read the rest when he had time—preferably as soon as possible. I gave Ed White much the same great deal, and he responded in the same generous fashion. My thanks also to Suzanne Clark and William Covino, whose close readings and detailed commentary were invaluable. I also thank two people who have known when and when not to ask about how the project was going: Andreas Hansen and Rick Moreland. Thanks also to Malcolm Richardson, the right chair at the right time. Finally, I thank Karl Kageff, who expressed interest from the start, took time out from the controlled chaos of the book exhibit at MLA to discuss the manuscript in detail, and has displayed a remarkable combination of professional acumen, generous support, and timely suggestions. That blend of professionalism and generosity has equally been a hallmark of my work with Carol Burns, Barb Martin, Wayne Larsen, and Marie Maes. My thanks to them and the press. I am also grateful to Louisiana State University for providing a Council on Research Grant that allowed me to work at the New York Public Library and to whose staff I also offer thanks for helping me to work in their holdings on turn-of-the-(last)-century popular fiction.

There is more to this book, at least for me, than lies within its own boundaries, however. I've tried to acknowledge in my dedication the most important of those people without whose support, drive, and yes, work, this project would not even have been begun. But there are others who contributed in ways that they, and I, couldn't have known at the time. I need to acknowledge the impact on me of people with and for whom I worked as a member of the United Steelworkers of America, Local 3081, Union Carbide's Ferro-Alloys Division, Ashtabula, Ohio. The list is long and admittedly incomplete, but Chuck Elliott remains a first among equals. He put a lot of untried kids to work—and a lot of them through college—just because he believed we could and would do the job. Somehow, we did—in my case most probably because of the talents of the furnace men, mix men and crane operators, head tappers, and tappers' helpers, sample men, and admittedly even some of the foremen with whom I worked: Bill Brunty, Howard Campbell, Dead-Fly, Paul Frabutt, Walt "Hatchet-Man" Harris, Clarence Johnson, Karl Keller, Bill Lovas and Wayne Lynn (on whose memories and work tales I rely even now), Lorne Merritt, Possum, Joe Rapose, Chris Savarese, Strawberry, Harry Whysong, Columbus Williams, and everyone else my poor memory has let go. I am indebted to you all. I owe a similar if more personal debt to those whose support was familial rather than shop floor, most particularly to Beth and Michael Goodwin, to Doris Massé and Gerard Byrne, and to their children. Solidarity, mutuality, support—those words work just as nicely in the family as in the workplace. Lastly, there is one more indebtedness and one more thank-you I need to declare. This book has been with us over a long and interesting period, and it carries some of our history as well. Thank you, Michelle.

RAGGED
DICKS

Introduction

After all, this is just a story about a kid from a good immigrant
family who studied hard and worked hard, who had some big successes and some big disappointments, and who made out fine in the
end because of the simple values he learned from his parents and
teachers, and because he had the good luck to live in America.
—Lee Iacocca, *Iacocca*

Rags to riches. Sons of truck drivers growing up to be millionaires.
It could only happen in . . . Finland?
 . . . Markus Jäntti, who teaches at the Academy of Finland,
surveyed existing comparisons of fathers' and sons' incomes in
Britain, Canada, Finland, Germany, Malaysia, Sweden, and the
United States. He found that the United States had less mobility
between generations than any country except Britain. . . .
 "The United States is exceptional," Dr. Jäntti writes, "only inso-
far as it has extraordinarily high relative income differences."
—*Chronicle of Higher Education*, 31 January 1997

AMERICA IS IN LOVE WITH THE MYTH OF THE SELF-MADE MAN—reports from
Dr. Jäntti and the *Chronicle* be damned. Neither of them has the audience—or the emotional appeal—of Lee Iacocca and his immensely popular self-portrait, one of many such tales that abound in Western and
especially American culture. Positive and negative, admittedly fictional
and ostensibly factual, narratives such as these are not only wide ranging but also durable, making the self-made man a central myth within
the history of the United States. Extending backward from Iacocca to
Benjamin Franklin, the most well known and stereotypical endorsements of the myth remain the late-nineteenth-century's broad, middle-
class stories of masculine self-making known as Horatio Alger tales:
morally uplifting stories that enact a successful struggle to overcome
less than spectacular origins and reap justly deserved economic and personal rewards.
 The Ragged Dicks of this book make up a brotherhood that is commonly exemplified in corporate magnates such as Lee Iacocca of *Iacocca*

1

fame or the prototypical self-made man of the Gilded Age, steel baron Andrew Carnegie as manifested in the pages of his own *Autobiography.* But self-makers and attempted self-makers are not always the rich and the famous—or even the successfully self-made. Also owing allegiance to the myth and its rhetoric are ironworkers and steelworkers such as Frederick Whittaker's nineteenth-century "Man of Iron," Larry Locke; Thomas Bell's ethnic immigrants and turn-of-the-century steelworkers George Kracha, Joe Dubik, and John Dobrejcak; modern African American furnace men and day laborers such as William Attaway's Big Mat, Connie Porter's Samuel Taylor, and Wideman's Harry Wideman; Preston's contemporary "Hot Metal Men"; Cameron's futuristic and literally hot metal man, Cyberdyne System Model 101 (a.k.a. "The Terminator"); and myriad such characters and figures from mid-nineteenth- and twentieth-century autobiographies, biographies, novels, obituaries, op-ed pieces, films, and most every form of cultural enactment available or imaginable.

Neither corporate barons nor ultimately self-made men, these steel-working men and literal men of steel are yoked to their corporate brethren by more than the myth's broad appeals to success. The rhetorical dynamic performed by all these figures is part of a vital cultural discourse that moves the story from components and claims about masculine self-making and into the process of making masculinity itself. The myth of the self-made man is, in short, a particular part of ongoing rhetorical practices that are constitutive of society, culture, and subjects—in this case, of the specific activities known as masculinity.

Masculinity is rule-governed practice, I am arguing here, a practice performed and maintained—culturally and individually—through and in terms of preset rhetorical arguments. In Judith Butler's terms, gender practice is "a public action" whose performance "is effected with the strategic aim of maintaining gender within its binary frame—an aim that cannot be attributed to the subject, but, rather, must be understood to found and consolidate the subject" (*Trouble* 140), although not to totally determine it. That maintaining of gender may be effected, of course, through direct rhetorical regulation—laws concerning marriage are one ready example. Such maintenance is a form of visible social argument, a clear maintaining of what masculine practice is and is to be. But at least equally important to gender maintenance are more complex rhetorical arguments and enactments that serve to naturalize gender practice, cultural arguments that rely upon nonconscious assent to underwrite and validate their particular enactment of masculinity. In Bourdieu's terms, gender is a set of internalized rules, attitudes, and performative behaviors, a body of "mythico-ritual representations" whose enactment produces *doxa,* a "quasi-perfect correspondence" between an assumed objectivity in the natural world and a subjective experience of the social and the cultural (164).

Ultimately, both direct and indirect forms of gender maintenance—laws and myths, for example—are dependent upon arguments that are motivated and underwritten by *doxa,* a complex set of desires, needs, rituals, beliefs, and practices that are internalized, and naturalized, by the members of a society. As I use the terms here, *doxa* operates as the "self-evident givens" of masculinity, and the myth of self-making is a particular form and reinforcement of *doxa.* Any specific enactment of the myth, such as Iacocca's opening claim, can never be innocent, then; it is always implicated in the overall mythic and doxic rhetoric, whether a particular enactment is seen as supportive or subversive. Experienced within this framework, masculinity is an oscillation or negotiation (as in negotiating a minefield) between a dominant mythic rhetoric and the particulars of a personal situation, "a reenactment and reexperiencing of a set of meanings already socially established . . . [and] the mundane and ritualized form of their legitimation" (Butler, *Trouble* 140). The particular rhetoric enacted by and through the myth of the self-made man (in culture and in this study) engages just such a set of historical, material, and psychological meanings in order to argue masculine success and successful masculinity.

My use of myth to describe this particular form of gender enactment is not intended to reduce such practices to the level of simple, personal fantasies or even cultural delusions. I do not separate mythic rhetoric from social realities or see mythmaking as a primitive cultural function replaced by later rational processes. The persuasive power of the myth of masculine self-making exists precisely because, in Laura Mulvey's words, it "flourishes at the point where the social and the psychoanalytic overlap, redolent of fascination and anxiety and generating both creative energy (stories, images) and the 'taming and binding' process through which collective contact with the unconscious is masked" (166). The particularly complex "taming and binding" of the myth of the self-made man is revealed by its own dirty little secret regarding masculine self-making. The deep irony of masculine self-making lies in its claim to offer the ultimate in freely formed, self-created individualism, while it actually serves to establish a social subject, a set of behavioral patterns and expectations that are already prescripted, as it were. Rephrasing Butler, the myth of self-making and its paradoxical claims for an unfettered act of personal self-making really enact a masculinity that "'works' to the extent that *it draws on and covers over* the constitutive conventions by which it is mobilized" (*Bodies* 227).[1]

In order to explain the capacity of the myth to cover over the glaring contradiction between its enactment of bounded gender practice within an argument of self-making, I am arguing that the rhetoric achieves not a little of its persuasive power by actively engaging desires and anxieties about masculinity and agency readily describable through—because ascribable to—the engendering process noted in the psychoanalytic narrative of preoedipal separation, oedipal conflict, and "proper" post-oedipal self-definition and socialization.[2] Variations and emphases, such as a gender-based preference for oedipal or male-centered motifs of individual struggle rather than preoedipal or female-weighted descriptions of mutuality, or the stressing of craft over industrial labor even in the face of historical change, serve to reveal the active, "maintaining" nature of myth's rhetorical activity and its role in refusing to acknowledge tensions and anxieties within masculinity about self-making or being made. These combined social, psychological, and rhetorical dynamics are reinforced, I'm also arguing, by a Lacanian sense of the constitutive power of language and rhetoric, a power that while not necessarily completely causative is undeniably formative in culture and society, and in the individual subject's relation to them. In using psychoanalysis as a basis for rhetorical analysis in this way, I basically am attempting to weave a relationship between rhetoric and the domains of the cultural, the social, and the personal.

The specific myth of self-making offers a particularly useful door into that complex relationship, providing a "fixed" form of reference to interrogate the fluidity of gender suggested by Bourdieu's ritual practice and Butler's performativity. But even though I am limiting my concern to the particular myth of masculine self-making, I have to admit that I can't introduce all the materials that make up its myriad versions; the myth is simply too ubiquitous in American culture. My decisions concerning how to focus the discussion further are partly experiential. Simply stated, my own training as a man makes me most familiar with the gendered emphasis of this version. That experiential emphasis is also related to my decision to center most of the materials that I discuss on steelmakers and steelmaking. My experiences as a steelworker in Union Carbide's Ferro-Alloys furnaces and as a member of the United Steel Workers have fostered a particular interest in this industry. In addition, I believe that doing justice to workplace description requires focusing on aspects central, and perhaps particular to, the workplace itself, an assumption that necessarily limits the variety of work that can be discussed. Finally, and perhaps most importantly, the steel industry has a long-standing history as a premier arena for not only rhetoricizing masculinity but also enacting masculine values seen as central to—indeed too often equivalent to—national values. Steelmaking and its dangers; its raw power, huge consumption of energy, and Promethean drive to produce a product seen as alternatively molten, malleable, and the backbone of the nation's economic and urban rise—all these images contribute to the centrality of steel in masculine mythmaking.

Such masculinized imagery and experience is regularly rewritten to align it with middle-class white experience, demonstrating a ready rhetorical process that appropriates or drowns out other voices in order to maintain not just a myth of masculinity but the dominant myth of masculinity. That appropriative process is a key concern in this study. I am not, finally, using my focus on masculine self-making to privilege an already privileged discourse. Like Judith Butler, I am aware that focusing on not only a heterosexual matrix but also heterosexual masculinity is to "run the risk of narrowness." But accepting that risk also helps reveal masculinity's assumed "priority and autonomy as a form of power" (*Bodies* 19). My overall purpose is thus not to privilege the myth of masculinity nor its dominant form but exactly the opposite: to display the conventional and problematic nature of what passes as a representation of "natural" masculine behavior, the product of a valid, "natural" frame as in reality an aspect of a much more complex and multiple cultural discourse.

That impulse motivates my contrasting of the dominant, middle-class myth (as exemplified in Carnegie's *Autobiography of Andrew Carnegie* or Preston's *American Steel: Hot Metal Men and the Resurrection of the Rust Belt*) with other variant or subversive forms, such as those with deepseated allegiance to working-class concerns (works such as Whittaker's *Larry Locke: Man of Iron; or, A Fight for Fortune: A Story of Labor and Capital,* for example).[3] The restrictive "rules" of gender practice may not be immediately obvious in a dominant myth's direct and supposedly historically endorsed paean to free and open self-making, such as is readily found in Andrew Carnegie's *Autobiography.* There, the rhetoric of self-making is conflated with the rhetoric of success, and troubling concerns over the agency ostensibly enacted through one's own self-making are allayed by this vision of unalloyed success. Such coverage can slip, however in a labor-oriented work such as Whittaker's *Larry Locke,* in which the dominant myth's rhetoric of masculine individuality and singular aggression may conflict with other arguments enacted by working-class needs for mutuality and solidarity, and even with labor history itself.

Such variant and possibly subversive forms of the myth, in which masculine self-making often is troubled by issues of class or race, offer intimations of alternative masculinities at odds with the dominant myth. And even the most ostensibly untroubled versions of the myth enact a masculinity to which most individual subjects have a nonsymmetrical relationship, exacerbating ongoing tensions between personal experience and the *doxa* of masculine identity. But the subversiveness of any rhetoric of self-making is limited by a variety of factors, not the least being a basic complicity in the broad project of masculinity that any subversive form threatens to reveal as a construct in toto. Committed to that overarching cultural practice, and often lacking the means to break out of the essential frame of its rhetorical practice, subversive versions not only repeat basic elements of the dominant frame but can even be co-opted as examples of the need for more effort in self-making, a more thorough performance of the masculinity argued in the dominant myth. Mythic rhetoric, I am arguing in the end, is a means by and through which masculinity is always—even though incompletely—enacted and maintained in and by both society and subject so as to preserve some felt measure of acceptable identity.

These complex tensions, desires, and needs—and their nonresolution—characterize the mythic rhetoric of masculine self-making and serve to motivate the basic goal of this study: to reveal how enactment of the "self-made man" reproduces and maintains masculinity by entangling it in narratives of economic and family life. In taking up that pursuit in the rest of this introduction, I want to establish a pattern that I will follow through the rest of the book as a whole. First, if gender performance is to be seen as rhetorical (and therefore sociocultural and subjective) practice, it is important to do more than simply label it as such and then move on to interpretations of various examples. Since part of my argument is that mythic rhetoric functions by enacting sophisticated sociocultural and psychological dynamics, what I want to do at the outset, in both this introduction and the ensuing chapters, is discuss current connections between rhetoric and psychoanalysis that provide the basic foundation for my claims. No mythic rhetoric operates in a historical or material vacuum, of course. Having established the basic theoretical frame of my argument, I am going to concentrate the interpretive sections of this study (primarily chapters 3–7) on the myth within the United States, focusing on the period from 1835 to the present—key years as regards gender, social, and industrial formation—so as to discuss the impact of context on the overall pattern of the myth.[4] Taken all together, these elements make up what I put forward here as the activity of mythic rhetoric, specifically that rhetorical performance known as masculinity and most particularly its enactment in the myth of the self-made man.

Rhetoric, Social Myth, and Psychoanalysis

The importance of rhetoric and rhetorical thinking to issues of social construction and agency has been discussed extensively over the last twenty-five years. These studies make clear that to speak of a "rebirth" in rhetoric is to do serious disservice to history, not to mention departments of rhetoric, speech, and communication, where rhetoric has forged a largely unbroken chain extending from the Western classical period to the present. Nevertheless, there are two factors, each related by an interest in language as an activity rather than an entity, that I see as most immediately and usefully aligned with the growing interest in rhetoric and my purposes here. The first factor arises not from rhetorical needs per se but from the desire in many varieties of literary theory to shift critical focus from an apotheosized and sanitized "high" literature to an "interested" literature read in terms of its contextualized nature: material, historical, social, and so on. The second factor is also somewhat "external": the reconceptualizing of language from an innocent, referential medium to one deeply involved in the production and maintenance of culture and knowledge itself.

Such questions are, of course, part of the history of rhetoric and the reactions of society to it from its earliest formalization in the West. By participating in these concerns, rhetoric ensures its relevance to them all. At the same time, as helpmate to all, rhetoric risks becoming subaltern to all, losing its own status as a discipline worthy of study at a level of equal interest and intensity. Those familiar with rhetorical history recognize this dilemma from arguments as early as the Socratic dialogues. Even today, various studies regularly use rhetoric as a convenient, and conveniently undefined, term. Worse yet, rhetoric still is regularly presented as a mere system for conveying knowledge, commonly via the shopworn claim "That's nothing but rhetoric." I don't think it's necessary to resolve a twenty-five-hundred-year-old argument in order to adequately respond to this situation. Rather, the issue for me is one of providing complexity and emphasis adequate to current interests and needs. Rephrased once again in terms of my goals, contemporary rhetorical concerns must be defined so as to contribute to understanding the complicated psychosocial practices they enact, especially in complex dynamics such the myth of the self-made man.[5]

Once defined as a socially constructive process, rhetoric produces a key question: To what degree is that process determinative; to what degree does it allow for free agency—or self-making? In current terms, what is the role of language or rhetoric in subject formation? This issue has led to numerous connections between rhetoric and sociopsychological interpretation, such as those Mailloux uses to unite rhetorical pragmatism and cultural rhetoric. In his framework, "'culture' gets defined as 'the network of rhetorical practices that are extensions and manipulations of other practices—social, political, and economic'" (qtd. in *Reception* 54–55). "Rhetoric is not simply an expression or reflection of 'deeper' historical forces, whether psychological, social, political, or economic. Rather, rhetorical practices are (at least partly) constitutive of these other historical categories" (*Reception* 55). Within such a frame-work, "rhetorical criticism is a self-conscious attempt to uncover the text's efforts to constitute the social and to bring to the foreground what may have been subtle or covert, unconscious or masked" (T. Poulakos, "Recovering" 39).

My own sense of rhetoric agrees with Mailloux's and Poulakos's criti-cal programs in general, although all three of us have differing empha-ses and claims. Where I differ most significantly from each is in my par-ticular emphasis on subject formation, that is, on gender as a rhetorical construct. As I use the concept, cultural rhetoric, enacted in specific myths, allows and requires complex behaviors necessary for and adequate to the complexities of society and subject formation. At the same time, neither myths nor gendered behaviors are in a simple cause/effect relationship. My sense of cultural myth is not designed to argue rhetorical effective-ness as the ability to resolve society's often contradictory charges to its members. The rhetorical power embodied in a myth instead lies precisely in enactment of psychological and social conflicts (exemplified in the myth's own internal contradictions) that cannot be readily resolved.

This incompleteness is emphasized in Butler's own definition of gen-der: "a norm that can never be fully internalized; the 'internal' is a sur-face signification, and gender norms are finally phantasmatic, impossible to embody. . . . The abiding gendered self will then be shown to be struc-tured by repeated acts that seek to approximate the ideal of a substantial ground of identity, but which, in their occasional *dis*continuity, reveal the temporal and contingent groundlessness of this 'ground'" (*Trouble* 141). This discontinuity between doxic myth and individual experience means that societies have a vested interest in continually maintaining cer-tain forms of behavior and myths, and in doing so in both senses of the word. That is, societies not only validate certain behaviors in a tendency toward "maintaining" the status quo, they also do so by affirming or "maintaining" that such behaviors are beneficial, acceptable, admirable.

The "self-made man" provides an opportunity to think concretely about the ensuing issues of social construction, agency, and masculinity from within the framework of cultural rhetoric. At the same time, a variety of contemporary feminists and cultural theorists provide the means for using psychoanalytic frameworks for further clarifying the general rhetorical process.[6] Quickly stated, these critics see gender prac-tices as a series of constraints, and in some cases even direct social as-saults, on a subject's sense of agency, a series of restrictions, reductions, reenactments, and refusals that are resolved with greater or lesser diffi-culty depending on the issue itself, the particular resolution, and the individual subject. Rephrased in the terms of my discussion, gender behavior can be seen as a rhetorical act that keeps arguing itself out in an attempt to clarify its own dynamics. Positive appeals to masculinist aggression or mutual brotherhood, for example, are regularly aligned with ongoing psychological anxieties that if a man is not correctly masculine, then he is something else. The most encompassing negative appeal is to association with the feminine, and American cultural myths draw heavily and continuously on the desires and fears that surround the resulting stereotypes.

The regular enactment of these needs and fears of feminization and dependency is embodied in the appeal to self-making as freedom from determining physical origins—an escape from family, class, or race. A second, less blatant appeal encourages departure from the general realm of the feminine with its daily interpersonal concerns, and a subsequent movement into the mythical realm of the workplace and its individual battles with patriarchal figures. This basic dynamic is furthered through regular overemphasis on oedipal struggle as a positive, agentive movement toward masculinity. Conversely, anxious concerns with mutuality, nonindividuality, and lack of agency (all symptomatized as feminine) are matched with underemphasis on preoedipal care and dependency and even more troubling possibilities of forced separation rather than chosen agency.[7] These arguments for masculine self-making are symptomatic of long-standing needs to address anxieties over the broad process of social structuring. It is not just the individual on Freud's couch that suffers trauma; it is the culture as a whole. If the rhetoric of gender enacts a widely accepted but faulty cultural myth, historical trauma is a moment in which these fault lines are intensified and particularly visible.

The historical trauma itself may vary either in kind or in intensity. One broad trauma is that alluded to within Susan Miller's novel, *The Good Mother:* the transition from the ideal of nineteenth-century rugged individualism, especially entrepreneurial self-making, to the middle-class reality of modern corporate life. More particularized trauma can be noted within specific historical events, specifically labor struggles leading to job actions such as the 1892 Homestead lockout at Carnegie's vast Homestead steelworks and the subsequent clashes between workers, company thugs, and governmental forces. At such moments, the social frame and its cultural rhetoric come under more than ordinary strain, and the society finds itself face to face with the incompleteness of its representations, resulting in accommodations not only by individual myths but also, in extreme cases, by the larger sociocultural frame. Change is not necessarily effected in such cases, but the possibility still must be addressed. Mythic rhetoric, in short, is a function of general psychocultural frames and the historical/material context in which the arguments are enacted.

History, Myth, and Self-Making

Two early analysts of mythic self-making, John Cawelti *(Apostles of the Self-Made Man)* and Irvin Wyllie *(The Self-Made Man in America: The Myth of Rags to Riches),* begin their historical studies by noting how their original projects—analyses of shifting concepts of success—had to be immediately and drastically qualified.[8] Both Cawelti and Wyllie pursue focus and control by stressing success as embodied in self-making. To further focus their studies, they select particular figures and particular representations of the myth. Not surprisingly, because money supposedly marks undeniable success in U.S. culture, the entrepreneurial myth of the self-made man receives much of their attention. Cawelti's ensuing categories are useful both in themselves and as a means of focusing and framing my own opening arguments. Cawelti's early and groundbreaking *Apostles of the Self-Made Man* uses a blend of theme and traditional sociohistorical description in identifying three interwoven strands in the myth over the last two centuries. These strands, particularly strong in the United States, are (1) the conservative Protestant ethic, (2) the formation of individual and social virtue codified by Jefferson and later embodied in the Emersonian dictates of self-reliance and the Chautauqua assemblies, and (3) the popular definition of the self-made entrepreneur, often broadly and somewhat incorrectly described as the Horatio Alger myth (4–6). The first strand—the conservative Protestant ethic—contains only a weak sense of social mobility, and I won't address it here. It is the second strand, established via Franklin, Jefferson, and Emerson, and especially the entrepreneurial third strand, that together dominate the popular versions of today and are most important to my approach.

The historical influence of industrialism and entrepreneurial variants notwithstanding, the Jeffersonian thread of the myth regularly appears as the heart of a democratic ideal of the free pursuit of personal and social growth, and that ideal constitutes one of the myth's ongoing appeals.[9] Despite popular misconceptions that emphasize economic values, personal development is often stressed in Horatio Alger's fiction as suitable reward for striving to achieve intellectual growth. In Alger's tales, the autodidact is the ultimate hero, and the tales' dual focus on personal growth and economic success lays at least equal stress on the former. These proto-entrepreneurial tales assume that poverty's child will be satisfied by a leap upward into a clerk's position, a move not into riches but into respectability (Cawelti 101), and one accomplished through luck and a patron capable of recognizing the hero's incipient self-making. In Alger's *Fame and Fortune,* for example, Ragged Dick "spends his evenings in study, engaged in a program of self-culture so ambitious it would have shamed Chautauquans"—the latter becoming a byword for adult education and entertainment programs extending from the lyceum movement of the early nineteenth century and into the Chautauqua Societies of the twentieth (Scharnhorst and Bales 87).

But Alger's Franklinian stress on self-education often placed his stories at odds with other, growing emphases on action and aggression. Indeed, later-nineteenth-century "culturally elite" readers question whether Alger's fiction is "manly" at all. "On the dimension of character," Carol Nackenoff suggests, "Alger boys are losing male identities. Characterization increasingly aligns the Alger hero with the wrong gender and wrong class." For elite readers, "Alger's characters came to look like . . . female characters" (221). At the same time, the ensuing ascendancy of the entrepreneurial strand (which is now somewhat inaccurately seen as the real Horatio Alger tale), established the pure, self-made individual not as quietly overlooking but as actively distancing him- or herself from all trammeling institutions, not the least being those of higher education. The choice between individual growth and modest success (as defined by traditional nineteenth-century programs of education and Alger) and upward mobility via economic power (as defined by the entrepreneurs) was easy for aspiring self-makers when they considered that higher education's halls were not only hallowed but also class defined. Whatever weight was given to the role of knowledge in acquiring personal success, then, the type offered by college training was dismissed as out of date and enervating. As Wyllie notes, in nineteenth-century entrepreneurial rhetoric, "higher learning undermined the rugged personal qualities necessary for success":

> Success demanded a strong will, diligence, persistence, ambition, good health, and self-discipline, qualities which colleges allegedly crippled and dwarfed in their concentration on the development of mental faculties. . . . [The college man was] thought to be deficient in determination, drive, and backbone, . . . awkward, hypersensitive, impatient, conceited, pedantic, confused, tactless, bookish, and utterly impractical. (102–3)

Although culturally elitist and entrepreneurial visions are opposed on the grounds of classical education, they also clearly share a gendered separation of the "real" world of masculine work and action from the feminine world of books and interpersonal dependency. That attitude is clearly apparent in the portrayal of working-class figures as feminized by the historical loss of the craft tradition and the resulting loss of self and workplace control:

> Workers were dissociated from emerging class-based images
> of manhood by their dependence on employers; loss of
> control over their activities; intemperance, violence, and un-
> restrained passion; performance of simple, manual labor; ab-
> sence of cultural refinement; and restricted ability to con-
> sume. They were even often exchangeable in the workplace
> with women and children. Engagement in production itself
> seemed to estrange one from manhood. Producing the *self*
> made one a man; producing *goods* made one not-a-man.
> (Nackenoff 221)

Faced with the dominant rhetoric, working-class versions of the self-made man display variations on the linkage between institutional dynamics, class bias, and creativity. As formalized in working-class dime novels of the nineteenth century, the nature of an institution rests in hierarchical control. As labor becomes increasingly dependent upon corporations, self-making lies not in scoffing at but in actively resisting institutional definition—both its control and its attacks on making, whether of self or product. "Far from being accounts of self-made men according to bourgeois standards of success," Michael Denning argues, "the [dime novel] tales are closer to the ethics embodied in the principles of the Knights of Labor: 'men wholly developed in all the attributes of manhood cannot become accumulators. . . .' Job Manly is not a manager, speculator, or fox: he wants to 'make things'" (171–72). Self-creativity is necessarily tied to job creativity, or at least to personal control of the means of production.

Studies such as Denning's attempt to address the resulting complexities of masculine engendering within its historical context, and there is a growing body of such work on which to draw. Michael S. Kimmel's *Manhood in America: A Cultural History* (1995) provides a useful addition to works such as those of Cawelti and Wyllie. Like Cawelti's and Wyllie's, Kimmel's overview of self-making considers materials from the Revolutionary War to current times, but his primary concern is with using the myth to explore masculinity, or the manhood of his title, which Cawelti and Wyllie tend to assume. As a cultural history of masculinity, Kimmel's work offers myriad reinforcements of my own claims regarding the rhetoric of masculine self-making. Of particular interest is Kimmel's reliance upon David Leverenz's *Manhood and the American Renaissance*. Leverenz himself supplements Cawelti's framework, and those of psychoanalytic critics, by producing a set of categories for describing classed and gendered dynamics in fiction. For Leverenz (and thus for Kimmel), categories of patrician, artisan, and entrepreneur characterize major groupings and themes affecting the representation and development of masculinity in the United States during the period from 1820 to 1860. The dominant conflicts are to be found in struggles between the patrician "mercantile and landowning elite and the new middle class of entrepreneurial businessmen" (3). In this frame, the individual masculine development represented by Jeffersonian patricianism and programs of higher education clashes with the masculine economic success touted by the industrial revolution.

All these class-based taxonomies work well to establish basic forms for description. Like all categorizations, they work even better by showing where and how such frames are inevitably broken and blended. Where Leverenz, for example, suggests that working-class consciousness is "continuously co-opted by artisan norms of manhood and middle-class expectations of upward mobility" (4), Denning posits a two-way street. Denning argues for influence up the class ladder as well as down, as does Nackenoff, who suggests that through "the mid-century rise of the dime novel, new working-class symbols of potency and maleness were created."[10] Characters like Frederick Whittaker's John Armstrong, Job Manly, and Larry Locke were all part of a "company of many more working-class heroes in a battle to retain control over the very definition of maleness in the Gilded Age" (222). This linked concern with masculinity, workplace control and productivity, and self-making is clearly displayed in characters' names and titles from Whittaker's stories: (1) *John Armstrong, Mechanic; or, From the Bottom to the Top of the Ladder: A Story of How a Man Can Rise in America;* (2) *A Knight of Labor; or, Job Manly's Rise in Life: A Story of a Young Man from the Country;* and (3) *Larry Locke, Man of Iron; or, A Fight for Fortune: A Story of Labor and Capital.*

These titles provide seemingly stereotypical, albeit working-class, enactments of individual self-making. But their emphasis on single figures hides a key, class-based tension in masculinity between individual and collective agency—a question rarely facing a Ragged Dick but one constantly before a Larry Locke: that is, the question of the role of unions. Unionization represents a historically significant possibility for shifting the material bases of power and control. It also offers real possibilities for reconceptualizing masculinity as solidarity and mutuality rather than individual self-agency. Yet there is a clear, built-in conflict between dominant masculinity, defined as self-made singularity, and that defined in terms of union mutuality—a definition fraught with overtones of dependency. That conflict replicates the narrative of oedipal masculine struggle and success versus preoedipal feminine dependency and failure. In addressing this tension, working-class myths of self-making all too regularly find themselves resolving the argument by encouraging pseudoheroic self-sacrifice or sentimental visions of individualism.

In most cases, the representations end up displaying the tensions of the dominant masculinity better than they actually resolve them, all manner of plot devices notwithstanding.

With turn-of-the-century near disappearance of craft traditions in industry and the rise of the modern corporation, nineteenth-century industrial rhetoric's more blatantly masculinized motifs of fistfights between workers and managers usually give way to internecine, boardroom struggles for corporate success. The modern myth of corporate advancement admits to the importance of education while still ignoring institutional hierarchies and priorities—along with sex, race, and class biases. Contemporary versions of both working-class and middle-class entrepreneurial myths thus shift away from direct anti-institutionalism and toward representations based on a carefully maintained blend of institutional vagueness and corporate prowess. However the categories are combined and applied, it is clear that the world of paid work outside the home maintains its long-standing role as one of *the* arenas of masculine engendering. Throughout all these historical changes, the mythic rhetoric continues to maintain itself and its effectiveness. How it achieves that rhetorical effectiveness across historical, class, and psychological boundaries forms the main argument of this study.

The constitution of the myth, from out of all the issues that I have discussed above, rests on the sociocultural need to dramatize the ambivalent desires and conflicting goals that are part and parcel of personal and social growth or, more accurately, the performing of a particular subject position. Such enactment of needs is invaluable in maintaining social organization and durability. The paradoxical power of a myth lies precisely in the fact that it engages specific psychological and social conflicts even though it cannot resolve them. Nor is this engagement an act of self-delusion, an escapist ritual that addresses ineffable mysteries beyond the reach of a culture's descriptive power. The contradictions can be unmasked and experienced as contradictions. A cultural myth is no more and no less than an effectively constructed, rhetorical enactment of the social and psychological conflicts that it embodies.

The progression of these arguments and of the chapters that make them follows both a theoretical and a historical design similar to that used in this introduction. Chapters 1 and 2 offer the basic underpinnings of the rhetorical model being argued, via union of rhetorical and psychoanalytic theory. Chapter 1 establishes the particular motifs and tropes of the myth in relation to basic connections between rhetoric, sociocultural knowledge, and psychoanalytic theory. Chapter 2 extends the claims and definitions made in the last section of chapter 1, adding contemporary concerns with the constitutive power of language in both psychoanalytic and rhetorical practice, and in social maintenance as a whole. Chapters 3–7 are interpretive chapters that analyze fictional and nonfictional representations of the rhetoric of masculine self-making that begin with the 1835 birth and subsequent entrepreneurial career of Andrew Carnegie and end with the collapse and attempted resurrection of the U.S. steel industry at the close of the twentieth century. Individual chapters may overlap the historical period of another as they take up earlier or later historical periods in order to address particular issues about masculinity more fully.

Chapter 3 continues the work of the first two by examining Carnegie's *Autobiography* and its role as the dominant, middle-class version of the American myth of masculine self-making as entrepreneurial success and upward mobility from within the tightened focus of my argument, which is centered on steelmaking. In its arguments, the chapter outlines the frame of the dominant myth in terms of its emphasis on male exchange and revision of preoedipal loss and fragmentation into an active separation to be lauded as the first step on the road to masculine self-making. Chapter 4 is paired oppositionally with chapter 3 and begins the process of analyzing nondominant variations in mythic rhetoric. It undertakes to demonstrate, via working-class enactments of the myth, the subtler gender dynamics that actually are at work in the particular rhetoric of masculine self-making and in cultural *doxa* as a whole. Concentrating on historical and conceptual shifts in steelmaking and its workplace, the discussions are of working-class versions whose own nonsymmetrical relation to the dominant myth serves to clarify general tensions and concerns in masculinity that *doxa* attempts to mask.

Chapters 5 and 6 further consider variations on the dominant myth via a key concern: separation as necessary to the acquisition of correctly masculine behaviors. Both chapters look at variations in this concern—immigration and ethnic/racial separation—in terms of their impact on both the desire for and the possibility of self-making. The book closes with chapter 7's discussion of mid- and end-of-the-century strains on self-making embodied in institutional and social shifts occurring over the period and in particular versions of the myth that subsequently are offered, again primarily narrowed to representations from within the steel industry. All the variations extol the virtues of masculine self-making, and all display its deep-seated contradictions. All, then, are active attempts to enact, consider, and understand the myth even as resolution or closure keeps moving beyond their boundaries. That, of course, is also the movement of this book.

1
Effective Rhetoric/Rhetorical Effects: Maintaining Masculinity

> My grandfather smiled at my father, the kind, condescending smile of a teacher to a particularly backward child. "I'm a self-made man, David. Let me tell you what that means. That means no . . . pension plan, for example. No company ladder to climb, to protect you every step of the way. No *company*. That's what self-made means." He paused. Then: "You. You're a company man, David. A company man. . . . I just thought you ought to be aware of that distinction."
> —Susan Miller, *The Good Mother*

> Plato . . . hated the lying myths of the poets so much that he had to invent new myths of his own to express his philosophy.
> —Robert Eisner, "Fantasy Islands," *New York Times Book Review*

THE BASIC MOTIFS OF MASCULINE SELF-MAKING are all suggested in the epigraph taken from Susan Miller's *The Good Mother,* her 1986 novel about the nuances of personal relationships and family life. At the outset of this particular scene, sons-in-law, daughters, and grandchildren are gathered about the family patriarch, who listens quietly to his "moderately successful" sons-in-law. Finally, one of them declares himself "just a self-made man" (36) and must be put in his place. In a verbally withering display of masculine aggression and competition, the grandfather forces his son-in-law to acknowledge the inadequacy of his middle-class claims of self-making—and his equally inadequate versions of masculine power and institutional independence. The grandfather represents the real self-made man of the nineteenth and early twentieth centuries: "a powerful and powerfully driven man [who] sought new and challenging engineering tasks in widely separated regions. When the initial challenge was met, he handed the task over to others, and moved on. His wife saw him only for an occasional impregnation. His sons could not keep pace with him and were left as respectable settlers by the wayside; only his daughter was and looked like him" (Erikson 312–13). As for modern nonmen, they are easily dismissible, "company" men with few of the traits, talents, or tendencies of their forebears.

The scene's descriptive and emotional accuracy rests on its use of a very common opposition—no company equals self-made; corporate equals dependent. But the real rhetorical power and effectiveness of the passage rests on its ability to trigger a deep set of cultural beliefs—and anxieties—that fully enact the myth of the self-made man and the masculinity that it encapsulates. Initial description of those dynamics is best done through two related disciplines—psychoanalysis and rhetoric—and several terms from each—oedipal and preoedipal, myth and *doxa*.

Oedipal and Preoedipal Rhetoric

The overall exchange between David and his father-in-law is recognizably that of the basic oedipal drama, an enactment furthered by its occurrence within the essential psychoanalytic frame—the family. As a quieted scene of male dominance, Miller's passage enacts David Leverenz's basic thesis about masculinity: "that any intensified ideology of manhood is a compensatory response to fears of humiliation" and the deepest fear, male/male humiliation, is essentially an enactment of the oedipal dynamic, emphasized in "man's experience of each other at work, where most American men measure themselves" (4).[1] Like Leverenz, Michael Kimmel stresses the high degree to which masculinity is "largely a homosocial enactment" (*Manhood* 7), and one that engages "a model of manhood that derives identity entirely from a man's activities in the public sphere" (*Manhood* 16–17). Ultimately, these arguments declare, workplace "humiliation," and the related need to avoid it in order to maintain adequate masculinity, echo the original oedipal defeat by the father.

Other arguments grow out of this frame, making subtle use of psychosocial appeals to encourage accepted, if somewhat questionable, masculine behavioral traits and social roles. Extolling a trait such as initiative, for example, meliorates the myth's less savory appeals to aggression and competition. Additional implications further accrete around the initial oedipal motifs. If anyone is free to climb the ladder of success, the argument declares, then those who do not do so can be ignored by defining them as lacking in personal force of will. Appeals to personal freedom and development, then, are also appeals to self-interest, aggression, and class and ethnic bias—emotions that tend to provide a sense of both personal satisfaction and guilty ambivalence. As the myth of masculine self-making is engaged by Miller's patriarch, these ambivalent desires and conflicting goals, which are part and parcel of individual and social masculine development, are also engaged, and colored by the broad argument that success is the final evaluative norm.

This basic oedipal dynamic, and its enactment of forms of dominance and aggression, are regular aspects of the essential rhetoric of masculine self-making. At the same time, specific historical and material contexts affect the particulars of individual and social identity argued in the general rhetoric. As Miller's grandfather makes clear, the modern rise of corporate, institutional power complicates any easy appeal to masculine action as the heart of manliness. The workplace is no longer under individual worker, craftsman, or even owner control. The individual acts and one-on-one battles so easily ascribed to nineteenth-century corporate titans are no longer readily available within contemporary corporate monoliths. The pleasures of direct oedipal reenactments are thus lessened. But if direct violence is commonly removed, the aggression in the "new" myth is no less keenly honed, and no less devoted to the essential tensions of the oedipal frame. All these dynamics are identifiable in Miller's enactment of her patriarch's arguments, which make full use of the major oedipal components of the myth's rhetoric.

This emphasis does not paint the whole picture, however. If we move to the second half of Miller's narrative scene, we begin to recognize further currents, additional workings out of masculine dynamics that must be characterized in terms beyond male/male oedipal exchange. Along with the classic male exchange, another highly complex enactment of masculinities is achieved through the women in the room. These dynamics demonstrate that masculinity consists not solely of an oedipal struggle for individuality and success but at least equally of a conflicted need for and aversion to feminization or the feminine. In a passage immediately following the above, Miller explicitly shares rhetorical emphasis between the gender dynamics of the oedipal and the preoedipal. The emotionally aggressive struggle between the grandfather and David serves to establish a sense of the danger inherent in not being a self-made man, in not being able to rise to the demands of the oedipal conflict. That failure in turn raises a lurking concern over being something else—and that something else is rife with overtones of preoedipal framing and a dangerous closing of a culturally declared gap between masculine agency and feminine dependency.

The shift can be found in a variety of references, such as the grandfather's sense of his sons-in-law simply as those men who had "compromised his daughters' lives" (35), a definition that effectively subsumes them under the figures of their wives. But the most telling dynamics occur between David, his wife, and the narrator of the novel—David's daughter. These dynamics are captured in two moves that allow us to agree that Leverenz's and Kimmel's concern with male/male shame and humiliation is a key component of masculine identity, while also arguing that such behavior is not simply male rivalry arising in the oedipal workplace but part of a much earlier process of mothering and subsequent, forced antifeminization. In fact, what the scene most displays are the complex and anxious negotiations among men for dominance and equivalency—as evidenced through relations to women—that Eve Sedgwick includes as a central component in her description of male homosocial behavior *(Between Men)*.[2]

The first move introducing this male anxiety occurs as David's wife refuses her role as helpmate of her husband. The daughter describes both the role and its implications: "I wanted her to defend my father, to cleave unto him, forsaking all others, as both she and I knew she should do. But she sat. . . . By her silence, I felt, she contributed to my father's shame, and I hated her" (37). These mother/daughter dynamics demonstrate what not only a good daughter but also a good wife stereotypically should be. A defense of David's self-made status by his wife might contain a further feminizing of David, but it would effectively be hidden by her institutional status as "wife" (a role the daughter makes clear by echoing language from both Bible and Christian marriage ceremony). The wife's passive refusal of this dynamic moves David perilously close to a neutered status—demasculinized by his father-in-law and unhusbanded by his wife, whose nonprotective silence underlines David's needs and shame.

David's possible regaining of masculinity through (or at the expense of) an acceptably gendered, feminine role for his wife is thus closed off. Masculine identification with the self-made grandfather already has been effectively denied. In Sedgwick's words, David's situation is "dire"—he risks being "feminized or suffer[ing] gender confusion within a framework that includes a woman" (36). Desperate, David asserts his nonfemininity and weakly reasserts his masculinity by separating himself from another woman's offer of support—that of his less powerful daughter. Attempting to occupy the vacant role of wife, David's daughter goes to her father and leans toward him. Responding to this even more feminizing (because nonadult) offer of solace, David "move[s] away from contact" with her. Masculine denial and separation having actively begun, David finishes his remasculinization by establishing both personal and linguistic dominance. He "irritably" asks his daughter why she doesn't go and "play with one of my cousins. 'Grownups are trying to *talk* here,' he whispered sharply to me" (37). Thus, a modicum of classic masculinity is remade: Separation from the female is declared and a broad postoedipal role (adults speaking) is announced.

In many ways, the scene is a direct fictional reprise of the tension between the interrelational, mutualistic quality of the preoedipal and the individualistic emphasis of the oedipal. Threats of feminization as well as oedipal defeat are only too clear. Luckily for David, that defeat and its underlying threat—banishment from the oedipal masculine and return to the preoedipal feminine—can be masked through a successfully chosen rejection of his daughter. David cannot defeat or equal his self-making father-in-law, but he can at least announce his independence from the support—and situation—of a representative of the maternal. Such reliance upon a rhetoric of masculine independence and singularity demonstrates a deep need to maintain masculinity as a man-to-man relation, a need that permeates all arenas in which social and cultural beliefs are maintained. But while emphasis on the oedipal is clearly useful to an initial characterization of the myth, that emphasis alone serves only to repress and reinforce anxieties over separation from the feminine that are themselves central to masculinity.

The rhetoric of self-making paradoxically addresses the anxiety hidden in masculinity's own insistently binary frame (male = not-female) by downplaying or ignoring the preoedipal, normally the maternal and feminine, characterizing such separation as a subset of "real" masculine struggle with the father and other males. In short, oedipal struggle with the father (vaguely motivated by pursuit of self-making rather than competition for the mother) is emphasized so as to mask and replace a prior, required preoedipal separation from the feminine with a later, supposedly chosen movement away from the feminine and toward necessary, "proper" struggle with other males. Erikson's self-made patriarch literally/geographically mimics this movement, while modern self-making, as voiced by David, attempts to rewrite this movement as entrance into a mythical realm of corporate battle.

But Miller's example makes clear that the separation between home and work, women's world and men's world is not as clear as it might be. The setting for this male/male work discussion is, after all, a family gathering.[3] Indeed, even as Leverenz defers feminist psychoanalytic revisions of masculinity in order to make his claim for male oedipal behavior as supreme, he admits to the presence of preoedipal concerns. "I think male rivalry is a more basic source of anxiety," he states—and then admits that "the language of manhood makes ample use of maternal scapegoating" (4). Leverenz also notes that while the essential humiliation may be "usually" rooted in male/male exchange, the basic fear is cathected to many sources: "The sources of humiliation may be diverse, in parents or the loss of class position, in marketplace competition or other fears of being dominated. A preoccupation with manhood becomes a compensatory response" (72–73). Such complications and qualifiers demonstrate how emphasis on the oedipal struggle with the father tends to overvalue, and thus promulgate, that aspect of masculine development. In Conway-Long's reworking of Bourdieu, "One naturalizes male dominance in social practice and discourse, claiming orthodoxy for its known rules, and rarely if ever reaches the underlying doxa of male insecurity and fear of returning to the original embrace of the mother and the feminine" (74–75).

The myth of masculine self-making enacts radical possibilities for such avoidance. But while it argues a deep separation from nurturance and the female, it also demonstrates the importance of those elements by using them as a reference point for the level of masculinity achieved. In protesting so much his separation from all that is feminine, the self-made man only suggests a conflict over and desire for that feminine. "The conflict of masculinity appears, then," according to Butler, "to be precisely the demand for a full recognition of autonomy that will also and nevertheless promise a return to those full [preoedipal] pleasures prior to repression and individuation" (*Trouble* 45). Explaining preoedipal and oedipal influences equally would argue for different patterns of gender formation, different requirements for rhetorical maintenance of social norms, and different or extended psychoanalytic models, of course.[4] Directly melding the issues, for example, Nancy Chodorow notes that "masculinity and sexual difference ('oedipal' issues) become intertwined with separation-individuation ('preoedipal') issues almost from the beginning of a boy's life" (106).

Yet the emphasis on male/male oedipal conflict in masculine rhetoric requires that the complex intertwining of masculinity and femininity be resolved in terms of a simplified myth of masculinity alone. The results of this requirement are not only the more blatant mythic enactments of masculine self-making but also wholesale valuing of behavioral norms within social critique itself. Although they are ostensibly more analytically designed than narrative myths of masculine self-making, traditional scales of masculine development nevertheless offer many of the same value features as the myth itself. Even analytic and descriptive characterizations, such as Leverenz's critiques or Erikson's scales of social development, are themselves part of the rhetorical mythologizing of masculinity. Erikson's characterization of the stereotypical self-made man, for example, is quite accurate. But even more interesting is his related concern over the historical shifting of the male role from that of self-making patriarch to company man.

In Erikson's argument, as entrepreneur becomes corporate drone, and father-figure becomes "Pop," visions of the purely oedipal model begin to waver.[5] One of Erikson's own solutions to this oedipal waver is the notorious portrait of "Mom," who usurps her husband's masculine role and becomes an oedipal father in place of the lesser male (312–13). Needless to say, it requires a lot less theoretical straining to describe separation and anxiety in terms of preoedipal dynamics than to insist on translating the role of mothering into that of fathering as well, just to maintain an oedipal emphasis. Yet the desire to represent masculinity as primarily male/male exchange makes complications in theory much easier to accept than changes in the larger cultural rhetoric.[6] In short, these varied rhetorical enactments of masculinity further emphasize the ongoing workings of *doxa* as they themselves repeat preset, oedipal arguments enacted by the mythic rhetoric.

Carol Gilligan's now-classic critique of this process demonstrates how stereotypical masculine behavior has been naturalized and incorporated into supposedly objective scales of human development. In Gilligan's example, the "fully developed" individual of Erikson's and Lawrence Kohlberg's scales of development is defined through masculinity-based traits such as independence, self-containment, and an ability to operate on the plane of the abstract and the rule-based in forming behavior and moral judgment. Within this binary interpretive frame, the supposedly less fully developed feminine identity concerns itself with responding to the world in terms of interpersonal need and exchange, in terms of the concrete and supposedly mundane situation rather than the abstract. The scales' assumptions thus not only repeat but also maintain the validity of the self-made man's attempt to bury the conflict between nurturance and self-creation, dependency and personal agency by declaring the identity of the independent male to be the highest form of individual development. Said in light of mythic self-making, the scales resolve conflicting identity needs by offering a definition of individual behaviors and exchange in which the desire to be independent of institutions and of feminine modes of behavior is attached to the "healthy" male and his desires. Erikson's and Kohlberg's own immersion in masculine engendering thus leads to a descriptive argument that overvalues and overinvests in singularity and individuality, portraying a self capable of maintaining inviolability at the expense of mutuality.

Ironically, then, the dominant motifs or components of masculine self-making are readily describable by reading the myth both from within and against a traditional psychoanalytic frame. That description, unfortunately, still has two related shortcomings. It tends to flatten the description into a set of taxonomic features or images, and perhaps more problematically still, it offers at best only a rather simplified connection between the individual narrative or myth and the individual psyche. Such a connection does not adequately address my concerns with seeing rhetoric as a sociocultural project for maintaining—arguing, preserving, and indeed naturalizing—cultural practices, specifically masculinity. In order to extend that initial descriptive movement, then, I want to take up another set of terms, these taken directly from rhetoric and its history and/or historiography. The terms I have in mind—myth and *doxa*—have already been suggested earlier as a means of making the move from particular components (oedipal and preoedipal, for example) and the myth to cultural practice and rhetorical performance.

The usefulness of myth and *doxa* in forging links between personal behavior and individual appeal or response on one side, and rhetorical action and cultural practice on the other, is visible not only in arguments concerning the concepts but also in their particular positioning within discussions of rhetoric itself. In the case of myth, that position is, or at least has been for a great deal of rhetorical history, one to be escaped, moved beyond, so that rhetoric can more fully (or ethically) flourish. The impact of that orientation within the discipline of rhetoric is readily visible in Ernest Bormann's attempts from 1972 to 1982 to link fantasy, rhetoric, and psychoanalysis.[7] The disciplinary minidrama surrounding Bormann's discussion of fantasy-theme analysis demonstrates both the benefits of aligning psychoanalysis to cultural rhetoric and reasons behind resistance to such an alignment. Faced with two key complaints— his use of psychoanalytic arguments at all and, more subtly, his willing extrapolation of individual behaviors to group behaviors—Bormann eventually denounced the psychoanalytic component in his thinking. Under attack, he declared that while "nonrational aspects need to be taken into account . . . to my mind, a rhetorical approach involves the conscious drafting of messages with an eye to audience conditions" ("Ten Years Later" 291n). The sociocultural dynamic in his portrait of rhetoric was to be drawn thereafter as a supposedly verifiable, conscious, and reasoned process of exchange.[8]

I want to set aside until later the issue of individual versus group exchange. As for the issue of rational versus "nonrational," Bormann's capitulation is part of a larger, ongoing concern over whether rhetoric is to be characterized in terms of deliberate persuasion and use of a relatively innocent language or whether it is to be broadened to include a much more active sense of rhetoric and language and their constructive, even constitutive capacities. At the time of Bormann's arguments, rhetoric's narrow focus on a supposedly readily definable "conscious drafting of messages" could not be balanced by contemporary rhetoric's interest in the full range of social persuasion and its equally full sophistic inheritance. But current thinking is quite different, and ongoing interest in sophistic rhetoric makes for a more complex melding of social practices and rhetoric. The traditional, linear description of society marching toward a supposedly enlightened rationality—commonly presented as a historical progression from *mythos* through *nomos* to *logos*—is being rewritten to address the wide-ranging activities of what I am calling mythic rhetoric. What the following arguments over the concepts of myth and *doxa* demonstrate, then, are particular positionings or moments in a revitalization of rhetoric, a renewal fostered not solely by rhetoric itself but also by related—and perhaps unanticipated—concerns in cultural studies, gender studies, and psychoanalysis.

Contemporary Perspectives on Rhetoric and Myth

Mythos, Nomos, Logos

In establishing the importance of myth and *doxa* to my interpretive method, I want to return again to Bourdieu for both definitions and impetus, since he links both together within an overall continuum of societal self-maintenance. As I noted briefly in the introduction, Bourdieu declares that the collective actions of a society eventuate in "'realized myth,' . . . the reconciliation of subjective demand and objective (i.e., collective) necessity which grounds the *belief* of a whole group in what the group believes, i.e., in the group" (163–64). In addition, he goes on to define such forms of group belief in terms of the situation in which a society experiences "a quasi-perfect correspondence between the objective order and the subjective principles of the organization (as in ancient societies)," a situation in which "the natural and social world appears as self-evident." "This experience," Bourdieu states, "we shall call *doxa,* so as to distinguish it from an orthodox or heterodox belief implying awareness and recognition of the possibility of different or antagonistic beliefs" (164). Bourdieu's sense here of *doxa* and myth extends, while remaining consistent with, contemporary considerations of rhetoric as actively constituting, rather than merely reflecting or rationally urging, cultural practice.

Common assent to the latter position remains deep seated, however. Rhetoric has long been one of many disciplines that narrate Western history, and especially the rise of democracy, as a progression out of a nonrational world of myth and superstition and into a world of reason and rational discourse, with transitional stages in between. Drastically simplified, the typical progression argues for a three-part (or three-term) movement out of superstition *(mythos),* into and beyond opinion (*nomos* or group think, as it is sometimes disparaged), with the ultimate destination being the freedom of individual reason and rationality *(logos).*

This model of linear progression regularly implicates specific value judgments. The full movement from *mythos* to postsophistic or Aristotelian *logos* (or even more fully to an idealistic Platonism) involves a move not only from the designated sources of laws or knowledge but also from "mythic-*poetic*" social practices to "humanistic-*rationalistic*" knowledges (Schiappa, *Protagoras* 31; emphasis added). The implication is that democracy is paired with the rise of a reasoning populace and escape from the emotionalism of a myth-prone society. Further extensions of the argument often reveal underlying biases toward immature cultures in pursuit of modernity, biases often echoed in turn in gendered images of nonrational, ostensibly feminine modes of conception versus hard-minded, supposedly masculine, reasoning abilities. In Bruce Lincoln's delightful summary, the transition from *mythos* to *logos* is part of a "creation myth that makes all good things come from Greece" and thematizes the transition itself "as the paradigm of the dynamism, progress, science, and rationality that are supposed to characterize and distinguish Europe forever after" (209–10).[9]

Those biases are echoed in specific cultural appeals such as those put forward by Miller's patriarch. His claims, although deeply rooted in cultural anxieties and needs, actually seem to rest on the irrefutability of their logic, a rationality manifested primarily in techniques of definition and opposition. A near-syllogistic pattern informs the basis of his own assertion of self-making and his denial of that status to his son-in-law:[10] (1) To be a self-made man you must succeed without the aid of a company ("no . . . [*sic*] pension plan, for example. No company ladder to climb, to protect you every step of the way. No *company*"); (2) I succeeded without the aid of a company; and (3) I am a self-made man. David, of course, is provided with an opposing premise that declares "You did NOT function without the aid of a company." Since David is irrefutably in conflict with the definition of self-made man, he therefore is irrefutably not a self-made man. Q.E.D. The psychocultural appeal of such formal arguments rests on socially reinforced attitudes toward the truth value of logical proof, a process directly engaged in arguments that attach sociocultural growth to the presence of such proofs. In Erikson's and Kohlberg's particular descriptions, for example, the male child's use of logic demonstrates a move toward rational decision making and the possibility of full social development, while the girl's failure to follow that pattern dooms her to an alternative path.

Approaches less committed to seeing history as a march toward enlightenment (or rationalism as the sole means of understanding) tend to see such descriptions—and the inviolability of their arguments—with a more jaundiced eye. Among rhetoricians, such questioning is visible in the ongoing battle over the status of the earliest known Western rhetoricians, the Sophists. As early as 1971, Lawrence Rosenfield's self-declared "autopsy of the rhetorical tradition" declared the progression as stressing a not-useful opposition between socially negotiated knowledge or *nomos* (the middle term of the *mythos/nomos/logos* triad) and language-antagonistic idealism associated with Platonic *logos*. In essence, Rosenfield was rejecting the idea that social knowledge, or generally agreed upon principles, were merely a weak or even false substitute for rational truth. But while these fifth-century B.C.E. rhetors have provoked great interest in some rhetorical circles recently, they also are often relegated, in Schiappa's words, to the level of "transitional figures" (*Protagoras* 201) who operated between a nonrational mythic period and the rise of abstract reasoning, the latter positively paired with the rise of rhetoric and a more democratic environment.[11]

In such readings, it is common practice to reinforce the differences between *nomos* and *logos* by minimizing the importance of the former as social agreement or practice in relation to the ostensibly more foundational, taxonomic knowledge linked to *logos* and its pursuit within Platonic dialectic. For example, Rankin contrasts Platonic and sophistic thought by declaring sophistic *nomos* to be "mere agreement" (80).[12] But new readings of the Sophists argue for a less ready separation and valuing of each concept. A more complex and more useful characterization sees *nomos* as part of an overall sophistic design for a "nonformal epistemology of rhetoric," a discourse practice that recognizes "the contingencies of interpretation and human nature that are inherent in any social circumstance . . ." (Enos 83). The importance of *nomos* rests in this latter application and its resulting definitions, especially when used to characterize the historical progression drawn from *mythos* through *nomos* to *logos*.[13]

When placed within the traditional opposition between the divinely inspired poetry of *mythos* and the rationally conceived argument of *logos, nomos* serves at a minimum to complicate the traditional, binary divide placed between the tribalistic/mythopoetic and the democratic/rationalistic. As described by Ostwald, *nomos* is not simply majority opinion but rather a sense of society endorsed "without question," achieving "general if not universal acceptance." Schiappa underlines that role in discussing the importance of Susan Jarratt's work on *nomos:* "The virtue of Jarratt's *mythos-nomos-logos* framework is that it acknowledges the sophistic advances over the mythic-poetic tradition while resisting the habit of equating sophistic *logos* with the sort of formal rationality one finds, for example, in Aristotle's works on logic . . ." (Schiappa, *Protagoras* 201).

Reconsiderations of the progression are based on more than just correcting a too-easy separation of each term in the triad, however. Rhetorical critics are building links between a poststructuralist and neosophistic interest in language as practice, arguing for a wide-ranging reconception of the Sophists and their relation to the social construction of knowledge. John Poulakos, for example, is less interested in "saving" negotiated knowledge by aligning it with a rationalistic *logos,* and more interested in heavily qualifying the ostensible objectivity of rationalism by linking contemporary thinking on language as a structuring medium with sophistic attitudes toward knowledge as contextually and historically negotiated. Within such a framework, social constructs are a function not only of a referential *logos* but also of an interpretative process that depends, in Mailloux's words, upon the "webs of belief and desire that constitute our rhetorical context" (*Reception* 10). Mailloux's use of "belief" and "desire" complicates even further the supremacy of *logos,* suggesting how fully the *mythos/nomos/logos* progression should be and is being problematized. Issues regularly seen as central to current concerns with discourse practice—texts as sites of a struggle over meaning, gender and subject performance, the roles of desire and belief, and so on—all can be used to reinforce rhetoric's social and critical value by rooting the discipline in an active social dynamic. Jarratt indicates the degree of rethinking underway:

> With the sophists, *nomos,* a self-conscious arrangement of discourse to create politically and socially significant knowledge, enters as a middle term between *mythos* and *logos.* This addition to classical rhetorical terminology might be used to displace the Aristotelian focus on rhetorical arguments with heightened attention to narrative structure, changing dramatically the status of arrangement and collapsing the discrete categories of *logos* and *pathos.* (*Rereading* 60)

The full import and value of Jarratt's arguments for my own concerns lie in her emphasis on "displacing" rhetoric's Aristotelian emphasis on argument with emphasis on "narrative structure," and in the resulting implications for the supposedly discrete categories of *logos* (reason) and *pathos* (emotion). With these actions, it is possible to defer not only a supposedly necessary and historically segmenting progression toward rationalistic *logos* (and by implication out of *mythos* and *nomos*), but also an easy removal of narrative (and of myth, as a form of narrative) from the realm of rhetoric. In like fashion, the reintroduction of *pathos* begins to hint at lurking gender values to be found in the drive toward apotheosizing reason as well. Refusal of discrete divisions between social norm and "rational" law, narrative enactment and rational argument, *mythos, nomos, and logos,* allows for a wide-ranging discourse practice to be put at the center of the construction of culture, society, and the subjects of them.

This reconsideration of *nomos* does not resolve immediately all the concerns I have in regard to defining cultural rhetoric in relation to myth, *mythos* and *nomos.* In speaking of *nomos,* for example, Jarratt herself separates it not only from rationalism but also from Plato's organic form and incantatory mythic: *Nomos* is that "self-conscious arrangement of discourse" in which "the composer and his co-creators, the audience, are fully aware of the craft" (*Rereading* 60). But Jarratt's overall goal is to complicate the idea of discrete forms of consciousness found within discrete historical periods, and she relies in her definition of *nomos* upon Ostwald, for whom *nomos* encompasses meanings ranging from "rule" to "customary practice" to "belief," the last usually held "unself-consciously and without question" (60). That definition once more places rhetoric, and rhetorical use of language, at the center of a mixed rhetorical activity devoted to the construction, maintenance, and challenging of "received" knowledge. It does so, moreover, without limiting rhetorical language to the realm of reasoned discourse alone, allowing for Jarratt's emphasis on *pathos* and on narrative—and for my emphasis on myth.[14]

A further, quick interpretation of Miller's scene clarifies both the usefulness and the need for complicating and expanding the categories in this way. I've already noted the grandfather's use of the cultural appeal of reasoned argument to put forward his claims. But such reasoned argument is hardly sufficient to produce assent on its own, nor does such a characterization of the rhetoric explain David's reaction. To understand that reaction, we need to again go beyond the formal, descriptive logic of the argument and note its nesting within complex psychological and sociocultural attitudes. The heart of the denial of David's self-making appears to be an argumentative given, for example, that individual drive and aggression ("no-company") make for a truer masculinity than can be achieved in modern, corporate spheres. *Logos* alone cannot explain or explain away that "given." To do so it is necessary to move beyond the definitions given by Miller's patriarch and enter into a larger cultural critique. Certainly within the United States (and indeed within different classes within that grouping) the meanings encouraged by the idea of "company" are simply too complex to be limited to the level of formal logic.

To explain this scene and its enactment of the complex rhetoric of self-making, then, we need to assume that a complex culture does not move away from the full range of its rhetorical powers—including the use of narrative, myth, *pathos*—but rather that a complex culture will contain all of these components in its acts of rhetorical self-maintenance. *Mythos/nomos/logos* describes not a progression but an accumulation; a culture and its rhetorical practices are not linear but accretive. At a minimum, Jarratt suggests, such complex rhetorical appeals require the addition of *nomos* as a component in cultural rhetoric. Moreover, Jarratt goes on to reject easy separation of mythic and logical modes and to argue for mixed discourse as a central form (*Rereading* 37). Finally, if we return to Laura Mulvey once more, we are reminded of her claim that myth "flourishes at the point where the social and the psychoanalytic overlap" (*Visual Pleasures* 166). Indeed, ostensibly formal critique itself demonstrates the concurrent presence of all three. Even as it moves to-ward explanation of the myth of self-making, critical analysis of mythic rhetoric is regularly implicated in its own subject matter—witness Erikson's arguments for what constitutes adequate masculinity.

This complicating of rhetorical categories and their supposedly dis-crete forms of knowledge is not the same as arguing that discourse prac-tices are uncontrolled or wholly deterministic, however, nor in the re-verse—that the constitutive power of rhetorical performance opens up a realm of total free play. Oscillating between its own arguments for a masculinity rooted in a naturalizing essentialism and a masculinity avail-able as a context-free performance, the rhetoric of the self-made man is subject to recognition and possible subversion and yet still beyond the range of easy rejection. To rephrase Bourdieu, the combined endurance, variability, and social effectiveness of such a myth exist not solely within its components but also within the myth's active enactment of cultural desires, needs, and behaviors—an enactment by society and individual that produces and maintains "the field of *doxa,* of that which is taken for granted" (166). Myth, in this definition, is the visible enactment of the field of *doxa.* The obvious question, then, is how to characterize *doxa* itself in ways that connect it to cultural myth, rhetorical practice, and masculine performance.

Doxa

Definitions of *doxa* are complicated by the same issues of cultural prac-tice, social structure, and disciplinary argument that complicate discus-sions of myth. These complications also provide the same opportunities for reconceiving both the concepts and the role that rhetoric can play in social action and cultural interpretation. Rosenfield's autopsy of rheto-ric again provides one such example, if not necessarily the complete answer. Early in the essay, Rosenfield considers negative attitudes in rhetorical theory toward *doxa* and suggests that a more adequate con-sideration of the concept requires replacing its "unfortunate" transla-tion as "opinion" with a more adequate sense of it as "that aspect of the whole of reality which the individual recognizes and shares with others" (*Prospect* 65).[15] At the same time, Rosenfield is insistent in his rejection not only of logical positivism and behaviorism but also, most tellingly, of what he describes as the Hegelian destruction of "the dis-tinction between being and appearance" (72). Social reality exists; in-tellect is "reified in acts of discourse: thought is indistinguishable from its public display" (67). Within this frame, Rosenfield believes it is pos-sible to achieve "distance," "impartiality," a form of "objectivity" that allows the individual to "interpret, indeed to evaluate, the reality given to his reason" (66).

Defining *doxa* in this way allows Rosenfield to step back from his autopsy and imagine a different rhetoric to replace the corpse lying before him. In classical Greece at least, rhetoric rested on a different *doxa,* a "degree of 'common sense' . . . [shared] among members of the *polis*" that gave rise to "the arts of discourse (rhetoric, poetic, dialectic)" (65). Such a vision of rhetoric leads naturally to Rosenfield's decidedly contemporary declaration that "had this [pre-Socratic] conception of man as speaker persisted, rhetoric's place might well be as secure today as when it was taught and practiced by Protagoras, Gorgias, Solon, Aristotle, and Isocrates. But accidents of history preserved instead the Platonic attacks on Sophistry and upon Athenian life in general and left for us only suggestive fragments of the dominant Sophistic motif" (67). In short, Rosenfield's interest in *doxa* encourages a historical revision similar to that pursued by current complicators of the common *mythos/ nomos/logos* progression.

Yet although Rosenfield clearly wishes to use *doxa* to reconsider the role of the Sophists, his angle of approach to language, rhetoric, and *doxa* as a whole is rooted in that sense of social reality as available, addressable, clearly present in some nonsubjective form. Social construction is seen as activity directed primarily from within the "commonsense" intentions of the citizenry, and Rosenfield's sense of societal exchange remains rather neo-Aristotelian and suffers from connection to the primarily rational sensibilities often associated with it. For all his concern with the impact of the pre-Socratics on the body of rhetoric, then, Rosenfield stops his postmortem too soon, leaving largely unexplored the complicated connection between discourse and the social and cultural reality it ostensibly reflects and directs. Said another way, Rosenfield's call to effective rhetorical action within the "sector of public action" (73) leaves both rhetorical action and especially its space of operation too thinly defined, never approaching, for example, Mailloux's spoken concerns with the beliefs and desires that form rhetorical contexts and, by implication, the societies that use them for self-maintenance. Rosenfield thus clarifies the problem if not the solution, at least in terms of my own concern with uniting myth and *doxa* under the aegis of a socially active, culturally formative rhetorical practice that moves beyond shared reason and common sense.

Ironically, a combination of these concepts that is closer to what is needed can be found in yet another postmortem on the old rhetoric. In "The Old Rhetoric: an aide-mémoire," Roland Barthes calls for what Lynn Worsham restates as "a thoroughgoing critique of Rhetoric's complicity with the emergence of nineteenth-century mass culture and the hegemony of twentieth-century consumer culture. This critical project, sub/versive in its anti-Aristotelianism, would continue the demystifying work Barthes began in *Mythologies*" (Worsham 150). Barthes's linkage of the discipline of Rhetoric and bourgeois hegemony will be addressed later, but for now it is important to note that the demystifying work in *Mythologies* to which Worsham refers not only defines *doxa* but also links it to myth. Barthes himself explains the connection in a later discussion of *Mythologies:* "Myth consists in overturning culture into nature or, at least, the social, the cultural, the ideological, the historical into the 'natural' . . . ; under the effect of mythical inversion, the quite contingent foundations of the utterance become Common Sense, Right Reason, the Norm, General Opinion, in short the *doxa* (which is the secular figure of the origin)" (*Image* 165–66). Here is a full unification of myth, *doxa,* and cultural self-maintenance that appears adequate to describing the power of rhetoric, language, and social desire.

There is, of course, a glaringly obvious problem in relying upon this delightful unity. Rhetoric, myth, and *doxa* are all under attack by Barthes. He means to display them as tools of a bourgeois hegemony complicit in the furtherance of mass culture and thus destructive of healthy social functioning. As summarized in additions to the overall history he provides, Barthes grants the activities of *doxa* and rhetoric a powerful but problematic cultural position by providing a complex definition of the relation between language and social practices. He sees "a kind of stubborn agreement between Aristotle (from whom rhetoric proceeded) and our mass culture, as if Aristotelianism . . . survived in a corrupt, diffused, inarticulate state in the cultural practice of Western societies: . . . everything suggests that a kind of Aristotelian vulgate still defines a type of trans-historical Occident, a civilization (our own) which is that of the *endoxa* . . . ("Old Rhetoric" 92).

In all candor, I don't necessarily see this view of rhetoric, when used to describe its active use in and by society, as a problem standing in the way of a more utopian project. In certain ways, I do see rhetorical activity as complicit with society's attempts to maintain a certain status quo. Indeed, as I define the workings of myth (and certainly a particular, dominant—that is, middle-class—myth such as that of masculine self-making), I am establishing them as an active practice of cultural and societal self-maintenance, a self-maintenance that by definition insists upon a certain version of myth and masculinity, to the exclusion of others—with working-class variations being the most obvious example to be analyzed later. My own project, then, is similar to what Linda Hutcheon posits as the working of postmodern critique: "adapt[ing] Barthes's general notion of the 'doxa' as public opinion or the 'Voice of Nature' and consensus . . . [so as] to 'de-doxify' our cultural representations and their undeniable political import" (Hutcheon 3).

I shift somewhat from Barthes's project on two further grounds as well, the first being his underlying purpose in defining rhetoric as he does and the second simply being temporal. Ultimately, Barthes's judgments on rhetoric are based in his own critical desire to produce a new form of discourse, to reduce rhetoric "to the rank of a merely historical object; [to seek] in the name of *text*, of *writing,* a new practice of language" ("Old Rhetoric" 93).[16] While neither agreeing nor disagreeing with the feasibility of that goal, it simply is not mine here. My purpose is to characterize certain terms and concepts—at present those of myth and *doxa* (along with oedipal and preoedipal)—in order to produce an interpretive model of rhetoric capable of engaging in the sort of cultural critique Hutcheon argues as possible through Barthes. I am not yet prepared to dismiss this type of rhetorical critique as ethically unsupportable. Indeed, it participates in a deconstruction of rhetorical and sociocultural practice that seems less utopian than Barthes's project, or operates at least as preamble to it.

I make that claim, moreover, without feeling overly complicit in certain forms of rhetorical action because of the second ground, that provided by time. I have already noted how current arguments concerning pre-Aristotelian rhetoric, specifically those concerning the Sophists, provide an environment for arguing out these issues that was enjoyed by neither Rosenfield nor Barthes. Simply put, current discussions more fully situate issues of myth—and of rhetoric—within a broader field of cultural analysis, arguing that social structure is indeed arbitrary, and our experience of that structure is not a simple function of negotiation or reasoned discussion. *Doxa* as cultural belief and need precedes and far exceeds our own actions. Likewise, society's "systems of classification" are part of a power dynamic that operates to encourage, for example, a myth of self-making that serves to mask factors such as birth, sex, education, wealth, and so on. The ensuing contradictions between personal experience and mythic rhetoric are regularly noted by the citizenry—and then are not reasoned out but ignored or even embraced because *doxa* and its rhetoric exceed individual experience.

This is the sense of *doxa* Bourdieu provides—and with which Barthes actually seems to be in substantial agreement. In Bourdieu's frame, "nothing is further from the correlative notion of the *majority* than the *unanimity* of doxa, the aggregate of the 'choices' whose subject is everyone and no one because the questions they answer cannot be explicitly asked" (168).[17] By offering a range of doxic awareness and linking its components to cultural hierarchy, Bourdieu establishes a sense of the dynamic tension in and ongoing maintenance of sociocultural practice. In Bourdieu's taxonomy, "the boundary between the universe of (orthodox or heterodox) discourse and the universe of doxa, in the twofold sense of what goes without saying and what cannot be said for lack of an available discourse, represents the dividing-line between the most radical form of misrecognition and the awakening of political consciousness" (170). *Doxa* thus covers a wide range of cultural belief and awareness, of active concealment and "visible" enactment of social knowledge.

That process is part of what Victor Vitanza looks at when he, like Jarratt, rejects the easy segmentation of concepts and periods and instead stresses that "it is Plato who separates *doxa* (opinion, appearance) from *episteme* or *physis* (knowledge as certainty or of reality), thus destroying the pre-Socratics meaning of *logos,* by insisting on the concealment of *doxa* or by insisting on its being projected onto the Sophists. . . . But it is Heidegger, however, who attempts a return to *logos* as both *doxa* and *episteme,* as concealment/unconcealment" (*Negation* 183). For Vitanza, this mixed mode of knowing, as it were, is a "productive state of confusion . . . which did not denote/connote the *separation* of *physis/ logos* from *doxa,* but its inclusion. Again, as Heidegger says: 'The essence of being *[logos/physis]* lay partly in appearing *[doxa]*' (*[Metaphysics]* 103)" (*Negation* 178).

Doxa, within this Heidegger/Vitanza framework, is more than mere opinion; it is an aspect of being, indeed of transitory moments of glory. Echoing Butler's description of performance as "'work[ing]' to the extent that *it draws on and covers over* the constitutive conventions by which it is mobilized" (*Bodies* 227), Vitanza notes that ultimately, "*logos* speaks *doxa* which is an unconcealment and simultaneously a concealment of *some aspect* of *episteme*/truth, which can never be completely gathered, or unconcealed. Unless rudely forced!" (*Negation* 177–78). *Doxa,* then, is not a state in which full awareness is missing or lacking but rather a condition of existence, of the productive processes of rhetorical performance. Such a condition is not necessarily negative or positive, but it does deny easy separation and/or rejection of myth, *doxa,* rhetoric, and language as active practices in society.

Mythic rhetoric as restated here, then, is the ongoing participation of society and its members in a self-maintaining *doxa,* most particularly, for my study, the *doxa* of masculinity. *Doxa* is made visible, moreover, in the particular patterns of specific social myths, such as the myth of the self-made man. Miller's patriarch, his son-in-law David, and their joint embracing and enacting of the myth of self-making are all components of social behavior that I am calling cultural rhetoric; they are visible embodiments of *doxa* in action, repeating social forms that serve to maintain certain arguments concerning society itself. As such, cultural rhetoric and its recognizable myths are not an arena of false consciousness from which we escape. As repeated forms, mythic practices—and their doxic underpinnings—do open themselves up to variation and critique, with possible responses ranging from simple enactment to disruptive play to cultural critique. At the same time, any and all of these forms are by default part of the cultural rhetoric that already exists and already mitigates, co-opts, and maintains itself.

This sense of *doxa* and of myth complicates, I hope, the easy dismissibility found in some uses of both, along with specific usage of them in characterizations of rhetoric. In particular, it is important to avoid two related reductions: reducing myth to a set of easily noted narrative components or, the opposite, presenting myth not as a visible social construct but as a primitive, nonrational form of sociocultural order—*mythos*—happily left behind. Myth is, in fact, active engagement and visible enactment of any society's and culture's *doxa,* a form of practice that is a regular part of a society's attempts to maintain its own framework and practices—both for itself and for its members. The cultural discourse that promotes that self-maintenance engages not discrete categories or kinds of knowledge but multiple aspects of awareness in which doxic, naturalized belief, orthodox awareness, and heterodox subversion meld and coexist with each other and, indeed, with "rational" thought.

It is according to this characterization of society and culture as a set of actively maintained practices and behaviors that I want to consider rhetoric's role as a necessary means of maintaining—and at the same time challenging—the doxic frame in general, and specific cultural myths such as that of the self-made man in particular. Comments made by Edwin Black clarify the situation well: "The process of incorporating a social identity has rhetorical characteristics that transcend the particular case. Those characteristics recur in the form of a limited number of idioms through which the issues of social identity are regulated and, by means of argument at least, sometimes resolved" (*Questions* 23).

The tensions produced by these doxically induced "regulations" or limits on masculine development are nowhere more visible than within a key motif (and desire/anxiety) enacted by the myth of masculine self-making: the question of agency. The degree to which agency remains a key question is visible in the degree to which the myth of self-making insists that masculinity equals the ability to "do"—the "what" of that doing being less important than the personal control of the act itself. Happily for my arguments, in taking up so insistently the argument that verbal behavior is so central to masculinity, the myth of self-making goes straight to the heart of current concerns and arguments over subjectivity and agency and, in doing so, also opens its rhetorical processes up to analysis, revealing even more fully the links between rhetorical, sociocultural, and psychological processes and practices. My purpose in the next chapter is to use the question of agency to move from the definition of rhetorical and mythic components to discussion of rhetoric and myth as practice and performance.

2
Dominant Myths/Myths of Domination: Masculinity and Agency

> COLLEGE STATION, Texas—Liquor Tycoon Bert Wheeler, an eighth-grade dropout from Louisiana who struck it rich in the real estate business, has died after a long illness. He was 83. . . .
>
> He once said he hated rags-to-riches stories, calling them "nine-tenths prefabricated."
>
> Yet Wheeler personified the poor-boy-makes-good story.
>
> —"Liquor giant Bert Wheeler dies in Texas."
> *Baton Rouge Advocate,* July 30, 1996

BERT WHEELER'S OBITUARY EXEMPLIFIES MYTHIC RHETORIC BEING performed in the public arena. While alive, Wheeler refuses to endorse tales of rags-to-riches, rejecting the rhetoric of self-making as a fabrication. Yet after his death, his own life is offered as exemplary proof of the myth. Who was right? is the first question that springs to mind. But right/wrong questions only screen the real dynamics at work. For his part, Wheeler ostensibly wants control over who he is and how he is represented. On the other side, the writer of the obituary is so eager to engage the myth of self-making that he usurps Wheeler's life, claiming that the classic story has more truth to it than the claims of the man who lived the life. Since the obituary writer has the last word on the subject, Wheeler as doxic argument now speaks at least as powerfully as Wheeler did in person. The question Who was right? fades as the rhetoric of self-making takes charge.

As an example, this exchange may be more humorous than definitive. But even minor elements of the story demonstrate rhetorical processes at work. We're told, for example, that Wheeler owned an extensive collection of historical documents. Given Wheeler's own endorsement of the "real" over the mythic, it's possible that he saw his collection as material validation of the past, as linkage to actual history. But Wheeler's collection of historical materials is certainly no guarantee of the "real," and historical papers are no defense against a mythic rhetoric capable of swallowing up Wheeler and his collection as well.

There is more than a little irony in the obituary's closing linkage of Wheeler to a document signed by Abraham Lincoln. By introducing Lincoln, the reporter effectively inserts Wheeler into a rhetoric of self-making more potent than Wheeler's own personal history. The irony is furthered by Wheeler's own use of *prefabricated* to describe the tales of self-made men. Prefabricated life stories, like prefabricated homes, are not built to fit the site—they are prior creations, life stories formed in advance according to preestablished practices. Individual lives have to match those practices or be altered to fit, a paradox underscored by the obituary's rhetoric as it inexorably removes Wheeler's individual control and agency over his story in order to write him up as a self-made man.

The obituary may be a minimal enactment of the myth. But it displays a major concern at the heart of masculine self-making, a concern that also lies at the center of much current thinking in rhetoric and psychoanalysis regarding subjects and selves: the status of agency in a world arguably constituted by cultural rhetoric and practices. In what follows, I take up this issue in relation to both rhetoric and psychoanalysis in turn, using both to explore not just the components of the myth but its active sociocultural dynamics and persuasive capacities.

Society and Agency, Subjects and Self-Making

Wheeler's brief obituary may not engage every motif of self-made masculinity, but it raises the key question, Who's in charge of the making? Said more formally, How much control does cultural rhetoric have over a particular story line and, at least equally important for a myth extolling masculine self-making, over the individual agency that the myth of masculine self-making extols?[1] Echoes of that concern can be heard in Paul Ricoeur's *Hermeneutics and the Human Sciences: Essays on Language, Action, and Interpretation*. Ricoeur is searching for a means of operating between Cartesian *cogito* and Nietzschean "subject," as well as defining the status of self in relation to others and self as individual. In a move useful to rhetoric, Ricoeur characterizes the self and self-awareness as embodied in the action of verbal testimony and performance. Both cases "can be summed up in two expressions that are at once descriptive and emblematic: *character* and *keeping one's word*. In both of these, we easily recognize a permanence which we say belongs to us" (118).[2] Ricoeur roots his epistemology and its concomitant sense of self in language-based social action. But equally interesting is the way in which Ricoeur, intentionally or unintentionally, drifts into the language of self-making.

The acts of verbal self-definition suggested by Ricoeur are regularly hyperbolized in tales of self-made men. The "knack for plain talking" and saying what one feels are offered there as emblems for self-making and authenticity. The claim that "*Iacocca* reads like Iacocca talks" is typical (*Iacocca,* jacket commentary), and a host of similar anecdotes make clear that attitudes toward agency, social behavior, and rhetoric as public discourse all come together in particular ways around issues of masculinity and, more specifically, the performance of masculine self-making and its particular role in social self-maintenance.

In arguing for a self available through speaking that self, the myth encourages and maintains a vision of verbal self-making. But at the same time, ceding such rhetorical effectiveness to language threatens the very individual agency and free play that both Ricoeur and the myth argue—witness Bert Wheeler's plight. Language use cuts both ways, then. As Debbora Battaglia suggests in her *Rhetorics of Self-Making,* the appeal of self-making, and in this case particularly that of verbal self-making, is an appeal based not solely on a positive desire for self-making but on an equally negative need to deny being made (1–15).

The last appeal is at least as effective as the first, since most of the masculine anxieties attached to the pun are fully operative in beliefs about masculine identity and its necessary free agency. Inaction, passivity, being made—all these possibilities represent feminization within models rooting masculinity in agency, a core aspect of the myth of self-making. It is with good reason, then, that the myth attempts to offset the potentially determining power of cultural discourse by extolling and engaging in self-creative—often verbal—activity:

> If the "cause" of desire, gesture, and act can be localized within the "self" of the actor, then the political regulations and disciplinary practices which produce that ostensibly coherent gender are effectively displaced from view. The displacement of a political and discursive origin of gender identity onto a psychological "core" precludes an analysis of the political constitution of the gendered subject and its fabricated notions about the ineffable interiority of its sex or of its true identity. (Butler, *Bodies* 136)

This unresolved tension over agency and subjectivity clarifies why the myth of masculine self-making aligns so well with broad concerns over masculinity and rhetoric as sociocultural practices. As practices, both masculinity and rhetoric face the same question: What is the level of agency allowed, or subjectivity required, within their respective practices? The myth argues that the sky (or one's personal mettle) is the limit. Most modern rhetorical theorists tend to suggest more limited possibilities or, in some cases, very few possibilities at all. Of those who claim the latter, the most notorious might be Paul de Man, whose literary rhetoric has made him both poster child and whipping boy for issues related to agency and cultural determinism.

Historically, de Man's concern with figural language is a sensible outgrowth of linguistic and literary-critical (semiotic) discussions of 1960–1980 and beyond. What is intriguing in de Man's case is his further insistence, to the dismay of traditional rhetoricians, on conceiving of literary figures "as the language most explicitly grounded in rhetoric" (109). De Man is not merely endorsing a second sophistic or Renaissance figurist position; he embraces recent theories of the figural aspect of language in such a fashion as to unite rhetoric with literature. "I would not hesitate," he declares, "to equate the rhetorical, figural potentiality of language with literature itself" (10). In verve alone, de Man easily outstrips more reserved claims for granting narrative and poetics a role within rhetoric.[3] For my purposes, the importance of de Man lies in his direct raising of problematic connections among concepts of language, rhetorical action, and, by extension, the place of *doxa* and myth in cultural and individual practice and behavior.

De Man's particular sense of rhetorical action begins within an intratextual frame that establishes his rhetoric as one of tropes and figures, not a study of "comment or of eloquence or persuasion" (6). Working from that core component, de Man slowly incorporates all linguistic externals (most easily considered as the referential "world") into the realm of the figural, into which he then absorbs performance, action, and history as well. Said in a reversed image, de Man's rhetoric slowly excludes the referential world from all of language's ostensible acts of reference, ultimately containing all that is knowable within language. The resulting difficulty, at least for rhetoric and its revitalization, is that de Man's stance seriously qualifies rhetoric's relation to effective action. Placing all acts within rhetoric, de Man appears to endorse Farrell's negative view of neosophistic rhetoric by fully collapsing *nomos* and *doxa* into linguistic determinism and historical relativism. The action or agency of self-making belongs to language, not its user.

De Man seems to signal as much when he finds in Nietzsche's critique of metaphysics "the deconstruction of the illusion that the language of truth *(episteme)* could be replaced by a language of persuasion *(doxa)*" (130). This attitude cuts to the heart of current desires for an "interested" rhetoric and literature, since both the renewed study of sophistic rhetoric and de Man's theorizing grow out of the same current theoretical milieu and its stress on discourse as central to human activity. The question is not so much de Man's claim that tropes and figurative structures are "the linguistic paradigm par excellence" (105). The question is what happens when epistemology is a function solely of that same linguistic paradigm. More specifically, the issue becomes one of whether such conceptions of rhetoric and discourse eliminate nondetermined, effective action and individual agency.

For de Man, figures, especially metaphor, serve to paper over the gap between word and world. "Metaphor," de Man states, "overlooks the fictional, textual element in the nature of the entity it connotes. It assumes a world in which intra- and extra-textual events, literal and figurative forms of language, can be distinguished, a world in which the literal and the figural are properties that can be isolated and, consequently, exchanged and substituted for each other." Such is the power of language, but it is a power that de Man immediately qualifies as "an error, although it can be said that no language would be possible without this error" (151–52). Much of the emphasis in this last sentence, and in the work of de Man as a whole, stresses this element of error and the subsequent need to deconstruct the linguistic elements that encourage such misreading. That deconstructive need isn't necessarily troubling to a rhetoric rooted in contemporary theories of language and social construction—until it becomes clear that by extension all social constructs and all behaviors, including deconstructive reading, are themselves necessarily rooted in the same essential error. The thrilling challenge of no boundaries slowly becomes the defeated agony of no exit.

To salvage or offset de Man's sense of rhetoric as requiring "the recurrent confusion of sign and substance" and the open-ended "possibility of error" (136), critics stress that de Man assumes a framework in which textuality is an event characterized internally rather than socioculturally. As Arac notes, de Man's inability to look away from the errors of textuality results primarily from an insistence upon ignoring the "'human relationships,' the 'people,' and the 'long use'" noted by Nietzsche as "enabling" history (253), even if that be *a* history realized in the workings of *doxa* and myth. Key to the resolution, in other words, is how error is to be conceived: as an act of producing and interpreting texts (historical and otherwise) that fails to yield pure truth, or a given of how society maintains itself while pursuing admittedly limited self-knowledge.[4]

Because rhetoric begins with the question of social exchange and cultural maintenance, it has always been linked to the cultural and political issues of its effects and its effectiveness (excessive or limited). Attempts to resolve the deterministic versus agency-granting status of language are apparent in arguments of long-standing within the field, among the oldest being those over the Sophists' (perhaps "immoral") use of antithetical arguments and dissociation of concepts to reveal the error of an assumed factuality, to perform the constructedness of *doxa* and myth, as it were:

The dissociation of concepts could not occur without deception; that is, words had to appear to be synonymous with
experiences actually perceived and not their mere symbolic
representation. "For," as Gorgias argued, "that which is communicated is speech, but speech is not that which is perceived
by the senses and actually exists; therefore the things that
actually exist, which are observed, are not communicated but
[only] speech, but they are perceived by the senses." . . . In
order to structure antithetical relationships, listeners had to
be "deceived" into providing meaning for notions which did
not come from sensory experience. (Enos 79)

Although the investigation of "error" is itself achieved through deception, it is necessary deception in the service of knowledge. The implication for current epistemological and/or interpretive concerns is that
knowledge is actively and continually negotiated, not simply relative or
linguistically determined. In Mailloux's paraphrase of Schiller, "the pragmatic character of truth—its value or usefulness—merges with and is
completed by the rhetorical politics of society, its coercions and cajoler-
ies, its threats and persuasions" (*Reception* 30).

This attaching of general arguments over the nature of meaning to
cultural knowledge is motivated by more than the hope of rescuing rhetoric from cynical relativism, of course. Behind arguments for negotiated
knowledge lies a desire to enter the wider realm of effective social action. As Jarratt states, regarding Mailloux's neopragmatist project, the
question is "how to articulate a radical project of social transformation
which incorporates the philosophical insights of neopragmatism without falling into a relativist despair or political quietism" ("In Excess"
208). Said another way, Where is the ground on which to establish a
rhetoric of myth and *doxa*, a basis for actively negotiating social frames?
In answering that question, many rhetoricians look to Richard Rorty's
and/or Cornel West's attempts to replace foundationalist desires for
"truth" with a pragmatism that accepts "certainty" instead, itself negotiated through social discourse and exchange. Focusing on "the various
ways pragmatism, rhetoric, and sophistry overlap" (*Rhetoric, Sophistry,
Pragmatism* 2), rhetoricians such as Mailloux have joined neoprag-
matists in searching for a model of public action that might enhance not
only rhetoric's theoretical possibilities but also "the effectiveness of progressive political activity" (21). Jarratt even more explicitly unites rhetoric, agency, and *doxa* in referring to Cornell West's pragmatism. West,
she notes, "places *doxa* at the foundation of his philosophical praxis:
'the populace deliberating is creative democracy in the making'" (Jarratt,

"In Excess" 214; West 213). The advantages for achieving a desired agency are obvious, as are the further implications for rhetoric.

At the same time, many critics such as Tom Cohen and Jarratt herself find Rorty's and West's ideas of social dynamics overly "genteel." As was true with *doxa* and *nomos,* there is a tendency toward a homogenized and simplifying vision that fails to speak to "specific social differences" (Jarratt, "In Excess" 209, 211).[5] Jarratt grants West awareness of this problem, noting his attempt to shift Rorty's broad liberal humanism into a more specific cultural criticism and linking his prophetic and romantic pragmatism to popular, cultural feminisms. Her goal is to create a space for each, offering an open-minded recognition that "the strengths of these romantic pragmatisms lie in their powerful rhetoric of love and transformation" (216). At the same time, there is a recognition that whatever the validity of the stance, there is a social utopianism here, a gap in neopragmatism's description of society that hampers its usefulness in describing rhetoric's role in maintaining society at large.

The problem in defining society on these grounds is visible in the way neopragmatism characterizes individuality versus subjectivity. There is a tendency in Rorty, as Cohen notes, to replace the troubling "subject" of continental theorizing with "a certain self or American 'identity'" (98) more agreeable to American pragmatism. In Cohen's eyes, while West may recognize Rorty's move, his subsequent failure to follow up with anything more than "a theologized self, only now communitarian" (100), is yet another key moment lost, a reinstatement of "the integral human subject and a seamless model for action to boot" rather than a study of the self in relation to a constitutive rhetoric (103). Cohen's implications are clear. Neopragmatism may attempt to avoid simple rationalism, cynical relativism, or linguistic determinism by moving toward negotiated knowledge, agency, and a rhetoric of effective action. But the move eventually founders on vague representations of both society and subject. As Cohen says elsewhere, "neopragmatism . . . end[s] by reinventing a privileged interiority or self" that is suspiciously free of the actual dynamics of society's power for self and subject construction and maintenance ("Diary" 162).[6]

Cohen's own rhetoric resolves Rorty and West's U.S. identity-self versus a Continental subject-self by endorsing the latter as a means to performative action against those doxic processes that mask subjectivity in the guise of self. The emphasis is on the necessity for "more *pragmatic* interventions." In short, we cannot achieve self; but we can attack the processes of subject formation. It is an interesting proposition, but such a move toward postmodern play is problematic on grounds ironically similar to those I noted in regard to Ricoeur. Cohen's delightfully over-the-top call to be "a pirate disrupting the commercial trade routes of . . . discourse" (108) tends to enact its own mythic rhetoric in order to subvert a deterministic situation. Individual agency is rewritten as a radical form of self-making. But wishing we can fly won't make it so, and open-ended calls for transgressive actions risk enacting a rhetoric of exuberant postmodernism whose surface appeal is not all that different from traditional, masculine appeals to entrepreneurial self-making.[7] "Just doing it" won't clarify what or who might be doing "it," nor does it erase the environment in which "it" is done. In Connell's words, "Recognizing multiple masculinities, especially in an individualist culture such as the United States, risks taking them for alternative lifestyles, a matter of consumer choice" (76).

Berlin likewise sees calls for agentive identity play as "narrative[s] told from the limited and exclusive view of a small segment of the comfortable classes." For the "vast majority of workers . . . glorying in the possibilities of floating subjects and indeterminate signifiers is unthinkable. Space-time compression for them means out of work and out of luck, not the frolic of simulated experiences from other places and times" (67). Ignoring such economic strictures, the entrepreneurs of self-help and success guides also encourage open-ended risk as a form of free play on the free market. But a *New York Times* headline argues the effects of class dynamics on the free play of the marketplace with a thumping dose of Dickensian reality: "Hard Work Can't Stop Hard Times" (A1)—and "free" play doesn't come without cost. The social frame, as Layton notes, is ignored or weakly defined at one's peril. In the call for ludic agency, "the pain of this fragmented self is forgotten or bracketed and [the subject] is rather figured as able to subvert the system by enjoying, rearranging, and playing with her fragments; . . . [Such portrayals] paradoxically leave the reader with the sense that their protagonists are in total control of their fragments, that they are auteurs who pick and choose how they wish to represent themselves at any given moment" (108–9). Calls for free play, in short, enact appeals similar to the rhetoric of self-making and its elision of the powerful presence of *doxa*.

This is not to say that it is necessary to endorse once again the opposition between self-agency/determinism by moving to the other half of an assumed binary. The question is not one of a society in which doxic behavior is wholly determined or opposable only by open-ended acts of self-making.[8] Rather the issue is one of degrees of agency within the rules of subject formation, of complicating the binary opposition in the same way that Jarratt has done by revisiting the overly easy triad of *mythos/nomos/logos*. Such complications serve, as Judith Butler notes, to define identity as neither "fatally determined nor fully artificial and arbitrary"

(*Trouble* 147). Within such a social and rhetorical framework, the subject "is not *determined* by the rules through which it is generated because signification is *not a founding act, but rather a regulated process of repetition*" (145). Agency as effective social action performs according to those rules of repeated representation even as it offers its own patterns of asymmetrical and subversive repetition. Restated in language specific to my argument, agency should be characterized in terms of a subjectivity practiced and performed through particular acts of social and cultural representation (such as myths of self-making), which enact the larger *doxa* of masculinity in general.

If masculinity is to be seen as a body of gender practices—practices that can be seen as continually enacted and maintained as cultural rhetoric—then disciplines specifically concerned with describing actual behavior and practice are likely to be needed. Joseph Pleck's social psychology offers a useful starting point for that characterization, arguing that the individual does not develop proper masculinity by acquiring the necessary components *seriatim*. Rather, like cultural myths, gender is a varied body of subjective practices in constant tense contact with a larger concept that no one example or individual actually attains. As a consequence, emphasis is placed on tense negotiation or "sex-role-strain" between available cultural representations of masculinity and the individual members of society subject to those doxic arguments.[9] Restated in rhetorical terms, because *doxa* is realized in and through cultural myths that are inherently contradictory and inconsistent, there will be a high proportion of individuals who violate the arguments and representations put forward as proper masculinity, thus experiencing strain and tension over what society maintains and what they experience.

Such a frame implies an ongoing process of recapitulation and accommodation among subject-specific behaviors and desires and larger representative myths and social beliefs. At the same time, because both myths and individuals embody doxic contradictions, anxieties, and inconsistencies within their own rhetorical self-enactment, masculinity and its representations are in some ways "psychologically dysfunctional." The resulting disparity between doxic argument and personal experience results in feelings of inadequacy, feelings additionally strained by ongoing historical shifts that further impact on experience and *doxa*. Masculinity, in short, is an active interplay between society's ongoing, rhetorical self-maintenance and the members of that society who are themselves enacting, producing, and testing the mythic rhetoric that embodies *doxa*.

The shift by Pleck toward nonessentialism and practice in sex role models has obvious usefulness for conceiving rhetoric's role in such a dynamic process. But sex role theory as a whole still has several shortcomings. Role theory's regular division of gender into masculine versus feminine overemphasizes these two roles and tends to render the categories more static, often reinforcing the view of gender as a binary opposition based ultimately on biology (Connell, among others, 26–27). More problematically, role theory often implies role playing, an activity that I have already suggested tends to drift toward endorsing a certain level of agency and choice. Butler is arguing directly against this tendency when she insists that "performativity is thus not a singular 'act.'" Rather, it is "always a reiteration of a norm or set of norms, and to the extent that it acquires an act-like status in the present, it conceals and dissimulates the conventions of which it is a repetition." (*Bodies* 12).[10]

Masculinity, in short, is a project of self- and societal maintenance that is not determined by (yet cannot be divorced from) sex, or language, or genes alone; that's clearly too simple. Nor is it gender role playing or even cultural free play, given society's power to naturalize *doxa*. Finally, it cannot be characterized simply as the possession or the individual internalization of a lump sum of masculine traits—a possibility perhaps encouraged by my own earlier concern with describing psychoanalytic motifs and components of the myth and its rhetoric in light of male/male oedipal exchange. The enactment of gender rests within all these concerns as a bounded practice or, in admittedly strained materialist terms, a production attenuated by its means of production (bodily and institutional) and its larger context.

The myth of masculine self-making rejects such explanation, of course, insisting on the pure agency of independent self-fabrication as the heart of masculinity. It does so by endorsing mythic arguments for masculine self-making and also by providing the rhetorical performance itself as a premier means of doing so. Public enactment (via self-display) of "accepted" masculine behavior thus supposedly validates the myth as it performs it. Most contemporary rhetoricians tend to agree more with Bert Wheeler's view, however, seeing rhetorical (and personal) performance as more scripted, more dependent upon the cultural rhetoric itself. Battaglia is representative of many when she argues for a rhetoric capable of addressing the "*problematics of self-action* in . . . relation to issues of power," where power is defined as a highly complex, rhetorically maintained social arrangement, and the gendered self is seen as a "representational economy: a reification continually defeated by mutable entanglements with others subjects' histories, experiences, self-representations; with their texts, conduct, gestures, objectifications; with their 'argument of images,' . . . and so forth" (2).

As all the above arguments suggest, such a rhetoric of masculinity needs to address masculinity in relation to a material social frame defined in terms of agency, power, and the role of language in relation to each. At the same time, not only the reinforcement but also the etiology of the engendering process needs to be discussed. Since a great deal of the effective force of masculine rhetoric relies upon deep, unconscious assent to doxic beliefs, psychoanalytic concepts of gender and sexuality are central to characterizing the problematics of masculinity as cultural rhetoric.

Language, Psychoanalysis, and Rhetoric

The psychoanalytic work of Lacan offers some of the most complex discussions of the link between agency, gender, and language. It also offers potentially the least radical revisioning of masculine myths of self-making. As Jacqueline Rose admits, there is "no question of denying . . . that Lacan was implicated in the phallocentrism he described, just as his own utterance constantly rejoins the mastery which he sought to undermine" (Introduction 56). Because Lacanian discourse carries these gendered overtones, it has "the potential for setting in motion both feminist and virulently misogynistic analyses" (Sedgwick, *Between Men* 24). Fully explaining such paradoxes is beyond the scope of my purpose here, although their presence is useful in indicating again that cultural rhetoric and *doxa* are inescapable, even within fields attempting to explain the dynamics of both. In order to discuss Lacan in regard to both this dynamic and those aspects of his thinking that are useful to my own goals, I am going to present particular aspects of Lacan's ideas rather rapidly, always a danger with any complex theory, and even more so with Lacan.

For Lacan—and I am summarizing heavily here—the gender training that constitutes masculinity (and femininity, as well, although I am setting that aside) is part of the overall question of subjectivity. In Lacan, that subjectivity is continually characterized through a variety of related terms: *split, division, difference, separation, lack, alienation.* Throughout life, the subject is faced with innumerable moments or events in which a sense of wholeness or unity is rudely met with an awareness of a lack of unity, of partiality and separateness, external control and nonagency. In short, the subject is constantly faced with its own subjectivity, with the tension between a desire for wholeness and an awareness of division. Although this sense of division is basic and constant, there are key stages and moments in the forming of subjectivity, most particularly the mirror stage and the oedipal stage. It is these two stages, and their connection to language, that are most useful to my own concerns.

In the mirror stage, the child "sees" and experiences itself (literally through sight of itself in a mirror, although the visible reflection of this specific event is supported with other "mirrorings" by the world) as a coherent and unified whole. That experience is extremely fleeting, however, since the image is already outside of the child and beyond its control. The initial sense of coherence and its rapidly ensuing sense of division defines or establishes subjectivity, which henceforth contains a constant pursuit—and denial of—a fantasied identity that is a unified and ideal whole. This process of establishing and experiencing the dividedness of subjectivity, along with its nagging sense of nonagency, is extended by Lacan in his discussion of both the Oedipus complex and language, or more generally, the Symbolic. Like the mirror stage, division is a key issue in the experience of the oedipal phase. In Freud, the primary trauma of masculine engendering that is associated with oedipal desire and the threat of castration requires renunciation of desire for the mother and orientation to the father. Lacan's major contribution is to radically emphasize the role of language in these oedipal dynamics, making language acquisition, or access to the phallic/symbolic, central in the formation of subjectivity and sexuality. In Lacanian theory, the oedipal situation and its threats of castration are inseparably connected to language use, "when speakers enter language through submission to the phallus, which is a signifier [language], and separate from the preoedipal mother" (Roman, "Female" 12).[11]

Importantly for my concerns, the connections Lacan develops between the oedipal phase, its threat of castration, and the resulting need to relinquish a fantasy of wholeness through union with another, on the one hand, and language acquisition and entrance into the Symbolic, on the other, are clearly gendered. Unable to fulfill a fantasy for a dyadic wholeness, the male child enters instead the realm of the symbolic order, an order whose definition is the law of the father, the phallic law. That gendered description may not be produced by psychoanalysis or, even ultimately, by Lacan. Lacan's characterization of the Symbolic as phallic can be described as evidence of patriarchal culture and cultural rhetoric at work, precisely the tack taken by Rose following her admission that Lacan's descriptions are undeniably "phallocentric." Whatever the source of the descriptive rhetoric, within its gendered frame, language, law, and social power can be readily equated with masculinity, albeit a masculinity defined in terms of an externally divided subjectivity reinscribed by the very phallic language and Symbolic that is now entered and used. In summary, the achievement of masculinity gives rise to a subjectivity deeply characterized by issues of separation, limited agency, and language, but one with privileged access to a gendered hierarchy that provides opportunities and means to repress that sense of fragmentation.

Given these descriptions, Lacan's theorizing on language and sexuality clearly bears on theories of rhetorical action and masculine self-making—both directly and indirectly. As is true with Erikson and Kohlberg, Lacan's language-based Symbolic and its ties to oedipal struggle, separation, and agency not only describe but in some ways reinscribe mythic desires in masculine self-making. As Lacanian theory outlines the processes by which masculine subjectivity and agency are controlled by language use, it also establishes the very means for denying that division. In order to repress the forced separations and external controls in masculine development, language as self-making or subject making is reversed in the myth of the self-made man. External control of the subject by language is introjected as control of language—and self, and others—by the self-making man. It is because of this dynamic that Lacan's theory provides the means, in Sedgwick's double-edged claim, for "talking about the relation between the individual male and the cultural institutions of male domination that fall usefully under the rubric of representation" (24).

In particular, Lacan's model serves to highlight the import of regular declarations by avatars of self-making that they "speak themselves," and do so with self-made authenticity. As I have noted in regard to Ricoeur and to Miller's patriarch, there is a recurring scene or motif in dramas of masculine self-making: the validity of one's word as public stand-in for the authenticity of one's self. In fact, the presence of this theme is nearly ubiquitous in portrayals of masculinity, and it may occur either as a direct enactment of speaking/authenticity or paradoxically as the opposite, where correctly performed taciturnity serves to validate the importance of speaking nothing but one's masculinity.

Once more, Miller's grandfather provides a useful perspective on the process. Within the oedipally weighted frame of male/male exchange, the historically dominant, individualistic masculinity of the grandfather is achieved via his use of the entrepreneurial, noncorporate card: "no company." David's self-proclaimed fantasy of corporate independence is easily trumped by his father-in-law's declared status as a true lone male, a unitary, unified self with no reliance upon that modern support frame—the corporation. That mythic status is further reinforced through his control over the discourse itself and its capacity to place David both outside the frame of true, self-made masculinity and outside the frame of a controlling "I." Miller's patriarch smoothly establishes a dominant "I," a role clarified through opposition to others, here specifically the other discourse-active male in the room: David. The secondary, son-in-law status of David need only be noted by the *paterfamilias* to make it so, while the grandfather's repetition of "I . . . you . . . you . . . you. You're . . ." (36) nicely reinforces the dynamic of dominance and separation. The oedipal reigns—as a victory for the father and his law.

The discourse performed by David's father-in-law may not place full control of language in his hands, but it certainly establishes David's masculinity as subordinate to the phallic symbolic and the law of the father. It is worth remembering, in light of this positioning of David, that he himself repeats the process in separating himself from his daughter: "'Grownups are trying to *talk* here,' he whispered sharply to me" (37). It is with this clear grasping of the phallic symbolic that David attempts to establish, if not his fantasy of a unified, self-made masculinity, then at least some measure of dominance and masculinity. He does so precisely because belief in masculine agency and authenticity is strongly maintained and regularly represented within Western cultural rhetoric as inseparable from straight talk and verbal domination.

This continually recurring scene in the myth of self-making may not be primal, but it is of primary importance in many renditions of self-making and masculinity—both popular and analytic, pro and con. In its related concern with language acquisition and identity, Lacanian theory helps explain the needs driving these dramas of masculine discourse. By declaring that separation and the resulting sense of conflicted identity are inscribed within the phallic/symbolic order, Lacan clarifies the doxic concern by linking masculine agency to rhetorical control. But it is the job of masculine *doxa* to set aside the trauma of separation in Lacan by linking language use not to the anxiety of separation but to the joy of authentic masculinity. David is revealed as only fantasizing himself as self-made, but *he* is rejected as inauthentic, not the myth. His relation to his father-in-law and subsequent behavior only serves to prove the doxic rule.

It is important to stress that those rules are themselves reinforced through emphasis on the oedipal. Having been separated from an original sense of union and wholeness (whether a result of defeat by the father in the Freudian oedipal or entry into the Lacanian Symbolic), the myth of self-making urges the conflicted male child to attain—and to voice—a masculinity that is experienced and expressed as a sense of a personal, authentic wholeness neither separated from nor determined by the external world. Linguistic power becomes evidence not of a forced separation or a subsequent defeat but of a desired and intentionally pursued masculinity. To control language, in line with this sense of masculine action, is to have personal agency and social power. The importance of the motif is evidenced by the flexibility granted to the varied forms of linguistic control that are espoused. Thus, spellbinding oratory, plain speaking, and even a refusal to speak (classic Gary Cooper taciturnity) are all evidence of masculine control because all are evidence of linguistic control.

Operating within the presence of this long-standing masculine rhetoric, the Lacanian representation both critiques the doxic argument and risks becoming a creature of it. Lacan may establish the acquisition of the Symbolic as an incomplete resolution of a sense of nonwholeness. But that sense tends to be overshadowed in the ensuing emphasis on successful grasping of the phallic/symbolic and society's granting of real value to that move, just as preoedipal separation is overshadowed in traditional psychoanalytic emphasis on the oedipal. From this angle, Lacan's language-based model of oedipal drama can be seen as functioning similarly to Erikson's and Kohlberg's scales: All critique, and all are implicated in, masculine desires and uncertainties enacted within the rhetoric of masculine *doxa*. This is not to say that concerns over language, self, and reality are solely masculine concerns. They are, in fact, central to any discussion of human development.

What is key in Lacan, of course, is his insistence on reading language and subjectivity not as stages in a developmental progression but as constitutive processes—specifically processes rooted in a sense of loss, lack, and—in regard to the oedipal—defeat. The myth of self-making argues precisely the opposite and does so via language as both medium and motif for performing masculine self-making. Summarized once again, masculine self-making partakes of a preset rhetoric of masculinity—as well as a real set of social values attached to both myth and masculinity. What we continually see, then, is a process by which *doxa* incorporates concerns into its cultural rhetoric so as to mask flaws in its arguments, to defuse anxieties over a masculinity that the rhetoric claims is flawless and the height of individual agency and achievement. Lacan clearly establishes the nature of some of those anxieties, as related to language and his Symbolic, while for its part the myth clearly relies on an opposing cultural rhetoric to establish elements of its general appeal. What Lacan provides, finally, is a means for adding to the portrait of myth and rhetoric as deeply, complexly, and regularly involved in maintaining masculinity.

I began my argument by noting that cultural rhetoric can best be explained as an ongoing act of doxic self-maintenance in which individuals and society perform acceptable genders. On one level, that explanation provides a particular explanation of the myth's effectiveness. A positive representation of the myth, such as the Alger tales or Lee Iacocca's autobiography, could be explained in several ways. Admittedly, the myth can be effective as a simple fantasy. For the individual whose situation does not match the myth (i.e., most male readers), the particular example could provide pure imaginative escape from his own situation: Enacting the myth provides temporary solace. Or, as the myth really tries to argue, it could provide incentive to further match fantasy with one's own experience: to perform the myth in depth.

But these explanations of rhetorical effectiveness simplify both the range of audience response and issues of concern regularly enacted in even positive versions of the myth, issues such as failure and self-destruction. Negative enactments of the myth recognize those outcomes and argue them directly, of course. As I will discuss in upcoming chapters, narratives oriented toward steelworkers as laborers regularly signal the presence of flaws in the myth, both directly and indirectly. Bell's Dubik is burned to death in the mill while pursuing his goals, and the entrepreneurial Kracha is socially and economically exiled; Whittaker's Larry Locke is beaten up and believed dead; Attaway's Big Mat sadomasochistically destroys himself; Porter's Mikey faces self-denial and a lifetime of separation from his working-class family. Even the most emblematic success stories display tensions within the rhetoric. Carnegie himself will be forced to admit defeat, relinquishing personal control of the wealth that made him what he was to institutional minions and subalterns. At least he closed with a suggestion of a choice. Liquor tycoon Burt Wheeler didn't even maintain that level of agency, becoming in death a good example of what he denied in life.

Given these complications and qualifications, the rhetorical enactment of the myth of self-making must consist of more than identification with and supposed public enactment of a simple fantasy of heroic masculinity. Rather than simply offering escape, the myth's wide-ranging effectiveness instead appears to lie in its ability to enact the full range of repressed anxieties and pleasures embodied in masculinity, all the while maintaining an argument for masculinity as untroubled, individualistic, agentive. To explain how and why the rhetoric of masculine self-making so effectively maintains that myth, it is necessary to delve into a hotly denied component of masculinity—masochism—and explain its connection to a myth that would appear to argue the complete opposite of such behavior.

Social Myths and Sadomasochism

One of the characteristics of masculinity that I have been stressing throughout this chapter is its performativity, its continual, tense enactment of gaps between cultural ideal, social situation, and particular experience. The myth of masculine self-making mirrors and repeats that process in its paradoxical reliance upon socially validated portraits of masculine agency and control and its simultaneous refusal of closure, a willful inability to produce a full sense of resolution in the portrait of masculinity that it extols. Internal conflicts arise, I've declared, because the myth is an attempt, by both society and subject, to perform the inherent contradictions of the *doxa* as they are embodied in cultural rhetoric. That description begs a question. If the myth is contradictory, what is the motive force behind allegiance to the myth and to *doxa*?

Together, psychoanalysis and rhetoric provide an answer—not just in theory but in performance. Paraphrasing Silverman's arguments, allegiance to *doxa* depends upon its ability to "extend itself into the deepest reaches of the subject's identity and unconscious desire," thus "successfully defining what passes for 'reality' at the level of the psyche" (*Male Subjectivity* 16, 21). How then do we define the means by which *doxa* "extends" itself into the psyche? To describe that process, Silverman undertakes a move similar to Jarratt's introduction of narrative into culturally formative rhetoric, offering "the dominant fiction" as a means for connecting individual identity and social practice, personal belief, and *doxa*. Similar to Lyotard's "grand" narratives, Silverman's dominant fiction "not only offers the representational system by means of which the subject typically assumes a sexual identity, and takes on the desires commensurate with that identity, but forms the stable core around which a nation's and a period's 'reality' coheres . . . " (*Male Subjectivity* 41). In short, a dominant fiction or myth enacts the pattern for a subject's earliest engendering and thus lays the groundwork for ongoing affirmation of the rightness (or wrongness) of the ensuing gender performance, individually and in general.

Silverman's choice for the dominant fiction of masculinity—the Oedipus complex—is particularly useful to my own arguments concerning the rhetoric of masculinity, even without Lacan's connection of the oedipal and the symbolic. As is so often the case, psychoanalytic narratives of the individual match very nicely with general cultural narratives. The match is not really surprising, however, since psychoanalysis—like rhetoric—attempts to explain how individuals are persuaded that cultural fictions (myths) are their fictions or, more radically, their selves.[12] Psychoanalysis, in my terms, describes the *doxa* that rhetoric embodies through particular myths. In the particular case I'm discussing here, authentic masculinity is embodied in self-making, achieved by emphasizing what *doxa* maintains as the correct pattern for doing so: struggle with primary embodiments of desired masculinity, the father and/or his authority.

But outlining the operations of dominant fictions and myths does not fully resolve the question as to why there is allegiance to a contradictory myth such as masculine self-making. It is relatively easy to assume that a noncontradictory cultural fiction or myth (as an embodiment of *doxa*) could be readily practiced by a society and its individual subjects. The oedipal dynamic (which the rhetoric of masculine self-making depends upon) really only works in its ideal form, however. The process is perfect only where society and psychoanalysis assume a complete, residue-free enactment of the oedipal dynamic. That assumed, masculinity moves freely forward into active, aggressive, unified postoedipal behavior. There is an oddity, however, even on a theoretical level, in the Freudian implication of an ensuing melioration of anxiety or guilt following oedipal resolution. It speaks a repression that is more than repression. Nevertheless, following Freud, many psychoanalytic descriptions regularly suggest what appears to be a doxic wish to characterize masculinity as a natural progression in development, a move toward healthy agency and away from unhealthy (and feminine) passivity.

Unfortunately, this idealized representation looks suspect from the start. The underlying implication of the whole rhetorical framework is that the oedipal dynamic dictates that the male child achieves masculine status by suffering the key defeat of his life—defeat by the father through the threat of castration. That traumatic threat and subsequent defeat are necessary and supposedly effective, in the oedipal model, because they lead to the ultimate formation of a realistic attitude toward life and life's possibilities. But the further implication for the child is clear: Having been defeated by the father, the child's active powers have already been called into question on a fundamental level. In its most visceral form, the myth makes that excruciatingly clear: "Yes, you may have the opportunity to display masculine agency and generativity, but only if I don't cut off the penis that supposedly will enable you to do so." In short, the oedipal defeat sets up a deep threat of passivity or, in terms of a related anxiety, an uncertain feminization of the male child. Silverman captures the situation nicely:

> There is a fundamental impossibility about the position in which the male subject is held, an impossibility which has to do with the self-canceling structure of the Oedipal imperative. The only mechanism by which the son can overcome his desire for the father is to . . . attempt to *become* the (symbolic) father. However, this metamorphosis is precisely what the super-ego prohibits by decreeing: "You may not be like [your father] . . . you may not do all that he does; some things are his prerogative." (*Male Subjectivity* 194)

The basic rhetoric of masculinity thus contains an inherent contradiction: You must be masculine, but you have already suffered a defeat that marks you as "not-the-father," a defeat that also hints at nonmasculinity or feminization.[13] That defeat is further exacerbated by an engendering process that insists upon an essential dividedness within subjectivity, a lurking awareness of separation from a prior sense of wholeness. Whatever the specific etiology of this lost sense of wholeness, both Freudian and Lacanian descriptions argue that masculinity desires (even as it denies) that original wholeness as union or reunion with the mother, the maternal, the feminine. Defeat, feminization, dividedness, passivity—these are deeply dangerous and deeply denied aspects of masculine engendering. Not surprisingly, then, the tensions and anxieties that result from their presence—and their necessary and continual representation in the myth of masculine self-making—are ultimately central to explaining the myth's appeal.

That paradox can be explained in light of a particularly good example of the full nature of the myth's complicated appeal: "The Bicentennial Man," a short story by Isaac Asimov. Not only does Andrew Martin wish to make himself a man in this narrative, he intends to do so as the ultimate hot metal man—a robot. The entire plot of "The Bicentennial Man" rests on the ensuing conflicts between what society designs Andrew Martin to be and what he literally attempts to make of himself. To flesh out Martin's development, Asimov makes use of some common motifs. Martin is portrayed as struggling with language, for example, and in need of instruction in its use. Language thus initially reinforces Martin's separation from the human. But his full entry into the symbolic is primarily audodidactic, and once control is fully attained, Martin's use of the symbolic to achieve his own ends becomes unquestionable and unquestioned within much of society. In his pursuit of self-making, Martin uses language to control not only his own literal relationship to laws of the father (early on it is his argument that leads to his being declared free) but also to control others—robot and human alike. In this and other ways, the story takes up key concerns in masculine engendering that are typically traumatic and threatening—and converts them into marks of self-making success. In the end, however, the masculinity pursued by Martin rests on a conundrum hidden deep in the *doxa* of masculinity: to make himself fully a man, Andrew Martin must kill himself.

Andrew Martin's self-making death clearly makes him a self-made man in a deeply paradoxical way. Yet it is important to note that the *doxa* of masculinity makes such a sadomasochistic ending both sensible and right. From the start, the rhetoric of self-making provides Martin with two options if he is to be truly a man: to strive to achieve as no one else ever has or to destroy himself in the process. As he says, his self-destruction will bring him either "humanity" or "an end to striving" (171). The final irony of the story—and of the myth of the self-made man—is that the doxic rhetoric of masculine self-making has always made the two choices one and the same. It is not really an either/or question. What the myth of masculine self-making offers is the opportunity to strive to achieve as no one else ever has *and* to destroy oneself in the process. Anything less is a defeat, since continued immersion in masculine *doxa* produces both an invitation and a requirement to continue the struggle, continue the aggression and dominance, the pursuit of masculine self-making—a self-making whose definition finally rests not on declaring what masculinity is so much as using the pursuit to avoid what masculinity may lack or may not be.

The tensions and contradictions underlying that insistent need to pursue self-making are made clear in the close of "The Bicentennial Man." As Andrew Martin dies, he "desperately" seizes at his last thoughts. "Man! He was a man! He wanted that to be his last thought. He wanted to dissolve—die—with that" (172). Martin's last act of agency, killing himself, is to be matched in his mind with declaration of what that agency has produced: a self-made man. Yet his actual last thought is something else entirely: "One final fugitive thought came to him and rested for a moment on his mind before everything stopped. 'Little Miss,' he whispered, too low to be heard" (172). What Martin's last, "fugitive" thought underscores is that his ceaseless drive to make himself a man is not primary. His two-hundred-year pursuit of masculine self-making only covers up a buried fantasy of wholeness, of indivisibility imaged not in terms of oedipal individuality but in terms of return to and nonseparation from a woman. The story's close thus echoes psychoanalytic descriptions of masculine engendering as a series of separations and defeats, revealing at the same time that the myth of self-making is itself masking a fantasied self-unity and agency.[14]

The presence of these contradictory arguments and experiences are the source of a whipsawing that unites self-making and self-destruction, creating a masculinity whose sadomasochistic undertones run throughout the oedipal in general and the myth of the self-made man in particular. Such a claim quickly raises objections. Masochistic pleasure traditionally has been considered a feminine (or even female) behavioral pattern, a pattern that is clinically aberrant only when excessive in a woman—but supposedly aberrant in most forms for a man, given its passive characterization. The presence of what appears to be endorsement of masochistic behavior in figures such as Andrew Martin qualifies this easy separation of masochism along gender lines, as does Silverman's discussion of the irresolvability of the Oedipus complex.

It still is possible, of course, to argue that Martin's self-destruction reveals the highest form of postoedipal agency and self-making. In David Savran's more colloquial phrasing, "the subject, torturing himself, can prove himself a man" (33).[15] But Savran himself qualifies any easy reversal by contextualizing and historicizing masculinity. For Savran, masculinity is sadomasochistic not simply in terms of its fundamental basis in oedipal training but as an ongoing aspect of masculine behavior attached to the rise of mercantile capitalism and its emphasis on self-denial and self-abnegation—and also on its ruses of power.[16] Following Savran, I would and will argue that the myth's contradictions are often most apparent in versions told by and about nondominant groups—such as the steelworkers' narratives I noted above. But if Andrew Martin is admittedly operating as part of an economically dominant class, his arguments for self-destruction as self-making are themselves framed by an equally dominant mythic rhetoric whose arguments about masculinity—men should suffer pain and ignore socially determined failure—already determine what Andrew must do to attain his goal, and his goal is to destroy himself. The ultimate choice is the logical end in a series that outlines a process of masculine engendering that may be privileged but is neither open ended nor individually agentive at base. It is, however, a choice so well aligned with the rhetoric of masculine self-making as to appear to be satisfying.

That interpretation leads to a troubling question. If the myth's persuasive power relies upon a hidden, masochistic self-destructiveness that lies at the heart of masculinity, then is the myth's appeal based solely on its ability to enact a related masochistic pleasure? I am more than willing to agree that the myth does allow for that form of behavior. But I am hesitant to assume that every enactment of the myth and its masculinity is fully successful or solely devoted to reinscribing masculine sadomasochism. For one thing, I've already defined both myth and masculinity as flawed and incapable of an untroubled enactment of *doxa*. In addition, I've suggested that class differences do affect response to particular myths. Finally, I would argue that repetition of the myth not only serves the subject as a means of testing his own masculinity but also serves as a means of testing the myth as well—even if such testing does not yield understanding.

In completing the answer as to why a flawed myth of masculine self-making enjoys such allegiance, then, I would follow Michelle Massé's answer to a similar question. Discussing the immensely popular genre of the Gothic in light of feminine gender issues, Massé points to an immediate dilemma: What is the pleasure, especially for women readers, to be found in a genre regularly devoted to the brutalization of women? The answer has traditionally been that of female masochism. Not satisfied with such a negative description of the *doxa* of feminine identity, Massé has proposed the Gothic not as a complex form of escape or ritual enactment but rather a working out, through the writing and reception of the fiction, of cultural gender training—a gender training rooted in the society's and the individual's attempts to embody needs and beliefs incorporated within that training. "We must consider 'normal' feminine development," Massé claims, "as a form of culturally induced trauma and the Gothic novel its repetition. That repetition is not generated by masochistic pleasure but instead, like the response to other forms of trauma, is an attempt at mastery and a revised reality principle" (7).[17] Such an interpretation saves the activity from becoming simply a willing acceptance of and pleasure in masochism.

At the same time, it is important not to use such an explanation to sanitize or even erase masochism within the performance. Cultural myths are not merely readily occupiable arenas for self-exploration; they are dangerous repetitions of the sociocultural frame itself. As Massé argues in light of her own concerns, "The Gothic plot is thus not an 'escape' from the real world but a repetition and exploration of the traumatic denial of identity found there. Both the nightmare status of the protagonists and the all-enveloping power of the antagonists are extensions of social ideology and real-world experience" (18). Performance of the myth remains necessary to maintaining a culturally defined subjectivity, which explains why a particular myth would, indeed must, be performed, even when threatening and potentially destructive. Stated similarly by Butler, enactment of an "I and its position can be secured only by being *repeatedly* assumed, . . . whereby 'assumption' . . . is a question of *repeating* that norm, citing or miming that norm" (Butler, *Bodies* 108), whether the norm be self-making or self-destruction. Social behaviors signal, reinscribe, and maintain doxic norms or patterns recognizable in themselves and productive of a subject's sense of self. Whatever their specific differences, Silverman, Savran, Massé, and Butler all agree with such a characterization. To be masculine, then, is to perform the accepted practices of masculinity, with all their contradictory arguments and related effects:

> What distinguishes psychoanalysis from sociological accounts of gender is that whereas for the latter, the internalization of norms is assumed roughly to work, the basic premise and indeed starting-point of psychoanalysis is that it does not. The unconscious constantly reveals the "failure" of identity. Because there is no continuity of psychic life, so there is no stability of sexual identity, no position for women (or men) which is ever simply achieved. Nor does psychoanalysis see such "failure" as a special-case inability or an individual deviancy from the norm. . . . Instead, "failure" is something endlessly recreated and relived moment by moment throughout our individual histories. (Rose, *Vision* 90–91)

As a particular version of this dynamic, the rhetoric of the self-made man reenacts the argument of oedipal structuring and defeat in an attempt to validate what is beyond the immediate validation or rejection of individuals or even full societies. Males participating in the myth's rhetoric can sense the incompleteness of the process, yet they cannot completely reject the dynamic without rejecting societal endorsement of the particular structuring that has produced their own sense of identity.

There are thus good reasons for the vociferousness with which purveyors of the myth of masculine self-making insist on real/phony representations of manliness—it signals a deep defensiveness. Hidden within the rhetorical performance of the myth and the *doxa* that it embodies are incomplete resolutions of both oedipal defeat and preoedipal division and separation. Ironically, uncertain awareness of the myth's contradictions and its nonsymmetrical relation to personal experience is itself a motivation for insistence on the myth's validity. Saying otherwise would require investigation of the very identity being extolled. Awareness and avoidance of that possibility are visible again and again in the myth's insistent enactment of its own arguments in the face of their contradiction. David's Nobodaddy father-in-law succinctly, effectively, and rhetorically dominates him with all the cultural power of history and all the psychological power of oedipal rivalry over the daughter/wife. Then David mimics the process. Andrew Martin pursues self-made masculinity only to arrive at a masochistic self-destruction that has a fantasied return to wholeness at its heart. Bert Wheeler attempts to deny self-making and is swallowed up by the rhetoric of self-making, while Iacocca's self-making verbosity is the product of a ghostwriter. Anxious recognitions occur within such representations, but not resolutions.

The unresolvable tensions between personal experience and cultural rhetoric are not relegated solely to the psychic, of course. They are reinforced and reenacted on class and racial grounds and are equally affected by shifting historical arguments concerning these social constructs. In the nineteenth century, *doxa* was already producing differing versions of the myth—one for the middle class and one for the working class. Miller's tale likewise alludes to the tensions produced by historical stresses and change. For a myth that claims ready access to a universal masculinity, the presence of multiple versions is an embarrassing admission of contradictions and boilerplate arguments. It is also dangerous, since such contradictions threaten society's structured performance of masculinity. The goal of *doxa,* after all, is to make its dominant myth not just the most popular but also the only game in town, eliminating excessive anxiety and social strain by eliminating clearly contradictory versions. In the remaining chapters, I critique particular examples of those variations, dominant and subversive, to gauge their impact on the basic framework of the myth, its arguments about masculinity, and the power of cultural rhetoric to maintain them both.

3

A Father Is Being Beaten:
History-Making Selves and
Self-Making Histories

> From a strictly statistical point of view, around 1835 appears to
> have been the most propitious birth year for a poor boy who hoped
> to rise into the business elite.
>
> —Irvin G. Wyllie,
> *The Self-Made Man in America: The Myth of Rags to Riches*

> Andrew Carnegie was born to bitterly poor parents in Scotland in
> 1835. His family emigrated from Dumferline, Fife, in 1848 when
> his father, a master weaver, lost his job.
>
> —Sean Dennis Cashman,
> *America in the Gilded Age: From the Death of
> Lincoln to the Rise of Theodore Roosevelt*

> Nothing stranger ever came out of the *Arabian Nights* than the
> story of this poor Scotch boy who came to America and step by
> step, through many trials and triumphs, became the great steel
> master, built up a colossal industry, amassed an enormous fortune,
> and then deliberately gave away the whole of it for the enlighten-
> ment and betterment of mankind.
>
> —Editor's Note, *The Autobiography of Andrew Carnegie*

THE EPIGRAPH FROM CHAPTER 2 DRAMATIZED BERT WHEELER'S assumption
into the realm of the self-made man and its myth. These epigraphs en-
capsulate the coalescing of the dominant version of that myth in the
United States. Carnegie the man ranges from his role as a "strictly sta-
tistical" point of reference to the mythical "Carnegie," the immigrant
child who, beginning work at 14 as a bobbin boy, eventually becomes
if not "the richest man in the world," as proclaimed by J. P. Morgan,

certainly the man with the world's greatest liquid assets (Wall 790–91). A number of happy conjunctions lead social historians to peg Carnegie's birth in 1835 as the opening act in a drama that produces the poster boy of the prototypical rags-to-riches story: the opening of the West in the United States, technological changes in industrial production, a rise in immigration related to both, to name a few.

Yet even as authors acknowledge Carnegie as a particularly useful focus for the myth, some take pains to underscore their sense that details of Carnegie's experience don't quite fit the dominant myth's broad outlines of open-ended self-making for any and all. As Wyllie notes in discussing the *Autobiography* and its role as foundation of the rags-to-riches theme: "Carnegie was not simply justifying maldistribution of wealth under a capitalist economy. He was also romanticizing the circumstances which had surrounded his own childhood and that of many other business leaders of his generation" (Wyllie 25; also Ingham, *Iron Barons* 13; Swetnam 18; and Wall 83–84). Even Carnegie could admit at times that his economic origins were not dire (*Autobiography* 13). No matter; detailed discussion of material inequality would only bury the mythic struggle in a mess of bureaucratic details.

Rhetorical self-revisionings by Carnegie and others are not, however, simple lying or self-delusion. Carnegie no more creates the myth as a false argument than his life actually provides the specific moment for its inception. Popeye can declare "I y'am what I y'am" all he likes, but like Bert Wheeler, the figure "Carnegie" is a creature of the myth.[1] Getting completely outside of the doxic frame would require the impossible task of getting out of the social process itself and, by definition, outside of yourself. In Jonathan Potter's words, then, "Histories," and certainly personal histories, "cannot be produced without drawing on the techniques of narrative and character construction which are so well developed in the fictional domain" (94). But if historical factuality is itself a function of desire and cultural structuring, as Potter, Foucault, White, and numerous others suggest, the proffered—and withheld—details of history and of histories are worth noting, particularly to see how specific details are enmeshed in the mythmaking process itself.[2]

As an exemplary argument for masculine self-making, Carnegie's traditional portrait is in many ways a well-wrought version of the dominant myth. The conflicts and contradictions that appear as misalignments in other versions here are more thoroughly masked because reinforced by the full power of middle-class *doxa*. Let me reiterate that in defining the mythic Carnegie in this way, I do not mean to suggest that Carnegie was himself materially middle class but that Carnegie's mythic portrait offers the dominant version of the self-made man in full postoedipal individualism, a well-maintained success produced in and by his own chosen and pursued self-agency. In his version of the myth, complications all fall down before the active, decision-making agency of the self-making, undefeated, postoedipal son.

There are moments in which the smoothness of the facade shudders if not cracks, however. The emphasis on the activity and making of self is enacted both within the childhood frame of family and home and that larger, public arena for mythical self-making—the workplace. Each arena offers myriad opportunities to display masculine self-making, and both enact tensions and contradictions as they engage the dominant rhetoric. Not surprisingly, those moments appear most regularly when the masculinity Carnegie enacts comes closest to revealing the underlying framework of its rhetorical appeals. The contradictions that show through this doxic maintenance hint at underlying concerns with preoedipal desires and anxieties, oedipal needs and guilt and their attendant sadomasochism, the negative suggestion of institutional dominance and determinism rather than singular agency, and the related but ambiguous attraction of union mutualism and support.

Carnegie's written acts of self-creation are thus rife with opportunity for unintended self-deconstruction. But as rags-to-riches apostles from Franklin to Iacocca continue to demonstrate, the risk involved in self-contradiction and public self-revelation is offset by the value attached to verbal self-making. Such performances clearly satisfy more that just the need for historical self-representation. As a genre, autobiography provides a premier venue for masculine self-making, one in which the writer supposedly is free to play with both content and medium, to perform verbal self-making as much as describe it. Control language, control the situation, control the self—all add up to masculinity within the *doxa* of masculinity. Enacting that belief, along with so many paradigmatic aspects of self-making, Carnegie's *Autobiography* provides a template for the dominant myth and a standard against which all other variants can be studied.

Andrew Carnegie and Middle-Class Myth

Carnegie certainly took great pleasure in the power of language. On a simple level, rhetorical ability is obviously useful in a career dependent upon selling one's reputation or products for cold cash—or at least lines of credit. "Bubbling with enthusiasm and full of brass," Matthew Josephson writes in *The Robber Barons,* "[Carnegie] intruded himself everywhere, buttonholed everyone, listened to everything. He cajoled and flattered the influential men he knew . . . with telling effects" (qtd. in Wolff 55). But Carnegie's pleasure in verbal play extended beyond making deals. "Like so many persons with a limited formal education but a genuine interest in intellectual concerns," Wall notes, "Carnegie had an exaggerated notion of the power of the pen to influence human behavior and to direct the course of history" (429). The resulting drive to use language to represent both ideas and self produced a deep attraction to writing that was displayed in a wide variety of forms: a happily noted boyhood letter to a newspaper, an aborted attempt to change British politics by owning newspapers, countless travelogues and essays, and several books.[3]

The *Autobiography* as a whole is a culmination of Carnegie's acts of verbal self-making, an activity he furthered within its pages by developing scenes of verbal play: conversations, joke telling, rewriting popular stories. Many of these vignettes are offered as ways of achieving masculine camaraderie, but Carnegie's activities go beyond the simple pleasures of fraternal exchange. A sense early in his career that "the pen was getting to be a weapon with me" underscores Carnegie's eager, aggressive willingness to embrace linguistic representation as a way of life— and a form of dominance (*Autobiography* 78). Verbal gregariousness, often a mask for power seeking, helps establish one's status in complex, gendered ways—a dynamic to which Carnegie often had recourse as he "subdu[ed] his partners and dominated his quiet, capable brother" (Josephson 55). Beneath manly exchange and masculine camaraderie lies the larger dynamic of participating in a culture's gender-making machinery. Achieving dominance over others through rhetorical performance is a way of validating one's relationship to *doxa* and its complexities. It also seems to provides a means of revising the Lacanian equation so that defeat by the controlling law of the father and entry into the Symbolic are conflated into control over language, control over others, and movement into the position of the father alone.

Rags-to-riches tales in general, and the life of Carnegie in particular, expand on this revision of Lacanian self-making by using language to sell the ultimate product: the man himself. In *A Nation of Steel: The Making of Modern America, 1865–1925*, Thomas Misa says as much about Bessemer, whose process provided the basic groundwork for mass-produced steel in the first place. Bessemer's "considerable flair for publicity and patronage," Misa notes, "was as important to his overall success as his original technical conception" (5). Selling the self becomes a part of selling the product, or said another way, self and product combine in the overall rhetoric. That process is clear in the way in which entrepreneurs regularly use their products to bolster the masculinity maintained in their rhetorical stance. To sell minivans, after all, Iacocca stood next to a Jeep.

The nineteenth century provided ample opportunity for the shift from direct linguistic self-representation to indirect self-display via production and product. Cecilia Tichi notes, for example, that "engineering 'muscle' was amply evident" in the steel-framed [originally cast-iron] bridges of the eastern seaboard and the Midwest (*Shifting Gears* 104). Tichi's bridge-building muscle is likewise displayed by Job Manly, the aptly named workman-hero in Whittaker's novel *A Knight of Labor.* Manly "is not a manager, speculator, or fox: he wants to *make things*," and in making them, make himself (Denning 172).[4] Given the prevalence of such motifs, Carnegie's connection to steel (and to bridge building) offered him innumerable possibilities to flex some steel-augmented muscle within his own portrait.[5] He chose instead to root his masculine self-making in his activity as a manager—and verbal manipulator—of men. It is a revealing choice, one that signals Carnegie's primary rhetorical allegiance to a middle-class, ultimately entrepreneurial version of the myth (one not yet troubled by the emasculating power of middle-class, middle-level jobs dependent upon huge corporations).

Within that basic framework, Carnegie's overall verbal and rhetorical performance enacts two particular aspects of masculine self-making. One component emphasizes the "making" of the myth of self-making, the dynamic, aggressive activity of pursuing self-made status through acquisition of verbal power and, by extension, monetary strength. This version dominates the first half of the *Autobiography.* The second form displays the achievement of that self-made status; here the portrait is of the established corporate head. In the latter, achieved masculinity is maintained as control and even fatherly concern rather than manly aggression and drive—young, self-creating entrepreneur is replaced by *paterfamilias.*[6]

Whichever rhetoric is being enacted, one basic tack taken by Carnegie is recognizable from the start of both career and self-portrait: the hugely positive representation. That gregarious style provides an upbeat tone in concert with the plot's movement from nobody to somebody, from rags to riches. Carnegie always has a firm arm around the shoulders of his audiences. Yet even given his own economic dominance and his myth's paradigmatic place in masculine *doxa,* Carnegie's rhetoric of self-making cannot fully control basic, conflicting components in the larger narrative, particularly when those components are so clearly linked to psychic tensions within the very *doxa* the myth performs.

The Family Romance[7]

Preoedipal Separation

In addition to the basic rags-to-riches plot, Carnegie's motifs are rooted in the tensions common to masculine development in general and the myth of self-making in particular: separation and division versus unity and mutuality, personal victory over other men versus oedipal struggle and defeat, individual agency versus institutional determinism, masculine versus feminine "rules" of personal behavior and exchange. Contrary to the myth's stated claims—and Carnegie's enactment of them—the typical motifs of the myth do not resolve these doxic oppositions. But Carnegie's particular use of them does help to clarify the jumbled collection of fantasies, needs, and anxieties within masculinity that the myth's rhetoric attempts to simplify or flat out deny.

In rewriting anxieties over separation (from a sense of self as whole and its related separation from unqualified nurturance), for example, Carnegie cannot engage a typical vignette—willed separation from the mother—since he shared a home with his mother throughout his life. Indeed, on the surface, Carnegie's sentimental and somewhat vague representations of his mother appear to argue against preoedipal separation as a powerful component in masculine self-making:

> The [Morrison's] second daughter, Margaret, was my mother, about whom I cannot trust myself to speak at length. She inherited from her mother the dignity, refinement, and air of the cultivated lady. Perhaps some day I may be able to tell the world something of this heroine, but I doubt it. I feel her to be sacred to myself and not for others to know. None could ever really know her—I alone did that. After my father's early death, she was all my own. The dedication of my first book tells the story. It was: "To my favorite Heroine My Mother." (*Autobiography* 6)

But the simple representation masks some greater complexities. Even given the level of sentiment common to the age, these descriptions stretch their appeal to the limit, and their fulsomeness has raised some questions, especially among biographers.[8] Equally intriguing are discrepancies between Carnegie's representation and those of others. Wall, for one, notes that the other main woman in Carnegie's life, his wife Louise, "confide[d] to Carnegie's biographer, Burton Hendrick] that Mrs. Carnegie had been the most unpleasant person she had ever known" (404).

Whatever their actual behaviors or interpersonal exchanges, the women in Carnegie's self-portrait of self-making simply occupy a minor, sentimentalized role. Briefly stated, Carnegie's heavy sentimentalization of Margaret Carnegie as nurturing mother adequately feminizes the woman as a blend of Joan of Arc and Victorian-angel, a form of reduction (if not outright erasure) of the individual woman through a stereotypical femininity. Sufficiently feminized/canonized, Margaret Carnegie's formidable strengths—integrity, grit, frugality, tenacity—can be introduced and represented as reflecting admirably on the strengths of any self-making, dominant man, since the figure "Margaret Carnegie" exists in the *Autobiography* to demonstrate the value of the son. The rather stock portraits of her may hint at greater complexities in development, as Wall suggests, but Carnegie's self-making is relatively safe alongside them, since it successfully operates within the larger cultural rhetoric of achieved masculinity.

The full mythic frame still requires a motif of chosen separation, however, and Carnegie enacts it in a classic American gesture, one that effectively allows for preoedipal anxieties to be suggested while they remain surrounded with a postoedipal frame of achievement and agency. Carnegie's separation is not from the mother but from the mother country. To the free-floating feelings of sympathy, empathy, and anxiety associated with separation, Carnegie attaches the positive, masculinized sentiment that accrues to the immigration myth as a whole: active struggle for a different role, real distance and achievement measurable in miles traveled, political institutions rejected, old attitudes thrown aside. In short, although his Scottish hero worship often leads to manly evocations of the old country, Carnegie generally uses immigration to engage the rhetoric so central to masculine myths of self-making—separation from all that is nurturing—while avoiding direct enactment of preoedipal anxiety (and fantasies) connected to separation from the caregiver/mother. If Scotland was and ever will remain wonderful, then the separation can be portrayed as traumatic—providing it sets the stage for dramatizing a masculine surmounting of separation. Not surprisingly then, according to the sailor who puts the 13-year-old in the launch, Carnegie's departure for the United States "was the saddest parting [the sailor] had ever witnessed" (27)—even though Carnegie's entire nuclear family leaves with him.

It is an appeal that Carnegie can use so well because societies heavily impacted by immigration (such as the United States) endorse it so thoroughly. Lacking literal separation from the mother, Carnegie just moves himself and his audience from one country to the next, individual agency and integrity neatly intact. Immigration thus operates as the main repository of and appeal to a rhetoric of willed separation from the feminine through which Carnegie's masculine self-making is argued. As a safe signal of that separation, it is also highly effective. Other separations are more problematic, however, especially those regarding the father.

Oedipal Dominance

Carnegie negotiates issues of preoedipal separation early and easily in his *Autobiography* by using immigration to enact the rhetoric of masculine self-making. But his engagement of the next stage of the traditional family narrative—oedipal defeat by and accommodation to the father, along with subsequent postoedipal victory over actual economic conditions—is not so smoothly enacted. While Carnegie has some general success in masking family issues throughout his self-portrait, he fails dramatically when these issues are further troubled by class tensions. There are two scenes in particular within the autobiography in which such misalignment occurs: (1) Carnegie's interview for a position as telegraph messenger and (2) his chance meeting of his father during the elder's unsuccessful attempts to sell his weaving. In each case, the son is represented as moving further and further up the self-made ladder of success while the father is slipping further and further into masculine failure, into Wall's description of him as a "weak, ineffectual father who had been unable to provide for his sons" (*Andrew Carnegie* 417).

The first scene describes a crucial step toward success for Carnegie, since the job interview will eventually position him to meet his patron, Thomas A. Scott of the Pennsylvania Railroad. Carnegie cannot know the job's importance at the time, of course, but he portrays himself as sparing no effort in obtaining it, and he describes his actions as another complex form of separation—along with adding a flavor of dominance and hierarchy in relation to his "improperly" oedipal father. Immigration again shoulders major rhetorical weight in masking these family dynamics and emphasizing masculine agency and self-making, while both of the latter activities are themselves rooted in Carnegie's control over a new order of language.

The interview scene is quick and fairly simple. Carnegie and his father walk to a telegraph office so Carnegie Jr. can pursue a job that his father is unsure his son should take. Upon arriving at the telegraph office, Andrew Carnegie tells his father to remain outside. Carnegie Jr. asks this, he declares, because although he remains proud of being "Scotch," he is nevertheless becoming "something of an American," most notably in his lessened accent. Carnegie notes disingenuously that "I imagined I could make a smarter showing if alone with Mr. Brooks than if my good old Scotch father were present, perhaps to smile at my [verbal] airs" (*Autobiography* 36).

Carnegie's vision of a bemused father notwithstanding, any child of immigrants who has been told to "Speak English!," or who has cringed at the unmistakable accents heard rolling from relatives' mouths, or who has been the recipient of ethnic or racial linguistic prejudice will not pass lightly over this scene. There are too many denials and separations crammed into too short a space. To offset this blatant repudiation of ethnicity and origins, and its even more explosive implication of a successful supplanting of the oedipal father, Carnegie senior is quickly reinstated in the next paragraph amidst the core elements of middle-class myths: the supportive nuclear family, with mother washing and ironing the Sunday suit used as interview clothes and father fighting "the good fight" and encouraging his son. But the damaging statements have already been made. There is a self-making aggression here that cannot quite free itself from the guilt drifting behind the achievement, and guilt does not usually show up in paeans to self-making.

It shows up here with a vengeance, coming forward to break the myth's doxic frame by rather too vigorously hacking away at still-clinging vestiges of father and national origins. Rather than an accommodation to oedipal defeat by the father, Carnegie's scene appeals to a full fantasy of oedipal elimination of him. For all its self-aggrandizement, the brief scene exposes both the deep oedipal desire to supplant the father and its attendant guilt, followed by a rapid move to bury both. The bland assertion that opens the subsequent paragraph, "The interview was successful" (37), fits the hurried and deflated tone. We are being encouraged to move on quickly, accepting this description of demasculinized father and masculinized son through a meliorating rhetoric of postoedipal achievement. Indeed, Carnegie's own earlier references to his father as one of "nature's noblemen" and a "saint" take on ironic tones here, as we recognize whose hand is responsible for his father's metaphoric martyrdom (32).

A second, equally brief, equally masculinized, and even more clearly victorious scene of paternal reversal and dominance occurs shortly after the job interview. Carnegie has become an accomplished telegrapher and is in Steubenville to aid in flood recovery. Learning that his father is traveling by barge to Steubenville and Wheeling to sell tablecloths he has woven, Carnegie goes to meet him. In order to save money, the elder Carnegie (who may have the masculinity attached to craft production but is now locked in an economic order with little use for it) has decided to ride on the open decks rather than book a cabin. Carnegie, as embodiment of the new order of production, declares himself "indignant" at this situation, and promises that soon his father will ride in his own carriage. His father responds as required:

> "Andra [his father murmurs], I am proud of you."
>
> The voice trembled and he seemed ashamed of himself for saying so much. The tear had to be wiped from his eye, I fondly noticed, as he bade me good-night and told me to run back to my office. These words rang in my ear and warmed my heart for years and years. We understood each other. How reserved the Scot is! Where he feels most he expresses least. Quite right. Silence is more eloquent than words. My father was one of the most lovable of men, beloved of his companions, deeply religious, although non-sectarian and non-theo-

logical, not much of a man of the world, but a man all over
for heaven. He was kindness itself, although reserved. Alas!
he passed away soon after returning from this Western tour
just as [his children] were becoming able to give him a life
of leisure and comfort. (60–61)

Read quickly, this is a moment of father/son recognition deepened by
the father's declaration of the achievements of the son. Not prodigal, the
son is nevertheless returning from a journey of masculine self-making.
At base, though, such returns and the praise that they garner often carry
a hint of competition. Wall, for one, finds more than a hint. "Carnegie
was right," Wall declares. "Silence can be more eloquent than words.
For all of the eloquence of his own words in recalling this scene, it is
doubtful if [Carnegie] ever did understand his father or ever did realize
that there could be both pain and pride for the man in this encounter
with his son. . . . Not knowing failure himself, Carnegie would always
be insensitive to the feelings of those who had failed" (105). Indeed, that
lack of empathy is directly visible in Carnegie's own ready movement
from representing his supposedly deeply understood father to a broad,
third-person generalization of Carnegie Sr. as the generic "Scot."[9]

Wall's comments are on the mark, then, but they're also unusually
harsh for him, and that harshness is its own signal of the tension of this
scene. It is a moment in which the masculine myth of self-making, up
to now moving inexorably forward, momentarily breaks down. Like the
earlier victorious self-making through usurpation of the father's oedipal dominance, this scene skates perilously close to crushing the father
beneath the son's achievement. Enactment by the reader of the scene's
self-making success, however willing, is conflicted at such a moment, and
a male reader is especially likely to find himself struggling with oedipal
anxieties and guilt. Wall's tone is thus that of angered male biographer
who now is willing to believe he knows his subject well enough to engage, if not in "amateur Freudian" depth psychology, at least in broad
characterizations of Carnegie's "insensitive" personality.

Wall may be right in claiming that Carnegie is capable of deep self-
delusion, but more to the point is that masculine *doxa* is inherently conflicted and therefore contains an insensitive, because conflicted, myth.
Carnegie is, after all, performing the rhetoric of self-made masculinity.
The degree to which he is personally and psychologically invested in the
myth is only a partial concern here. More important is recognizing what
are by now the equivalents of common fault lines in the mythic rhetoric. Investing in the activity of becoming masculine, of attempting to
dominate fathers and father-figures, does produce guilt and require later
insensitivity. In more specific terms, it encourages both masculine mas-

ochism and sadism, as I argued in chapter 2. Because the myth contains within itself tensions and contradictions that it is meant to gloss over (such as father beating or being beaten by the father rather than a safer, family-free self-making), there is every chance that individual enactments of the myth will not only recapitulate but also too directly reveal internal tensions and contradictions rather than setting them aside.

In line with this reading, the passage immediately following the barge meeting and its description of the death of Carnegie's father is transitional in more ways than one. Having separated completely and victoriously from his ambiguously oedipal father, Carnegie now develops an equally ambiguous father-figure common to Alger's tales: the patron, in this case Thomas A. Scott. Carnegie will need to address Scott as a father/dominant figure throughout the rest of the book's argument, often erasing or eliding or inventing Scott's paternal role and its possible "re-feminization" of Carnegie as dependent subaltern and/or insufficiently postoedipal male. But in figuring his further success in light of the individual man, Scott, Carnegie gains the benefit of setting aside the growing presence of huge, late-nineteenth-century corporations derided by Sue Miller's father-in-law. In masking the presence of institutions and the crucial role of others providing him with status within them, Carnegie again enacts the self-making rhetoric of personal agency in order to enact doxic masculinity via the dominant rhetoric of masculine individuality and postoedipal success.

Postoedipal Success

A Foucauldian look behind the curtain of the general myth and its motivating *doxa* easily displays institutional powers greater than those engaged by the rhetoric of postoedipal masculine self-making. Ingham, for example, has thoroughly studied the actual social and economic powers of Pittsburgh's so-called "Iron Barons." The tale he tells of Carnegie's ethnicity and personal anti-institutionalism evokes some empathy and sympathy, albeit on different and more subtle grounds than that of Carnegie's portrait of aggressive, postoedipal individualism:

> Despite the popularity of the Andrew Carnegie archetype, only five Pittsburgh steel men were immigrants from poor backgrounds. Since two of these were Andrew Carnegie and his brother Tom, only three men outside the Carnegie family (less than 1 percent of the total) reflected this archetype. Further, all five men were officers in the Carnegie mills; thus, outside of this establishment in Pittsburgh, the poor-immigrant-to-steel-mill-owner syndrome never occurred. . . . Although there were a fairly large number of immigrants or sons

of immigrants among the Pittsburgh steel entrepreneurs, only a handful, at best, conform to the "rags to riches" myth. The majority either had skills which gave them ready entrance to elite status, or they had family connections, money or education to assist them. (Ingham, *Iron Barons* 32–33)

To the argument that this merely proves Carnegie's success and the validity of the mythic argument, there are further qualifiers to note. The preestablished frame of Pittsburgh society produced a system of social exchange that Carnegie, renowned for discerning the abilities of men, is not likely to have missed. Nor is it likely he failed to notice, on some level, the resulting social evaluations of himself and his family. Yet such details do not fit the mythic rhetoric, and their representation would describe limits on masculine agency and achievement that *doxa* and myth do not allow. Thus, while Carnegie happily mentions golf in his autobiography, cultural rhetoric requires that he omit mentioning the various golf clubs of Pittsburgh, the typical exclusivity encouraged among the more elite clubs, the obvious sense of privilege they would foster, and his own membership in a less prestigious club like the newer, second-tier Pittsburgh Country Club (Ingham, *Iron Barons* 121–27).

Nor does Carnegie's regular valorization of his heritage address the fact that in Pittsburgh at this time there were Scots, and then there were Scots. Indeed, Ingham has argued that the real cultural shift in Pittsburgh was not a movement from rags to riches but a movement of old-money Scottish immigrants from the role of social outsiders to social insiders— a shift Carnegie's more recent immigration denied him. "Thus," Ingham notes, "when Pittsburgh emerged as the center of the iron and steel industry, its entrepreneurs—largely Scotch-Irish—seemed to be men on the move; and, indeed they were." But these men differ significantly from Carnegie: "It was not poverty they were forsaking; it was a negative cultural stereotype. As such it was a very important form of mobility, but sharply divergent from the standard myth"—and equally divergent from Carnegie's blithe portrait or actual situation (Ingham, *Iron Barons* 7). For all his enactment of the myth, Carnegie has not moved as far away from his father or his immigrant accent as his income would suggest.

One last signal of the apparent gap between mythic argument and personal experience rests in Pittsburgh's reaction to Carnegie's philanthropy. In many cases, the city elders seem to have reacted as negatively to his giving away of money at the close of his career as they did to his too-eager desire to make it earlier in life. Henry Frick, on the other hand, may have gained few friends by being a Carnegie partner or by his central role in Pennsylvania labor disputes, especially the deadly Homestead battle. He nevertheless had one edge on Carnegie—he was from an established family. Moreover, as Ingham notes, Frick had married into "the eminent Childs family." Unlike Carnegie, then, "Frick was an impeccable member of the city's Core [sic] upper class and possibly as a result of that status did not experience the same negative response to his philanthropies" (*Making Iron and Steel* 178–79).[10]

Clearly, the old-money rich are not "just like the rest of us," no matter how strong the desire to realize cultural myth through personal portrayals of origins overcome, effort expended, or masculinity achieved. What the myth offers is a broad argument for achieving masculine success. What it omits are any clear scales of measurement, any sense of differing scales for differing people, and any complex description of what one acquires when one acquires success. Usually, the gains are power and status or, in a culture that values capital acquisition, both in the form of money. But that motif only begs the question again. Doxic rhetoric does not really address what one makes when one makes a masculine self; it only provides signifying markers that it then essentializes.

The irony is that the dominant rhetoric of masculine self-making prevails because specific characterization of success and/or its means of achievement would threaten the myth. Fully characterizing the complex manipulations required to achieve institutional power, for example, would qualify more than the success of the self-made man. It would demonstrate restrictions on and possible alternative means for attaining masculinity—some of which would hint at possibly nonindividualistic, possibly even nonmasculine—behaviors. Part of the usefulness of masculine arguments of self-making thus rests in the deep need of both society and individual to maintain the status quo. Success, by definition, must be a matter of individual effort and personal agency, since it is easier for society at large to consider its conflicts to be those of individual men struggling with individual, personal contradictions than for society to reconsider its own *doxa*.

On the other hand, individual failure to achieve victories comparable to the myth does not produce rejection of the myth's vision of masculinity; failing actually provides an opportunity to experience the pain that is argued as "natural" in the struggle for masculinity. The presence of such negative experiences thus becomes desirable as a "nonperversely" masochistic validation of the ongoing struggle for masculinity. No pain, no gain. Normally, however, self-conscious masochism is not directly forced upon the reader. Nor is sadism brought too fully forward. Instead, both are rewritten by a mythic rhetoric devoted to self-making masculinity characterized as a vague but justifiable form of separation achieved and postoedipal dominance and success attained. Carnegie clearly could not dictate Pittsburgh's view of his self-made masculinity. So he elides it, and the myth's focus allows him to do so—indeed encourages it by declaring social success an unnecessary complication, an achievement not worth having. Inherited status, according to the middle-class rhetoric of self-making, has no adequate struggle to signal the success. Masculinity resides in effort, and in keeping with the rhetoric of willed separation from family and support, individual effort in the workplace is a prime arena in which to enact it.

Workplace Ethos

Individual Agency Versus Institutional Control

As Leverenz notes, the workplace provides an arena in which masculine success is publicly performed. But the rhetoric of self-making faces difficulties similar to the family context in maintaining its emphasis on personal masculine agency as a marker of oedipal, man-versus-man, struggle. Appeals to masculine agency only work when the self-made man neither is controlled by nor depends on institutional limits and levers—or any patriarchal males controlling either. Witness George Bush Sr.'s need to deny Connecticut and Yale and embrace Texas and oil rigs in his presidential campaign, or George Bush Jr.'s similar need in his campaign to avoid mentioning that most of his success was bankrolled by father and friends. Related conflicts and contradictions in Carnegie's rhetoric of self-making point to basic tensions in the dominant myth, exemplified in the *Autobiography* in regard to both Carnegie's corporate mentor and his reliance upon institutional manipulation.

In Carnegie's version, the traditional Alger patron is Thomas A. Scott, superintendent of the Pittsburgh division of the Pennsylvania Railroad. He is positive replacement (and reward) for Carnegie's defeated father, not barring the door to desires and fantasies of power and dominance but instead opening a gateway to a young man of merit who is eager to charge through it and make his own way. The role played by Scott in Carnegie's life and success certainly is hard to ignore. It is imperative, however, that Scott not appear too much the patron, in which case the positive appeal of self-making would be replaced with the negative argument of patronage. Scott merely plucks Carnegie out of his telegrapher's role, makes him his assistant, and gradually introduces him to a wider intellectual and economic life. Both the occurrence and the results of that favoring are to be seen simply as a product of hard work and effort.

Not surprisingly, the overall process—for Carnegie as well as most others—tends to be much more complex and thorough going. For one thing, being from the wrong class or cultural background in mid-nineteenth-century Pittsburgh did not simply set the stage for self-made success; it actually "made success in the business world that much more difficult"—and difficult to achieve through simple effort (Ingham, *Iron*

Barons 221).[11] As women so cogently demonstrated and litigated in the 1970s, what may pass as social—private clubs—regularly encompasses the corporate. Analysts who completely separate the social and the economic miss "the realities of power in the situation": "The functioning of men's clubs in the various cities are [*sic*] a good case in point. Membership in these clubs was essential to the businessman who wished to rise above a certain point in the business hierarchy. So much business was done over lunch, or late in the afternoons in these clubs, that if a businessman did not belong he would miss out on many of the important transactions in his industry" (Ingham, *Iron Barons* 226). It is a mark of Carnegie's economic success and power that he could, in fact, not only overcome but also actually ignore many such social arenas. But that does not mean that Carnegie succeeded without sponsorship and by effort alone. Like any good self-made man, he got someone else to help him pull up his bootstraps.

Scott provided that support in innumerable ways. As mentioned, he took Carnegie from his telegrapher's job in Pittsburgh and made him a personal assistant.[12] He placed Carnegie in his first position of responsibility at the Pennsylvania Railroad. He provided Carnegie with his first insight into and opportunity for stock speculation. Most importantly, Scott directly underwrote or indirectly influenced, personally and in his position with the Pennsylvania Railroad, a vast majority of Carnegie's ventures during the formative years of the Keystone Bridge Company and Carnegie's steel mills. Clearly, Carnegie's rhetoric of self-making needs to address the role that Scott played, but how? Ignoring Scott entirely would destroy credibility. Portraying him in a role that clarifies Carnegie's dependence would devalue Carnegie's self-making by default, emphasizing a dependency even more problematic because it reinstates a father-figure. Finally, there is the risk of clarifying the place that abstract institutional power occupied in Carnegie's success, which could heavily qualify the rhetoric of individual action with that of institutional status.

Carnegie's particular mythologizing offsets these dangers of patronage and institutional power through a simple *ad hominem* technique rooted in the nature of the myth itself: He energetically emphasizes his own actions and decisions while downplaying the importance of all other aspects. Since the myth demands a masculinity defined by singular and singularly decisive action, it is a simple enough matter to reinforce the validity of that desire by reducing the details of the contexts in which one acts.[13] When complicating features or aspects of the context cannot be eliminated, they themselves can be incorporated into the action by emphasizing their positive dynamics rather than hedging their presence. The process is apparent in a large number of Carnegie's dramas of masculine action. One brief event—Carnegie's notorious dramatization of his role in the sleeping-car industry—makes clear the rhetorical process of melding mythic structure and doxic appeal.

Carnegie's involvement in the Pullman Company was made possible by his investment in the work of T. T. Woodruff and the Woodruff Sleeping Car Company. Both Burton Hendrick and Wall agree in seeing this investment as the beginning of the Carnegie fortune (Wall 138), and Carnegie's description of it in the *Autobiography* (and *Triumphant Democracy; or, Fifty Years' March of the Republic* 297–99) portrays a marvel of masculine decisiveness and self-making agency. Carnegie is on a business trip when he is approached by "a farmer-looking man" who turns out to be the inventor T. J. Woodruff; Woodruff pulls a model of his sleeping car from out of a bag; the importance of the invention "flash[es] upon" Carnegie, and he convinces Scott of the value of his vision; Scott agrees, and Carnegie is rewarded with an offering of an eighth interest in the forming company; he "boldly" applies for a loan from a local banker to make his payments; the banker recognizes this budding self-maker and grants the loan (*Autobiography* 83–84). According to Wall, it is "a typical Carnegie story, replete with all the stock situations of popular melodrama" and all the stock characters and props: "The shy, unworldly inventor, the crude, hand-made model. The chance meeting with the bold young business executive, who in a flashing moment of truth recognizes genius when he sees it. There is even the mysterious green bag, in which the stranger carries his invention. It is all too pat and too familiar, but those commentators upon Carnegie's life who have dealt with this incident have accepted his story in every detail" (139).

For his part, Woodruff contradicted most aspects of the story, and Wall prefers to believe him rather than Carnegie. Wall's own generally less mythic narrative notes that Woodruff was already an accomplished inventor who had made and sold a number of his cars prior to formation of the Pullman company. Wall also feels that it is probable that Woodruff's account of meeting first with Thomson, the president of the Pennsylvania Railroad, is the accurate account. Finally, it appears likely that the one-eighth interest Carnegie supposedly earned with his flash of insight and decisiveness was actually set aside for him by Scott. In Wall's version, the agency and appeal of the entrepreneurial myth disappears under the language of corporate negotiations and personal patronage. The acceptance of Carnegie's Algeresque version by many biographers becomes even more noteworthy in light of such depressingly mundane representations. It is obvious that the preferred version is the one in which the myth functions as it ought. Repetition of the story by others is as much evidence of the self-maintaining actions of *doxa* as it is evidence of scholarly error or sloth. Bert Wheeler's obituary has made that clear.

Carnegie presents a similarly doxic enactment of manly decisiveness and agency in the workplace through his account of the construction of the St. Louis Bridge. As I noted above, such construction feats were regularly aligned with westward expansion and the flexing of both national and individual muscle. Echoing Cecilia Tichi's description of the nineteenth-century's "manly" engineers, Wall notes that Carnegie readily declared that his Keystone Bridge Works had "always been a source of satisfaction to me" (*Autobiography* 116). That satisfaction is initially described by Wall in terms of the quality of product produced by the bridge works: "Of all his many activities in the early postwar years, the one that apparently gave him the most satisfaction in retrospect was that of bridge building. Here at least he could feel that he was instrumental in building the kind of permanent monument appropriate to the new industrial order in America" (226). Wall's characterization purports to reveal Carnegie's underlying emotion, but it also suggests Wall's own participation in the rhetoric of masculine craftsmanship. Carnegie may suggest some pride of craft in his description, but he actually spends a great deal more time describing deal making. The most particularized vignettes that Carnegie offers in regard to the Bridge Works revolve around descriptions of his dealings with men and of forming contracts with corporate and governmental boards. Thus while Tichi describes the actual bridge architect, James Eads, as an exemplar of the "structural artist-engineers" of the day (*Shifting Gears* 141), Carnegie portrays him as "an original genius *minus* [the] scientific knowledge [needed] to guide his erratic ideas of things mechanical" (Carnegie's emphasis, *Autobiography* 114). Intellectual control and masculine leadership, not artisanship or working-class craft, are the issues that Carnegie emphasizes.

To support his own role as leader, Carnegie provides himself with a cast of followers and figures like the "grand fellow" Colonel John Piper, an engineer and a Keystone partner, but one whom Carnegie nevertheless represents as more horseman than businessman. There is more than simple competition here. Jovially spinning tales of "Pipe" enables Carnegie to establish not a corporation but a spirit of workplace camaraderie, an air of doing business that consists of knowing men, and knowing how to be the most manly of them. The dynamic is further represented in the settling of a contract for the Dubuque bridge with "Mr. Allison, a great senator." With the contract in jeopardy, what is required is fast thinking, luck, and verbal skills. Having failed to provide the lowest bid, Carnegie lingers after the meeting to talk with board members, who were "delightfully ignorant of the merits of cast- and wrought-iron." "Providence" intervenes by providing a board member who can personally verify, via a recent car-lamppost encounter, the fracturing problems of wrought iron. The contract bid is reconsidered and re-let.

As further reward for his verbal control and decisiveness, Carnegie establishes "a lifelong, unbroken friendship with one of America's best and most valuable public men, Senator Allison" (119–20).

The lesson to be learned here is ostensibly one of how business success hangs on and requires attention to "trifles" (118). There are other lessons, of course. One is the power of cleverness and rhetorical ability; another is shrewd dealing. The last lesson provided is supposedly the lesson of friendship. That this lesson is offered through the boyish good spirits (and ultimate infantilizing) of Pipe, along with the rather smarmy, sentimental portrait of lifelong friendships, signals the rhetorical churning of masculine *doxa* at high temperature. Friendship, after all, is acceptably masculine, but only as long as it does not impinge on individual action and lone decision making. What these vignettes offer is masculine exchange and friendly—at times aggressive—bonhomie. They offer a hint of mutual exchange, without raising the specter of mutual support or, worse yet, intimacy. What they overlook is institutional manipulation, which is not so easily accommodated by the rhetoric of masculine self-making.

A different enactment of the activities involved in these bridge projects reveals the degree to which Carnegie engages the rhetoric of self-making in his own performance. According to Wall, those involved in the St. Louis Bridge included not only Pipe and Eads but also Carnegie's patron Scott, who "use[d] his influence with the St. Louis Bridge Company to have J. H. Linville, the bridge engineer for the Pennsylvania Railroad, appointed chief consultant to Eads for the design of the bridge." It was another of those happy acts of Providence, Wall rather sarcastically implies, that "Linville was also a director of [Carnegie's] Keystone Bridge Company" (Wall 271). Equally telling is the fact that Carnegie was interested in not only building the superstructure but also taking part in its lucrative financing. "As always," according to Wall, "he turned to Scott and Thomson for support" (227). In his description, Wall again eschews the rhetoric of self-making in favor of the language of corporate manipulation:

> The building of the St. Louis Bridge clearly reveals the intricate pattern of business activity with which Carnegie would surround most of his Keystone contracts. First, he would establish a sound alliance with those railroad companies who would be the chief clients of the complete bridge. Then, if possible, he would invest directly in the business syndicate holding the charter for the bridge. The contract for the bridge's superstructure would then be awarded to his Keystone Bridge Company, which would, in turn, subcontract the

iron structural parts to Carnegie, Kloman, and Company. For
frosting, there would be the commission to Carnegie, bond
salesman extraordinary, to negotiate the financing of the
bridge in New York and Europe. (278)

There is nothing particularly underhanded in all of this, nothing directly
illegal at least, in the intricacies. If anything, the rhetoric of individual
exchange is merely traded for one of corporate shrewdness. That shrewdness still contains an air of masculinity, even if it is a bit limp in comparison to the vigorous, lone agency enacted by Carnegie's doxic rhetoric.[14]

But Wall demonstrates his own disengagement from the dominant
rhetoric through some shockingly blunt imagery. It is not the activity of
masculine self-making that he sees in all of this. Instead, he portrays a
"vast intricate web of finance, manufacturing, and transportation [hang-
ing] on these bridge strands, and across the network Carnegie would
move with amazing alacrity, always ready to rush in any direction where
something of value had been caught in the fibers of the web" (269).
Wall's portrait of Carnegie as spider is a strikingly negative conceit, especially powerful within the ostensibly unbiased confines of Wall's biography. This is not a portrait of a self-made man at the center of power
but of an avaricious insect scrabbling after victims caught in its web. Fed
up with Carnegie's use of the mythic rhetoric, Wall has provided some
metaphors of his own.

Yet the aggressive and evocative power of Wall's language fades rapidly once we are back in the *Autobiography*'s culturally endorsed myth
of self-making. It is difficult not to be caught, or want to be caught, in
its performance of postoedipal masculine power and self-definition.
Within that doxically validated myth, nepotism, patronage, ethnic fa-
voritism, corporate gamesmanship, and other such issues become something else entirely. Advantages and disadvantages attached to ethnicity
can be sentimentalized in Scott's friendly admiration of his "little white-
haired Scotch devil" (*Autobiography* 69). Nepotism and patronage actually come to mean standing by one's family and being recognized for
one's unique efforts and energies. Business as an institution fades before
the masculine good spirits of men engaged in the give and take of aggressive business among the boys, "hustlers" all (335).

It is an engaging portrait, and one still common in contemporary
representations of the inner circles of corporate success. But as the nineteenth century moved into its final quarter, the dominant *doxa* of masculine self-making as individual agency in the workplace was endangered
by a slowly growing awareness, initially among blue-collar and gradually among mid-level workers, that desire and effort did not necessarily
produce satisfaction. Self-made men were more and more clearly occupy-

ing seats of economic and institutional power rather than pursuing individual challenges and agency.[15] That particular shift could be accommodated so as to mitigate resulting conflicts in the rhetoric. But direct clashes between laborer and corporate head produced much deeper and more immediate threats to masculine *doxa* at all income levels, threats culminating in national trauma and international outcry over the Homestead lockout of 1892—a trauma that further strained a myth increasingly redolent of class difference.

Individual Agency Versus Mutual Support

In 1892, Homestead was a borough just south of Pittsburgh and the location of the Homestead Steel Works, which Carnegie had purchased in October of 1883. The works were organized by the Amalgamated Association of Iron and Steel Workers, and the mill was a focal point for Carnegie's and Frick's attempts to eliminate union labor from their mills, at Homestead through use of a lockout and the importation of strikebreakers. The ostensible reason for the lockout was labor's refusal to accept Frick's new sliding-wage scale. But the long preparations for the lockout and an open letter declaring all Carnegie's works nonunion as of July 1892 belied any real desire on the part of management to negotiate.

The collapse of negotiations in July was followed by Frick's importation of Pinkertons as strikebreakers, a move vigorously and violently opposed by most if not nearly all of the inhabitants of Homestead (many of Homestead's civic officers were also workers in the mill). Following the death of approximately ten steelworkers and Pinkertons in the first days of the work stoppage, Pennsylvania's state militia seized control of Homestead from its elected government on July 10 and reopened the mills. With Carnegie still secluded in Scotland, Frick was shot and stabbed in his office on July 23 by the anarchist Alexander Berkman. Frick recovered, but the union did not, and the job action collapsed after nearly five months. On November 20, the remaining workers went back, and the union was effectively crushed, in Homestead and throughout the steel industry. Individual power, as embodied in Carnegie and Frick, maintained ascendancy over the mutual strength argued by union solidarity.

The job actions at Homestead in particular, along with labor disputes in general, thus enact a specific tension in masculine *doxa* that their essential structuring necessarily produces: that of individualism versus mutuality and the way in which each is to be defined. The goal—realizing a satisfactory sense of self-worth—in both cases equates to feeling adequately masculine. In a capitalist culture, there are two obvious means for achieving such a goal: (1) economic power (self-made fortunes/corporate wealth) or (2) shared strength and mutual support (organizational power or unionism)—the latter a clear option to the dominant, middle-class self-making we have been looking at thus far via Carnegie. But engaging that alternative option is complicated by the pervasive rhetoric of "proper" masculinity and its motifs: self-control, personal power, direct action, decisiveness, and so on—most of which not only connote but also may require individualism.

Mutualism, which potentially dissolves the barrier between self and other, carries not only the appeal of combined strength but also the complicated question of a possible return to preoedipal dynamics, desires, and anxieties. As a result, emphasis on an oedipal and postoedipal struggle for individuality and personal power usually can be made to seem at least partially preferable and potentially more satisfying no matter what one's actual class position. In such a framework, mutualism becomes second-level masculinity, at best.[16] Not surprisingly, then, Carnegie regularly manipulates and emphasizes individuality versus mutuality as a motif in portraying his dealings with union men in general, and especially when discussing his dealings with labor in the Carnegie mills.

As Carnegie clearly knew, one of the major moves in breaking a labor union is to destroy the mutual support and worker identity offered by a union so as to replace it with a socially endorsed individualism. That move is especially sinister, since once individualism is embraced by a worker, the self-made man can next threaten the same worker with a negative individuality, that is, singularity. Individualism thus can be portrayed as an opportunity for agency (act on your own like a real man), while singularity provides for the threat of easy dominance (you're on your own, so don't test the company's good will). As Rotundo notes, "it is a mistake to confuse individual action with solitary action," and for all his emphasis on individualism, Carnegie was well aware that the "work world created by the market economy was a fundamentally social one" (195).

Alert to these dynamics, Carnegie's *Autobiography* manipulates each side of the argument so as to bias its conclusion in favor of the agency and power of the self-made man in action. The process is clear in an early, specific enactment of the struggle between individual self-made man and mutualistic laboring force: an impending strike of the Pennsylvania Railroad in 1856. The details provided are sketchy, but the form of their presentation establishes the key issues in the rhetorical dynamic and demonstrates how Carnegie enacts the situation as a positive argument for self-making. To begin, overtones of corporate control that are attached to the event itself need to be addressed. Essentially, Carnegie is taken aside at night by a blacksmith and told that the shop men are organizing and planning a work stoppage. The divulging of this inside information results in elimination of the threatened work stoppage. Wall puts his finger on one significant difficulty with this vignette when he sarcastically notes that Carnegie "had come a long way from his life in Chartist Scotland, where the most hated name had been that of the company or government spy"—a form of company man beneath contempt (136).

Yet Carnegie demonstrates no conflict as he constructs his self-portrait in later life, nor does he bother to mitigate the harshness of Scott's subsequent notice "that all men who had signed the papers, pledging themselves to strike, were dismissed" (*Autobiography* 81). At no point, in fact, is there any indication of a felt need to offset possible negative overtones to these acts. Problem solving, and especially quick action in problem solving, carries its own cachet within masculinity, and Carnegie uses its appeals to carry the weight of his argument. In a rapid, one-paragraph description, Carnegie declares that "there was no time to be lost" in countering the now-revealed strike plans. Scott prints dismissal notices "at once." That same day, "the threatened strike was broken" (81–82). Labor organization and disputes presumably argue against themselves; an assumed problem, they simply are to be solved. Said another way, a reader is left to empathize with the authority vested in Carnegie by his self-making or to side with what are not only lesser achievers but also possibly recalcitrant children.

Yet the appeal of such active agency is not completely without tension. Carnegie's portrait of active resolution is similar to his earlier quick dismissal of a "negligent" train crew (*Autobiography* 70). Wall tellingly connects this second incident to Carnegie's earlier declaration that young men should be forgiven errors, such as his own near-loss of the company payroll (*Autobiography* 65). Noting this contradiction, Wall finds Carnegie wanting in regard to practicing with his men what he preaches to his audience (Wall 122–23), a lapse all the more noticeable because Carnegie's antiunion actions appeal to a personal agency that is very clearly enacted through controlling the agency of others. The result is a performance of oedipal dominance—enforce the law of the father and grant benefits to your defeated children—that threatens to emphasize not only the father's manly action but also the son's basic defeat. That incipient tension is both clarified and exacerbated in Carnegie's summary moral to the strikebreaking incident—"No kind action is ever lost"—which underwrites Carnegie's self-dramatization as powerful but benevolent father (*Autobiography* 82). That Carnegie's role emphasizes dominance more than benevolence is clear in the way he uses this nostrum to link his earlier action of helping the blacksmith/informer get his present job with the worker's further opportunity to become a company spy, a nice side benefit for management that enables Carnegie to sever the strikers from their jobs.[17]

Carnegie's disproportionate blend of aggressively active decision making and genial paternalism intentionally loads his rhetoric so as to simplify a complicated argument. As union mutualism begins to complicate the mythic dynamic of manly individuals dealing with each other one-on-one, the rhetoric is rewritten in terms of a specific, gendered hierarchy. Union workers, depending on a suspect preoedipal mutuality, are aligned with women and children—then "rightfully"—even "naturally"—defeated. The blacksmith/stool pigeon, for example, verifies Carnegie's patriarchal victory by acting as beneficiary of the more powerful father's largesse. Placing the informant in a dependent position, Carnegie temporarily shifts his agency from its upward pursuit of self-making to one that moves in a decidedly different direction: down from above, a power dynamic furthered by Carnegie's supposedly positive reference to the blacksmith as one of "the humble" (82). The self-made man has control here, and if the control is sadistic at base, the lesson is clear: It is better to hold the rod than to be beaten with it. Mimic the self-making father, in short, if you want to forget having been the defeated son.

Carnegie's subsequent representations of labor disputes from 1884 to 1892 at the E. P. Thomson and Homestead mills continue to argue the benefits of self-made individuality, adding to them a further emphasis on the nonmasculine dependency of workers who rely upon union mutualism.[18] Manliness is characterized by standard appeals to shared ethnicity and pseudoequivalency, verbal power and aggression, and ultimately to the motif of one-on-one, individual struggle, even when the exchange occurs in a mass meeting numbering in the hundreds. Carnegie's use of such scene setting is revealing. As is true with any formal meeting, dominance can readily be achieved by anyone with actual or claimed facts and specific data; paper, not dialogue, rules a meeting. Likewise, the individual ostensibly acting as himself has an advantage over any committee that needs to debate, discuss, and vote. The committee must act as an institutionalized, representative body and thus must address structural complexities, complications and delays, legal redefinitions and legal restrictions. The lone individual, on the other hand, engages in the simple, direct action of deciding and acting solely by and for himself. With these dynamics as backdrop, Carnegie's responses to labor unrest are paradigmatic representations of masculinity in action.

As master of the phallic symbolic, Carnegie delights in his ability to use language to dominate men. Under the guise of formal meeting rules, Carnegie achieves a "safe" intimacy that implies the presence of individuals and coequals. But it is a pseudoequivalence that is achieved by using meeting etiquette to dictate behavior: referring to any and all present as "Gentlemen" (when it suits the need), taking control by calling (jovially) for order at (in)opportune moments, making decisions, and giving one's word—which is never to be gone back upon. Captured by the verbal display, Carnegie's audience sees a unionized workforce, defined earlier as the natural aristocracy of labor, silently morph into individualistic abstractions: "the true American workman," "the self-respecting American workman" (*Autobiography* 232).[19]

What is being maintained in these representations of manly behavior are not the particulars of labor questions but the correct form of masculine exchange. Recognition by and voyeuristic participation of those who understand how to behave in manly ways enacts a rhetorical moment of friendly male aggression. When the performances mesh, the rhetoric of individual masculinity underwrites the workplace—and the reader's experience of it—as a series of one-on-one, manly exchanges: The repartee defines a man who becomes one's "stanch [*sic*] friend and admirer" (234). When the exchanges go wrong, it is because workers (and again, by implication, the reading audience), like "women," can have some "queer kinks in them" (231).

This underlying men-versus-women emphasis is not incidental to the overall rhetoric and its reinforcement of oedipal and postoedipal masculine individualism and dominance as different from feminine, preoedipal nonseparation and mutual support. Since jokes create "a theater of domination in everyday life, and the success or failure of a joke marks the boundary within which power and aggression may be used in a relationship" (Freud, "Jokes" 102; also qtd. in Lyman 150), joking can ritually enact culturally gendered behavior that neatly unites social organization and masculine needs: "Rule-governed aggression . . . is very useful to organizations, in that it mobilizes aggressive energies but binds them to order by rules." Participants assent to that binding, moreover, because "the male sense of order is procedural rather than substantive . . . the male bond is formal (rule governed), rather than personal (based upon intimacy and commitment)" (Lyman 161). Within this ritual behavior, verbal dueling for dominance is encouraged in order to establish who is adequately masculine. The dangers of such aggression are reduced by ostensibly erasing the personal from the exchange and enacting individual rhetorical dominance within the frame of widely accepted and rule-governed, hence abstract, behavior. Individual behavior is sanitized as a particularized set of general values, of subject positions within the established social hierarchies of work, all of which allow for aggression and competition while displacing direct physical attack into corporate-level playing of the dozens, verbal sparring based on industrial positions and identities.[20]

Carnegie's owner/labor negotiation passages thus enact one of the major rhetorical moves—and major paradoxes—of the rhetoric of individual identity, demonstrating why it so important to masculine *doxa* and so useful to large institutions. First, Carnegie performs Lacanian oedipal dominance through masculine joking. This visible defeat of a specific opponent is then translated into (and meliorated by) the abstract frame of general masculine, rather than personal, behavior. His defeated opponent is really no opponent at all but a catalyst for performing masculine behavior. With the stage thus safely cleared of all but abstract opposition, Carnegie's performance of abstract rules of masculine self-making is placed in the spotlight—ironically as an argument for authentic individuality. Rhetorical enactment and legitimizing of masculine dominance of this kind plays a key role in Carnegie's antilabor rhetoric. By mixing direct self-performance with abstract rules of engagement, Carnegie and Carnegie Steel (itself a giant institution) can be portrayed as a single, forthright figure: "Carnegie."

The achievement of this quicksilver blend of personal and abstract is subtle and paradoxical but readily endorsed by masculine *doxa*. Under the aegis of that endorsement, Carnegie is even free to replace the actual workmen with a generalized abstraction—the individual American worker—both in the *Autobiography*'s general rhetoric and the rhetoric of this scene.[21] Having achieved this creation of self and other, Carnegie is in a position to intensify the rhetorical appeal of individualism by threatening his workers with reconstitution as a faceless, unionized mass if they refuse the dominant rhetoric. The rapid oscillation between self-made, masculine individuality and faceless, union mutualism additionally underwrites Carnegie's portrayal of his destruction of unions as an act of true (because individualistic) democracy, neatly hiding the fact that unions are themselves representative democracies. Thus, when union representatives consent to sign an agreement, Carnegie also agrees with a hearty "certainly, gentlemen!" (237). At the same time, he refuses their authority as union representatives through the pseudoindividualistic rhetoric that "each free and independent American citizen should also sign for himself" (238).

The appeal to patriotism is almost not needed, given the impact that the appeal that individuality itself will have, especially for a male audience. Lost in the discussion, of course, is the fact that by signing individually, rather than through an organized, representative body, each worker is not so much individual as singular, while Carnegie, ostensibly an individual, actually represents the corporate power of Carnegie Steel. Nor does his reference to "American" workers note that the United States is itself not a pure democracy but a constitutional, representative democracy—designed to function more like most unions than a corporation. This form of argument, regularly offered today as "Right to Work" laws, uses the confusing, doxic contradictions of masculine individualism to offset the clear, corporate dominance that is being enacted in the guise of individualism.[22]

The effectiveness of the enactments of masculine rhetoric in the workplace is made doubly apparent in their absence. Carnegie's self-chosen isolation in Scotland during the entire Homestead lockout precludes his using the rhetoric of active, direct manly exchange in the *Autobiography*'s retrospective portrait of that event. His literal and metaphoric self-distancing from Homestead in 1892 ironically reinforces his growing difficulty (at the time of writing in 1914) in representing himself in the paradigmatic, hands-on guise of the nineteenth-century self-made entrepreneur. In fact, the chapter of the *Autobiography* devoted to Homestead is notable for its contrast to chapter 18's hearty self-portrait of labor disputes manfully resolved.[23]

The difficulty of maintaining the dominant mythic frame is partly due to the severe shock to *doxa* that was produced by the Homestead events—the lockout, deaths, trials, and general loss of faith in the rights of workingmen everywhere. Homestead alone did not trigger this shift, but it focused the underlying tensions of the time, allowing the concerns to erupt on a scale sufficiently massive to impact on national and international labor concerns, and beyond.[24] Almost fittingly, given his rhetorical focus on individual action as the heart of industrial activity, the ultimate focus of the attention was Carnegie himself. The vituperative, antibusiness/anti-Carnegie rhetoric that ensued had been prepared for by Carnegie's own insistent selling of himself as a premier self-made man and Carnegie Steel as an embodiment of him.

From within that established frame, Carnegie's complete absence from Homestead during the lockout emphasized as much as anything that he was an industrial manager, and a physically distanced one at that. In Wolff's sardonic description, "Mr. Carnegie and his wife were secluded in a lonely lodge on Loch Rannoch, Perthshire, Scotland, thirty-five miles from any railroad or telegraph connection. Having shut himself off from the outside world, he killed time by firing at grouse from a shooting box" (95). It didn't take much work by labor or the press to engage a telling rhetoric concerning this lordly absence: There was something unmanly in Carnegie's behavior. One particularly pointed comment from the *St. Louis Post-Dispatch* is noted by James Bridge, Wall, and Harold Livesay in turn: "One would naturally suppose that if he had a grain of manhood, not to say courage, in his composition, he would at least have been willing to face the consequences of his inconsistency. . . . Say what you will of Frick, he is a brave man. Say what you will of Carnegie, he is a coward" (Bridge 233–34; Wall 573; Livesay 143). Fictional portraits were no better: any manager now could be characterized positively simply by having him despise Carnegie "as an opportunist, a hypocrite, a poseur and a coward—this Carnegie who ran away to hide from the results of his own written word in the Homestead revolt, and left the putting out of the conflagration to abler and braver and more sincere men than himself" (Kelland; qtd. in Blake 98).[25]

In the *Autobiography,* Carnegie struggles mightily to offset the antimasculine rhetoric of these representations, offering arguments similar to his antiunion statements. In less than two pages, he declares that "three thousand men . . . were anxious to rid themselves of the two hundred and eighteen" in the union; denounces the "unjust demands of a few union men" while trumpeting "the opinion of the three thousand non-union men that they were unjust"; and rather darkly hints at the might of "three thousand men as against two hundred and eighteen" (221–22). But instead of sounding convincing, Carnegie merely sounds a bit hectic and shrill. There is no actively dominating male—Carnegie having absented himself from the role—to speak the needed masculine rhetoric in these portraits. Indeed, the few opposing union men begin to look a little heroic in their outnumbered and now ironically more individualistic struggle against a dangerously faceless group of three thousand.

Carnegie's appeals to pseudodemocracy are a bit ragged as well, since the vast majority of Carnegie's "best men as men" opposed his policies, no matter the attitudes Carnegie tries to speak for them.[26] All in all, it's a portrait that underscores the lurking danger that paternalism introduces into the rhetoric of masculinity as self-making individuality. In the previous descriptions of labor disputes, Carnegie set himself in his activist role, aligning aggression with the decisive masculinity of the lone, self-making male. Here he struggles to close as paternal master, but the move fails.[27] Faced with incredible vituperation in the press, among the general public, and even in Congress, Carnegie and the *Autobiography*'s rhetoric noticeably stagger. But while the historical events of Homestead allowed a spectacular outpouring of antipathy to be focused and expressed on the self-made man, "Carnegie," the dominant fiction of masculine self-making was shaken but hardly replaced. Carnegie's status as rightful heir to the myth became questionable, but the myth as a whole remained viable, both inside and outside of the workplace. It did so because masculine *doxa* required that society maintain the myth by addressing these tensions or risk the task of questioning *doxa* itself.

Maintaining Doxa *Through Mythic Variation*

Even prior to Homestead, end-of-the-century strains on *doxa* were intensifying the need for more active maintenance of the myth—by Carnegie and society. In style, tone, and motif, Carnegie's own self-justifying descriptions of earlier labor resolutions engage the rhetoric of active self-making. But other books and essays, particularly *Triumphant Democracy; or, Fifty Years' March of the Republic* (1886), already begin to revise the masculinity argued for earlier, now offering the economically well-made Carnegie as *paterfamilias*. In these representations, the masculine doctrine of personal self-growth and risk taking is joined by the related doctrine of achieved—but enlightened—economic might. Carnegie is attempting to become a patriarch, shifting his rhetoric from oedipal son attempting to get what rightfully is his to postoedipal father trying to defend against those who would take what they wrongfully see as theirs.

That appeal to patriarchal economic power, although still rooted in somewhat problematical calls for aggression and hierarchy, can be substituted for that of hands-on action—provided the negative overtones are mitigated. Philanthropy offers one such means of mitigation, but its implication of audience infantilization and feminine dependency must be muted. Carnegie does so by bolstering the rhetoric of self-making with specific intellectual arguments, finding the most useful of these in the philosophy of his friend, Herbert Spencer. Spencer's social Darwinism, and its particular uses and effects, various elements, broad attitudes, and general beliefs that came under its sway—survival of the fittest, the benefits of subsistence-level struggle, laissez-faire economics, Algerism, self-improvement, rags to riches—is marked by the usual complexities and contradictions (Cashman 42–43). Aligned with muscular Christianity, social Darwinism produces a rhetoric appealing to aggression and masculinity, while adding a touch of paternal care for the lesser and less worthy.

Such a philosophy enjoys an obvious symbiotic relationship with the dominant myth of masculine self-making, and it would only be surprising had Carnegie not made use of it. That he did is not particularly noteworthy, but the timing and the response are. To offset the now inappropriate language of entrepreneurial agency, Carnegie fully shifts from active, self-made industrialist to active, self-made public figure. In the last third of his life (and long before the *Autobiography* appeared), Carnegie produces a wealth of writing that propounds a neopatriarchal gospel of self-making, thus publicly enacting the rights of the father to language, self-representation, and verbal dominance.

Among these works, the success of Carnegie's *Triumphant Democracy* marks not only the popularity of its Spencer-based ideas on the struggle of self-making but also the position of its author as public elder justifying both the myth of self-making and his relation to it.[28] Carrying the belief even further and more famously was the subsequent two-part essay, "The Gospel of Wealth," which reappeared along with a number of former articles and a speech in *The Gospel of Wealth and Other Timely Essays*. The title essay of the last collection is, in Swetnam's words, "a typical late-Victorian essay, complete with all the trappings: the masses do not deserve money because they are unable to use it wisely;

those who have made money know how to use it and what is best for the poor; property is equated with civilization, success with goodness" (89). Carnegie's philosophy, and with it his particular representation of masculine self-making, has come a long way from that of simple, verbally adept entrepreneur. But only some of the particulars of the rhetoric of self-making have really shifted, in part to address the impact of time and situation, historical as well as personal. *Doxa* does not change overnight and not very substantially even over time.[29]

For his part, Carnegie continued to engage very traditional features of masculine rhetoric where they proved useful. As Wall notes, in speeches and essays offered in the 1890s, Carnegie could still hold forth a version of pure self-making and institutionally free, masculine rites of passage:

> In an article entitled "How to Win a Fortune," written for the New York *Tribune*, [Carnegie] had been even more blunt. "The almost total absence of the [college] graduate from high position in the business world seems to justify the conclusion that college education as it exists seems almost fatal to success in that domain. . . . It is in this field that the graduate had little chance, entering at twenty, against the boy who swept the office, or who begins as shipping clerk at fourteen." (835)

But if self-growth through experience and autodidacticism mark Alger's heroes and Carnegie's self-making bobbin boy, at the turn of the twentieth century, higher education—even of a liberal or classical sort—was no longer the house of enervation still being portrayed by Carnegie's rhetoric of self-making. Higher education in general, and not just of a technical nature, was becoming more important to an increasingly complex world and corporate environment. There were others with Carnegie's experience who saw the changes coming. Edward Atkinson, Carnegie's "fellow entrepreneur," "found all of this prattle about 'the self-made man' a bit too thick" (Wall 835). "You started young without a classical education," Atkinson suggests to Carnegie, along with admitting that "I did the same thing." But although they both have accomplished a great deal, Atkinson reaches "radically different conclusions. I should recommend every boy of capacity to make the utmost sacrifice possible and to devote the time up to twenty-three or twenty-five if necessary, to getting the benefit of a thorough University training" (qtd. in Wall 835–36).

For all his use of the ever-popular anti-institutional rhetoric of self-making, Carnegie himself was aware of the shift that was coming, much as he may have continued to portray a masculinity antagonistic to some of its elements. The individual corporate lion, his drive and energy embodied in his company, still remains a key aspect of middle-class myths of masculine self-making. But the rise of the twentieth-century institutional corporation introduced a need for more complex enactments.[30] Indeed, the Carnegie Steel Company, and the individualistic role Carnegie portrayed as his place in it, faced dissolution at the same time:

> Most immediate to Carnegie's sense of a shattered world was the sale of the Carnegie Company, Limited—limited not just in precise, corporate, legal sense, but limited in ownership and management. The small band of Carnegie associates, who had directed this great empire under the watchful paternalism of the Old Man himself, had been replaced by a vast super-corporation, owned by thousands of stock investors and managed by salaried specialists, by bureaucrats sitting in committees, and by an intricate web of interlaced financial interests that no one would ever understand or untangle. (Wall 798)

Carnegie's own words following his retirement offer yet another portrait of patriarchal masculinity and beset individualism: "Trial bitter—father bereft of his sons—abandoned & alone—no more whirl of affairs, the new developments in—occupation gone" (Wall 797).

The shifting social framework even adds an ironic touch to Carnegie's philanthropic activities and their implications for masculine, workplace agency. Toiling energetically at disbursing his huge fortune, Carnegie finds himself unable to give it all away by himself. In 1911, he finally bows to the inevitability of twentieth-century institutionalism and creates the Carnegie Corporation of New York, a foundation established for the giving away of his fortune. It is a telling blow not only to Carnegie himself but also to his status as avatar of middle-class, masculine self-making. The very act of disbursing his self-made money now lacks the hands-on behavior of self-made masculinity. As Wall succinctly states it, "No matter how actively [Carnegie] might participate in the organization and establishment of a particular foundation, he could not, in the role of founder, be the policy maker, the man of action" (911). In the end, Carnegie as lone agent cannot give his own money away directly and decisively; it takes a foundation.

Carnegie's twentieth-century admission that liquidating his nineteenth-century fortune is best left to a corporation closes the books on his attempts to elide institutional presence from his own portrait of self-making. Post-nineteenth-century proponents of self-making ignore the presence of social institutions only at the risk of their own plausibility— witness what happens to Sue Miller's David. Altered middle-class myths of masculine self-making would have to adjust their dominant rhetoric—

or their ostensible middle-class roles—to argue this new manhood in relation to powerful institutions. Ironically, possible means for doing so rest in working-class myths from Carnegie's own era. Labor had long been faced with institutions and corporations whose dominance produced clear tensions between a doxic, middle-class masculinity defined in terms of individualism and a blue-collar experience encouraged to see mutualism as a means of opposing corporate power. Not dominant and thus not as fully nurtured and maintained by middle-class *doxa,* the rhetoric of working-class myths addresses much more directly the tensions between self-making and group support, individuality and mutuality, postoedipal claims and preoedipal needs. Their attempts to consider that opportunity and that conflict in a reworked rhetoric of masculinity are the subject of the upcoming chapter.

4

Beyond the Buddy Principle: Individual Struggle and Masculine Solidarity

> Now is the time when you, the wage earners in the iron and steel industry, must feel and know how helpless you have become. You have acted as individuals. Do you know and feel how powerful you could become if you were to unite and become organized?
> —AFL organizing circular, 1912, in David Brody,
> *Steelworkers in America: The Nonunion Era*

> Why did you do that? Don't you understand? I was on my way up. It was my first fucking interview in six months.
> —Gerald to Gaz, *The Full Monty*

> Everyone in the steel mill was GAY!
> —Homer Simpson,
> "Homer's Phobia," *The Simpsons*

THE DOXIC RHETORIC OF MASCULINE SELF-MAKING emphasizes individual struggle in a male-dominated workplace as a central form of masculine engendering. But as these epigraphs make clear, *doxa* cannot maintain full control over masculine rhetoric, and the dominant myth's contradictions allow and even encourage variant forms and testing of the cultural rhetoric. At the same time, such testing still must be carried out in relation to the overall framework of doxic masculinity. The AFL circular, for example, certainly intends to promote a sense of manliness. Its primary appeal, after all, is to overcoming weakness and helplessness in the face of big business—a passive, "feminine" role to be avoided. But in locating the source for this manly power in mutual support, the AFL runs head-on into a key tension. The dominant rhetoric of masculine self-making as individuation easily opposes mutuality by rewriting the latter as dependency and feminization.[1]

The same issue is enacted in *The Full Monty,* a popular 1997 film portraying unemployed steelworkers who are struggling to maintain their uncertain connections to each other while fully involved in the dominant myth of individual advancement.[2] In the epigraph above, Gerald's vision of personal advancement (and a job) has just been destroyed by the boyish pranks of a group of fellow workers. But the most parodic questioning of mythic rhetoric may be that of *The Simpsons* episode. As the steel mill reverberates with shirtless men singing and dancing to "YMCA," Homer's phobia finds full expression in his anxieties about the homoerotic implications of hard-bodied masculinity. Real men can't be gay and can't be dancers; gay men, dancers, and the like, being effeminate, can't be steelworkers; hard-bodied, muscular men can be steelworkers but can't be gay; hard-bodied, muscular men must be narcissistic and thus might be latently gay; and so on *ad infinitum.* The fun—and anguish—in these parodies and testings lies in their clear undercutting of myriad expectations and stereotypes about masculinity.

Such testings of workplace masculinity and self-making are produced by any number of historical, racial or ethnic, and economic misalignments between mythic rhetoric and personal experience. But even as these particular labor-based tensions are mythologized and remythologized, masculine *doxa* is maintained across class boundaries. As exemplar of the entrepreneurial self-made man, Carnegie demonstrates that class-erasing maintenance when he elides a variety of workplace elements from his labor-focused discussions of self-making in order to emphasize two issues. First, he ignores the craft of work (with its linkage to actual means and methods of material production) in favor of extolling the virtues of working in general or, more specifically, the value of effort itself. Second, he always implies that the work ostensibly being done is undertaken primarily by him as an individual.

For craftsmen and laborers, actual workplace dynamics and the historical shifts that they are subject to make it difficult and often unwise to embrace such generalized arguments—while the myth's dominance makes it equally difficult to reject them. Numerous attempts to represent and enact working-class masculinity display those difficulties as they struggle to combine a dominant rhetoric that emphasizes individual struggle with a variant rhetoric of mutual support and solidarity. Not surprisingly, these alternative portraits do not fully resolve the internal tensions that their enactments of masculinity produce.[3] They do, however, regularly emphasize that emphasis on individualistic, often violent struggle is paired with a related sadism in masculinity—and quite possibly a related masochism. In brief, the rhetoric of solidarity and mutuality threatens to unveil anxieties in masculinity that are written up as a set of naturally opposing pairs—agency or nonagency, victory over or defeat by the father and/or his law, sadistic aggression or masochist self-effacement, solidarity and mutuality or dependency and intimacy—and a lurking feminization that lies at the heart of all these oppositions. For its part, the dominant masculine rhetoric, deeply invested in maintaining male/male exchange as the key to male identity, attempts to mask not only these anxieties but also any and all possibilities suggested by alternative rhetorics as well.

Work Shifts/Mythic Shifts

Steel mills and steelworkers are often used to embody masculinity *par excellence,* and workers have fostered that sensibility throughout the history of their industry. Ironworkers relied on traditional self-figuring in calling themselves the Sons of Vulcan, as did nineteenth-century general laborers in naming themselves the Knights of Labor. Contemporary portraits enact similar appeals. Richard Preston's *American Steel: Hot Metal Men and the Resurrection of the Rust Belt* offers up a modern vision of masculine power amidst the self-focusing intensity of steel:

> Live steel can come to a boil in a flash. The term for that is a carbon boil. A severe carbon boil can shake a steel mill to its foundations. Something horrible churns against the furnace's walls, trying to escape, throwing steaming hot metal out the door. Ambushed by a carbon boil, Iverson backed away from the furnace, sparks monsooning around him, drowning his outline in fire, and then he was just another hot metal man lost in a hot metal rain, with eyes like two black coins, staring into the blackbody light. (10)

Mythic overtones—danger, controlled violence, mystery, and heat—abound in this contemporary, epic portrait of masculinity. Interestingly, Preston is portraying not a common laborer, a twentieth-century "Son of Vulcan," in his example, but the mill's manager. In addition, the "Resurrection" of Preston's title points to the mid-twentieth-century collapse of the steel industry in the industrialized West and its assumed rise from the ashes. The historically variable workplace thus continues to enact the basic myth while supplementing its individual arguments and motifs in ways suitable to the complexities of the situation.

The late-nineteenth-century shift from craft-based to mass-produced steel remains among the most significant of such historical changes. Earlier production of steel was essentially group controlled, consisting of teams of workmen concentrated around three primary activities: puddling, heating, and rolling.[4] The resulting ethos was a question not simply of group tasks but of mutually agreed upon behaviors that often relied upon masculine hierarchy and literal paternalism. As Couvares notes, "The ethic of mutualism extended beyond brothers in the craft. Indeed, a form of paternalism marked relations between craftsmen and their helpers. In part, this reflected the not uncommon experience of fathers hiring their sons as helpers" (20). This vision of patrimony provides a particular enactment of mutualism as a properly oedipal dynamic: Son acknowledges the authority of father and thereby earns the right to participate in and eventually inherit the father's authority. In his autobiographical *The Iron Puddler: My Life in the Rolling Mills and What Came of It,* James Davis earnestly embraces this vision as the true form of masculine development. Puddling iron is a skill "handed down from father to son, and in the course of time came to my father and so to me. None of us ever went to school and learned the chemistry of it from books. We learned the trick by doing it, standing with our faces in the scorching heat while our hands puddled the metal in its glaring bath" (91). Masculine knowledge, growth, and authority merge seamlessly as life's hard experiences are enacted by father and son, in turn.[5]

Within craft production, craft knowledge provides leverage, control, and agency to workers defined in terms of their membership in a group. In turn, the masculinity associated with these interdependent behaviors is attached to craft knowledge itself, making craftsmanship not simply a form of knowledge but an essential component of the masculine identity of those who possess it.[6] At the same time, the craft tradition encourages repetition of paternalistic patterns that include not only experience, growth, and reward but hierarchy as well. The latter half of that equation rests on an exclusionary system that replicates and validates itself by devaluing other forms of work—an argument repeatedly used by owners in their turn to devalue all nonmanagerial work, skilled or unskilled, as well as to counter any incipient rhetoric concerning a masculinity attached to solidarity or mutuality.

By the last quarter of the century, these tensions between worker solidarity and craft exclusion were exacerbated by shifts in technology that devalued craft in favor of general labor, with both tensions and shifts being mirrored in the growth and makeup of unions themselves. Only two years after their 1874 contract negotiation with Columbus Rolling Mills, the Associated Brotherhood of Iron and Steel Heaters, Rollers, and Roughers combined with members and former members of the United Sons of Vulcan, Pittsburgh's Iron City Forge, and the Iron and Steel Roll Hands Union to create the Amalgamated Association of Iron and Steel Workers, the craft union organized in the Homestead Works.[7] Despite its increase in size, the formation of this union was an attempt to maintain some semblance of self-control and agency embodied in the earlier frame of craft-based masculinity. Unfortunately, the sense of agency provided by union solidarity continued to be limited by the insistence in many unions like the Amalgamated on admitting only skilled or craft workers. The reasons for this exclusionary policy (a clear weakness, given the ongoing shifts in actual production) are complex and multiple but more than minimally based on a lingering and nostalgic tie between craft and masculinity.

Such craft-based arguments were already becoming moot by the time of the Homestead lockout, however. As craft-based jobs and their related values and identities were eliminated or segregated, the large degree of interpersonal, group-centered control and exchange afforded by an admittedly hierarchical but nevertheless worker-controlled, craft-oriented system of labor came to play an increasingly minor role in the high volume production of steel exemplified by Carnegie's Edgar Thomson Works. Steelmaking had progressed from a production dependent upon small crews producing small batches of wrought iron to massive blast and open-hearth processes in which laborers essentially became functions of the furnace. All labor historians concerned with steel address this technological shift, differing mainly in their claims as to the degree to which some measure of control and agency was maintained, complete loss of it forestalled, or compromises somehow achieved by workers—each instance usually depending upon the nature of the factory and its own particular production goals and technologies.[8]

It is certain, however, that a huge industrial complex such as Carnegie's Homestead mill did not lend itself to maintenance of masculine *doxa* in the same fashion as father-and-son dominated, craft-oriented mills. What was needed to produce steel in these factories was not a group of skilled puddlers but a large workforce of unskilled laborers. Craft and trade unions thus were torn between their own craft identity and the need for leverage and agency in a workplace being revamped by technological changes. Open unions, of which the Knights of Labor were the most successful, did welcome any and all workers regardless of skill or job type. Yet even here certain exclusions took place. The loss of worker control and knowledge produced by the shift in steelmaking from craft-based to unskilled laboring became readily linked to ethnic and racial tensions as owners, faced with skyrocketing needs for unskilled labor, relied on transoceanic and South to North migration for a ready supply of generally unskilled labor.[9] The impact of all these pressures on workplace structure and masculine ethos was enormous.

> Between 1865 and 1897, a whole range of orthodox values
> and community structures were shattered by the rapidity and
> extent of economic and social change. Individualism, equal
> opportunity, democracy, and liberty assumed new forms and

implications in a society increasingly dominated by giant corporations and urban concentrations of population. Clearly,
individualism and democracy had different meanings for John
D. Rockefeller and for his refinery hands, or for Andrew
Carnegie and the men who sweated before Homestead's open
hearths. (Dubofsky 30)

Such wrenching changes among working-class labor directly threatened
dominant, middle-class representations of masculinity and the myth of
the self-made man. As Daniel Rodgers notes, "The arc that ran from
Edgeworth's cautious acknowledgment of upward mobility, to Alger's
celebration of ambitious individualism, to the school story writers'
ambiguous code of group solidarity reflected something of the rise, triumph, and final disarray of the idea of success in nineteenth- and twentieth-century America" (150–51).[10]

But the *doxa* of masculinity is not readily overthrown. What varies
is its particular realization in specific myths of self-making. With these
issues in mind, it is worth asking with Dubofsky, "What was more important in determining a worker's attitudes and values—the immediate
circumstances of his work, family, and neighborhood life, or his knowledge of a few men who had made good?" (27). The answer, not surprisingly, is that historical and technical changes in steel production both
allowed and demanded shifts within worker sensibility and representation in relation to the dominant rhetoric of self-making. But the basic
myth refused to give up its doxic power and its emphasis on individualistic, one-on-one battles with father-figures, as myriad enactments of
working-class masculinity and its ethos reveal.

Whittaker's Larry Locke: A Story of Labor and Capital

Captain Frederick Whittaker's *Larry Locke: Man of Iron; or, A Fight
for Fortune: A Story of Labor and Capital* first appeared in serial form
in the premier pulp venue *Beadle's Weekly,* running from October 27,
1883, to January 12, 1884. As Grimes notes, "In the early 1880s the
Knights of Labor were multiplying rapidly, and the story papers reflected
the current enthusiasm" (11). In a brief two-year period, Whittaker
wrote seven novels capitalizing on this interest in working-class heroes.[11]
All are representations of laborers or craftsmen in search of work that
will provide them income and, more importantly, identity and satisfaction—essentially a chance to make themselves. As such, the tales enact
a characteristic rhetoric of American labor and self-growth and are often considered classic representations of the Algeresque tale, both in content and venue.

The stories certainly do begin in good Algeresque fashion. In *Larry Locke,* the hero possesses the quintessential prerequisites for self-making. He is poor, jobless, and, importantly, an orphan. He is also hard-working, generous, devoted to personal growth, and, again importantly, lucky in meeting the right people. Grimes summarizes the features nicely:

> Although written for entertainment, Whittaker's stories are latter-day morality tales, with one uniquely American requirement: the honest young mechanics or carpenters must work their way up the ladder of success from humble beginnings. Education and self-improvement become practically a religion. . . . Without exception, Whittaker's heroes are abstemious, industrious, honest, and gallant—Horatio Alger types. (12–13)

But if Whittaker's Larry Locke has many of the same qualities of Alger's Ragged Dick, there are differences worth noting in these labor-oriented myths of self-making. Ragged Dick's break into the world of valued work is a movement into a white-collar world. Like so many Alger heroes, Dick moves into the middle of an institution, if not directly into the middle class. The effect of that move on the hero's actual work is little noted, however, since Alger is rarely interested in portraying the workplace per se. As Rodgers and Denning note, Alger's interest (like that of Carnegie) is not in actual labor but in success (Rodgers 39, 144; Denning 172).

That alone is a signal difference between the heavy middle-class bias of Alger and the attempted working-class orientation of Whittaker. In texts like *Larry Locke,* there is a clear effort to validate not just the hero but the work of the class to which he belongs. For a hero like Larry Locke, then, a good bit of his masculinity is attached to labor and the place and way in which he performs it. Strength, power, and physical struggle of a regular and regularly violent form are stressed. Achievement of masculinity (or the respect due the father) is not to be signaled primarily through external markers, such as movement into and acceptance by a "higher" class, but by manly performance within the framework of honest labor and physical effort. If that honest labor should be matched with economic gain and/or dominance over lesser men, so be it. But the labor itself must first be validated as difficult and honorable. The emphasis, then, to reverse Alger's 1869 "Luck and Pluck," is on pluck more than luck.[12]

In addition, the eager leap into a white-collar job that signals Ragged Dick's middle-class self-making enacts a point of major concern in working-class rhetoric. The tension between pursuing personal upward mobility versus maintaining group solidarity—union or craft-based—is one of the key issues Whittaker faces, and his rhetoric clearly displays the strain in its contradictory enactments of individualistic and mutualistic rhetoric. It is within and at times against the dominant rhetoric's mythic portrayals of individualistic, masculine aggression that the uncertainties and tensions of union organization and mutuality must be read.

The presence of the dominant myth and its power to define masculinity is clear from the outset of *Larry Locke*. As happens so often in these tales, the rhetoric of separation from both family and class is quickly conflated. Locke is the proverbial street orphan, first seen walking along a country road toward the steel-mill town of Holesburg. Such total removal of background provides clear benefits. Literally eliminating family and class history allows the traditional family drama to be rewritten as a romance of self-making. The reader (usually a young adolescent, quite often male as regards these particular dime fictions) is encouraged to enact Locke's adventures and translate the fiction's underlying argument (the more troubling description of growth as a family-based struggle) into the social myth of independent struggle for selfhood, masculine questing, and so on. Placed before the reader with no previous family or institutional history, Locke need not separate from the attractions of mother, renounce the authority of father, or (as in Carnegie's case) offer deeply sentimentally portrayals that anesthetize the self-maker's relation to either or both. In Rodgers's terms, the tales allow "the eradication of parents from boys' stories [and] the triumph of the chivalrous, heroic virtues. . . . In one act of skillful daring, [the heroes leap] directly into manhood" (144).

Yet what is so striking about *Larry Locke* is that what is replaced is most emphatically not the entire family drama so much as the presence of the caregiver/mother. It does not require much reading to encounter a central fact about *Larry Locke*: The book's ostensible emphasis on heroic self-making is rooted in multiple appeals to and versions of the father/son dyad. This is very much a book about men and oedipal struggle (failed and otherwise). At the head of these pairings, we have the nineteenth-century version of Miller's patriarch and Erikson's grandfather: Elisha Skinner. A classic, mid-nineteenth-century Carnegie figure, Skinner began as a blacksmith and wheelwright until, "by dint of hard work, scheming and saving, he had risen to be the heaviest steel manufacturer in Pennsylvania" (145). In occupying that position, Skinner senior has a dual role to play. He is the unhappy father of the novel's villain—Marcellus Skinner—and the doting grandfather of the novel's secondary hero—Paul Van Beaver, nephew of Marcellus. Each of these three figures, in turn, engages a father/son rhetoric lying at the heart of this supposed tale of an orphaned, self-making boy.

This rhetoric of father/son exchange and aggression produces myriad pairings throughout. After abandoning his family and going to sea, Marcellus Skinner returns to reveal himself as a decidedly nonbiblical prodigal son, signaled by the fact that Elisha blanches (155) rather than rejoices at his son's return. Elisha Skinner has good reason to question the reappearance of this infernal prodigal. Marcellus has no intention of returning in order to beg a position as one of the hired servants (Luke 15:19). Indeed, although he is provided with a position at the mill, his ultimate goal is to "get back his rights" (163), which will be his *when the old man's dead*" (Whittaker's emphasis, 164). With his mother, wife, and sister occupying the ever-convenient role of dead women, and his father established as the classic, precorporate self-made entrepreneur, Marcellus's character slides readily into the position of ungrateful and undeserving son who wants the father's power and status without honest effort. Truly prodigal, his arc of development reveals only too negatively the buried fantasy of eliminating the father rather than embracing the broadly endorsed rhetoric of phallic acknowledgment, acceptance of defeat, and subsequent personal achievement.

It is a negative oedipal display that Whittaker reinforces through Marcellus's own abandoned son, Tom Trainor. Dim-witted and hulking, Tom helps the plot by being beaten up by Larry Locke (who thereby wins his job in the mill) and by serving as a convenient foil for the positive, male-centered, postoedipal family model that Whittaker and masculine *doxa* argue. Like many of the characters in the novel, Tom has no clear relationship with his mother, who was abandoned (along with Tom) by Marcellus. Indeed, although technically a bastard, Tom grows up as one more of the book's numerous male orphans. His prodigal father's return subsequently eliminates any brief and temporary emphasis on the absent mother, and it allows Whittaker to reinforce the father/son framework that is central to the rhetoric of masculine *doxa*.

From within this general rhetoric, Marcellus and Tom demonstrate the dangers of perverting the father/son relation. Just prior to cementing their plans for gaining control of the mill, Marcellus caustically denounces Elisha's attitude toward him. "I'm the only son," he rages to Tom, "and he give me the grand bounce. His *son!* d'ye mind that?—his *son*" (163). Determined to recover from this admitted paternal defeat, Marcellus's fantasy begins by blatantly envisioning the deaths of his father and his nephew Paul. He then delightfully compounds this wishful patricide by urging his own son Tom into a lively cursing fit over the prospect: "Oh, curse 'em, curse 'em, curse 'em, Tom!" he hollers. "Nothing loth, the boy obeyed, and for a good minute father and son blasphemed with a virulence perfectly Satanic, till Marcellus shook his son's hand, saying: 'Thankee, thankee, Tom. It does me good to hear ye swear like that.'" Thus united in good Lacanian fashion by the phallic pseudo-power of a perverted logos, father and son agree to "shut up" (163–64). Thoroughly established in the reader's mind as powerful (and powerfully twisted) prodigal and abandoned sons, eager for the death of father, nephew, and cousin, and bonded through their demonstrated control over an impressively infernal logos, Marcellus and Tom quietly brood over their oedipal fantasies (164).

The focus of their cursing is not only Elisha Skinner. It is also the third motherless son in Whittaker's triad of Larry Locke, Tom Skinner, and Paul Van Beaver, the somewhat effete grandson of Elisha Skinner and Tom's cousin. If the young male reader is encouraged to peer into aberrant oedipal dynamics through Elisha, Marcellus, and Tom, he is also encouraged to compare their behaviors to that of Elisha and Paul. The young Van Beaver is, in his own way, another ne'er-do-well son, but in a genteel and genial way. It is not Marcellus alone who senses class issues in Paul, "that cussed young snob" (164). Spoiled, the spendthrift child of "a lazy, improvident gentleman who had lived on his relatives" and whose death was regretted by "no one" (166), Paul is the heir apparent to his grandfather's business and a card-carrying member of the upper-middle class. His class negatives are nevertheless tempered by Whittaker, who establishes him as a good (grand)son via the explicitly loving relationship he shares with Elisha.

Van Beaver thus initially plays a cautionary rather than a negative role for the reader. Not a battler like Larry Locke, Paul drifts perilously close to the feminine, finally being rudely reminded of the need to pursue masculine self-making when he loses his inheritance and his leisured status. He will only begin to regain both when he learns the masculine values of work and self-definition. Like Marcellus and Tom, then, Paul enacts a series of ambivalent arguments within the dominant rhetoric. He is "left an orphan at an early age" (145), but he has a father-figure in his grandfather. He is "the living link which connected the plebeian manufacturer [Elisha Skinner] with the aristocratic Patroons of Beaver-wyk" (145), but the loss of his inheritance will force him to make himself over again with the ostensible help of no one. Paul, Marcellus, and Tom thus offer the reader a multifaceted reflection of the self-made man, a set of impure desires hidden within "proper" masculine development and self-making that Whittaker reveals as tainted by linking them to twisted family dynamics and class temptations. So colored, they are even more fully overshadowed by Whittaker's true, working-class hero and model of masculine self-making: Larry Locke.

In making Larry Locke the only "true" orphan and the only "true" working-class male, Whittaker has reserved for him the initial twin characteristics necessary for maintaining real working-class, masculine self-making: He is completely without family and thoroughly at the bottom of the economic scale. As orphan, Locke is not attached directly to the tension and guilt involved in the full family dynamics of masculine training. Instead, Locke offers a halcyon innocence that only a spectacularly self-making figure can provide. When read this way, Locke's relation not only to the absent parents but also to the other male characters is further clarified. The other "father/son" sets (Elisha/Marcellus, Marcellus/ Tom, Elisha/Paul) serve as object lessons that reinforce the preferable status of the motherless/fatherless Locke. In this case, no pain—much gain: The figure of Locke offers male readers a safe position from which to reject Whittaker's three determined representations of how not to act like fathers and sons.

Such a position allows readers to watch fathers beat (or be beaten) without the underlying oedipal concerns and anxieties being directly enacted. Acknowledgment—however buried—and testing of these issues are eased along through low-level sadomasochistic voyeurism. Readers are encouraged to enjoy feeling scorn for the warped or sidetracked masculinity of Marcellus and Tom, both pleasure over and pity for Elisha's weakened paternalism, and sympathy for Paul's untested masculinity. There is even the rhetorical *frisson* of listening to Marcellus's hopeful call for the death of his father. At the same time, the true masculinity and self-making that is embodied by Locke remains as positive foil to the warped manliness of the rest. With the other figures serving to ease anxieties, Locke remains both the dominant figure of Whittaker's argument and a socially acceptable embodiment of the desires, tensions, and contradictions of the father/son oedipal emphasis in the myth of self-making. With that "safe" status established, Locke is free to indirectly enact struggle with other men through two motifs central to Whittaker's novels and to working-class fiction in general: the fistfight or wrestling match and the labor strike.

The regular occurrence of these two motifs is a commonplace. They are key because they not only represent historically valid, working-class behavior in the plots but also are a means by which authors engage the dominant myth's masculinity. The use of these motifs both to engage and to meliorate negative overtones is readily visible in James Davis's jolly sketches of boardinghouse fights among the guys. Highly juvenile, the conflicts provide Davis with a useful means of representing individuals fighting over food rather than the mom who typically prepares it or the father who "owns" it (as well as avoiding portraits of groups struggling against corporate power). Davis's stagy, autobiographical scenes often mitigate their violence through self-deprecating attempts at humor, such as his names for a succession of boardinghouses, which range from the sublimity of "The Pie Boarding House," to the flatly clichéd "Greasy Spoon" (where the men are admonished by the landlady to "Stop yer fightin' before I hack your hands off"), and finally down to the pirate play of "The Bucket of Blood," from which Davis claims to be ejected for reading at night by being literally tossed from a second-story window (148–49, 153–55).[13] The description of this fight closes, of course, with Davis as Wiley Coyote: He gets up, dusts off, walks away.

This sort of over-the-top juvenilia tends to so comedically bludgeon the emphasis on manly battles for dominance that it risks parodying the fight motif. Other working-class stories tend to offer more conflicted attempts to consider the masculinity Davis purportedly is so sure about. *Larry Locke* is fairly typical. Locke's first act of note is to defend himself—not through fistfighting in this case but by beaning an older man with a rock. That description doesn't quite do justice to Whittaker's portrait, however, nor its clear David and Goliath overtones. As "Terror Jim" chases him, Larry picks up a stone and stops, waiting until "his enemy" is less than ten feet away. "Then, with a force and precision amazing in one so small . . . he cast the stone full in the tramp's face, taking him between the eyes with a crack like that of a whip. Not a sound came from the tramp, who stumbled and dropped in the road like a slaughtered ox" (141). It is the first of myriad such encounters, and they all tend to be relatively violent, albeit in that boyhood, war game fashion in which all and sundry somehow get up and rejoin the fray, charging back into the (take your pick) gang of bullies, crowd of police and strikers, barroom-brawling cowboys, shrieking savages, whatever.

Although the scenes are both violent and juvenile, Whittaker is deadly serious in using them to establish the rhetoric of successful manly battle. Very shortly after his first encounter, Larry attempts to secure a job at the mill. Lacking a craft arena (and a father) through which to negotiate Locke's battle with authority, Whittaker is both constrained by the shifting industrial workplace and free to substitute a screen event with the requisite overtones: Larry fights Tom Trainor for the right to work in the mill. Initially overwhelmed by "his big antagonist," the smaller Larry "bucks" Tom with his head, sending blood "streaming from his nose and mouth," bites him, drops him headfirst on the "hard ground with a terrible thud," and "like a little demon" again bucks his head ("Crack, crack, crack, crack!") into Tom's face, "savagely crying" for Tom to call it quits (150–52). Given Locke's need for a job, the reader is clearly being asked to enjoy Locke's prowess and eventual victory on those grounds. But there are other pleasures. Carnegie quieted his acts of replacing the father by emphasizing his mouth and his money. In a world defined by industrial needs, Whittaker quiets the oedipal quality of Larry Locke's battle by concentrating on Locke's use of his fists, feet, head, and whatever else is necessary to win a job. But if Whittaker's rhetoric of battle is fairly direct in its violence, it is also not-so-indirectly oedipal in its argument: By beating the hell out of the right authority figures or their surrogates, you can make yourself a man.

For his prowess, Larry is given a job, that key trait of working-class masculinity, wins the praise of his eventual wife when he returns to his newly found home, and polishes off the day by saving, club-in-hand, his preset family household from a gang of toughs led by a still angry Tom Trainor (158–59). All is right in this masculine version of the world where the purportedly mutualist ethic of fighting and boxing that Denning describes is enacted through a decidedly noncovert sharing of masculine delights in a personal struggle for dominance and advancement. As Denning's own comments suggest, then, fights occupy a somewhat ambiguous middle ground between mutualism and individuality, a means of earning supportive solidarity and brotherhood through display of individual personal dominance. In short, the appeal of these scenes relies heavily on the masculine rhetoric of self-making, which translates masculine struggle with (and hidden defeat by) the father and his law into workplace victory achieved over a safe male figure.

But there is another current flowing in the background activity in this scene, and it is one that recognizes a class difficulty often missing from middle-class versions. As Larry fights, the mill owner and his grandson are blithely betting on the outcome of what is metaphorically and perhaps literally a life-threatening situation for Locke. Like Ellison's Invisible Man, who is forced to fight in a "battle royal" with his peers, Locke provides sport for those gathered around and betting on him. Locke's prize will not be Invisible Man's fake coins or even (thanks to the speech Invisible Man gives later) the middle-class version of success—college and a briefcase. Locke's working-class reward is a job at the mill. But both teens are forced to fight with members of their own class (and race in IM's case) in order to enact the middle-class rhetoric of individual struggle and personal advancement.

In his scene, Ellison directly reveals that the myth of masculine self-making is another way to "Keep This Nigger-Boy Running" (33).[14] But the sadomasochism that Ellison makes so apparent is not offered as such in the background betting of Larry's fight. Even as Whittaker presents his outside bettors, he appears intent on putting the fight forward as part of a positive performance of masculine rites of passage. For all its suggestiveness, the betting is ultimately represented as being at the service of Locke's masculinity; like the correct bettor, the reader (especially the male reader) knows the "natural" outcome of this story and the inevitability that Larry will win. Paul Van Beaver's bet simply signals Locke's (and Paul's) worthiness through a natural recognition of manliness. But the voyeuristic figures in the background nevertheless hint at another level of control and another appeal in fighting. What they reinforce is a sense that Whittaker's novel considers, while not directly celebrating, the sado-masochistic underpinnings and anxieties that underlie the dominant myth of self-making. Ultimately, this scene, like the earlier exchange between Larry and Terror Jim, serves to enact what Rotundo describes as "curious veins of casual hostility and sociable sadism" that underpin "the pleasure that boys took in fighting and even stoning one another" (35–36).

As Rotundo's description makes clear, to characterize the fight scenes as even lightly sadistic is perhaps to do no more than repeat a long-standing link between masculinity and male aggression. But this characterization of male aggression is no less long-standing than the desire to repress that description behind the code of manliness itself, to replace the negative of sadism—as the achievement, usually via violence, of dominance over others—with the positive of male aggression as a societally endorsed reversal of dependency on and/or dominance by others. This masking displays not simply psychological and doxic flexibility; it also demonstrates the anxious need for a defeat-erasing victory in the first place, an admission of sadomasochistic complexities that ultimately are compounded by the presence of preoedipal as well as oedipal anxieties.

Sadomasochism and Self-Making

The general tendency to characterize fight scenes as common components in male aggression (the "boys will be boys" motif of Davis) is often accompanied by the sense that, since there is no direct sexual activity depicted, genital or otherwise, to call the scenes essentially sadistic, let alone masochistic, is to engage in overreading. Freud's own definition of what he eventually calls sadism proper—a "general instinct of mastery . . . in the service of the sexual function"—notes the dual focus while not necessarily resolving the question ("Economic Problem of Masochism" 163). There can be little argument that the first half of Freud's equation is clearly at work in all of Locke's battles. At the least, these fight scenes establish Locke's aggressive, even violent, mastery of his own existence. In addition, self-mastery is regularly performed in terms of an equivalent mastery over others: Terror Jim, Tom Trainor, Marcellus Trainor, the bosses as a whole. There is, then, a distinct pleasure in the violent dominance of others offered to the reader by the hero of this story.

That pleasure is not directly signaled as sexual, but libido is not solely in the service of genital sexuality. Moreover, as LaPlanche and Pontalis note, Freud does "at times" use the term *sadism* to describe certain forms of violence, "whether or not it is accompanied by sexual satisfaction," and this sense of the word "has attained wide currency in psycho-analysis" (401). As described by Lynn Chancer, such violence is sadistic, or masochistic, or both: "The sadomasochistic dynamic . . . is a very particular but common social relationship based on power and powerlessness, dominance and subordination."[15] That description fits a capitalist workplace neatly, of course, where job dependency and power over labor exist as a matter of structure. These less directly sexual forms of sadomasochism are not lesser or incomplete versions of a truer, more obviously sexual version, however. Their subtle sadomasochism serves rather to provide a general rhetoric of sadomasochism in situations where more blatant linkages of sexuality and violence might disconcertingly display the presence of the underlying dynamics.

Reasons why doxic rhetoric often prefers to provide less obvious ways of maintaining connections between masculinity, self-making, and sadomasochism are made very clear in Robert Olen Butler's *Wabash* (1987), a contemporary novel about Depression-era steelworkers. Butler's main character is Jeremy Cole, a steelworker limited to short turns at the mill, who is slowly turning in on himself. Emotionally separated from his wife, Deborah, by the loss of their daughter and the tenuousness of his job, Cole's main recourse is immersion in the remnants of physical work to which he has access and explosions of violence—both of which are finally united in Cole's killing of a company goon on top of a furnace (a rather different end from that provided for Carnegie's stool pigeon). As the only means Cole has to maintain contact with his emotions, these fights serve a sense of masculinity that is disturbingly minimal and bleak, unmeliorated and untempered by a doxic rhetoric of self-making. The very motives in which Butler roots Cole's violence—worker brotherhood/worker powerlessness, hatred of but inability to counter unalloyed corporate power, repressed fears of emotion and emotional weakness, and sexual frigidity—don't so much underwrite the violence as demonstrate not only an incipient sadism but a deeply threatening masochism resting directly alongside. Chancer characterizes Cole's situation well:

> The structural situation of factory workers . . . permits no possibility of exercising simultaneous independence and dependence: striking out, literally and figuratively, may indeed result in loss. . . . Too often, workers feel that there is no place to direct anger except inward, at the self that feels inferior and is consequently more likely to accept the conditions of psychic and social dependency. (102)

Violence, in other words, is a result of agency denied, a point Butler himself argues. Both Jeremy and his wife are repeatedly required by the institutions and events around them to engage feelings of passivity and powerlessness. Cole's friends have been beaten up and evicted by the mill owner; Deborah's family is dysfunctional and nonsupportive; together they have been unable to save their young daughter from dying of pneumonia. This is the reverse image of self-making; these people try as hard as any, and yet they fail. The result, Butler argues, is masculine violence—violence directed sadistically outward but also masochistically inward until a crisis point is reached. At that moment, masculinity demands either salvation or suicidal behavior, sadism directed outward toward a socially acceptable oedipal target or masochism focused internally on guilty self-punishment.

Butler's final resolution of these warring concerns—Cole's sexual reunion with his wife—reinstates masculine *doxa*. But it also reveals clear complications in both the dominant myth and its doxic underpinning. Cole is frustrated in his goal of murdering his boss by the intrusion of his wife, who seeks connection with Cole rather than victory over injustice. Cole solves that problem by "mistakenly" punching Deborah in the mouth. Literally with one blow, Cole comes to his senses. But this rather bizarre form of renunciation of the female does not adequately enact an oedipal rhetoric that requires (fantasied) victory over or (realistic) defeat by the father. The story line thus continues with the socially necessary correction of this "error" as Cole now accepts Deborah's *wifely* offering of a substitute oedipal figure, Spud the foreman. Deborah holds the admittedly murderous Spud at gunpoint until Jeremy can approach. She then backs away and nods at her husband: "Jeremy had good leverage; he set himself; he felt a quick bright flare of desire for the touch of his wife and he understood what they [*sic*] had to do and the strength poured into his fist and he hit Spud at a slight upward angle on the point of the chin and the man flew backward and fell and did not move" (229). Butler's insistence on the connection between masculine violence and marital desire is further reinforced several pages later, after Cole and his wife make good their escape. But the novel's closing sex scene is almost an afterthought, a finalizing of the equations in a formulaic scene of "correctly" postoedipal, heterosexual coupling.

Within the larger workings of this novel, it is hard to argue that endangered masculinity does not necessarily produce violence of some sort. It is even difficult to argue that it is not warranted; Cole himself has been threatened with murder, and one attempt has already been made. The difficulty a reader experiences with Butler's tale, then, is not the plot-based proof he brings to bear on the motivation for violence. The difficulty is that the story resolves its argument by revealing the direct connections and contradictions in masculine rhetoric's linkage of self-making, sexuality, and violence. The links among dependency, aggression, and acceptable heterosexuality are just so plainly *there*. Moreover, unlike the violence of Whittaker's tales, this representation of masculine aggression is not explicitly validated through the rhetoric of self-making. Because of these missing screens, the novel's final representation of masculinity is less easily embraced than a doxic representation in which masochism and dependency are elided in favor of sadism, sadism is quietly transmuted into masculine aggression, and aggression is a naturalized motif in the mythic rhetoric of masculine self-making.

The underlying appeal of Locke as a mutable figure and his fights as exemplary testing behavior can be best understood when considered in this light. The pleasure to be found in Locke's battle for self-made status depends on masking Butler's direct demonstration of sadism and its role in denying masculine masochism. Figuratively family-free in his orphaned status, Locke safely repeats the reader's desire to battle incessantly so as to avoid not only revisiting but repeating masculine gender training rooted in initial oedipal defeat, preoedipal dependency, and ultimately the feminization attached to each. As a premier, self-made "man of iron," Locke's high energy activity offers temporary avoidance of all those issues. His incessant battling produces a series of father-figures to be happily overcome, and each fight invites the reader to occupy the role of the beater. All that is required is will, effort, and a body of iron—as both Davis's near-parodic and Whittaker's versions suggest.

That process is not fully sustainable, however—not historically in terms of the nature of the workplace and certainly not at the level of the plot for Whittaker. The focus on individual, physical battles temporarily deflects attention away from institutional effects on issues of masculine self-making. But as later struggles in the novel suggest, the real fight for mastery is not with other individual men but with a world dominated by money and institutional power. Locke's initial performance of adequately individualistic victories—Terror Jim, Tom Trainor, the Black Hawk Gang—is balanced by another triad of physical tests, one a victory that leads to a defeat, one a victory over the idea of fighting, the last a defeat that leads to a victory. All address masculinity in separate but related ways, and all complicate a basic rhetoric that lies at the heart of masculine behavior: singular victory over embodiments of power.

Solidarity, Mutuality, and Unionization

The victory by Locke that leads to temporary defeat provides a specific rewriting of cultural rhetoric and its emphasis on achieving manhood at the expense of another male. In this case, Locke initially defeats not the mill owner's son but the mill owner himself, Marcellus Skinner. In doing so, Locke also acquires full adult status, as signalled in his winning the name "'Man of Iron' by a single blow . . . as he had that of the 'Boy of Iron' six years before" (176). Sent to bed with two broken ribs, Skinner the man is unfortunately not defeated as Skinner the boss. Locke loses his job not over the fight alone but also because he refuses to work at reduced wages. Only he and the other skilled crane men refuse, however, and Skinner successfully repeats Carnegie's ploy of reducing wages by defeating the men's solidarity.

This clear defeat is temporized by masculine agency of a different sort. Locke simply goes to Ohio by himself and gets a new job, while Molly and son, conveniently self-contained, easily adapt to such a situation. In his masculine separation and mobility, Locke finds some similarity with Erikson's self-making and peripatetic patriarch. For such figures, a challenge is simply an invitation to further effort, and answering the call can be as simple a task as moving on. But Erikson's figure is an engineer, a middle-class entrepreneur more in the Carnegie vein, and he bears few marks of defeat by the fathers or anyone else. Locke may be mobile, but he is not middle class, and Whittaker is determined to address his class status, not alleviate him of it. As a defeated worker, then, Locke is free to find work elsewhere, which he does. But in the end, he has to face up to institutional power if he is to achieve real victory, and he must return to Holesburg in order to do so. If he does not, mobility contains overtones not of agency but of escape. Locke does return, of course, arriving once more in the nick of time to save Molly from Tom Trainor. More importantly for working-class, masculine self-making, he also returns as the region's Master Workman of the Knights of Labor.

The strike and Locke's role as Master Workman of the union that organizes it signal the height of Locke's power over the bosses. Together they are used by Whittaker as an indication of Locke's maturation and movement into his own form of postoedipal, family-based masculinity. These last two battles thus serve as a transition in masculinity as well as in plot. Having established an ability to literally beat the fathers, Locke now appears to have achieved a new masculine stature, one capable of maintaining itself through organizational victories over dominating institutions. But the masculinity that accompanies this shift from physical to organizational prowess is not quite so lavishly embellished as the fight scenes, nor is the solidarity it offers in place of the individuality of the fistfight as completely argued. That is not to say that Whittaker is not attempting to positively reinforce this move. The complication lies in the way the rhetoric of labor organization and strikes recapitulates masculine anxieties even as it partially echoes the dominant rhetoric of masculine self-making.

Locke's return signals Whittaker's argument for a self-made man in revised form. Locke has adequately demonstrated his independence and ability to separate by moving to Ohio. Those markers of masculinity having been acquired, he is free to set aside physical force in favor of power through language and union solidarity. In adopting this stance, Locke essentially beats the bosses (and their individualistic masculinity) at their own game. By adopting a different form of middle-class dominance (through language rather than fists), while coupling it not with individuality but with working-class mutuality, Locke is ready to enact a new form of masculine behavior by performing its most recognizable act—organizing a strike.

Whittaker takes pains to argue that this is a form of masculine self-making with greater value than the violence of the earlier fights. Although masculinity remains a value that accrues to Locke as a powerful individual, it roots itself in mutual recognition by a brotherhood of equal (or near-equal) manly figures. The most blatant demonstration of this new linkage occurs in Locke's returning battle with Hargous, the watchman at Skinner's mill. Notably missing in this representation is the cheap violence and sadism of the earlier fights. Here, Locke and Hargous only "wrastle," and the battle is over quickly. More importantly, it is a battle that also describes a different masculinity:

> The unexpected dignity of the watchman—for there is dignity in the acceptance by a man of a contest in which he knows he will probably be beaten—compelled a certain amount of respect, and Larry in his turn began to feel that he had gone too far in bullying the man who, after all, was only doing his duty with extra rudeness.
>
> However, there was no help for it now, so he only said, as he stretched out his arms:
>
> "You said you'd break my back. Now let's see ye do it."
>
> The next moment the men grappled, and Hargous was thrown with a violence that knocked all the breath out of his body for several seconds, when Larry helped him up, saying kindly:
>
> "No malice, I hope, friend. You and me ain't a fair match. Besides, why should we fight, when we're both workingmen? Our kind ought to stick together against the bosses." (217)

The union as the source of Locke's newfound self-knowledge is apparent in this blend of masculine domination and brotherly solidarity. It is not sufficient, of course, simply for Locke to call for equality. Masculine recognition still must be earned in a battle in which possible defeat is admitted but successful dominance is apparent. Locke's earlier physical dominance of boss Skinner ultimately only led to defeat—Locke became jobless. That defeat is now replaced by Locke's current dominance of Skinner's man Hargous, a victory that serves as precursor of the new drama in which workers search for masculinity not solely in individual physical battles in which they must ultimately repeat the oedipal trauma (safely suggested in Hargous's "embrace" of his own possible/certain defeat) but also in labor-based battles in which they can win through solidarity with other men. Montgomery summarizes the conceptual as well as historical shift: "This self-improvement was aimed not at promoting individuals out of the working class into the ranks of the wealthy, but at personal and public enlightenment, so that all might see the falsity of the individualistic beliefs that had come to be taught in high places and to understand that 'an injury to one was the concern of all'" (Afterword 329). In short, what is offered is a masculinity that is not only attached to the rhetoric of middle-class, individualistic self-making but also rooted in both the rhetoric of personal battle and the rhetoric of solidarity and mutual interdependence.

Such a rhetoric runs counter to doxic myth. But as Montgomery makes clear, it is not only labor history that supports Whittaker's argument. There also is clear psychological value in the rhetoric of union solidarity and mutuality, which offers a means of avoiding a repetition and reinstatement of the damage done to masculinity by the initial defeat of the bosses'/fathers' phallic authority. Whittaker clarifies that issue by describing the differing attitudes between Locke's firmly set union consciousness and that of the rest of the men, in whom the mutual brotherhood of unionism has not yet produced a revised and/or renewed sense of masculinity: "The months had made a difference in them and in him. They all looked sullen, downcast, and discontented, while Larry held his head up as proudly as ever, and his sturdy figure seemed the personification of strength" (214). Locke apparently possesses a strength based on a realistic attitude toward authority and power, a "properly" oedipalized reality quotient, albeit with a shift. Masculinity is achieved, or at least further marked, through a mature embrace not simply of wife but of brotherly mutuality and solidarity.[16]

In enacting this new rhetoric, Whittaker's strike revises several aspects of the male/male exchanges that Carnegie took delight in producing as proof of his entrepreneurial dominance over union men. Whittaker replicates Carnegie's rhetoric of individual manhood but reverses the images. Carnegie's self-aggrandizing demonstration of verbal control and individual phallic authority is matched with constant reference to Locke's quiet power as based in his responses and own training in group dynamics. Locke knows how to speak as an individual representative, not as a lone figure. Indeed, Locke is praised for using parliamentary tactics to ensure that the men's resolve doesn't collapse too quickly (273). Whittaker even provides a version of Carnegie's hat-negotiation scene, again with the phallic capacities reversed. When Carnegie tells the story, he achieves dominance by refusing to recognize the union spokesman, ridiculing him for not removing his hat when he stands before Carnegie and the group (*Autobiography* 239). In Whittaker's scene, Locke recognizes the bosses' intransigence, and "put[s] on his hat instantly, an example imitated by his followers. 'I'm Larry Locke, Master Workman of this district of the Knights of Labor,'" he declares, and demands to be treated with the respect accorded that group, or he intends to leave (239–40).[17]

These are moments of masculine assertiveness and group solidarity. But in small, individual victories, Whittaker also signals larger, group dangers. Well-trained, Locke knows Skinner's ultimate tactic. He will try "to breed disaffection between Larry and his friends" (240). The danger, of course, is of the strike collapsing—and Locke failing—through a failure of solidarity and mutual support. Whittaker reinforces that equation by explicitly basing the failure of the bosses' "union" on the same grounds. Mill owner Grynde, unable to meet his contracts, is forced to ask for support from his fellow bosses: "A hard man himself, like all rich men who have made their money, [Grynde], for the first time, found himself in a position when he had to ask a favor of his friends, and it was in a pleading voice" that he was forced to do so (239). No longer hard, Grynde shifts from dominance to dependence and finds not friends but more dominance. Skinner responds to Grynde's pleading by cursing him for his weakness and the workers for their attempt to gain mastery over all the bosses. Unsuccessful in gaining support from his fellow owners, Grynde will be forced to reopen his mill at the negotiated wage scale, a failure of solidarity and mutualism that Whittaker explicitly links to Leverenz's sense of workplace humiliation as a central dynamic in masculine behavior. Grynde must leave the room (from which Locke has just defiantly departed) "very pale, and seeming to be much ashamed of himself" (241).

Clearly, Whittaker intends his discussion of solidarity and mutual support to be more than an argument for the economic and political necessities of unionized strikes. He also is working with the implications of mutual support as a new role for masculine representation. In Denning's terms:

> On the [one] hand there is the ethic of solidarity and mutualism, of the unity of the workers in a strike, of the readiness of the older workers to teach the hero, an ethic that is often tied to manhood based around the sociality of the saloon and the code of the most popular sport (to judge from the *National Police Gazette*), boxing. On the other hand, there is the more individualist ethic of hard work and raising oneself, what David Montgomery (*[Beyond]* 1967, 204) has called "the ideological syndrome of 'free agency,' self-improvement, and temperance." Though the narrative patterns are bor-

rowed from pre-existing generic conventions, they are
adapted to work out a genuine ideological antinomy in pro-
ducer manhood—how to reconcile mutualism with self-advancement. (171–72)

Larry Locke makes clear that Whittaker is addressing this issue. It
also makes clear that he is uncertain over how to replace individual self-
making with that of union solidarity. The portrayal of Locke's clear leadership role, for example, suggests a familiar pattern of upward progression and individual differentiation, even if one achieved within the frame
of union solidarity. Signals of that pattern are apparent in Locke's own
questioning of his "fighting for other people" rather than pressing self-
advancement (253). Further tensions are visible in Locke's concern over
the men's commitment. They "don't seem to know anything about saving money. They go spending it on beer, and pawning their clothes to
live with." Still, the strike can be won if the men do not lose heart. "If
they were all *men* it would soon succeed" (Whittaker's emphasis, 249).
These sorts of comments inevitably separate Locke in the reader's sympathy from his fellow workers, and that undercuts the appeal to solidarity and mutualism even as the argument is being made. No such
questioning ever arose while Locke was beating the tar out of someone.
Nor is it likely to have. Locke as boxer is alone, independent, and safely
masculine within the dominant middle-class rhetoric of individualized
agency and aggressive self-making.

Whittaker's attempt to take up the question of mutuality and solidarity as masculine behaviors entails more than just substituting one behavior for another, then. His testing of where solidarity and mutualism lead
is also a testing of whether the appeal to nonindividualistic modes of
masculinity also implies dependency, with its further suggestion of feminization and, in some cases, possibly even masochism, as the latter is
culturally inscribed within the doxic architecture of Western society.
Given that framework, it is significant that the final testing of Locke and
masculine *doxa* occurs in Locke's last physical fight, one in which he is
beaten. To be sure, the fight is an unfair one. Locke is lured to a supposed meeting with the bosses, only to be set upon by Terror Jim and a
dozen other thugs. Hit from behind, it is Locke's turn to be felled like
an ox and considered dead by the coroner. Here, of course, is true martyrdom. Disgusted by the failure of the men to hold fast, Locke has nevertheless been willing to risk death for them (or at least for Paul, who
has been revealed as the mill's inheritor should the strike continue).

If the pleasure to be taken from Locke's former successful beatings
was lightly sadistic, here the emotion tested is that of mutual solace at
best—admission of Locke and reader into the masculine fellowship of

those defeated by a dominant power—and possibly even recognition of masochistic impulses within masculine *doxa*.[18] The novel has prepared the reader for this moment in the earlier lesson learned from by Locke's defeat of Hargous, the mill's security man. Whittaker has told us that "there *is* dignity in the acceptance by a man of a contest in which he knows he will probably be beaten" (Whittaker's emphasis, 217). Yet there Locke still won. Here Locke's defeat produces anger because it is inherently unfair—boss over employee, boss's many thugs against one, blows delivered from behind the back or behind a desk. But even while the unfair beating produces anger, it also suggests hidden awareness of that initially unfair oedipal defeat central to masculinity. Both are delivered by institutionally powerful fathers and bosses, authorities socially and culturally defined as capable of defeating the strongest individual will and effort at every turn.

Locke's apparent defeat establishes more than that oedipally colored frame, however, since it occurs within a narrative not only of individual self-making but also of solidarity and mutual sacrifice. Whittaker clearly is testing solidarity's replacement of the rhetoric of individualistic self-making with that of group interdependence, and it has led him inexorably to martyrdom, and even to the possible masochism that such radical self-sacrifice entails. With all these complexities fully laid out, Whittaker veers away. Locke rises from the mistakenly dead and is immediately threatened with arrest and imprisonment. Recognizing that their leader has been seized, the strikers move to attack the police. Only Locke's newly found verbal skills and quiet power enable him, in what is now blatantly Christlike fashion, to convince his followers to let the police take him to court: "Larry, who had been shaken more than he cared to show by the blows he had received, nevertheless had preserved his coolness, and made a peculiar signal with his hand, which procured instant silence" (288). His control established, Locke provides a short but well-turned speech that disperses the men and underwrites his stature not only as a physical fighter but as a leader who wins with a power rooted in language and self-control.

Whittaker may be attempting to use Locke's status as union man to balance the individualism at the heart of the middle-class myth, but this behavior echoes Carnegie's middle-class rhetoric of personal dominance through language. Locke's near martyrdom too quickly becomes a precursor to near messianism—a state far removed from either solidarity or mutuality, and farther still from masochistic self-erasure. Whittaker's further struggle to alleviate the tension between a rhetoric of masculine independence and that of a now weakened masculine mutuality produces an argument in which the strike succeeds and Locke remains a worker, a significant closure offered by none of his other novels. Only in this story does the hero "resist the lure of the ladder," as Denning describes it (173), turning down the Pisgah-vision of managerial promotion that so many of Whittaker's other workers accept.[19] Unfortunately, the return of Locke to the mill becomes secondary to Whittaker's continuing struggle with the dominant rhetoric of masculine self-making. Locke does not actually control his own destiny; he is saved from the courts—and replaced in the plot—by his lawyers, one of whom is the now adequately self-made, newly masculinized and middle-class Paul Van Beaver.

Metaphorically, then, Locke never really recovers from his last beating even though he wins the strike. Whittaker tests solidarity and masculinity, martyrdom and masculinity, and then shifts his rhetorical emphasis from Locke's invincibility to Paul's rebirth—a rebirth of the self-made man in its doxic, middle-class individualism. Having hit professional bottom following his ejection from the mill by Skinner, Paul has learned to make it on his own. He has in his face now "the solid look of a man who respected himself and felt that he had a place in the world, could earn his own living and owe no man anything" (250). He also has the verbal ability and institutional knowledge needed for the courts of law, and before those kinds of abilities, Locke's role (and masculinity) shrinks. In Locke's world, worker solidarity is operative but with qualifiers. Union solidarity replaces physical aggression, only to be met by issues of personal legal competence and linguistic control. With Locke's dependence on Paul, hands-on craftsman yields to verbally adept, institutionally alert lawyer. Paul, then, is in various ways the embodiment of shifts in masculine self-making from the nineteenth to the twentieth century, as well as from working-class, shop floor challenges to middle-class, institutional manipulation.[20] In short, Paul's middle-class myth of self-making serves to resolve, by setting aside, the tensions raised by Locke's working-class concerns with solidarity and mutuality and their possible divergence from the dominant rhetoric.

The capacity of middle-class self-making to co-opt and/or mollify these concerns is readily apparent in another novel of the period that is explicitly focused on the question of solidarity: Edward Bellamy's immensely popular, futuristic utopia *Looking Backward* (1888) and its dramatization of his Religion of Solidarity.[21] An attempt to resolve troubling social questions of the day, Bellamy's philosophy of solidarity envisioned an "industrial army . . . a strictly military organization staffed by officers and filled with rank-and-file workers who are the foot soldiers of the nation's industrial forces" (Thomas 57). Bellamy clearly intended solidarity to operate as a counter to the religion of individuality. As Thomas notes of Bellamy's vision, "True individuality . . . becomes possible only in a rational world that systematically leads the individual to an acknowledgment of his dependence on others" (59).

In one of the more long-winded of Bellamy's clarifications, Dr. Leete calmly explains this paradoxical truth to his time-traveling guest, the nineteenth-century Julian West. "Every man, however solitary may seem his occupation," Leete intones, "is a member of a vast industrial partnership, as large as the nation, as large as humanity. The necessity of mutual dependence should imply the duty and guarantee of mutual support; and that it did not in your day constituted the essential cruelty and unreason of your system" (178). That cruelty is rooted in the nineteenth century's failure to note the true meaning of solidarity. "If I should give you, in one sentence, a key to what may seem the mysteries of our civilization as compared with that of your age," Leete notes, "I should say that it is the fact that the solidarity of the race and the brotherhood of man, which to you were but fine phrases, are, to our thinking and feeling, ties as real and as vital as physical fraternity" (179). In Bellamy's novel, dependency is not aligned with feminization or masochistic passivity; it is seen rather as the beneficial offshoot of mutual support and solidarity.

Here, it appears, is a calm resolution of Whittaker's uncertainties, a demonstrated awareness of how to achieve what Larry Locke can only puzzle over. Unfortunately, or perhaps predictably, Bellamy's rhetoric of solidarity is underwritten by a deep "commitment to the patriarchal principle" (Thomas 61). The solidarity that Bellamy enacts is paired with an affectless and traditionally hierarchical masculinity, no matter how much Bellamy's rhetoric stresses mutuality and interdependency. Sliding easily between a rhetoric of solidarity and one of masculine self-making, for example, Leete agrees that "it is obviously important that not only the good but also the indifferent and poor workman should be able to cherish the ambition of rising. . . ." Leete continues on, sounding a note of upward mobility in a remark worthy of the finest myths of self-making. Those who never move out of the "lowest class," he notes, "are but a trifling fraction of the industrial army, and likely to be as deficient in sensibility to their position as in ability to better it" (174–75).[22] The language invading Bellamy's concern with solidarity is that of individual effort and just reward, heavily qualifying the rhetoric of mutual interconnection and support with that of a mythic brotherhood of proper struggle and effort.

The ability of the middle-class myth to override laboring alternatives in this way is partially explainable simply in terms of its definition as the dominant myth. Because its dissemination and repetition make it the most common argument for masculine behavior, the middle-class myth is capable of ignoring, denying, or co-opting labor's versions. But that explanation does not completely describe what occurs when Whittaker approaches the issue of solidarity from a laboring angle—and then backs off. Enacted from within a worker-oriented narrative, Locke's near martyrdom and Grynde's feminization open up for a moment issues not fully buried even by Bellamy's reliance on the dominant rhetoric and its emphasis on masculine struggle and victory. Grynde's failure as mill owner may be expected, given Whittaker's sympathies with labor and unionization. Grynde is beaten by the workers, and his beating is ascribed to his own failure to negotiate the needed move from independence to solidarity and mutuality. Tellingly, however, in that failure, Grynde slides right past its possibility for a new masculinity and ends up with a "pleading" dependency that is clearly marked as a defeat dangerously close to femininity.

It is this threat—an unstoppable slide from self-making to solidarity and mutuality and into weakened dependency and its implications of feminization—that troubles Whittaker and reinforces his retreat back to Paul's middle-class self-making. Whittaker may wish to differentiate positively between the failed solidarity and mutuality of the owners and the successful solidarity and mutuality of the workers. But in the case not only of Grynde but of Locke as well, the concern that solidarity and mutuality leads away from masculinity (as declared by *doxa* and its myth of self-making) and into something vaguely nonmasculine is clearly visible and clearly operative. Bellamy's middle-class myth masks that concern with its heavy reliance on the middle-class rhetoric of individual effort. He also masks it with Leete's own verbal style and argument. As Thomas so cogently notes, Leete allows for the question of dependence in solidarity by immersing the concept in the rhetoric of rationality.

That rhetorical frame serves to offset the threat of nonmasculinity hovering about the move toward solidarity and away from individualism. If the move from independent masculinity to solidarity and mutual dependence is a reasoned move, if it is not colored with lack of control or emotionalism, then doxic masculinity can accommodate the shift. But if an admission of noncontrol or nonagency is made, or more threatening still if emotion threatens to enter the equation, then those lurking concerns that dependency is a "necessary" slide toward femininity will come forward. Bellamy's middle-class rhetoric of rationality does not let that happen. But Whittaker's working-class rhetoric has more room in which to address these concerns, and to provide opportunity for questioning of *doxa*. Ultimately, Whittaker drifts back to the dominant rhetoric of individual self-making, but he has begun to demonstrate why labor-based rhetoric is central to understanding tensions in masculinity. Whittaker's replacement of Grynde's defeat with Locke's near martyrdom is the clearest example of the basic opportunity—and the basic difficulty—provided by the attempt to look into issues in masculinity that ultimately are rooted in what are commonly considered preoedipal concerns.

Intimacy and Dependency

In the various defeats of Locke by Skinner's institutional power, the dream of personal omnipotence suggested by Locke's early battles and victories is temporarily replaced by a sense of self as beaten or beatable. Whittaker's rhetoric thus clearly shifts from the dominant myth of masculine self-making, with its determined equating of effort and victory, to a self-making masculinity that addresses the possibility of defeat. Solidarity has been offered as an alternative route to power, but not to its ultimate masculine form, that is, self-sufficient, individual agency. Moreover, like the historical issues facing unionization, the power being invoked is no longer rooted in free self-assertion but colored with overtones of forced response. As Couvares notes, "The power of [workers'] mutualistic values need not be exaggerated. . . . When Pittsburgh workers mobilized their resources—both moral and material—they did so in an act of collective self-defense against a series of external threats from employers" (22).

Whittaker's simplest resolution of such underlying conflicts with doxic masculinity is to blend individualistic masculinity with generalized solidarity, to combine issues of union organization with leadership and self-growth. Unfortunately, within this representation, solidarity is subject to mutation back into the rhetoric of self-made masculinity, albeit with a bit more awareness of the real doxic appeal of advancement and individualism. Having engaged a rhetoric of nonindividualistic masculinity, Whittaker finally cannot entirely offset the dominant myth. The union's successful strike quietly gives way to Locke's individual dynamism and effort, and then his laborer's virility is replaced with that of Paul Van Beaver's middle-class, institutional knowledge. The resolution offered by solidarity and mutuality remains elusive and vaguely threatening, at least in the works noted here.

Reasons for that elusiveness, however, have been made clearer by the novel's enactments of working-class versions of masculine rhetoric. Whittaker's nineteenth-century enactments of solidarity and mutualism do more than just shift the tenor or emphasis of individualistic self-making; their representations of masculinity enact basic concerns that are regularly ignored or tensely devalued within the cultural rhetoric. By definition, mutualism and solidarity are concepts that border on the realm of interpersonal support and dependence, and as such, they are rooted not only in the complexities of oedipal struggle with authority but even more strongly in those of preoedipal connection and intimacy as well. The dominant myth's emphasis on aggressive opposition to the paternal serves to effectively screen these other issues in masculine engendering. But the resulting nonconsideration and nonresolution of intimacy and dependency also make investigation of closely related concepts—such as mutuality and solidarity—deeply problematic to the rhetoric of masculinity. *Doxa* ensures that it is more efficient to oppose solidarity and mutuality with individuality and self-making than to consider the dangerous question of masculine intimacy—with women or fellow men.

Nevertheless, union rhetoric still remains as an alternative argument even at the close of the twentieth century. Discussing male/male mutuality and interdependency, for example, Montgomery argues that "once on the job, a laborer found personal friendships and loyalties as important to his psychic and even physical endurance as they had been to locating employment in the first place" (*Fall* 89). To reinforce his point, Montgomery is willing to make use of some decidedly loaded language that leaps the solidarity/mutuality/intimacy gap with ease. Echoing contemporary film and novels that have made a commonplace of the unique bonds formed among police officers who are lifelong partners, Montgomery adds a near-marital tone in describing longshoremen who also have worked together for years. "For such a working couple to part company created a scandal among their workmates," Montgomery declares. "Consider also the photographs left from this epoch by Lewis Hine and others; notice how some individuals in every group leaned toward or touched each other. Such intimate work groups set the tone on any job" (89).

Here the rhetoric of masculine solidarity and brotherhood moves readily across a whole spectrum of interconnections and forms of support within the workplace.[23] But even Montgomery is subject to the pressure of the dominant rhetoric. Once his discussion shifts to job actions and the sense of agency and action they entail, his rhetoric takes on a differently gendered tone. The masculine intimacies that characterize ethnic "labor consciousness" are no longer aligned with the needs of successful labor actions. The rhetoric of masculine partnership and intimacy in the workplace that occurs within Montgomery's larger discussion of ethnic laborers is paired instead with description of their collective nonaction and the failures of union organization among them (91). Since job actions involve confrontation, one could argue that job actions by nature require such a rhetoric of opposition and aggression, and hence a different rhetoric of solidarity. But organizing among female laborers does not appear to carry the same requirements and necessary separations of the rhetoric of home and workplace, community and union hall, intimacy and solidarity: "Despite all the individual, cultural, regional, industrial, and racial variations in women's employment, both household and factory experiences drove home to daughters a message of interdependence among family members and placed greater value on solidarity and loyalty than on their personal achievements" (*Fall* 139). Here is an almost idealized version of worker unity, an enactment of interdependence and selflessness rather than individual selfishness. Yet speaking it requires a gendered division that Montgomery can only affirm. "If working men's experience introduced them to class first and foremost through conflict at the workplace," he suggests, "women's lives placed daily before them a panorama of goals and pleasures that required joint efforts, of loyalties to 'one's own kind' . . . and of interdependence with neighbors, as well as with workmates" (140).

Montgomery's separate rhetorics for men and women echo society's own doxic maintenance of male/female dichotomies by discovering gendered differences between the two as labor forces. It is a divided sensibility that encourages Montgomery to follow Whittaker's one-hundred-year-old path, albeit doing so in reverse. Montgomery begins with recognizing the importance of intimacy in masculinity, then he goes on to address tensions between male solidarity, mutuality, and intimacy through a progressive movement from intimacy to solidarity to brotherhood (and an eventual separation of each into its own category) so as to provide a doxically acceptable emphasis on masculine forms of agency and action, on direct struggle with the powers that be. With intimacy as a masculine dynamic gone or at least quieted down, anxieties attached to its place in proper masculinity can likewise be quieted. Ultimately, doxic representation quietly elides any need to reconsider concerns (and fantasies) regarding intimacy and dependency in relation to male preoedipal development and, thus, elides that threat to the myth of doxic masculinity as individuation, agency, and self-sufficiency. At such a point, myths of self-making are even free to engage nostalgia for the "real" masculine intimacy of the patriarchs. One need only look at the readiness with which current men's movements such as the Promise Keepers embrace the question of the father amid stadium-sized exhibitions of intimacy. These mass demonstrations of men hanging with men to resolve their emotional and psychic needs ironically demonstrate an unconscious understanding of the threat involved in addressing the issue of intimacy. Characterizing and enacting the anxiety as a deep pain over the missing father, a pain to be addressed primarily in the company of men, only reinforce the insistence on eliding preoedipal, feminine issues and focusing instead on oedipal, buddy-based frames.[24]

Doxic self-making pairs well with this overall process, given its own emphasis on separation from the familial and personal struggle in a masculine workplace as central to masculinity. In Erikson's words, men who would "fit into the image of the self-made man and the self-made personality, and who would create and 'adjust' their ego identity as they went along, did not have much use for protective mother love. Indeed, where they received it as children, they had to repudiate it later. Where 'Mom' did not exist, she had to be invented; for such is the historical importance of 'griping' in this country that a man, to stand on his own feet in a powerfully changing world, must keep himself up by his own gripes" (305).[25]

Erikson himself ascribes to "folklore" the idea that separation from the mother is a function of "systematic maternal rejection" (305) and provides instead a process in which masculinity oscillates between two explanations for this unresolved tension over intimacy and nurturance. On one side of this unresolved conflict "appears that deep-seated sense of having been abandoned and let down by the mother. . . . [T]here was no use regressing, because there was nobody to regress to, no use investing feelings because the response was so uncertain. What remained was action and motion right up to the breaking point" (296). In this use of the motifs of self-making, agency and action are linked to separation from nurturance as a move necessitated by rejection. That is only half the narrative, however. "But wherever our methods permit us to look deeper," Erikson argues, "we find at the bottom of it all the conviction, the mortal self-accusation, that it was *the child who abandoned the mother*, because he had been in such a hurry to become independent" (296). Here rejection is denied and the unresolved tension over separation is instead written up as guilt over a chosen departure.

Whichever argument is provided, an essential, unresolved problem in masculine engendering—loss of connection and intimacy—is met with the same motif—emphasis on agency and action. In essence, separation and loss of intimacy produce an essential motivation for the basic rhetoric of masculine agency and self-making. Even Erikson's own scale of normative masculine development contributes to the myth's rhetorical de-emphasis of connection and intimacy in favor of action and struggle. In that scale, as characterized by Carol Gilligan, "for men, identity precedes intimacy and generativity in the optimal cycle of human separation and attachment." As a result of the emphasis on separation, "in this male life cycle there is little preparation for the intimacy of the first adult stage. Only the initial stage of trust versus mistrust suggests the type of mutuality that Erikson means by intimacy and generativity and Freud means by genitality. The rest is separateness, with the result that development itself comes to be identified with separation . . ." (12).

This general devaluation of intimacy and mutuality, and the assumption of normative masculinity as a project rooted in separation and individual agency, is not only described but oddly validated by Erikson's further assumption that interpersonal issues will be resolved by the adult male through a move back to intimacy at level six of the eight stages of development. In an argument akin to early psychoanalytic claims that oedipal defeat can be set aside with minimal effects, Erikson implies that it will be just as easy to take up again the concern with intimacy that was buried by the move toward separation and the intervening stages of identity formation. Yet much recent discussion tends to argue against the ease that Erikson posits, noting that a key tension in masculinity is how to address intimacy—with either sex. As if to address such concerns, Erikson offers a wide range of possible intimacies. He foregrounds the traditional psychoanalytic concern with heterosexual "generativity" or reproduction but allows intimacy in general to be experienced "in the solidarity of close affiliations, in orgasms and sexual unions, in close friendships and in physical combat, in experiences of inspiration by teachers and of intuition from the recesses of the self" (263). These terms run the gamut from "orgasm" to Lockeian "physical combat." In between lie congruent forms of intimacy: "close friendships," "experiences of inspiration," and, worthy of note, "the solidarity of close affiliations."

Defined in this fashion, solidarity is a form of limited intimacy sensible and sufficient for many situations. But even a sanitized and "innocent" solidarity, such as union membership, will still raise the same concerns linked to the general, and generally problematic, category of intimacy. Doxic masculinity tends to resolve the concern by erasing the connection. Erikson's dominant term, *intimacy,* tends to drop out of the discussion, while *mutualism* and *solidarity* are melded and merged, alternately separated and alternately joined, finally drifting toward a vague sense of manly, acceptable brotherhood.

The implications of such consistent emphasis in the cultural rhetoric of masculinity are clear enough. If an inadequately understood and vaguely threatening masculine solidarity is forced to operate as screen behavior for closely connected concerns over interpersonal dependency and masculine intimacy, then solidarity itself is likely to be weakened as an arguable form of acceptable male behavior and to be less persuasive as an argument against the masculinity of individualistic self-advancement. That, in fact, is precisely what we find in looking at Whittaker, Bellamy, Butler, and countless others. The myth of self-making works so effectively not solely because of what if offers but because its narrative of separation and individuation removes the need to address the implications of masculine solidarity, let alone the issues of intimacy and interpersonal (effectively feminine) concerns. Enacting *doxa* and its cultural rhetoric of masculine self-making makes repetition of the trauma and damage of self-made struggle both natural and, equally important, preferable to further investigation of the myth itself. Faced with the threat of considering issues of mutuality and separation, the myth prefers to maintain a vague sense of inadequacy and defeat—of being beaten—safely entombed within a mythic rhetoric of action and necessary separation.

As a result, the possible subversive emphasis of a rhetoric of masculinity rooted in mutuality and solidarity all too often is left to struggle with an ambiguous brotherhood while the institutional organizing power of unionization reduces to the rhetorical equivalent of an action-image—the strike. As unions are destroyed at the end of the nineteenth century, all the complexities of solidarity are balled up into a single act of masculine struggle and defiance—and then historically tossed aside. Most historians see the defeat of the Amalgamated at Homestead in 1892 as the death knell of union organization in steel for nearly forty years, "the beginning of the end for the Amalgamated and for unionism in an important segment of the iron and steel industry" (Ingham, *Making Iron and Steel* 136). But popular fiction had begun to shift away from the rhetoric of labor-based self-making even earlier.[26] Whittaker's own attempts to use the openings offered by working-class fiction follow the historical arc well. After 1884, he simply stopped writing novels of heroic mill workers. "Story papers and dime novels had seemed quick to hop on the bandwagon of labor," Grimes notes sardonically, "and they were equally quick to alight" (14). For his part, Whittaker shifted to novels with western heroes. Key to that enactment of masculinity, as Erikson himself notes, is a continual emphasis on separation and mobility. As the next chapter shows, those emphases convert separation and loss of intimacy into yet another opportunity for masculine agency and self-making, and reenact individual struggle as the primary answer to masculine anxiety.

5

Moving Up or Moving Out:
Separation, Mobility, Agency

Make good money, five dollars a day.
Made any more I might move away.
                    —Robert Hunter, "Cumberland Blues"

The able man had little fear of losing a job, except in depressed
times, because he could always get another. Among railway repair-
shop machinists, transient "boomers" were legendary. . . .
                    —David Montgomery,
                    The Fall of the House of Labor

Charles Loring Brace proposed [in 1877] that a pass system should
be adopted, along the lines of the French or Belgian *livret,* to reveal
a man's employment record and his *bona fides,* if he claimed to belong to a craft in which traveling was commonplace. . . . In what
may have been the country's first campaign for uniform state legislation, [delegates to the conference] urged that similar statutes should
be adopted in all states to leave no advantage to moving about.
                    —David Montgomery, *Citizen Worker: The Experience
                    of Workers in the United States with Democracy
                    and the Free Market During the Nineteenth Century*

IN TALKING ABOUT THE RHETORIC OF SOLIDARITY and intimacy, I've also referred to its opposite—separation. Larry Locke's classic wandering on
the road and Carnegie's immigration from Scotland are two particular
examples. Related to each of these are more abstract separations: economic or class separation and separation from an ethnic or racial group.[1]
As varied and variant enactments of society's complex arguments about
masculinity, these categories and motifs test, reconsider, or directly challenge doxic arguments. The Grateful Dead's miners and Montgomery's
transient machinists don't want to move up; they want to move out.

Yet as I argued in the previous chapter, even the most directly subversive rhetoric is regularly co-opted by the dominant myth so as to reinscribe the original self-making rhetoric and its forms of masculine agency and individualistic struggle. Such co-optation is aided historically by a related loss of craft-based labor, increases in external control of the workplace, and legal limits on worker mobility and agency. Journeymen may envision moving at will, but Charles Loring Brace's call for legal regulation of the workplace directly maintains doxic masculinity by allowing for only one form of mobility—upward within the corporation.

However the variations may differ, they do tend to share one essential purpose. As willed separation and agency are argued, they simultaneously screen off—and indeed actively set aside—related anxieties and concerns produced by suggestions of earlier separations from nurturance, support, and a sense of wholeness. These redefined separations and their attendant mobilities provide feminine-free markers of a supposedly desired—rather than a painfully required—engendering process. Separation thus becomes a valued goal, and movement or mobility becomes a mark of masculine agency in all versions of the myth, while paradoxically reinforcing the final control of masculine *doxa* and the dominant cultural rhetoric.[2]

Journeyman/Craftsman Masculinity

The historical tensions and doxic assumptions that are visible in Whittaker's attempts to address working-class masculinity in terms of solidarity and intimacy are likewise visible in his enactments of separation and mobility. In presenting Locke's midplot departure from Holesburg and Marcellus Skinner's mill, Whittaker bases Locke's masculinity on an appeal to willed separation and its attendant mobility—the free agency of a skilled journeyman—that is both historically accurate and broadly acceptable to *doxa*. Such mobility remains potentially subversive of the dominant rhetoric, however, since Locke's movements and agency set aside the middle-class rhetoric of upward mobility, economic growth, and control over others, replacing these appeals with a masculinity enacted through control over oneself and one's job.

In an era of craft-based labor, westward expansion, and stable or expanding job opportunities, there is validity to Whittaker's argument. Skilled workers' ability to move pairs nicely with their further ability to negotiate and subcontract their labor. Even large mills could be seen as "congeries of individual workshops . . . run by a relatively autonomous, highly skilled craftsman. . . . [In] the typical iron mill, managers were in no real sense in charge of production . . ." (Couvares 11). This sense of workplace independence, when coupled with expanding frontiers, implies marketability of skills and related mobility, which in turn completes the equation by implying masculine agency. Dependencies of job and place are erased, replaced with a willing separation from one workplace and the easy movement into another. In such an environment, "machinists celebrated the self-direction of the 'practical mechanic.' . . . They defended their own notoriously migratory propensities as necessary for their self-education and for their economic security . . ." (Montgomery, *Fall* 191–92).[3]

This subversive rhetoric of horizontal mobility, coupled with the *doxa* of individual agency, provides a powerful appeal, and Whittaker engages it when Locke, having been fired and robbed of his nearly completed mortgage savings, considers his future: "Under such circumstances most men would have despaired, . . . but Larry had not earned the name of the 'Man of Iron' without deserving it." Manliness having been fully raised as an issue, Locke enacts his hold on it by confidently declaring "If there ain't work here, there's work in Ohio. . . . We've got health, strength, and the rest will come to us" (*Larry Locke* 205). Skill and effort inevitably couple with real job prospects for such men.

But there are specific historical and psychological tensions being masked here that can be exemplified in conditions within the steel industry. After the industrial transition to mass-produced steel, the craftsman/journeyman rhetoric of willing separation from one job and ready horizontal mobility fit few situations and fewer skills. Even when skilled men remained in a position to bargain for work with a manager, that manager embodied capital investment in a physical plant where workers' skills would be plied. There is an obvious limitation, then, built into certain crafts such as puddling steel: "The nature of the steelworker's skill also limited his independence. Unlike a machinist or bricklayer, his training was valuable only in a steel mill, frequently only those turning out the same product. Moreover, steel plants were largely isolated. Even in the Pittsburgh district, mills were too distant for a man to conveniently live in the same residence after changing jobs" (Brody 87). The availability of work was thus tied directly to the presence of an operating steel mill, while mobility was limited to the small number of towns where such a mill existed. Equally obvious is the need for the mill to be operating. Since the steel industry was prone to periods of production and shutdown, real instability in the workplace tended to test even a skilled worker's faith in Locke's rhetoric of individual effort and mobility, in simply "moving on" to the next job that needs a man of quality. Craft-based independence remained fairly strong as a motif in masculine rhetoric, but weak in its capacity for social enactment.

The rhetoric of craftsman mobility also faced negative implications that the dominant rhetoric exploited in order to undercut the masculinity of this particular form of separation and movement. Like many nine-teenth-century journeymen, Locke hits the road whenever he needs to pursue his future. Each time, however, he invariably runs into Terror Jim, who is his own form of mobile man—a bum. Whittaker's purpose in contrasting Jim and Locke is to address an ongoing complication in working-class performance of separation/mobility—that is, the ability of middle-class rhetoric to equate craft mobility with shiftlessness. Both Larry and Jim, after all, are on the same road, jobless, with no visible family ties and no visible means of support. To differentiate between them, Whittaker must add positive masculine value to one and remove it from the other. Once again, the dominant rhetoric provides those values. Locke's mobility is that of the man who pursues self-advance-ment by embracing both hard work and effort. Terror Jim's mobility, much like that of Marcellus Skinner with whom he once sailed, reveals an unwillingness to cleave unto either.

Whittaker's use of the motif of tramping, so common in fiction of the period, thus displays complex tensions over separation and agency that are common to both worker and dominant rhetoric. In this particular case, Whittaker does not so much investigate these tensions as displace them onto the masculinities of individual characters. Locke tramps to find work, and he does so readily. Leaving behind wife and child, he nevertheless continues to occupy the traditional family narrative with himself at its head. He engages, in short, the rhetoric of a correctly post-oedipal male. Terror Jim tramps to avoid work and responsibility, and he does so constantly. He refuses middle-class self-making and thus re-fuses postoedipal masculinity. He enacts, in short, a threat to both work-ing-class and middle-class masculine rhetoric. Ultimately for Whittaker (and the dominant cultural rhetoric), pursuit of work and its enabling mobility must signal not wanderlust but agentive masculinity and its centrality in the family framework, while absence of these values must argue moral and masculine failure—refusal of appropriate, postoedipal agency and rejection of the familial.

The continual pressure of such historical and doxic arguments on working-class rhetoric is fully represented by Locke's nonfictional twin in self-making, James Davis, whose parodic self-making and sadism were noted in the previous chapter. Proffering myriad endorsements of sepa-ration and mobility, effort and agency throughout *The Iron Puddler*, Davis enacts a mixed rhetoric of craft-based masculinity. An expert pud-dler (having learned the trade as apprentice to his father) now in search of the highest steady wages, Davis "d[oes] not wait" for a temporarily closed mill to reopen, but takes "the first train for some other mill town" (120). This rhetoric of youthful questing leads to encounters with fel-low workers of various abilities and levels of effort: thieves, con men and—worst of all—Communist "intellectuals" who mistake him for a *"tramp"* akin to Terror Jim rather than a horizontally mobile, self-making man like Larry Locke (127).

Like Whittaker, then, Davis intentionally compares and contrasts right and wrong forms of separation and mobility. Further mimicking Locke, Davis sets forward his own "need for a broader education" in labor organizing (131) and likewise argues the value of joining "the Amalgamated Association of Iron, Steel and Tin Workers of North America" (134). In addition, Davis's narrative moves beyond the exemplary drama of a single lockout and into the employment problems facing labor as a whole. Trained through the basic paternalism of craft-based iron production, Davis nevertheless cannot expect to inherit his father's furnace because his father "was good for twenty years more" (114). Davis's separation and mobility thus are admittedly forced upon him by hidden impediments to craft labor, late nineteenth-century job markets, and the need to respect the authority of the father. Nor are Davis's acts of self-making as readily rewarded as Whittaker claimed was true for Locke. "After a period of prosperity the hard times had come again in 1891 and '92" and "jobs were getting scarce as they had been in 1884," when even his father's mill had closed (114). By 1892, the year of the Homestead lockout, Davis decides to leave his father's mill in Sharon and go to Pittsburgh's mills to find work.

These are clear qualifiers on the ostensible free agency of craft-based separation, mobility, and self-making. Faced with such strictures, Davis needs to revamp the basic rhetoric of masculine agency. He does so not by reforming craftsman rhetoric so much as by deeply coloring it with overtones of the dominant myth. As he had earlier granted control of the workplace to his father, Davis now cedes the Pittsburgh workplace to married men with families and goes to Niles, Ohio. His postoedipal credentials correctly established via (1) supposedly chosen separation and movement and (2) endorsement of family values, Davis still is forced to admit that he is unrewarded for his virtue. "I worked a few weeks and the mill [in Ohio] shut down," he notes. "I wandered all over the iron district and finally, deciding that the North held no openings, I began working my way toward the iron country in the South" (115). Through all of this, Davis and his brothers urge their father to stay at home and attempt to keep the family house, which he manages to do: "If he had wandered around as millions of us did in those days," Davis notes, "he would surely have lost it" (117). The advice is economically sound, postoedipally correct, but a bit troubling to the myth's arguments about ready self-making for the eagerly questing male.

Davis does survive, of course, and indeed manages to find work. Still it is not steady, it is not always at his craft, and it is certainly not the ready horizontal mobility suggested by journeyman rhetoric. Clearly the vision owes as much to the rhetoric of western expansion and masculine self-fashioning as to the actuality of the late nineteenth-century workplace. These were transitional times, and the rhetoric of skilled craftsmen moving independently according to their will and ability no longer fully meshed with the actuality of large-scale steel production.[4] Even Davis's partial successes are a select representation, since he works in the specialty areas of wrought iron puddling and tin production, where craft traditions held out longest. Davis's story, for all its elaboration of self-sufficient masculinity, balances tenuously on a moment of historical shifting in workplace control, and his rhetoric likewise teeters between the language of personal craftsmanship—with its rapidly closing opportunities for horizontal, physical mobility—and the language of upward mobility—with its lurking suggestions of corporate control and worker dependency.

Davis ultimately embraces the last option, melding his supposedly labor-oriented rhetoric with the fully engaged doxic power of the dominant middle-class rhetoric—along with its capacity for masking corporate nonagency. Arguing his self-made masculinity, Davis is somewhat like Whittaker and decidedly like Carnegie, finding much to endorse in the rhetoric of willed separation and upward mobility. Like a latter-day Carnegie, Davis has emigrated from Great Britain as a youth (1881), and like Carnegie, he demonstrates upward mobility, eventually finding himself secretary of labor in the cabinets of Harding, Coolidge, and Hoover and an exemplary figure of labor achievement. But as a late nineteenth-century steelworker, Davis's mobility owes a great deal to institutional connections (union related and then political), and the masculinity he enacts is ultimately a reworking of both Carnegie's and Whittaker's rhetorics. As I noted in the previous chapter, Davis masks the tension between these mythic rhetorics, and between their arguments and his experience, with the dominant rhetoric of hearty masculine aggression and effort. Indeed, the autobiography finally reads best as a good old moralizing story for the adolescents of Davis's schools rather than as a mature representation of Davis himself.

In its most disingenuous moments, the dominant rhetoric appears in full cry—entrepreneurial questing, appropriation of craftsman individuality, upward mobility as validation and reward. In its most strained moments, a different appeal surfaces, however. Having enacted much of his tale of self-making through the rhetoric of manly brotherhood, Davis dramatizes his appeals to upward mobility through a rhetoric of masculine dominance. Normally, such forms of dominance are represented as innocent offshoots of a natural hierarchy of merit. Sexual components are reduced, made visible only in blatant enactments like that of Butler's Cole. But in Davis, the sexual moves forward again—this time as a means of establishing not only masculinity but also separation from the non-masculine, male or female. This particular form of separation and mobility is nowhere more strongly argued than in Davis's narcissistic and homoerotic rhetoric of male physical power, as found in both oedipally tinged fight scenes and direct paeans to the body.

These scenes are intended to unify Davis's increasingly prevalent rhetoric of separation, individual aggression, and (upward) mobility. Like Larry Locke, Davis faces not only familial separation but also the class separation initiated by becoming a self-made leader in the union. Unlike Locke, who attempts to address the issue via the rhetoric of a troubled solidarity, Davis fully engages the rhetoric of individualism. He does so with a Lacanian power blend of newfound oratorical skill, wily negotiation, and an interesting display of the manly body, enacting his individual masculine effort not as mutualistic self-erasure or masochistic martyrdom but the reverse—narcissistic display and pleasure in dominance.[5]

Early in the book, in a paragraph chock full of the Franklinesque aphorisms that comprise his style, Davis describes his own postimmigration arrival outside of Pittsburgh. Dirty and tired, he "learned then that food is the first thing in the world . . . and without food man loses his cleanliness, godliness and everything else worth having" (53–54). It is an equation that he will continue throughout the book; food equals a good body, a good body equals a good worker, and good workers hard at labor equal the height of masculine brotherhood. With this rhetorical formula as their base, paeans to hard work, hard eating, hard bodies, and the resulting personal (and national) development run throughout the book. Disputing those reformers who might find fault with working conditions in the mills, Davis declares that he "went in a stripling and grew into manhood with muscled arms big as bookkeeper's legs." Noting that he "lusted for labor," Davis declares that his work was "no job for weaklings, but neither was tree-felling, Indian fighting, road-making, and the subduing of a wild continent . . . done by the whole tribe of Americans" (87). It sounds like more fun than a wild-man weekend.

Davis carries the rhetoric of physical self-making even further, however. In his world, intellectuals, communists, naysayers, and reformers are invariably physically impaired "bookkeepers" (87) visibly marked as nonmasculine by their excess theorizing, wrong thinking, and poor bodies. As the title of chapter 35 declares, uplifters who lack masculine power and control are "ruled by envy" (199). Like Comrade Bannerman who does no work, they have feminized bodies too weak to serve the larger body of the nation. They cannot do so, in another example of Davis's simple but constant rhetoric of the physical, because they don't know how to eat. "Good board," Davis opines, "consists in lots of *greasy* meat, strong coffee and slabs of sweet pie . . ." (145). Reformers who think otherwise are simply like the "dyspeptic" muckraker who does no work himself but "trie[s] to force his diet upon us and ma[ke] us as weak as he was" (151). In an extension of the analogy noted in Tichi's "engineering 'muscle'" (*Shifting Gears* 104) and Erikson's "wire guts" (306), the body itself becomes a mechanical device, "engines" moving westward fueled by the classic manly diet of hog fat and those "thick slabs of sweet pie" (Davis 151–52).

More important than Davis's interest in food, however, is his interest in displaying the body as a form of power and agency. Davis's final extension of his argument for physical self-development completes the masculinity/dominance/sexuality equation of Butler, but with a further homoerotic twist. Deeply invested in dominance over other men, Davis develops scenes of direct physical display, intruding a clear note of masculine sensuality as a means of separating from less-than-men (and by implication, the feminine). One such moment occurs as yet another nonman puts workers off their feed with negative discussions of meatpacking, corned beef, and "wienies" (197). Foolish in that regard, the reformer still more foolishly asks why the men work shirtless. Davis's reply is straightforward: "To withstand the heat we stripped to the waist. We didn't want to wear a shirt. It would have clung to our flesh and hampered our moving muscles. We were freer and cooler without any shirt to smother us" (198). It is a direct and relatively honest answer, perhaps a bit narcissistic in its tone of self-display, a bit foolish in its erasure of the danger of molten metal.

But Davis wants to present more than the value of clothing-free labor. What he really wants to do is trick the reformer into revealing himself as not only foolish but also actually envious of what Davis and his body represent. Arguing with the reformer over the value of beer on the job, Davis initially relies on an uncharacteristically non-American argument: "Iron workers in the Old World have used malt beverages for generations" and it hasn't injured them. "[L]ook at the worker's body," Davis declares. "It is four times as strong as yours." Suddenly, the metaphoric body standing before both reformer and reader becomes Davis's own. He notes "an envious look in [the reformer's] eye" and goes on to enjoy that gaze a bit more. Keeping the focus of reader and reformer on himself, Davis continues to pose. "'Of course I inherited a muscular build,' [Davis] apologize[s], 'and so I try to make the most of it in boasting to you fellows who haven't any muscle. But I really envy you. You have education and brain power. That's what I lack. . . . I haven't got any chance against you fellows who are born intellectual and have college training on top of it'" (201). Davis is hardly in an apologizing mood, however; he is out to get the reformer to reveal his own envy of Davis, and the ploy "works" (202).

Taking his own turn on the runway, the reformer displays himself briefly, but only as prelude to further references to Davis: "I really envy you. You are built like a young Hercules and are never ashamed when you strip. When I put on a bathing suit I am embarrassed. . . . I'd swap all my education in a minute for the mighty body and the healthy and lusty living that you enjoy. If you knew how much I envy you, you would never think of envying me" (202–3). The reformer has "blurted out" the naked truth and stands fully revealed as an envious false brother before and alongside the self-sculpted, Herculean Davis: "It wasn't the love of comrades that gave a motive to his life. It was envy that turned him inside out" (203). In Leverenz's terms, the reformer's pseudomasculinity has been revealed. He can be hounded out of the mill, thanks to his humiliating defeat in the workplace—defeat visited on him not through fighting or verbal exchange alone but through strutting and posing worthy of a beauty pageant.

It would be funny were the signals of Davis's pleasure in physical and sexual dominance of another male not so clear throughout. The reformer has been soundly defeated—shamed in the workplace—and on two grounds. He has displayed a lack of true manly feeling for his fellows, and he has done so by revealing a secret envy for the "clean and lusty" body of Davis, for the "mighty body and healthy and lusty living" that Davis enjoys. The pleasurable blend of homoeroticism and psychological dominance that Davis urges is reminiscent of the physical dominance and heterosexual coupling that Butler offers. Sensuality, dominance, shame—the hints of masculine sadism are all put forward, then quietly halted. With no further need to pose either himself or the reformer for the gaze of his readers, Davis closes the chapter. He will return to celebrations of strength and muscle, "street smarts" versus "intellectualism" at other points, but nowhere with such directness.

The equations and connections of this last argument for manly brotherhood, separation from the lower-status feminine, and visible masculinity represent the core of Davis's rhetorical appeal; all other discussions are essentially analogies leading to this point. Davis has established his masculine self-making with requisite degrees of useful separation: immigration, westward movement, separation from family. These and all other comparisons become secondary proofs, however; they reinforce the rightness of Davis's ultimate appeal to a masculinity rooted in dominance of other men. When fully engaged, Davis's rhetoric offers the ultimate in self-making—the self made into loved object both properly separated from vanquished, feminized nonmen and worshiped by equivalent real men. The solidarity and interdependency of worker brotherhood, with which Davis supposedly begins, closes as a narcissistic and homoerotic sadomasochism whose supposed appeal rests on aggression and dominance. As these sadomasochistic and erotic underpinnings are revealed, Davis's rhetoric hastily rechannels its own implications into arguments for work and effort and success. In the next chapter, Davis shifts from the brotherhood of journeymen workers and narcissistic display of his and the nation's physical development to discovering how "to get out of the labor field and into the field of management" (207).

It is in these short pages that Davis's tale most clearly encapsulates the shift from nineteenth- to twentieth-century forms of separation and mobility. Ostensibly the journeyman's friend, Davis in fact has spent a goodly portion of his argument extolling a heavy-handed absorption in physical dominance. Now his early masculine separation and horizontal mobility are replaced with subsequent explanations of his move out of labor into "management" via a Carnegie-like rhetoric of saving, shrewd investment, and wily politicking. Davis's opening focus on possibly subversive undercurrents within the rhetoric of craftsman separation and mobility (not to mention a truly subversive suggestion of homoeroticism as a form of masculine nonseparation and intimacy) has, under the guise of manly brotherhood, been quietly subsumed into the dominant modern motif of upward mobility within established institutional and corporate frames.

Ironically, this shift helps explain Davis's surprisingly insistent need to assert real manliness. The modern rhetoric of corporate self-making continues to echo masculine agency by emphasizing the role of the individual and minimizing the role of institutions and corporations. It does so for good reason. Clarifying the actual corporate role would implicitly lower the value of (and the incentive toward) a masculinity of individual achievement. Speaking of mill workers at Homestead, Schneider notes the "great emotion" with which workers spoke about "economic subjection" to Carnegie and his company. Significantly, workers also characterized their situation in terms of an additional, psychological loss, "namely that Company actions 'threatened' or 'insulted' their manhood, assaulting their very pride and self-respect as independent men" (57).

For all that Davis's argument extols both solidarity and individual agency, then, corporate dependency remains a real threat of external (and hence infantilizing or feminizing) control. Davis's homoerotic rhetoric engages more fully than most the tensions and anxieties behind these options of brotherhood, individualism, and corporate dependency or feminization. It does so because it is itself formed in an era of weak or absent unions and amidst historically shifting arguments for entrepreneurial, craftsman, and corporate masculinity. Uncertain of his rhetorical cross-dressing, Davis loudly declares his individual resolution of all tensions over self-making or being made. Later versions feel the same strains. But while they tend to provide a less erotic rhetoric, they also continue to follow Davis's essential equation by conflating the single male and the corporate body into an individualistic masculinity rooted in power and dominance.

Company Men and Corporate Power

As Davis's self-portrait makes clear, the usefulness of physical separation to the myth's rhetoric is qualified by two key concerns: (1) the impact on worker agency of growing corporate control over the industrial workplace and (2) the ongoing problem buried in the myth's half-realized logical contradictions over who can separate from their origins and rise (anyone) and who should (the best). Given these complications, some versions find it most effective simply to avoid hints of separation from home and hearth entirely while still stressing independence and singularity. These variations demonstrate necessary accommodations to, and explicit use of, shifting pressures on *doxa,* individual biases or agendas, and the historical complexities of the social frame. The complex rhetoric needed to interweave all these concerns with the myth's motifs of separation, success, and masculinity is readily apparent in Marcia Davenport's *The Valley of Decision* (1945), a best-selling, historical novel of Pittsburgh's steel industry that covers the years 1873 to 1941.

Davenport's huge and hugely melodramatic novel, which was successful enough to lead to a movie also released in 1945, is a singular display of tensions produced by belief in Jeffersonian self-making (the natural rise of the meritorious) and a further sense that the vast majority can make nothing at all, let alone themselves. In line with these beliefs, Davenport's argument is further conflicted in its nostalgic commitment to the individualistic, entrepreneurial rhetoric of the nineteenth century, its related commitment to attacking the rise of the modern corporation, and its ultimate awareness of the need to augment nineteenth-century entrepreneurial struggle with the historical inevitability of the modern company man's climb up the corporate ladder.

Like Whittaker and Davis, Davenport wishes to see those willing to strive move up the ladder of success. Unlike either's tale, her narrative tends to look steadfastly from the top down. The main figures of the book, even the Irish servant girl Mary around whom the novel revolves, are developed from within the frame of the mill owner's mansion. If not to the manner born, the best certainly have to the manor gone. Davenport's ultimate needs are thus as much those of justifying continued occupation of a position at the top as they are arguments for getting there. Her nineteenth-century mill owner and patriarch, William Scott, enacts precorporate, patriarchal masculinity; independent and hard driving, he is able to grasp the country's growing needs and rise with them.

From Davenport's 1945 vantage point, the elder Scott remains a shrewd, powerful, and generally masculine figure; known as the "Old Man," he is "gratified by the sense of dynasty and paternalism that the title emphasized" (32).

As a convenient but dated motif, Scott is provided with no immediately apparent mark of familial separation and struggle to motivate his masculinity. Scott's father was the immigrant. Moreover, Scott is not a pure entrepreneur; he grew up in the mill and inherited it from his father. He does have one stereotypical mark of self-making; he started "as a cinder monkey when he was fifteen" (28). But Scott didn't get his first job by chance or even by beating up another worker; he asked "dad" for it. William Scott is nonetheless represented with full entrepreneurial status, although with overtones of Paul Van Beaver's inherited opportunities. Eschewing the traditional entrepreneurial elements of separation from the nurturing family to motivate Scott's masculinity, Davenport instead chooses a psychological marker of separation. William Scott is represented as clearly manly in his separation from emotion. In the eyes of his own wife, Scott is "a just but not compassionate man" (17). A nineteenth-century patriarch, he is de facto separated from his emotions in a way that guarantees a stereotypical masculinity by eliminating any emotional/feminine capacities.

In portraying Scott in this fashion, Davenport adds negative tones to separation and its losses in ways that most enactments of masculinity as purposive agency prefer to screen. Yet even as Davenport comes close to naming the deep damage connected to separation in masculinity, she attaches the motif to such a doxically loaded, stereotypically entrepreneurial framework that the separation suggests not lurking anxiety over incompleteness and loss but only a slightly dated form of masculine power rooted in dominance and hierarchy. Scott's character is safely placed in the mid-nineteenth century, while his behavior is lightly critiqued according to twentieth-century mores—his masculinity is both admired and chided by Davenport. A dated figure, Scott is pointed to, recognized, and lightly dismissed from a safe historical distance. He is a distant and mainly admirable other.

Although Davenport's novel begins with nineteenth-century patriarchal masculinity, it is Scott's son Paul who expresses Davenport's primary rhetoric of self-making. In charge of the steel mill from 1884 to 1918, Paul enacts his middle-class masculinity by combining modern managerial power with earlier appeals to the craft-based making of steel. The equation is completed by uniting in Paul the best of his entrepreneurial father and the master craftsman James Rafferty, "the two passionate, powerful men [who] personified everything that made Paul's world" (176). Son of a nineteenth-century mill owner, Paul blends his inherited corporate power with a brotherhood of craft earned on the floor of the steel mill. Even as the era of craft-based steelmaking and his youth begin to wane, Paul remains "as eager, as able as ever to put on overalls and hand-leathers and take a turn on a heat at the open hearth. He retained all the physical comradeship with the men that his years of labor alongside them had developed." But Paul is also a boss, and "with his father's responsibilities had come, perhaps, unconsciously, some of his father's ways" (233). In short, Davenport's rhetoric melds middle-class entrepreneurial and working-class craftsman self-making into an impending corporate masculinity—the last achieved by adequately separating Paul from his now-dated "fathers."

Paul enacts the masculine growth ostensibly capped by that emotional and physical separation by becoming a college-educated man before he inherits the mill (and the modern mantle of the well-trained, upper-class male). Although Davenport is not facing an audience that equates college training with effete elitism, she sidesteps any lingering problems of nonmasculine intellectualism by graduating Paul as a brilliant metallurgist from the Sheffield Scientific School at Yale. A Yale man in a practical, "hard" science, Paul's masculinity remains intact. His education is in service to the technology of steel, and he uses it to shift the mill into the production of steel alloys and other "refined" products.[6]

Davenport plays a second card as well in her maintenance of Paul's increasingly modern manliness. If the growth of corporations threatens masculine independence, then a further means of maintaining Paul's somewhat divided status as creative steelmaker and corporate manager is to make him battle with the corporate model itself. Paul not only loathes "gigantic monsters like Carnegie's steel company" (293) but "of course" maintains Scott's Works as a family-held business (454). Davenport's repeated insistence on this personified line of argument marks both her desire for historical believability and her sense of corporate growth as problematic for the traditional individualism of masculine *doxa*. Carnegie and Henry Phipps represent men who "*used* the iron business . . . to amass money and power for themselves" (305). Paul Scott's power is offered instead as a symbiotic growth of man and management ultimately validated by the craft of steelmaking itself.[7]

Not surprisingly, the film version reinforces and streamlines many of these arguments as well, ultimately shifting characters and events to enhance the novel's other main plot, that of the love story centered on Paul and the Irish servant girl Mary. Fervently linking mill, manhood, and family, the movie provides an early close-up of Paul (played by Gregory Peck) as he refuses to sell to Carnegie, declaring the mill "as much a part of us sir, as well, the blood that runs in our veins." As he provides this speech, the camera cuts to both an admiring father, William Sr., and an eavesdropping Mary (Greer Garson), thus providing Paul with both a patriarchal seal of approval and proper love object.

Particularly interesting in all of this rhetoric of patriarchal power, craftsman masculinity, and pending emotional development are the character shifts and binary oppositions that the movie uses to reinforce its middle-class and corporate self-making. William Scott Sr. is directly contrasted with Mary's father, Pat Rafferty, whose crippling injury in the Scott mills has left him an embittered man dedicated to destroying the Scotts through union agitation. That characterization is noteworthy not only in its father/father, owner/union oppositions but also in its shifting of the novel's original worker/owner opposition in which Mary's fictional brother, Jim Rafferty, acts out union versus corporate masculinity. The change encourages much more direct comparison of correct and perverse behavior by the fathers than that suggested by the novel.[8] Moreover, with such a frame in place Paul is free to enact fully a rhetoric of adequately postoedipal male who is both craft oriented and corporately empowered, an empowerment validated by his ability to differentiate himself from either father.

These shifts serve to emphasize the degree to which both Davenport's novel and the movie ultimately address modern threats to masculine individualism not by revealing the corporation as an institution and its workings as complex but simply by condemning certain owners, buyers, and union rabble-rousers on the grounds of personal and individual immorality or perversity and improper paternal behavior. Corporations appear, union strength waxes and wanes, but these historic elements are only stage sets before which Davenport represents the doxically endorsed actions and agency of authentic individuals who naturally rise upward.

To enact that mythic portrait, Davenport appropriates the rhetoric of craft production, combines it with entrepreneurial rhetoric, and substitutes the resulting argument for any specific consideration of Paul as modern owner and his subsequent relations with labor.[9] As Davenport has Mary say of Paul, "You *are* the mill" (218), and that older entrepreneurial rhetoric is not Mary's alone but Davenport's as well. It is a moment devoted less to the issues of corporate power versus union power than to the characterization of Paul as individually powerful agentive male. He exists then as exemplar of the masculine corporate figure whom all should aspire to be—and cover-up for nonmasculine, institutional dependency. Indeed, the degree of focus is so individualistic that the film essentially sidesteps the threat of laborers rising (and uprising). Everyone is simply devoted to Paul and the mill he personifies, itself a "giant of a human thing [that's] got a heart and a soul" in his own eyes.

This complicated blend of mill, craft, and personal manliness is important not only to Davenport's novel and the movie but also to the dominant myth as a whole. It allows Paul, owner of the mill by birth, also to occupy the role of achieved embodiment of upward mobility, thereby providing the dominant rhetoric with further means for encouraging middle-class self-making among shop floor laborers who have been divested of craftsman control over their work and workplace and are unlikely to inherit a mill upon reaching manhood. Davenport does not begin her enactment of the myth with Davis's working-class affiliations, but she reaches the same end, arguing the need for personal struggle, separation from class, and company loyalty to achieve individual dominance.[10]

As long as the demand for work remained stable, skilled (often western-European) workers could embrace the cultural rhetoric of moving upward according to individual effort. Unskilled workers were provided with similar encouragements, although their separation and mobility had a particular twist that revealed several different forms of agency within the argument. In Brody's words, "The stability in the unskilled ranks . . . rested on mobility. The newcomers moved up into the skilled force; or they moved out at the first depression or with satisfactory accumulation" (108). Movement upward is the paradigmatic, middle-class myth. Movement out of the mill at a depression is self-explanatory—a new stability is achieved, as it were, when corporations match unavailable work with unneeded workers. But tales of unskilled workers who moved out and back to the country of emigration does have agentive value for workers, and even for concepts of self-making. The worker who returns to a native land with newfound wealth has clearly achieved a great deal. Not surprisingly, then, when the workforce is in short supply such narratives are downplayed, often by writing up such worker agency as a failure to assimilate the greater values of American masculinity and settling instead for a different—and suspect—European version of manliness.

At other times, mill owners were not unhappy to find that even skilled workers, whose increasingly nonunion status made them more likely to be committed to a rhetoric of individual advancement, could be conveniently laid off when work slowed or easily rehired after strikes were broken. The ease with which the owners shifted their behavior and their rhetoric to fit the situation suggests whom myths of class separation, struggle, and upward mobility best serve in the end. These easy shifts also underline the lack of a powerful dissenting rhetoric. Brody notes that during the absence of effective union activity from 1890 to 1920, "competition for promotion became fierce." In a time when job security and alternative rhetorics of masculinity were weak or lacking, workers hearing the ongoing song of masculine agency as realizable through class separation and upward mobility "came to identify their fortunes with the good will of their particular boss, and they behaved accordingly" (86–87).

Looked at through Davenport's eyes, identification with a boss like Paul merits high praise. But the reality of Carnegie and his mills provided a less personal, more institutional viewpoint that was rooted in a desire to encourage worker competition through the rewards of in-house mobility:

> [The Carnegie] company gradually but systematically devised a new managerial structure. . . . [C]raftsmen were, in the words of Mary Freifeld [551], "grafted . . . onto the bottom [of the firm's] own management structure, with their traditional supervisory work roles, and scientific and technical knowledge intact. . . ." What had been eliminated was collective, deliberative control from the workers' end. In its place the company cultivated a hierarchy of fiercely competing individuals. . . . (qtd. in Montgomery, *Fall* 41–42)

The value for a corporation in replacing a rhetoric of union mutuality and solidarity with that of class separation and individual competition is fairly obvious. Samuel Gompers, for one, "believed this eagerness to leave the laboring class was the Amalgamated Association's chief weakness" (Brody 86) and thus a corporation's chief strength in maintaining its own control at the expense of the masculine agency that its individualistic rhetoric supposedly endorses. The myth of self-making as class separation and upward mobility remains *doxa*'s best means for maintaining a sense of agency that offsets the empowerment offered by union mutuality or journeyman/immigrant mobility.

The most commonly accepted indicator of the ensuing rewards for class separation, upward mobility, and their attendant masculinity is that of income. But secondary markers—the items that the new income will buy—may be more readily visible. Of these, perhaps the most popular trope of advancement, beyond changing clothes, is that of purchasing a home. Dubofsky discusses the marker even as he downplays its linkage to notable upward mobility. "It has been shown," he notes, "that although individuals rarely rose from poverty to wealth, most residentially settled workers succeeded in moving slightly up the occupational ladder or in acquiring homes and savings accounts; their children sometimes discarded blue collars for white ones and rose from the working class to the lower middle class" (27). Homes, then, are an emotionally loaded trope that serves both to enact and to maintain the desire for class separation and upward mobility. Typically a place devoted to the domestic and maternal and from which men "ought" to separate, homes also can become an argument for adequate masculinity and reinstatement of the patriarchal. Schneider describes the situation well in discussing the Homestead lockout, where home ownership already had become a major aspect of worker rhetoric:

> The importance of "home and Homestead" as a symbol in the strike must be evaluated in relation to the symbols of craft and work, or their lack. Twenty years earlier, the symbol of home had not figured so strongly in iron and steelworkers' discussions. At that time, workers seemed to fasten upon their right to their particular jobs, rather than to a special place of residence. At Homestead in 1892, the sense of possession in jobs stemming from a craft identity was being replaced by a sense of possession in the *place*, a commitment to the town where workers hoped to build the good life of which their jobs were a necessary part. (62)

While this appeal undoubtedly carried great emotional weight for workers, counterpoints and tensions remained. "Both workers and industrialists might subscribe to the importance of home ownership," Dubofsky notes. "But what is one to make of Carnegie's multimillion-dollar Fifth Avenue mansion compared to the two-room shack of a coal miner?" (48). Even more troubling, homes as a marker of class separation and upward mobility might actually only mask a loss of individual agency. Drawing on Juliet Mitchell's *Woman's Estate*, Sedgwick describes the conflicting appeals behind the idea of home ownership that are encapsulated in the old saw "A man's home is his castle."

> [The image] reaches *back* to an emptied out image of mastery and integration under feudalism, in order to propel the male wage-worker *forward* to further feats of alienated labor, in the service of a now atomized and embattled, but all the more intensively idealized home. The man who has this home is a different person from the lord who has a castle; and the forms of property implied in the two possessives (his [mortgaged] home/his [inherited] castle) are not only different but, as Mitchell points out, mutually contradictory. The contradictions assuaged and filled in by transferring the lord's political and economic control over the *environs* of his castle to an image of the father's personal control over the *inmates* of his house. The ideological formation thus permits a criss-crossing of agency, temporality, and space. (*Between Men* 14)

In line with these arguments, home ownership could be and was used by corporations to reinforce direct economic dependency. Carnegie's vision of paternalistic corporate welfare, such as the subsidizing of home purchases by workers, was a direct means of offsetting a subversive rhetoric of worker mobility and agency. When companies held the mortgage on workers' homes, they possessed a considerable lever, not to say stick, with which to discourage worker independence.[11] It is no coincidence that after the Homestead Strike, the company quickly bought land and erected homes, which they encouraged employees to buy (Brody 87–88). If a home visibly argued upward mobility, class separation, and a certain independence from the workplace, it also helped tie one to a specific area and a job—and to the corporation's mortgage company.

Whittaker notes both dynamics when he joins Locke's sense of personal agency to the economic and civil problems that gather around his attempts to pay off his mortgage. Typically, Whittaker overwrites the positive in order to stress Locke's capacities. Most workers would face real difficulties in paying one mortgage while moving to a job in another town. Whittaker simply makes Locke's mortgage payments due later. In the end, though, keeping his home depends not so much upon Locke's personal power and agency as upon a lawyer's ability to keep institutional creditors at bay. Home ownership, then, is regularly argued by the dominant myth as a key marker of masculinity, an indicator of class separation and upward mobility. Rarely is it presented as discouraging the urge to move on and increasing dependency.[12] Also regularly downplayed are corporate moves to curb a recalcitrant workforce by first establishing the dependency of a mill town and then threatening it with a radical form of separation. As is true today, nineteenth-century owners "commonly threatened during labor troubles to remove their plants to more tractable communities" (Brody 87). In a town where work is scarce or movement from one mill to another unlikely, the departure of the mill itself would leave workers with a mortgage, no means to pay it, no buyers, and no agency whatsoever.

It is a grim irony that home ownership, like so many doxic arguments for masculine independence through class separation and upward mobility, is readily twinned with a reverse rhetoric that emphasizes the anxieties of nonagency and "feminizing" dependency. Being laid off or let go nastily underscores the worker's actual dependent position once the company decides that downsizing makes a different kind of separation useful to its goals. Ostensibly basking in a properly postoedipal family framework, the fired worker who faces forced departure from the workplace—and quite possibly the home itself—only too quickly reenacts defeats and required separations within both oedipal and preoedipal periods. This is not to say that home ownership, job stability, or increased income or status are in themselves negative because always threatened by loss. But it is important to recognize the ways in which particular motifs of masculine self-making such as separation and mobility are co-opted by doxic rhetoric so as to mask the complexities and downright contradictions contained within its own as well as variant myths. Such simplifications are readily visible in the motif of home ownership and deeply at work in yet another form of separation closely connected to masculine concerns with agency and mobility—that is, immigration.

Immigration and Agency

I discussed the ready applicability of immigration to dominant myths of masculine self-making in chapter 3, noting that "Carnegie" provides an excellent example, offering both physical separation from motherland and psychic/economic separation from class and origins as marks of achievement. At the same time, Carnegie's own reception by Pittsburgh's established Scottish families makes clear that physical separation from origins may be easier to enact than full social separation from class origins. However subtle the differences may be, *doxa* must deal with them insofar as they complicate the rhetoric of self-made masculinity, especially in light of those who do immigrate but fail to separate—even economically—from their class origins.

The ensuing complexities and internal contradictions in the mythic rhetoric are again visible as Davenport uses working-class immigration and class separation to argue for authentic masculinity and self-making. We know, for example, that as a master workman, James Rafferty is worthy of his sister Mary's love and Paul's adulation. Moreover, the level of his craftsmanship separates him from many of his fellow workers and even his fellow Irishmen (whom Davenport will consistently differentiate into "acceptable" Irish and the feckless rest). Rafferty is a steelworker with "unquestioned mastery of his craft," and as such, he is free to move at any moment to Jones and Laughlin or any of the other mills that have "made him offers at one time or another" (48, 121).[13] It is a form of masculinity reinforced within the film as well, where James Rafferty becomes Jim Brennan, and is paired with Paul as his equal in craftsmanship and love for Mary. Indeed, Paul and Brennan are seen as coproducers of the open-hearth process that establishes Paul's entrepreneurial masculinity as well.

While Rafferty/Brennan is praised as a skilled craftsman in both novel and film, it is in the novel that he is most thoroughly studied as a member of an immigrant group that (by the time of her writing) Davenport knows hasn't—as a group—noticeably risen. Many still remain working class, even after having been in America for a generation or more. As such, Rafferty and his fellow workers represent a potential counterargument to the myth of upward, corporate mobility for any and all who strive. The film, for its part, simply avoids the issue. There are the gentrified Scotts, and there are the Irish, the latter running the gamut from craftsman Brennan to stereotypical, friendly tippler Mac to twisted father Pat. But Davenport is concerned with addressing the historical complexities of immigration and its connections to the rhetoric of rising—or not. At the same time, her solution is fairly straightforward; like the "Carnegie" of this novel and the Carnegie of Pittsburgh and its elite, Rafferty can't separate and raise himself to the level of the Scotts because he doesn't have the right stuff.

Nevertheless, it is not sufficient for Davenport simply to argue some general innate inability in James Rafferty, since such essentialism contradicts the doxic rhetoric of ready rising for all. Davenport remains firmly committed to maintaining the mythic argument (Mary, after all, is Rafferty's successfully risen sister) and to leaving open the door to immigration. Rightly avoiding essentializing arguments then, Davenport instead reduces Rafferty through a rhetoric grounded in motifs of nonindividualism and nonmasculinity that are secondarily linked to immigrant issues. It is as a "misguided," working-class radical that Rafferty negatively separates from Mary and fails to align himself with Paul and the dominant rhetoric. The ensuing pressures of Rafferty's nonseparation from class and his false embrace of solidarity finally reduce him to an animal status that is both implied ("He stood half crouched, crazily at bay, his mouth twisted open, his back bent, his head lowered" [176]) and directly argued ("With an animal scream he leaped forward . . . gibbering and squealing" [177]). Initially displayed by Davenport as an emblem of craft masculinity and possible immigrant mobility, Rafferty ends the era that he and William Scott exemplify by shooting Scott and being beaten to death by his own fellow workers as a result.

Ultimately, both fictional and filmic versions argue that the unionizing Raffertys prove themselves incapable of properly masculine separation, struggle, and ascent. But where the film enacts Pat Rafferty as an example of literally crippled patriarchy, Jim Rafferty of the novel remains a prisoner mainly of his inability to choose to rise, much like the slatternly Irish servant girls that Mary is forced to fire—not the least because they question her authority to rule over them. In contrast with her brother's misguided union solidarity and its resulting failure of class separation and upward mobility, Mary's self-making (into a poetry reading, brogue-less savior and nonsexual mistress of Paul in this rather convoluted household) is based upon her refusal of an equivalency of status with her fellow colleens from down the hill. "I won't do it!" she decides. "I'll keep the upper hand if it kills me" (246). The truly self made recognize the importance of maintaining dominance over those left behind.

This is Davenport's counterargument concerning first-wave, Anglo and Irish immigrants who for some reason have separated from the homeland but not completed the sequence by reaching a level of rightful dominance. All are welcome, but the exceptional will quickly advance, thus "proving" that those left behind are less interested in (and possibly less capable of) self-making. The ostensibly nonethnic/racial qualities responsible for such failure (or success) are made even more apparent in Davenport's (and history's) subsequent attempt to deal with second-wave immigration (immigration from southern and eastern Europe) as a form of masculine advancement. Unlike the earlier immigration period romanticized by Carnegie and embodied in Rafferty, late-nineteenth-century needs for unskilled labor in steel mills like Carnegie's encouraged massive immigration from groups even less likely to be easily assimilated.

Large groups from southern and eastern Europe began arriving in 1880, and the masculine rhetoric of separation and mobility needed to accommodate the circumstances of these new figures for whom it was now to be argued. Davenport signals the shift by relying upon an often-used aspect of her already established argument for middle-class masculinity and success—mill owner Paul Scott. As established craftsman/corporate head, Paul is in a position to ignore earlier immigrants like Rafferty, not least because they represent a misguided, nonindividualistic masculinity that is embodied in a severely weakened, post-Homestead unionism. These workers already have been demonstrated as unlikely material for class separation, advancement, and masculine self-making. It is men like "the Hunky" Karel Hrdlička whom Paul/Davenport now moves upward in the mill, thus reenacting doxic arguments that the masculinity signaled by separation from the mother country will be further validated by willed movement upward through the job force.

Once again, this positive rhetoric of immigrational separation and mobility appropriates motifs of earlier, now nearly defunct, craft mobility. Karel/Charlie is "a skilled manipulator," trained at the Skoda works in Austria. Having established these qualities in Hrdlička, Davenport is free not only to help him advance but also to displace the issue of bias and racism onto the Irish themselves. Hrdlička is prevented from advancing by the ethnocentrism of his Irish and Scottish fellow workers (285). Incensed at this denial of a rightful advancement, Paul promotes Hrdlička, rooting the promotion in the rhetoric of a doubled masculine individuality, that of Paul's singular ability to recognize Hrdlička as a singular craftsman. "Most of 'em aren't much above animals, poor devils" Paul muses, "but this Charlie" is something different (315).[14] Fulfilling his role as a correctly valued and valuable immigrant, Hrdlička reacts to his shop floor promotion by producing "glittering" tears of gratitude in the corners of his "dark eyes" (286).[15]

This unselfconsciously qualified rhetoric of separation from homeland followed by separation from class and upward mobility continues throughout Davenport's historical novel as it moves inexorably forward through immigrations from eastern and southern Europe, the rise of U.S. Steel, and onset of World War II. In all the plot turnings, characters are identified as immigrants mainly so they then can be established as those whose natural class separation is enabled by an alert system of enlightened management. Nowhere is the issue of dependency or agency closely explored. The dominant rhetoric suffices to maintain the arguments, and their ongoing appeal is visible in both the novel and the film's ready engaging of them. That engaging is not without cost, however; it requires either the film's simplification or Davenport's masking and displacement of tensions, thus leaving unresolved questions to fester.

The results of that nonresolution are clear in variant enactments of the myth. Other texts study the same Pittsburgh steel mills as both versions of Davenport's tale, but they demonstrate much less commitment to the rhetoric and inherent blessings of immigrant separation, mobility, and self-making masculinity. Thomas Bell's *Out of This Furnace* (1941) is one of the best examples of a worker oriented novel that not only questions but also offers to subvert the dominant middle-class rhetoric of immigration and masculine achievement. Appearing four years before Davenport's *Valley of Decision,* Bell's novel opens with the requisite motifs: George Kracha emigrates from eastern Europe in search of work. He disembarks at New York in 1881 (the same year as James Davis) and, like Larry Locke and countless others in search of employment, finds himself confronted with "the necessity of getting from New York to Pennsylvania by the tedious process of putting one foot before the other" (5).[16] Having arrived, he finds work on the railroad at White Haven among his previously emigrated relations. But the work is not portrayed as craft-based, and the masculine self-making ostensibly attached to a willed separation from homeland and ready advancement up the corporate ladder is not a ready part of Bell's argument.

When Kracha's friends and relatives attempt, at various times, to find work in the steel mills, they are not instantly rewarded but constantly thwarted by the uncertainties of the workplace. Dubik is the first to decide to move from one form of laboring to another. He is motivated, to a small extent, by the chance to earn slightly more by working more hours. But he also "had been in one place long enough; it was time to move on" to Carnegie's mill in Braddock (21). He does so and, in fact, is readily employed as an unskilled laborer. But when Andrej and Francka decide to follow, they discover that deciding on mobility is not the same as achieving it. The mill is now closed and "Carnegie . . . did not intend to reopen [it] until the men accepted a wage cut" (23).

Bell's use of a historical lockout at Carnegie's Edgar Thomson Works in Braddock, Pennsylvania, is a comment on more than the mobility of craftsmen. Lasting five months, the strike also is the end of both "the union and of the eight-hour day in Braddock" (23). But Andrej and Francka are still eager to move and work in the mills. Having been thwarted for months because of workplace instability, they now choose to go to Homestead, where the union still has a contract. Kracha is eager to follow at this point. Yet his hoped-for mobility is halted for over a year by railroad accidents, floods, and vagaries in the workplace attributable to national elections. At last able to move to Homestead in 1889, he hears that another strike over wage reductions has been declared. Finally, he hears that the union has won the strike and leaves for the mill, naturally unaware of the lockout and deaths that will occur in 1892.

These vignettes clearly address the myth of masculine agency as rooted in chosen separation and mobility. Bell states his particular beliefs not in Davenport's rhetoric of ready self-making for all who enact separation and struggle, however, but more in terms of Davis's portrayal of the unstable job market of the Pittsburgh mills. Unlike either, he also is not committed to maintaining the dominant rhetoric, and his narrative shows it, beginning with neither patriarchal entrepreneurs nor skilled journeymen but unskilled immigrant laborers whose separation from home produces only further separation and wandering. Little of the dominant myth's linkage of agentive, immigrant separation and advancement is visible in this portrait—beyond the ever-present desire of those eager to embrace it. Faced with the dominant, middle-class rhetoric of separation and upward mobility, Bell emphasizes instead a variety of issues that lurk beneath the myth of masculine self-making. Given the myth's origin-erasing rhetoric, one of his most significant concerns is that of ethnicity and race.

Ethnicity and Race

Bell's rhetoric does not simply deny the dominant social myth of entrepreneurial and upward mobility. His portrayal of Kracha's various separations and temporary entrepreneurial rise is significant precisely because of what he does include of the myth and how he argues it. Briefly stated, Kracha's separations and movements are immigrational, horizontal (out of the mills), entrepreneurial, upward, and downward. All of these separations and their attendant mobilities are fully enacted by Bell. At the same time, his rhetoric casts a cool eye on the masculinity ostensibly achieved, explicitly questioning the separations, movements, and mobility of the dominant myth, viewing these motifs instead in the light of interpersonal concerns rooted in ethnicity. Where Davenport uses individual advancement to erase ethnic strains on mobility, Bell chooses to develop the issue in light of community, mutuality, and masculine intimacy.

Kracha's first job in White Haven enacts both a traditional motif of movement into the workplace and a questioning of the equation that individual effort equals advancement. Kracha works not because a Paul Scott sees in him a fellow craftsman, or because a brotherhood of the body recognizes him as a man. Kracha works because there is a large Slovakian community willing to take him in. It is the mutual support of Francka and Andrej that provides shelter and employment, not the beating up of a mill worker or the boardinghouse brawling of "The Greasy Spoon." Even the masculinity endorsed by a paternalistic passing on or recognition of skills is removed here. In this argument, then, separation from domesticity is not a precursor to masculinity but rather a stage before the next domesticity.

The actual hiring process clarifies the ethnic, communal base of this support. There is a procedure required to gain entrance as an unskilled laborer, and to outline it, Bell presents Davenport's view of the lingering control held by skilled workers over employment and economic mobility, along with her sense of the ethnocentrism that tends to limit the range of unskilled workers' mobility. To both he adds his own opposing rhetoric of nonindividualism. Kracha's successes in moving from job to job, mill to mill, come not through manly battling or corecognition by craftsmen/mill owners of individual merit but through a repeated ritual: A friend or relation arranges a meeting with a skilled worker; the worker (usually not middle-European and therefore a "godling," in Bell's sarcastic phrase) is given a bribe; Kracha is hired (31). Individual effort or inherent talent is not a primary issue in getting or indeed in keeping a job. In Montgomery's phrasing: "Woe unto the man who stood alone in this pitiless struggle for existence. Walter Wyckhoff, Alfred Kolb, Whiting Williams, and other upper-class writers who 'put on overalls' to share the experience of unskilled workers in America quickly discovered that both obtaining jobs and surviving on them required pals, kin, connections" (*Fall* 88).

Bell portrays Kracha as advancing, then, but not by engaging the dominant masculine rhetoric. Kracha is carried along by his ethnic ties. He works and minimally rises not simply through moments of masculine separation and agency—immigrational, individualistic, or skill-based—but via mutual support provided by a full community. At the same time, through displaying negatives that historically attached to Kracha's particular ethnic community, Bell enacts Kracha's mobility as limited both in scope and agency. In short, Kracha is upwardly mobile, limited in his mobility, and dependent all at the same time. Such conflicting currents clearly qualify the individualistic, agentive masculinity maintained by the dominant mythic rhetoric of masculine self-making.

In addition, Bell demonstrates the doxically enhanced ability of the dominant rhetoric to co-opt subversive rhetoric by portraying skilled labor's own qualification of a rhetoric of upwardly mobile, individualistic masculinity. As Bell makes clear via Kracha and his ethnicity, skilled workers enact a typical recapitulation of systems of dominance, replicating the dominant myth's hierarchical rhetoric by adopting managerial behaviors and attitudes that are destructive to the actual power and leverage of their own unions. Part of that stance results from skilled workers' anxiety over the threat of slipping backward into a "feminine" dependency and nonagency that job insecurity fostered. Unionized workers both loathed and feared second-wave immigrants, who were seen as pawns of mill owners and possible strikebreakers. Under such circumstances, it is not surprising that ethnic immigrants were, in Brody's words, "uncommitted to a permanent life in the mills, . . . [and] did not find the arguments for joining a union persuasive. . . . [U]nions spelled dismissal or at least a prolonged strike . . ." (136). Said another way, having experienced ethnic prejudice from skilled workers, immigrant laborers found unions' rhetoric of job control through mutualistic struggle to be somewhat unconvincing. Kracha himself presents such an attitude. Eager to work in the mills only to be faced with a strike, he evidences not solidarity or a concern for his plan of advancement but only shock. "Good God, do they strike in the steel mills every year?" he exclaims (24).

Internal union ethnocentrism, racism, and representation of unskilled laborers as lesser (or less than) men thus seriously damaged any insight into how union solidarity and communal mutuality could serve as a viable contrapuntal theme to the music of upward mobility. That damage was furthered not only by direct antiunion rhetoric but also by cultural rhetoric's enactment of masculine *doxa* to cloud the issue of ethnicity further. As was true in regard to the issue of intimacy among workers, current attempts by modern labor historians to characterize the situation demonstrate the rhetorical complexities within the doxic myth. Speaking of second-wave, formerly peasant workers, for example, Montgomery suggests that "nothing in capitalism's rural periphery had nurtured a programmatic sense of collective or even personal advancement" (*Fall* 91). Similarly, Brody states that "the mass of peasant workmen were, as they appeared, unpromising union material. Nothing in their agriculturalist past prepared them for collective activity in industrial America" (136–37). Both scholars are referring to what they perceive as a missing sense of organizational sensibility.

Yet ethnic laborers did organize, albeit not clearly along the lines of aggressive struggles with authoritarian fathers so often enacted in union rhetoric. By and large, Montgomery suggests, when laborers organized themselves as laborers, "their organizations were based on ethnic ties" (*Fall* 94). Brody agrees, developing the characterization further:

> The peasant looked on himself primarily as a member of a
> family and a village. He could not conceive of differing with
> group decisions, unanimously reached. Moreover, nothing
> mattered more than communal approval. Immigration weak-
> ened, but did not destroy, group consciousness. When, there-
> fore, immigrant workers were driven to strike, they were
> likely to persist until the general sentiment turned. They were
> effective strikers because they were peasants. (140)

This description raises some interesting issues. Stated in terms of masculine individualism, ethnic identification is just another form of un-
differentiated collectivism and, as such, comes close to emasculating
group-think. But stated in terms of solidarity, ethnicity is an immensely
powerful form of resistance. Clearly the question is complicated once
again by the need to produce an alternative rhetoric that sees as acceptable a masculinity tied to nonseparation and interdependence rather than
a masculinity engaged in terms of individual agency and the strike.

In searching for such a rhetoric, Bell intentionally opposes the dominant rhetoric of masculine self-making by using motifs of mutuality and
interdependence that Brody alludes to and Montgomery briefly raises.
Bell begins first by allowing Kracha to enact various forms of separation and related mobility. He is, after all, a Hungarian peasant who saves
his money so as to immigrate, later brings his wife over, moves to Pittsburgh and becomes a steelworker, raises a family, and, most important
of all, moves both horizontally and upwardly at the same time—having
quit the steel mills, Kracha buys a butcher shop and begins to acquire
property and status in the community. This last movement out of the
mills is a form of separation and mobility that is both subversive of the
myth of internal corporate mobility and at the same time suggestive of
one form of the dominant myth of masculine self-making, that of entrepreneurial individualism and agency.

Yet Bell also adds qualifying tensions to the full-blown myth and its
doxic underpinnings. Kracha himself sees his progress as differing from
that of the full avatars of entrepreneurial self-making. If owning one's
own business hints of such masculinity, Kracha is quick to debunk his
role as heir to mythical self-made patriarchs and their less than flattering real-life versions: "The big man who was for the little man didn't
exist, never had and never would. Kracha's distrust of big men, rich men,
rulers, was profound" (65). In his own mind, then, Kracha's pursuit of
class separation and upward mobility is not the limitless adventure of
the true, patriarchal entrepreneur.

Such a self-imposed limit on upward mobility is perhaps healthy,
because there are external limits as well. Bell is not singing the praises

even of Kracha's mixed form of separation and mobility, although his behavior has some of the elements. Poised to move into an entrepreneurial frame, Kracha's full mythic enactment requires the rhetoric of personal effort as voiced in Davis's, Carnegie's, and Davenport's middle-class means of mobility: saving, shrewd investment, and wily politicking. Unfortunately for the dominant myth, Kracha does not make these moves—nor, Bell suggests, can he without a subsequent shift in personality and masculinity. Upward mobility of this sort requires the talents of the bartender Perovsky: "One could tell from [Perovsky's] bearing that he, unlike Kracha, had never been surprised by his own success. He was known to be on the inside of things, with a finger in every pie. He was a saloon keeper and a coming Republican ward heeler but he could have been as successfully a confidence man, a priest or an actor" (93). It goes without saying that Bell intends these latter occupations to be seen as no more savory than the figure of Perovsky himself. Kracha is clearly out of his league, an ethnic entrepreneur who, while supposedly upwardly mobile, knows next to nothing about banks, institutional lending, internal politics, or how to really maintain class separation and upward mobility in this environment. It is not the sky that is the limit here but Kracha's educational and economic shortcomings. Knowing nothing but the generalities of the standard rhetoric, "in one sweeping avalanche of disaster [Kracha] . . . lost the Halket Avenue property, lost his business, lost his home; and when they let him out of jail he discovered that he had lost his wife too" (107–8).

Ironically—and significantly—the behavior that puts "paid" to Kracha's middle-class separation and mobility is his particularly full enactment of masculine *doxa*. In temporarily enacting the dominant myth of masculine self-making, Kracha has achieved a separation, most notably from the mutuality and interdependence of his ethnic community. But Bell argues that it is precisely this separation from those around him that both enacts the dominant rhetoric of Kracha's upwardly mobile, middle-class masculinity and reveals its inadequacy at the same time. Fueled by an inflated sense of himself and faced with a wife whom he physically and emotionally abuses, Kracha's newfound economic power frees him to indulge himself in keeping Zuska, the rediscovered, dark-haired beauty of his shipboard fantasy. Not a wife, Zuska is nevertheless a trophy, a mark of yet another emotional and physical separation. But in Bell's revised rhetoric of masculinity, Kracha does not deserve to gain but to lose his business because of the direct economic and social impact that this separation has on his family, the larger ethnic community, and the attitude of them all to each other. Bell argues that the separation that motivates Kracha's mobility is a form of avoidance or escape. Like Davis's self-absorption in his physicality, Kracha's struggle is truly masculine according to the full implications of *doxa*—narcissistic and sadomasochistic.

These are central components of Bell's argument, and he reinforces them, interestingly, by having already established Kracha's real emotional center as his relationship with Dubik. That may taint the argument with a suggestion of masculine buddiness, but it also provides enactments of a masculinity consistent with Bell's larger argument regarding ethnic support and mutuality. Dependent on the mutual aid of Andrej and Dubik to find work, Kracha also is tied psychologically to Dubik for his sense of self. Unlike a Davis who goes to the physical body for narcissistic separation and self-definition, Bell goes to the intimacy of Montgomery's workplace photos to establish Kracha's manliness—and its subsequent collapse. Work, intimacy, and domesticity are related throughout the novel, as Bell makes clear in Kracha's first visit to Dubik's home in Braddock. The description opens with a reference to a cradle at the foot of the bed, and the association continues in the description of Kracha's reaction to Dubik: "Dubik lay on his side, asleep. He had lost weight and even in sleep he looked exhausted. The boisterous shouts Kracha had meant to awaken him with died in his throat. He shook him gently. "Get up, lazy bum. You have company" (31).

This is a highly masculine and thus highly limited intimacy and mutuality, and it occurs in the relative peace of home. But its motive force also includes the workplace. Set in the domesticity of home, the visit actually centers around conversations about work: Dubik's unflattering views of Carnegie and Captain Jones, the need for more better wages, the uselessness of Carnegie's library, Dubik's desire for mobility in the form of self-education, separation from the mills, and escape to a small farm. This vignette thus both incorporates and expands Leverenz's definition of the workplace as key to reenacting oedipal struggle and masculine humiliation; beginning in the home, the scene establishes that site as an arena in which to consider the workplace as a related arena for enacting preoedipal mutuality and intimacy.

Bell provides this scene to contrast the dominant masculine rhetoric of separation and mobility with a subversive rhetoric of ethnic connection and masculine mutuality. Then he destroys the possible blooming of both. Dubik's immigrant's desire for an intellectual form of upward mobility—"to educate myself a little"—falls victim to his twelve-hour stint (34). Nor will Bell allow Dubik to own the small farm of his fantasies. Dubik achieves none of his wishes not because of a lack of separation and effort but because a blowout on his furnace burns and kills him. Bell's minute, narrowly focused description of Kracha and Dubik following the explosion suffers from a typical requirement that men demonstrate their connections only under moments of extreme stress. But the portrait achieves its emotional effect nonetheless:

> Somehow [Kracha] got Dubik's arms over his shoulders, his own body under his friend's. He was heavier than Kracha had expected. Grunting, his hands and knees scraping cruelly under the cinders, he got one foot against the ground, put his hands under Dubik's thighs, and rose. The muscles of his belly stayed tight for a minute after. "So." His knees were trembling. . . . Dubik's arms dangled before him, and over his shoulder Dubik's head, like a tired child's, moved gently with each step. Kracha could smell burnt skin. (52–53)

This scene relies heavily upon a traditionally limited, masculine connectedness. There are clear appeals to paternalism and power, and hints of masculine concerns with death and self-sacrifice; Kracha takes a gut check after lifting Dubik, and Bell makes the reader do the same when faced with Dubik's "burnt skin." But there remains nonetheless, or perhaps for that reason, a clear portrait of a masculine ethos of the workplace. It is easy, in fact, to link this scene with Montgomery's photographs, and even with Davis's self-portraits. Kracha's rising from his knees with the weight of Dubik is both intimate and an endorsement of masculine strength. The difference between this scene and Davis's portrait is the duty performed by that physical strength. Davis's body is portrayed in service to his self-congratulatory song of individual upward mobility, Kracha's to embracing and raising a dying friend.

Importantly, it is Kracha's loss of Dubik that marks both an end to Kracha's experience of masculine intimacy and ethnic mutuality and the beginning of his movement into individualistic, entrepreneurial mobility. A month after Dubik's funeral, Kracha "signed papers and became a businessman. . . . A little over a year later he owned two horses and wagons, had a man and two boys working for him, and in a steel box in the trunk in his bedroom he had nearly one thousand dollars in cash" (60). Kracha appears to have achieved an ethnicity-free, communally independent, self-made masculinity. But what follows is the slide I noted above; the drift away from family and ethnic community leads to adultery, an ill-advised investment scheme, and bankruptcy. Bell clearly argues that all these reversals follow upon the loss of Dubik and the mutuality that he represents. Having been forced into a viciously masculine separation from Dubik, Kracha's self-making eventually drops to the aphoristic level of a Davis. Kracha continues to argue his masculinity through the doxic rhetoric of separation, regularly announcing to any and all that "in two years I have lost my wife, my mother and my best

friend" (99–100). By this point, Kracha's pursuit of masculine separation has burned all bridges connecting him to his community and moved
him far down the path of an upwardly mobile, self-made narcissism that
will ruin him.

Bell spends a good deal of effort preparing us for this drift and the
negativity that attaches to its perverse portrait of middle-class, masculine self-making. From the start, Kracha has been represented as both
ambitious and self-centered. His treatment of his wife is unacceptable;
his enactment of the successful businessman role and affair with Zuska
is childish. Bell even denies Kracha some minor solidarity with the union
men of Homestead. As Brody notes, during the lockout at Homestead
the union lodges "were able to bring out almost the entire labor force.
But for the battle, the union might well have won the strike" (59).
Kracha, however, is portrayed as uninterested and uninvolved.

If Kracha's noninvolvement is not entirely accurate historically, it is
in keeping with Bell's ethnically alert treatment of the dominant myth
of masculine self-making. Bell is arguing for a different masculinity here,
one fostered by an ethnic mutualism both embraced and forced upon immigrants whose own rhetoric of mutuality and community is insufficiently argued and insufficiently heard. As Schneider notes, "The ten to
twenty percent of Homestead's workforce who were immigrants from
southern and eastern Europe and were in later years to play such a large
part in the steel industry, found no spokesman in the labor press in 1892,
and there is little record of what they thought or did" (Schneider 48). That
voicelessness fits Bell's purposes well. As a result of his immigrant and
ethnic status, Kracha cannot adequately articulate and enact either the
dominant or a subversive rhetoric of masculinity. In the end, Kracha fails
because he feels no allegiance to union or community and instead pursues—too eagerly and with too little opportunity—a mythic rhetoric he
cannot fully enact, that of individual control of his own self-making.

The absent working-class voice and its missing rhetoric recall Whittaker's pursuits as well. For Whittaker, elements of such an argument
might be found in the vague loyalty of Larry Locke to his fellow Knights
of Labor. But in the end, Whittaker himself is most comfortable with
individualistic masculinity and personal success. For different reasons,
Bell also does not put forward a mutualist argument for Kracha, primarily because the sense of solidarity or mutuality for all these characters
lies not in the union but in one of the reasons that they are absent from
the union—their ethnicity. To that end, the Homestead lockout comes
and goes in Bell's narrative with accurate and damning portraits of Frick
and Carnegie, but with no call for union solidarity at this point in the
novel. That will occur only later with other characters. For now, Bell is
content to let his characters' doxically colored dreams of ethnic mutu-

ality and worker solidarity provide suggestive counterarguments to the masculine *doxa* of class separation and upward mobility.

Historically, however, these suggestions are eddying currents in the larger waters enacted by a rhetoric of immigration, class and ethnic separation, and corporate advancement that comprises the dominant myth of masculine self-making. Normally *doxa* attempts to accommodate such currents by redirecting and merging them with the mainstream. When the variant myth can be appropriated (as with craftsmanship and immigration), the larger doxic flow moves forward. But when ethnicity and, even more regularly and terribly, race are constricted in their flow and blocked from the mainstream so as to become a separate and raging current, they can quickly drown the unsuspecting. The next chapter demonstrates how swiftly that can happen and the damage to masculinity that inevitably occurs.

6
Tapping the Heat:
Race, Racism, and Erasure

> I'd made my choices. I was running away from Pittsburgh, from
> poverty, from blackness. To get ahead, to make something of my-
> self, college had seemed a logical, necessary step; my exile, my flight
> from home began with good grades, with good English, with setting
> myself apart. . . . To succeed in the man's world you must become
> like the man, and the man sure didn't claim no bunch of nigger
> relatives in Pittsburgh.
> —John Edgar Wideman, *Brothers and Keepers*

> None of us has gotten where we are solely by pulling ourselves
> up from our own bootstraps. We got here because somebody—a
> parent, a teacher, an Ivy League crony or a few nuns—bent down
> and helped us pick up our boots.
> —Thurgood Marshall alluding to Clarence Thomas,
> *Newsweek*, October 28, 1991

IT CAN AND HAS BEEN ARGUED THAT one of the premier representations of
masculine self-making—of any form—exists in the self-portraits of
Frederick Douglass. On nearly every score, Douglass achieves more than
a Carnegie, fights and wins a more desperate battle than a Larry Locke,
demonstrates more integrity in success than a James Davis. His portrait
is, as Waldo Martin notes, that of "a peerless self-made man," "a model
self-made man" (253). The portraits certainly contain all the motifs
common to the myth. Technically not an orphan, Douglass has a childhood background typical of the insanities of slavery, starting with an
unknown father (but suspected to be his master Aaron Anthony) and a
mother from whom he is separated as a child. Undeterred, Douglass
seizes an opportunity offered him to learn to read and write. This personal, internal improvement is met with an equal desire for self-dignity.
The key moment for satisfying this desire rests in the mandatory fight

scene—but here with the added twist of his defeated opponent being notorious for breaking the spirit of recalcitrant slaves. Further physical separation and mobility follow these initial victories, with Douglass's immigration motif supplied by his escape to the nonslave North. Finally, Douglass's self-making engages the ultimate in rhetorical self-enactment: His autobiographical *Narrative of the Life of Frederick Douglass* leads to international recognition, social effectiveness in the war on slavery, eventual governmental positions, and comfortable wealth.

More problematically for the dominant rhetoric, Douglass's self-portraits also provide cogent demonstrations of the tensions existing in the myth of self-making, the masculinity enacted by it, and the larger *doxa* itself—a set of tensions exacerbated and magnified though the additional issue of race. As we have seen with Davenport and Davis, when the dominant myth of upward advancement faces the question of race or ethnicity, it may not erase race per se. In various arguments, the restrictions of race and of racism are minimized for the successful individual and maximized for the nonsuccessful at large. Race, then, can be introduced as a floating marker of difficult things correctly overcome, a signal of that which has been correctly left behind by the individual with the requisite masculinity for true self-making. Or race can be the reverse if it serves the doxic argument: a symptom of "natural" causes for failure by others.[1] As was true with separation, solidarity, or mobility, then, cultural rhetoric displays a powerful ability to alter the value of the motifs to fit the argument.

On the other hand, enactments of the myth less heavily invested in racial innocence may not only represent self-making as racially conflicted but may do so by qualifying and questioning the common motifs of separation, individualism, and agency that are provided by the dominant version of masculine self-making. Instead of encouraging identification with a figure who offers closure of the issue and reinscription of the dominant myth, subversive rhetorics rely upon a more qualified recognition of and assent to conflicts and anxieties normally overridden by the doxic rhetoric.

These rhetorical dynamics and their relation to the dominant, middle-class rhetoric of masculine *doxa* are clearly visible in the writings of Frederick Douglass, and equally so in Douglass's readers and interpreters. They are likewise visible in three other writers and texts of particular importance here: William Attaway's *Blood on the Forge,* Connie Porter's *All-Bright Court,* and John Edgar Wideman's novels and nonfiction works. As these works discuss masculinity, the steel industry, and the impact of steel and steel's demise in Pittsburgh and Buffalo, they enact points of tension and contradiction within the myth of self-making. In doing so, they not only enact well-known tensions regarding masculinity but also further link those tensions to deeper anxieties over sexual aggression and sexual dependency, sadism and masochism, separation and agency. Most importantly of all, they do so in light of the added difficulty of maintaining the myth when race is added to the rhetoric.

Frederick Douglass's Rhetorics

There can be no doubt that Frederick Douglass was well aware of the appeal of self-making and its ethos, especially in the United States. The most direct evidence lies in his lecture "Self-Made Men." Following its composition in 1855, the oration became his "mainstay" and was delivered "more than fifty times to audiences across the United States, Canada, and Great Britain" (Andrews 4; Blassingame and McGiven 544–46). The rhetoric of self-making in that lecture appears in the autobiographies as well—and in ensuing commentaries on them and on Douglass himself. In Benjamin Quarles's *Frederick Douglass,* for example, Peter Walker finds "a black Ragged Dick" (214), a Douglass "[brought] straight, ideologically, to the mainstream of a social theory for which Andrew Carnegie, the Scottish bobbin boy, was the peerless model and exemplar" (216).[2] But in Philip Foner's *Frederick Douglass,* Walker finds a class-based, anti-Carnegie attitude in Douglass's self-portraits, an oppositional stance ostensibly taken by a premier example of American self-making (218–19). Like the mythic rhetoric he enacts, Douglass and his writings are fraught with contradictions.[3]

Houston Baker provided his well-known answer to these contradictions by arguing that once an autobiographical voice, especially that of a minority figure like Douglass, begins to enact "the linguistic codes, literary conventions, and audience expectations of a literate population, [it] is perhaps never again the authentic voice of black American slavery" (*Journey* 43).[4] Both generic form and cultural rhetoric thus are at work in and through the rhetoric of masculine self-making that Douglass enacts. Described in such terms, Douglass's need is not to subvert the myth but rather to get it to accommodate his voice and rhetoric. As Sojourner Truth makes clear concerning women in "Ain't I a Woman?" (1851), the issue is not just one of getting people to recognize your capacity for achievement, but getting them to recognize you in the first place—in Douglass's case as a man, indeed as a human being capable of doing anything "manly" at all. To do so successfully requires speaking the dominant cultural rhetoric. In Robyn Wiegman's words, Douglass found himself gravitating toward those forms most amenable to a white audience "overwhelmingly convinced of the African-American's incapacity for rational thought or imaginative creation: . . . narratives of masculinity—of the heroic body, of democracy and the nation-state, of founding 'fathers'" (71).

Produced within these dynamics, Douglass's revised self-portraits provide an unusually rich demonstration of the contradictory strains (in both structure and argument) at work in the rhetorical maintenance of masculinity—and particularly the effects of race on both. Comparing versions of Douglass's famous fight with the slave breaker Covey from *Narrative of the Life of Frederick Douglass, an American Slave* and *My Bondage and My Freedom,* for example, Leverenz argues that alterations in Douglass's fight scene are indicative of an equivalent conceptual shift not simply in personal self-awareness by Douglass but in class awareness as well. In explaining the stylistic shifts, Leverenz twice notes that Douglass's earlier sense of an artisan's freedom "now uneasily coexists with an entrepreneur's sense of power" (108, 120). Interestingly, Leverenz himself sees in these differing modes a further complication in representing masculinity. For Leverenz, Douglass's newer rhetoric enacts more than a simple, manly brawl for self-respect. It is used "to affirm the self that has risen so far from that fight . . . , to exhibit his ability to control himself as well as his master" (118). Unfortunately, Leverenz also declares the voice of the later version "smug, pretentious, excessively genteel, even phony" (121). "The taut drama has been lost," Leverenz believes, "both at the level of action and at the more subtle level of voice, where the emotional tensions of the first version have given way to claims for self-control, mastery, and dignity" (121) and a tone of "high-minded prissiness" (119).

With such changes and other enactments of self-making, Douglass gives rise to a set of contradictory if not incompatible masculinities, depending upon the rhetoric engaged and the context in which it is performed. It is a not uncommon problem; the same need to appeal to what is seen as a correct or dominant masculinity and its related class dynamics is visible in many postemancipation manuals written (by well-intentioned reformers in many cases) to "train" former slaves in acceptable forms of self-making. As Saidiya Hartman makes clear, these guidebooks stressed that the middle class ideal of self-control was key to the process of self-making: "It appeared that only the cultivation of rationality and responsibility could [produce] the remaking or self-making of the formerly enslaved as rational individuals and dutiful subordinates (129–30)."[5] Middle-class values thus served as convenient markers of proper self-making. But the rhetoric they provided was hardly without internal contradiction, as Leverenz suggests in establishing his patrician, artisan, and entrepreneurial categories of masculinity and Douglass's relation to them.

What Leverenz describes as an artisan/craftsman world threatened by entrepreneurial power and industrialism is itself workplace specific, notable for its emphasis on artisanship, as much as its consideration of working-class craft. Douglass may well have been attempting to enact working-class issues in his later rhetoric, but the concept "artisan" rewrites the actualities of labor and laboring in class-ambiguous terms. In addition, Douglass's refashioned voice is closer to the rising institutional or corporate masculinity of the already entitled Paul Van Beaver than it is to the entrepreneurial with its anti-institutional, "outsider" masculinity. These conflicting voices are rooted in a variety of oppositions and anxieties that complicate the middle-class myth of self-making and deny any clear separations between patrician/artisan/entrepreneur frameworks, as *Larry Locke, The Iron Puddler, The Valley of Decision,* and *Out of This Furnace* make very clear.

For the majority of postemancipation slaves, in fact, a very particular sort of work was being urged in the self-help manuals—their rhetoric of middle-class self-making notwithstanding. As Hartman notes, these texts produced a specific double bind in their appeals to self-making. They on the one hand "advocated mastery and control over one's condition and destiny—autonomy, self-possession, resolve, and discipline—and to the contrary confused self-making and submission. Overwhelmingly mastery was given expression through the laboring body. . . . [T]he primary role of blacks, whether slave or free, [was to be that of] manual laborers" (134). The presence of this underlying sense of the labor available to blacks thus complicates the traditional middle-class narrative of free self-making with racially based, economic limits that Douglass himself may have too easily elided.

In addition to this complication, the general middle-class tendency to rely heavily upon male-centered characterizations as the key to masculine self-making produces the usual tensions for both Douglass and his critics. Once again, heavy emphasis on male/male exchange tends to involve doxically induced masking of preoedipal dependency and separation. But the rhetoric of male/male struggle and willed agency alone simply cannot encompass the full sociocultural complexity it purports to define, as much as *doxa* encourages the attempt. Jenny Franchot demonstrates this pressure on Douglass's enactment of middle-class rhetoric not only by noting a historical progression in his portrayal of women but also by suggesting that some of the roots of that shift lie in the preset rhetoric of self-making (149). Franchot carries the latter point further, suggesting that "because 'manhood' and 'freedom'" are regularly paired in Douglass's rhetoric, his move from slavery to "'Representative Colored Man of the United States' marks a transition from the afflicted feminine to the empowered masculine. . . . This gendered conversion paradigm unavoidably situates the feminine within the 'nothing' that precedes the acquisition of virile autonomy . . ." (153–54).[6] Douglass's autobiographies clearly stress self-making as an issue in becoming a man, then, while his rhetoric mirrors then-current tensions surrounding the dominant, middle-class myth of masculinity and other contending rhetorics.

The same tensions and processes are revealed in Douglass's "Self-Made Men" oration. Delivered in various forms from the mid-1850s to 1893, the lecture was performed during a highly fluid period in the rhetoric of masculine self-making. Yet as Martin notes, "Douglass's mature thought remained wedded to a simpler, romantic view of America. As a result, he never quite came to grips with industrialization and urbanization and their ramifications for black progress" (283). Ironically, it is this distance from the actual world of the noncraft, industrial laborer or corporate entrepreneur that enables Douglass to extol the necessary link between work and successful self-making, and to denounce those who do not succeed as likely to have refused to work.

There are even echoes of James Davis in Douglass's claims for the healthful properties of work, notable for their nostalgic image of craft labor. Apparently never having heard of the dangers of the blind stitch and other such extremely close, eye-hand work, Douglass is capable of such statements as this: "The eye of the watchmaker is severely taxed by the intense light and effort necessary in order to see minute objects, yet it remains clear and keen long after those of other men have failed . . ." ("Self-Made Men" 559). These are middle-class, managerial blandishments and clichés, appealing to a sentimental sense of craft that simultaneously hides the particulars of industrialized labor and its effects on masculinity.

Ultimately, then, it is not the actual work of laborers or even craftsmen that forms the foundation of Douglass's myth of self-made masculinity. It is the masculine rhetoric of willed separation, of movement from "without" to with and within that characterizes this self-making:

> Self-made men are the men who, under peculiar difficulties and without the ordinary helps of favoring circumstances, have attained knowledge, usefulness, power and position. . . . They are the men who owe little or nothing to birth, relationship, friendly surroundings; to wealth inherited or to early approved means of education; who are what they are, without the aid of any of the favoring conditions by which other men usually rise in the world and achieve great results . . . [men] who are not brought up but who are obliged to come up, not only without the voluntary assistance or friendly cooperation of society, but often in open and derisive defiance of all the efforts of society and the tendencies of circumstance to repress, retard and keep them down. (549–50)

The language is notable for its characterization via the negative; it is what these men originally are without that characterizes their later gain. This is a middle-class appeal to the *doxa* of masculinity as agency, as a willful struggle to separate, leave origins behind, and move toward the places and goods whose possession denotes a place at society's top rather than its bottom.[7]

Equally notable in the speech, however, are ways in which Douglass himself qualifies middle-class rhetoric even as he enacts it. Thus, he precedes this representation by noting: "Properly speaking, there are in the world no such men as self-made men. That term implies an individual independence of the past and present which can never exist" (549). To a degree, this denial is itself a device, a suggestion of human limitation that serves to forecast the ultimate success of those who face and yet move beyond limitations. But the clear rejection of context-free individualism cannot be missed, as is true for most of the quiet contradictions throughout the speech. Douglass extols work and rejects luck as the ultimate feature of successful self-made men. Then he quickly follows by refusing to "exclude other factors of the problem. I only make them subordinate" (560). He echoes the claim that the United States is the preeminent realm of self-made men because all can work and work equally at all levels. "The strife between capital and labor is, here, comparatively equal," Douglass's middle-class rhetoric asserts. Yet he quickly follows by declaring that labor "can never be respected where the laborer is despised. This is today, the great trouble at the South. The land owners resent emancipation and oppose the elevation of labor . . ." (570). He rejects those who overvalue the diploma, only to assert "no disparagement of learning" (574). In fact, he closes this last comment by noting: "With all my admiration for self-made men, I am far from considering them the best made men. . . . The hot rays of the sun and the long and rugged road over which they have been compelled to travel, have left their marks, sometimes quite visibly and unpleasantly, upon them" (574).

It is a highly contradictory display, perhaps annoying in its Gilded Age echoing of clichés of self-making, certainly confounding in its denials of what it supposedly argues. At times, those appeals and contradictions in race-based, self-making rhetoric are jarringly obvious: "Personal independence is a virtue and it is the soul out of which comes the sturdiest manhood. . . . I have been asked, 'How will this theory affect the negro?' and 'What shall be done in his case?' My general answer is, 'Give the negro fair play and let him alone. If he lives, well. If he dies, equally well. If he cannot stand up, let him fall down'" (557). Such a statement appears to directly enact the dominant myth of masculine self-making and Douglass's relation to it. At the same time, there is a subtext at work. Douglass is unlikely to have expected that such "fair play" was readily available, even as he calls for it.

It is difficult to believe that Douglass had totally lost sight of what Hartman refers to as the "burdened individuality" or "double bind of freedom" that lay at the paradoxical heart of calls for individualistic self-making offered to the black community, "being freed from slavery and free of resources, emancipated and subordinated, self-possessed and indebted, equal and inferior, liberated and encumbered, sovereign and dominated, citizen and subject" (117).[8] Nor is it likely that Douglass expected many blacks to "fall down" if equal opportunity suddenly were to arrive. If anything, then, Douglass's speech reinforces his representative nature as an exemplary self-made man—but not simply in terms of his success. He is most representative because his experiential and representational enactments of the myth range so widely, and attempt to master so fully, the conflicts and contradictions raised by the dominant rhetoric of masculine self-making.

Racism in the Steel Industry

It is as dangerous to assume that Douglass's audience would miss these contradictions as to assume that he was completely unaware of them.[9] The conflicts might not be heard initially in the midst of traditional appeals to doxic self-making, but contradictions were likely to be heard very loudly indeed when the audience (especially black males) later attempted to enact the self-making noted in the myth. Too often, the dominant rhetoric's insistence on the validity of the supposedly race-blind myth serves mainly to provide an arena in which race-based evaluations of workers in the workplace can be blithely ignored, directly denied, or paradoxically used to validate the myth itself. For example, in 1922, James Davis (still speaking as a former secretary of labor and a full twenty-eight years after Douglass's last formal delivery of his oration) puts forward his considered opinion that self-making perhaps is not and probably should not to be available to all. Immigration laws must take note that "racial characteristics do not change," and "[t]ribes that have swinish characteristics" in their native country will destroy any country to which they are admitted (28). Davis is able to ferret out such characteristics in various forms. Work attitudes are premier, of course, but Davis's abilities also let him discern racial and ethnic heritage on the basis of cockiness (Syrians), food (French), bathing habits (American blacks), warlike attitude (Germans), socialist tendencies (Native Americans), and excess populations (Chinese and Indians) (94, 156, 168, 264, 269, 272). Such masterful discernment is not always directly negative of course. In a double move, Davis praises a man who helps workers, having first identified him as one of those men who operate clothing stores with continual "SALES": "a Jew" (47).

Davis is clearly not yet ready to follow Douglass's call for egalitarianism. Nor does Davis agree with Douglass that all races have merit or can rise equally. He notes as much in a long, steel-puddling conceit that unites race and industrial labor more succinctly and obviously more distastefully than Douglass ever does:

> There isn't much use for pig-iron in this world. You've got to be better iron than that. Pig-iron has no fiber; it breaks instead of bending. Build a bridge of it and it will fall into the river. Some races are pig-iron; Hottentots and Bushmen are pig-iron. They break at a blow. They have been smelted out of wild animalism, but they went no further; they are of no use in this modern world because they are brittle. Only the wrought-iron races can do the work. (98)

It could be argued that Davis differentiates between Africans and sons of American slaves, as Douglass himself was wont to do. But it hardly seems worth the effort, given some of Davis's other statements. Indeed, it appears most likely that his attitudes bespeak a general antiblack, anti-immigrant racism not uncommon for the day, an attitude in some ways necessitated by Davis's earlier use of his own immigrant status as an aspect of self-making. If upward mobility is a given of masculine effort, and immigrant mobility is a positive foundation for such upward mobility, then the impending syllogism is clear to all: More immigration will yield more masculine self-made men. But if you have all the workers you need and want at the time, and if your own status would be reduced if everyone achieved equally, then you're probably going to want to limit general immigrant and upward mobility, so as to prove the rule in yourself rather than others.

It is in service to this argument for the exceptional proving the rule that the dominant myth of masculine self-making can and does put race and ethnicity to the service of masculinity. The desire for exceptions to the rule is most easily satisfied through attaching secondary values (provided by racist attitudes) to the primary values already argued by the myth. Thus it is easy enough for the dominant group to declare itself metaphorically (as well as ethnically, racially, and materially) separate from other groups by virtue of its own effort. Dominance becomes its own proof of the value and rightness of separation, especially in a masculine culture that defines itself in terms of self-made success. The myth of self-making maintains the validity of its key mobility—upward—by declaring that the limited movement of certain ethnic or racial groups is not inherent in social structure but rather proof of the dominated group's own internal and even natural limitations.

All of these self-justifying variations on the dominant rhetoric of self-making are part of the African American experience within the steel industry. At the same time, the power of *doxa* is also visible in reenactments of the myth by African Americans themselves, even as racial restrictions demonstrate that the myth is and was seriously flawed. These positive representations once more enact the main tenets of self-making, including willed separation, migratory mobility, and the search for upward mobility. Secondary forms and subversive arguments do occur in terms of craft-based independence, possible union solidarity, forced separation on ethnic/racial grounds, and return to the point of separation. But overall, the dominant myth manages to maintain its validity, and the validity of doxic masculinity along with it.

Given that dominance, the appearance of the myth and its common motifs among black steelworkers should not be any more surprising than its appearance among other groups of workers. Like the myth of self-making, the history of African Americans in the American steel industry is as old as that of American steelmaking itself, and their experiences follow the key technological changes from craft-based, puddled iron to mass-produced steel utilizing large quantities of unskilled labor. Black slaves reportedly were hired out as skilled puddlers by their masters in the South as early as 1842 (Dickerson 8; Spero and Harris 9), and they continued to work in those positions throughout the Civil War. Following the war, it became possible for skilled African American steelworkers to follow the dictates of masculine self-making, especially if they were willing to add familial separation to migratory mobility. Although black steelworkers were used by northern mill owners as strikebreakers as early as 1875, in most mills they arrived as trained puddlers.[10] Their willingness to migrate and their craft-based abilities did produce upward mobility, and many of these skilled workers "rose to responsible positions, and earned wages which frequently equaled those of Whites" (Dickerson 7–8).

But that final qualifying phrase tells the whole tale. The upward mobility of Dickerson's workers is gauged by their *near* equivalence to white wages. Added to this quiet limitation on upward mobility and self-making was an increasing obsolescence of craft-based skills. As puddlers, black craftsmen were already becoming anachronisms. When their skills became less important, their already small numbers dwindled to insignificance. The pre-mass-production experience of African American steelworkers is thus closer to the exception than the rule, and even as an exception, it contains inherent limits on self-making denied by the dominant myth. The more representative linkage of the myth of self-making and black steelworkers rests in the later movement of unskilled workers out of the South and into the area of western Pennsylvania.

The heaviest movement of black labor into steelworking came via the shift from puddled to mass-produced steel and its concomitant shift from skilled to unskilled labor. As I noted in chapter 5, the need for unskilled labor was initially satisfied by immigration from Europe, with succeeding waves arriving first from the British Isles and western Europe, followed by importation of laborers from central, southern, and eastern Europe. Throughout this period, northern steel manufacturers also recruited African American labor, in some cases to offset job actions and union activities throughout the industry. But the most substantial influx of black labor into steelmaking occurred as a result of World War I, as labor shortages during and shortly after the war produced the so-called "Great Migration" from the South and created opportunities in industrial cities for African Americans "to achieve their desire of freedom and social advancement" (Johnson and Campbell 86).

But arrival and even acquisition of a job did not eliminate discrimination and limitations on advancement, within and without the labor force. The experience of black laborers in general was complicated and reinforced by their ongoing racial exclusion from white-dominated unions, a situation that continued, with greater or lesser intensity and collusion, up to the mid-1960s. Much of this exclusion operated on both a national and a local level. Some attempts were made to offset racial antagonism. Early efforts by Powderly and his Knights of Labor, Murray and the CIO, and the Steelworkers Organizing Committee demonstrate a selective commitment to removing some forms of racism (antiblack but not anti-Asian, for example) from union activity. But racial separation and exclusion predominated. The result of this situation was to drastically limit if not eliminate unions' ability to produce a corrective or subversive rhetoric of masculinity in opposition to mythic representations of masculinity as movement up the corporate hierarchy.

Appeals to the dominant myth of self-making were additionally reinforced by antiunion, probusiness arguments put forward from within the African American community itself. Black newspapers "actively encouraged blacks to leave the South" (Yarborough, Afterword 297), regularly enacting traditional representations of upward mobility within the corporate frame. "Newspaper advertisements, mainly in the Black press, stressed the economic opportunities which the iron and steel industry offered to prospective Black migrants" (Dickerson 38). In 1917, the *Chicago Defender* invited anyone who wanted work and freedom to come north, declaring, "Plenty of room for the good, sober, industrious man. Plenty of work" (Johnson and Campbell 81). In the same year, the nationally known *New York Age* featured "special articles on opportunities" and "biographical sketches of some prominent Blacks" in the Pennsylvania towns of Sharon and Farrell (Dickerson 38). Among the portraits were those of African Americans "who had worked in the mills, and eventually became property owners and leading citizens in the Shenango Valley": "One was Charles Wayne, a Farrell resident since 1910 as well as an employee of the Carnegie steel works. . . . Another success story concerned Thomas H. Robinson, a migrant from Millwood Virginia. . . . Like Charles Wayne, the 'flattering sums' of money which he earned marked him as another prosperous member of the Black community of Sharon and Farrell" (Dickerson 38–40). Such reports, when matched with advertisements for opportunities in northern mills, helped provide a sense of turn-of-the-century upward mobility. The entrepreneurial heyday of a Carnegie might be gone, but masculine self-making within the corporate frame appeared to exist for those willing to separate from their homes and pair their migrant mobility with upward mobility.

This ongoing rhetoric of masculinity was augmented by arguments within black churches "espousing the work ethic and encouraging Blacks to value their jobs and obey their employers" (Dickerson 114–15). The companies themselves, eager to foster such antiunion, procompany rhetoric, regularly contributed financial support to churches and to social welfare organizations such as the Urban League.[11] Although alert to the importance of unionization and self-determination, the ultimate purpose of the league was "to get jobs" (Spero and Harris 140). Companies themselves encouraged these economic arguments for a middle-class masculinity defined as corporately upward mobility by adding programs of welfare capitalism, geared, "like Americanization programs for immigrant workers in preceding years," toward making black employees "dependable, efficient, and compliant laborers for the steel companies" (Dickerson 104).

The dominant rhetoric thus remained the middle-class myth of individual advancement and success in line with corporate needs. Masculine, individualistic self-making, verbally fostered and physically reinforced by the emigrated black worker's separation from home, family, and the population at large, produced a situation as well suited to reinforcing corporate control as to inculcating doxic masculinity: "Workers could be pitted against each other not simply because of ethnic and racial prejudices, which they were assumed to (and did indeed) harbor, but precisely because the environment mitigated against the creating and maintenance of strong social bonds" (Hamilton 151). In short, the mythic rhetoric of masculine self-making provided an argument heavily weighted toward acceptance of personal separation and company-based, upward mobility, no matter what the relation of one's personal experience to the myth and its attendant masculinity might be.

Conflicts within the dominant rhetoric did produce undertones within the doxic song. One of the more complexly subversive uses of the middle-class myth exists in the self-help rhetoric of Marcus Garvey and the Universal Negro Improvement Association (UNIA). Although it is often characterized simply as a "back to Africa" movement, Dickerson believes that the UNIA "clearly had greater mass appeal among Black steelworkers in the Pittsburgh area than the NAACP" (79). Part of that appeal relies upon aspects of self-making echoed in Garvey's emphasis on black pride and self-help. Taking up arguments against white unions, Garvey argues further that the black worker should side with his employer "until such time as he could achieve economic independence and become his own employer" (Spero and Harris 135). This last advice suggests the full complexity of Garvey's particular rhetoric of self-making: solidarity within the black community, personal upward mobility or maintenance of status via the corporation, and eventual separation from the white corporate world via entrepreneurial activity within the black community itself.

Even racially alert enactments of masculine self-making thus continue to rest on a bedrock of the dominant appeals. Garvey echoes the rhetoric of upward corporate mobility in the call to cooperate with (as well as to use) the employer and to reject direct union confrontation, even as he argues for eventual separation from the dominant culture through independent entrepreneurial activity. Garvey's argument thus is subversive primarily in regard to final separation from white society. Initially, power is to be achieved by rising within the dominant social institutions through full internalization of their call for individual, willed separation and struggle as key to identity. The ultimate success to be achieved in this process involves yet another willed separation—from the dominant institutional frames in order to achieve full self-making and black masculinity.

By leaving the basic form of the myth intact, however, such racially alert subversions continued to reinforce behaviors amenable to the dominant power structures and their myth. In addition, final separation was complicated by the fact that eventual removal from the white power structure could be extremely difficult to effect, not least because it depends upon a further engaging of dominant institutional powers—banks, credit organizations, corporations. The argument acknowledges the need for equivalent black institutions, but the recognition cannot fill the need. Like Kracha with his butcher shop, African Americans who effected some level of economic progress could find themselves simply overrun by the dominant institutional powers that preexisted their own smaller concerns. Ultimately it was not as fully independent self-made men that black entrepreneurs were most successful but as "middlemen" operating between the African American community and white institutional power.[12]

The resulting tightrope was compounded by a notable lack of areas in which initial success could be achieved within white institutions.

Corporations (and components of the black community itself) continued to encourage self-making via the dominant rhetoric of unfettered upward mobility through equivalency of effort, but that encouragement was only verbally open ended. A percentage cap on upward mobility often existed within companies. Where it did not, it often was unneeded because of a common practice of segregating departments; there was no need for a cap in any department from which blacks were excluded. As a result, "Black steelworkers experienced mobility within predominantly Black mill departments" (Dickerson 186), thus engaging a basic form of upward mobility while at the same time effectively contradicting the myth through "the perpetuation of black men's and white men's jobs" (Spero and Harris 180).[13]

For their part, companies regularly endorsed the dominant myth of self-making by arguing that the practice of separate and limited upward mobility was forced on management by racism among workers. Frustration over the contradictions between the dominant myth and the experience of racial exclusion were thus deflected from the myth and toward labor itself, a deflection not unaided by racist practices among white workers. But the overall argument is largely invalidated by management's generally negative history in regard to both proactive hiring at upper levels and advancement of black employees.[14]

In short, neither the dominant discourse of traditional class separation, upward mobility, and masculine self-making, nor alternative and possibly subversive self-making through union solidarity and brotherhood, nor even racial solidity and mutual support, fit the situation as the majority of African American labor experienced it. Once again, those contradictions need not necessarily lead to changes in the dominant discourse; in some cases, they are instead blatantly endorsed as a means of upholding racist views. Eventually, however, the constant pressure of such contradictions may well produce explosions. But even these blazing hot enactments do not necessarily bring down the edifice of masculine self-making as a whole.

Race and Self-Making, Separation and Sadism

In Octave Thanet's (Alice French's) 1905 novel *The Man of the Hour,* Johnny-Ivan, son of the owner of a foundry and plow-fabricating mill and himself a committed (if confused) Socialist, separates from his family and lives a life of constant internal struggle between commitment to capitalism or socialism. Finally, he is relieved to note that the "Anglo-Saxon in me has conquered" (438), and he returns home to claim his masculinity. In a version of the common strike/fight motif, Johnny-Ivan experiences his newfound masculinity through breaking a strike at the mill of his now-dead father, doing so by battling a knife-wielding Finn (462) and "Dago tricks" (436), and by employing such managerial tactics as importing strikebreakers and black scab labor. Thanet clearly intends to connect racial anxieties to labor's general fear that strikes can be broken with cheap, nonunion workers. Yet within Thanet's dominant, promanagerial rhetoric, Johnny-Ivan's tactics are marked neither as racial nor problematic; it's just good business.

The resulting self-exculpation is based on the attitude that scab labor may be seen, also in good business fashion, as nothing more than a tool in the hands of the proper, self-making man. Having won the struggle to let his Anglo-Saxonism come to the fore and with it the strike, the no longer hyphenated Johnny receives his one-hundred-thousand-dollar birthright. He now is in a position to acquire the mill and to "help people in the only true, sensible, American way, by giving them a show to help themselves" (475). Self-making is thus reinforced, but only for Johnny and the type of man he has come to know, respect, and, most importantly, represent. That masculine figure, Thanet's rhetoric argues, is "the best fellow in the world, the American workingman" (475), a workman who, like Johnny Ivan, is in a position to display not only his natural propensity for masculine self-making but the Anglo-Saxonism that lies at its base.

It might seem logical that Thanet's ethnic and black workers, who have supposedly migrated from their homes and into the workforce as common laborers, are also free to pursue self-making. Such suggestions don't match Thanet's prejudices, however, and must quickly be quashed. Thanet does so, mocking the manliness of ethnic and black laborers, and then simply removing them from the scene, preferring that method to an outright denial of Douglass's hoped for "fair play" (557). As necessary pawns, the black laborers are established as improper material for self-making, portrayed as "niggers," a "regular forest primeval of blockheads" (409) and "darkies" whom Johnny-Ivan amuses with stories (434); "coons" who flock to the white strikebreaker (435); workers as difficult to convince as "a mule" (457) and so superstitious that when faced with dynamite they declare "dat ar's conjure work and I gits!" (458).[15] Along with the other non-Anglo workers, Thanet's laborers thus move temporarily upward to fit plot needs, but the novel's concern with proper masculinity eventually sends them most assuredly outward—out of the mill and out of the novel itself. As soon as the strike is over, they vanish from the plot so that the "good" labor organizer can intercede for the now-chastened Anglo strikers and get them their jobs back (469).

Presented by Thanet's managerial voice as humorous figures to be gawked at, black men simply disappear when the strike is over, along with the extensive history of African American workers in the steel industry. William Attaway's *Blood on the Forge* (1941) enacts a different myth, to say the least. More complex and ultimately even more damning, his novel directly questions the myth and its masculinity within the frame of early twentieth-century steelmaking. Like Bell's discussion of ethnicity, this novel argues that mixing the dominant *doxa* of self-making with the subtext of minority experience can be lethal, even as it struggles to find a different rhetoric.

Attaway's rhetoric is rooted in historical data described in the previous section, while it adds the immediacy of individuals to the numbers. If that process of individualization carries its own taints of bourgeois romanticization, Attaway's unflinching judgments on race, upward mobility, and union solidarity remove any vestige of nostalgic glorification and sentimentalization. Attaway's novel is a brutal portrait of black migration to the mills of Pittsburgh during the 1920s—a movement culminating not in escape from poverty and oppression but into further external control and emasculation. In displaying those issues, the novel pursues at least two related goals that are clearly linked to Attaway's concern with the rhetoric of black masculinity. Deeply committed to labor and laboring issues, Attaway insists on (1) representing labor and laboring values as victims of capital and (2) portraying the myth of self-made masculinity as perverted by the economic system it touts.[16]

That two-part argument is enacted through Attaway's three main characters—the brothers Big Mat, Melody, and Chinatown—all of whom represent particular aspects of masculinity and particular ways of dealing with society's attempts to define masculinity to, for, and through them. As brothers, these men enact a literal brotherhood established through personal intimacy. It is the tragedy of this novel that their immigration to the North leads not to a furthering of masculinity and brotherhood in labor but only to separation from their families and a failure of brotherhood amongst themselves and the workforce they join. Ultimately for Attaway, the movement toward masculine self-control and economic mobility closes by revealing directly and vividly that its separations are not willed but forced and that they are attached to an underlying sadomasochism.

The initial separation and emigration of Attaway's brothers—from rural Kentucky to the mills of the Pittsburgh area—is necessitated by yet another fight—Big Mat's attack on a white riding boss. Importantly, that attack is a result of the recent death of the men's mother and Big Mat's subsequent emotional upheaval. The emotional weight of separation is thus effectively attached to the emotional loss of the maternal, while the fight also serves to establish a key aspect of Big Mat—that his great strength is matched with an inability to address his own emotional needs. In contrast, Melody is as deeply attuned to others as his name suggests.

He cannot fully understand the forces that shape, control, and deny his attempts at masculine self-making. Yet Melody works at pursuing that insight, and it is he who most sustains the intimacy among the brothers. Through this slowly disintegrating intimacy and Melody's own self-analysis, Attaway effectively argues that the reader's deepest connection belongs with this character. Chinatown, finally, is the least fully developed figure; youthful and fun loving, he is also less insightful and conflicted than Melody.

It remains Big Mat, however, who provides Attaway with most of the cause and effect movement in the plot. It is his fight, after all, which leads the brothers to their initial forced separation and migration. Unlike Larry Locke's battles, this is a fight that defines not supremacy but oppression and lack, as Big Mat is threatened with passivization and feminization by the dominant white boss. Big Mat is also threatened by his ongoing inability to preach, a Lacanian opportunity that (in the context of the novel) would supposedly eliminate his wife's miscarriages or at least the pain they cause. Yet whenever he tries to preach, "it all jest hits against the stopper in my throat and build up and build up till I fit to bust with wild words that ain't comin' out" (43). As his wife continues to insist that he might try anyway, Big Mat busts out in typical fashion; he hits Hattie.[17]

These quick events presage the full performance of Big Mat's doxic masculinity. Incredibly strong (a "he-man" [5], as the regularly beaten Hattie chants, seemingly without irony), Big Mat's horizontal mobility is inextricably connected by Attaway to acts of separation—emotional and physical—from mother, wife, eventually his ill-used mistress, finally his brothers, and most effectively from himself. The literal migration to the North is thus offered by Attaway not as an emblem of a proper separation necessary for masculinity but as a set of moves from that which gives a sense of intimacy and connectedness. When Big Mat leaves his Bible at the bunkhouse and goes to live with his mistress, the separation from Hattie, his brothers, and the thin-soiled but still life-giving land is effectively complete. With familial intimacy and connection banished, the only arena for establishing masculine self-identity will be that of work.

Having represented the myth's separation not as chosen agency but as forced flight, Attaway is ready to comment on the rest of the dominant myth—agency as a function of effort and will—and the masking of racism that its appeal achieves. Big Mat's physical power is linked throughout the novel to effort and competition. Yet even as Big Mat enacts the physical equation of all would-be self-makers and real men, he is limited by the racism of both management and his fellow workers: "Big Mat welcomed the heat. Through the long, hot hours he would do twice as much work as anybody else. In competition with white men, he would prove himself" (106). The rhetoric of masculine self-making and hard labor echoes Whittaker, Davis, Davenport, Douglass, and myriad others. Attaway, however, qualifies the call, and not simply by adding Big Mat's self-comparison to white labor. Having separated from all emotional ties, and yet still been denied success in the workforce because of his race, Big Mat will find not the liberating rewards of honest work but the ragings of sadomasochism.

Attaway's basic argument states that the erasing of race in a rhetoric of equal effort and equal reward is a mythic appeal that only augments separation from and removal of support and intimacy that is supposedly a necessary first step toward masculinity.[18] For black men excluded from power structures, Attaway argues, there is no open-ended opportunity for self-making, and no real opportunity for positive subversion of the myth's dominant rhetoric. Having migrated North, the brothers may dream of the reverse separation and mobility to be found in returning to Kentucky. But these are nothing more than fantasies. By the end of the novel, Melody knows the truth: "They would never go home" (290). Nor does Attaway put forward a working-class alternative to individualistic self-making such as self-definition via solidarity with the union. Attaway believes in the need for worker control, but he refuses to ignore a history that separated black steelworkers from any such brotherhood. Faced with the contradictory requirements and needs of a workplace and a landscape dominated by white males, Attaway's vision of masculine self-making is devastatingly bleak.

What Attaway is left to enact is the masculine destruction that occurs when the underlying motive forces of the dominant myth of self-making find no adequate or socially validated outlet. In Melody's case, separation finds expression in his loss of empathy and intimacy. He can no longer play music, and he fails both sexually and later emotionally with Anna, Big Mat's eventual mistress. When Anna declares him "not a man" (105) and goes to Big Mat, Melody finds "nothing could get past a fence" now between the brothers (138). Motivated to pursue self-making but denied a means for achieving it, Melody directs the underlying contradictions and inherent trauma of the myth at himself, allowing his guitar picking hand to be injured at the mill (166). That masochism reinforces his earlier distancing from the pure myth, as do his more feminine values of personal awareness and the need for connection. But Big Mat remains Attaway's purest embodiment of masculine self-making gone awry, and its ultimate effects on him are enacted during a strike at the mill.

In other novels, the strike can serve as unifying—as an opportunity at least for self-control if not self-making. But Attaway does not ask readers to envision a subversive, unionized mutualism or solidarity. Instead he makes clear the irony in which union practices of racial exclusion lead only to a gain in corporate control over all workers. Big Mat is separated from mother and wife, from home, from his brothers, and is kept separate from the union because of his race. As a result, he becomes pure effort and will, the ultimate tragedy of masculine agency, self-making and—as Attaway makes clear—the ultimate in masculine sadomasochism.

Hired as a strikebreaker, Big Mat initially directs his energy into a manic maintaining of the furnaces that up to now have controlled him: "Now these monsters that made metal were dependent upon the strength of Big Mat. It moved him to rush madly about the yards, knowing that only his will would keep a fatal crack from their big, brittle insides" (264–65). The masculine call to effort and action finds its last, ostensibly positive enactment here. But Mat's will and effort cannot control these furnaces any more than he could control Hattie's miscarriages, to which Attaway is clearly alluding. Defeated, Big Mat redirects his energy at the strikers themselves, finding a new brotherhood, a twisted "kinship with the brutal troopers" and their sadistic pleasure in producing "terror in the strikers" (266–67). Like Ellison's Invisible Man, Big Mat searches for a way to put violence to use for himself but only finds his violence put in the service of others.

As Attaway develops Big Mat's sadomasochism, he insists on connecting it to masculine sexuality and the enactment of both through the myth of self-making. With outlets for his masculine aggression thwarted, Big Mat "had drunk out of the deputies' bottles and he was blind with whisky and power. Like the deputies and troopers, he no longer needed reasons for aggression. Cruelty was a thing desirable in itself" (268). Having thus been reinforced in his views that masculine power resides in those who can beat, Big Mat decides that he is finally a "new man," a "boss," and returns with his newfound knowledge to Anna (269). But the scornful Anna sees power as more than physical force. The economics of the myth of masculine self-making are clear to her: "'You are a peon,' she kept on. 'I will not live with peon. . . . You are not *Americano*. *Americano* live in big house back in hills. . . . *Americano* have big car.'" Big Mat's reaction is to take his newly found masculinity (with its pleasure in unbridled cruelty) and direct it at Anna: "She went to her knees under the wild lash. 'They are not peon like you.' . . . Big Mat went hog wild and laid the belt across her face" (276).

Attaway moves close here to allowing Anna's words at least to effectively cause this beating, although not to justify it. A number of factors serve to offset such a reading: Big Mat's clearly announced sadistic pleasure in cruelty, Anna's unspecified but undeniable link to the strikers Big Mat beats, Big Mat's muddled recognition that he has become another "riding boss" himself, and finally Big Mat's self-initiated, masochistic death at the hands of "a young Zanski," whose own "repugnance for the blows he must deal" opposes his violence to that of Big Mat (287).[19] The novel ends, then, with Big Mat forcing his death at the younger Zanski's hand, the strike broken, and Melody and Chinatown headed into the Pittsburgh slums. Tapping into the blinding-hot frustration and anger produced by contradictions in the myth of masculine self-making, Attaway nevertheless insists that Big Mat's aggressive individualism is a false outlet for that frustration.

But while the dominant myth of masculine self-making is perverted in the figure of Big Mat, it is subverted by no single character. Writing in 1941 about the nature of work in the mills in 1919, Attaway refuses to do more than suggest that subversion might rest in refusing individuality in favor of mutuality, solidarity, and intimacy. Excluding those interpersonal values, his argument suggests, intensifies the frustrations generated by racism, while all the contradictions together repeat and effectively enhance the inherent and ongoing trauma of separation and exclusion endorsed by middle-class self-making, ensuring the repetition of sadism and masochism in masculine behavior and the maintenance of *doxa*.[20]

Race and the Collapse of Steel

Much has changed and much remains exactly the same when John Wideman and Connie Porter address the same questions of work, race, and self-making. Their late-twentieth-century works cover black upward mobility, the steel industry, and the neighborhoods that were dependent on both. Wideman covers nearly all of Pittsburgh's history in his wide-ranging corpus, with a major focus on the latter half of the twentieth century as lived and experienced by the residents of Pittsburgh's Homewood neighborhood, who like the mills themselves have been abandoned.[21] Porter's Buffalo-centered novel provides a portrait of steel's closing days as the ultimate heavy industry in the United States (roughly from the late 1950s to the late 1960s). Porter's novel adds the meliorating effects of civil rights legislation on union membership. Nevertheless, her portrait of mid-century black steelworker and son portends a problematic future; upward mobility achieved through separation from family also requires separation from one's own race.

In considering the effect of work, the workplace, and rhetoric, these fictional enactments attempt to resolve the desires and contradictions produced by the dissonance between the dominant rhetoric of masculine self-making and a broad spectrum of the African American experience. They do so by willingly enacting the dominant rhetoric of chosen separation, active questing, and masculine struggle with which Attaway likewise began. It makes sense, then, to consider these works as taking up questions posed forty years earlier by Attaway, and to link the emigration of Big Mat, Melody, and China to Pittsburgh with that of Harry Wideman, who "migrated from Greenwood, South Carolina, to Pittsburgh, Pennsylvania, in 1906" (*Brothers* 22), and to Porter's Samuel Taylor who, orphaned at ten, leaves Tupelo, Mississippi, in 1958 in order to "make good up north" and become a man (12).

Wideman may find a "raw, dirty, double-dealing city" full of "Dagos and Hunkies and Polacks" when he arrives. But like him, they'd "been drawn . . . by steel mills and coal mines, by the smoke and heat and dangerous work that meant any strong-backed, stubborn young man, even a black one, could earn pocketsful of money" (22). They may not earn pocketsful of money, but unlike Attaway's heroes, there is some measure of truth in the myth for these men and others like them who have moved to the northern mills in order to engage the dominant myth. Porter is likewise willing to enact the basic rhetoric. Samuel's separation and immigration is rewarded with a job at Capital Steel, and he saves his money, goes back to Tupelo for his sweetheart, brings her back to Lackawanna, New York, and settles into life on All-Bright Court.

A member of the "brotherhood" of the United Steelworkers of America (3), Samuel is free to eat at Dulski's, a working-class, mixed-race diner, where Porter opens her novel. Having finished the midnight shift at the mill, Samuel stops at the diner to collect his reward for good honest effort and labor—a reward provided by the restorative, almost domestic intimacy of a brotherhood of men and food, where Samuel enjoys the classic camaraderie of the working man's early morning breakfast. "At eight in the morning, Samuel Taylor was eating eggs. . . . [Y]olk ran down his chin. He was making a mess, but he did not care. All the men, the steelworkers, who came to Dulski's ate like this." These hungry men resemble Davis's in their refusal to be "kind to food" (1). But the masculine camaraderie of this diner carries none of the competition Davis also loves to portray. Quietly enjoying breakfast with steelworkers of all races, a correctly postoedipal married man, eventual father, and owner of an automobile, Samuel has all the minor trappings of the self-made workingman.

In both cases, the rhetoric suggests, effort and will produce some of the rewards of shared masculinity. But Porter and Wideman complicate the dominant rhetoric as readily as they introduce it. Their purpose is not simply to engage the middle-class myth, nor simply to deny it. Rather, what Wideman and Porter explore are the conflicts that appear, both in the dominant and in the subversive forms of masculine self-making. Most importantly of all, as they do so, they take Attaway's concern with the sadomasochism even further, pursing it to its ultimate source within the doxic realm of the domestic and its preoedipal concerns. A primary job of the dominant myth of masculine self-making is to avoid that buried concern in masculine *doxa,* of course, and in taking it up Wideman and Porter reveal and enact tensions both within the myth and within their own works as well.

Harry Wideman may enact the necessary rhetoric, for example, but his separation and migration also underscore a conflict between the middle-class myth of upward mobility and the experience of many black workers. In Pittsburgh as in Buffalo, the work does not last, nor does the dream of self-making. By the next generation, too many mills have become "hulking, rusty skeletons lining the riverfront" (*Brothers* 41), and the eager workers have moved to and through those mills and into the Homewood streets that Wideman often recites as a litany in his works: Tioga, Seagirt, Susquehanna, Homewood, Hamilton, Frankstown, Finance, Cassina Way, and Dunfermline.[22] As Wideman passes through these streets on his way to the various jobs he works to make ends meet, the presence of Carnegie's Dunfermline provides ironic commentary on black workers' relation to the dominant myth of masculine self-making.

For his part, Samuel Taylor's efforts in Buffalo do yield benefits argued by the dominant rhetoric, but they too prove insufficient to move him fully into the realm of masculine agency that self-making implies. By 1972, his status as a steelworker is clear: He is at the mercy of a collapsing steel industry and a complicit union. The mills are slowly closing or moving away. Dulski's burns after Martin Luther King's assassination and is not rebuilt. Saved not by legal prowess or union solidarity but by the luck of a job lottery, Samuel's dependency and his sense of self are only too obvious. The "gratefulness" the men feel over being spared by the lottery is "sanguine and sensual, as raw as the passion a man can feel for another man's wife" (145). As intimately tied to their sense of masculinity as is the sexuality to which Porter equates it, their gratitude only reinforces their singularity and missing solidarity, based as it is not on interpersonal, mutual brotherhood but on competition and forced dependency (145).

This rhetoric of failed mutuality and union brotherhood is one half of a reply to working-class attempts to subvert the dominant rhetoric. An answer to another of labor's possibly subversive rhetorics—craftsman/journeyman independence and agency—is taken up by Wideman. Among a variety of figures who enact this rhetoric, John French is the "standard" in Wideman's work "for assessing and understanding black masculinity across generations" (Byerman 13–14). A lingering representative of craft and journeyman masculinity, French carries his tools in a "canvas drawstring sack it takes a good man to heft" (Wideman, *Sent* 387), and he enjoys the respect of his fellow laborers. "Can't nobody hang paper like French," they say. "Even these hunkies know that. They all want French if it's a particular job" (392). But for all that skill and power, by mid-twentieth century neither the craftsman nor his myth are in control of most workplaces—shop floor or even craftsman's workshop. French must sit on the street corner and wait on work, hoping for a pickup truck and a job to roll up, grinning "like the white man gon carry you to Great Glory but you knowing all along he gon take you to some piece of job and pay you half what he pay one of his own kind" (387).

Like Whittaker, then, Wideman engages the mythic contradictions circulating around the working-class rhetoric of honest craft, agentive masculinity, and the dominance of both by institutional power. But Wideman's own rhetoric is affected by more than Pittsburgh's shift from craft-based steelmaking to mass production. His masculine figures are operating within an industrial frame that has collapsed almost completely, and they are doing so as black men. One hundred years after Larry Locke, then, Wideman uses figures like French and Mr. Tucker—"A workingman," as he describes himself (*Reuben* 189), to sound many of the notes of labor and craft used by Whittaker to establish Larry Locke's masculinity. French and Tucker are even more subject, however, to a lack of power, and as such, they even more fully enact conflicts in both dominant and subversive rhetorics. Tucker, for example, is both journeyman laborer and latter-day Kracha, a self-employed entrepreneur who has subcontracted a house salvaging. For his laboring efforts, Tucker too is jailed. But unlike Larry Locke, Tucker is not jailed for heroic union activity, and his masculinity is not attached to union solidarity. Instead, the primary contractors who hire him turn out to be rip-off artists stealing the salvaged materials, and Tucker is arrested in their place, an act that fully severs the rhetoric of honest labor from that of masculine agency.

As a black working man in modern Pittsburgh, Tucker—like French—does not and cannot engage the subversive rhetoric and possible power of a nineteenth-century working-class craftsman. Instead both men bespeak lingering echoes of journeyman/craftsman rhetoric. They are workers whose nonaccess to the larger power dynamics of Locke's union, coupled with racial bias and its regularly attendant economic limits, has put French on the street corner and Tucker in jail. What Wideman subverts, then, is not only the dominant myth but that of the craftsman as well, turning the rhetoric of agentive journeyman into that of dependent day laborer.

If history has left little room for enactment of the rhetoric of craftsman masculinity, especially among black men in the inner city, then history takes us logically to the last potentially positive aspect of Tucker's and French's status—to the entrepreneur whose authentic masculinity is developed through deep personal struggle and effort in the "real world." Clearly, their dependency on others to ply their skills does not enact that rhetoric fully, either. But in his autobiographical *Brothers and Keepers,* Wideman pursues a purer version of this myth, explicitly comparing his own educationally separated and upwardly mobile masculinity to that of his brother, the latter embodied as both activist and ghetto entrepreneur. When Wideman leaves Pittsburgh's "miles of deserted sheds" and the "old, rusty guts" of J & L Steel (*Brothers* 40–41) behind in order to attend college, he is enacting fully the doxic masculinity of the dominant, middle-class myth of self-making—separation via the institution of education and, by implication, upward mobility within pre-existent frames. It is Wideman's brother Tommy, then, who remains at home and voices the rhetoric of entrepreneurial authenticity.

In that role, Tommy argues that the "streets is out there. The hard-ass curb. That's why the highest thing you can say about a cat is he made his from the curb. . . . That's a cat took nothing and made something" (*Brothers* 132). Determined to enact this rhetoric of masculine self-making, Tommy masterminds a cocaine buy to start him and his crew on their way: "We all been working and saving up our cash. . . . We know our time is come. We just know we gon get our foot in the door and won't be no stopping us. We're on our way to the top just like Garth said" (122).[23] Tommy's rhetoric of active agency and street-validated authenticity are appeals to masculine *doxa* that Wideman cannot help but contrast with the more ambiguous masculinity of the self-made intellectual who has achieved separation, but in doing so also has left the authentic streets and their ostensibly refining fire.

Wideman engages those tensions by putting the returning intellectual in a Homewood bar with his uncle: "Tall dude act like he ain't with Carl now. . . . He don't say Rock or Bud or Iron like somebody got good sense. He have to go and say *Budweiser, please* like Violet supposed to set something different on the bar nobody else ain't drinking" (*Hiding Place* 270). The anxiety attached to inauthentic masculinity within cultural rhetoric is more than just suggested here. It is almost the given role of the middle-class, nonactive, nonauthentic male. But while these opposing masculinities (and nonmasculinities) are clearly of concern, Wideman also complicates the rhetoric by revealing the level of Tommy's entrepreneurial success. The coke deal goes bad; Tommy is arrested for murder; he is sentenced to life in a dreary prison west of Pittsburgh.

Clearly, Wideman and Porter are intent upon engaging all the major motifs in the myth of self-making—separation, immigration, craftsman agency, entrepreneurial authenticity, middle-class upward mobility—only to leave them echoing through abandoned shop floors or the now-disadvantaged inner-city streets of Pittsburgh and Buffalo. As is true for Attaway and even Douglass, Wideman and Porter name the conflicts only to demonstrate the power of *doxa* in maintaining its rhetoric of masculine self-making in the face of their naming. These works do not enact closure, then, but the underlying frustrations that race attaches to the myth and its always present, internal contradictions. More importantly, their further pursuit of the myth does not lead back to a revised version of the dominant, however, but rather to the psychocultural tensions that the rhetoric tries to offset in the first place. Porter and Wideman choose, in short, to pursue masculine self-making into the domestic arena and the full family romance, rather than remain in the realm of the workplace. What they find upon their arrival is sadomasochistic self-erasure.

Self-Making as Self-Erasure

Porter makes her move through Samuel and Mary Kate's son Mikey, who is to be placed by racially concerned whites into an exclusive private school in Buffalo. Samuel has been shown as choosing to separate from the South in order to eat at Dulski's, but he cannot fully separate from his race or his class. Now the dominant rhetoric suggests his son should want to do both. The middle-class myth of upward mobility thus remains Porter's main rhetorical focus, even though Samuel's racial experience has already partially subverted it. Indeed, what Porter reveals is the degree to which Samuel himself revivifies the myth through his son Mikey, the mid-century, middle-class embodiment of separation from family, race, and class in pursuit of mobility up the educational—and by implication class—ladder. The ensuing paradox of self-erasure through self-making is enacted through the same Lacanian action that Carnegie positively uses to demonstrate his rise—language or, more specifically, acquisition of the prestige dialect. Carnegie knows that to be really self-made he must control his language, and Mikey knows that too. Mikey begins to "talk . . . white" (177), "juggling" the "eggs" of his language, in his teacher's analogy (176). If his sisters tease him about his speech, his parents do not. They have become "proud of the way he spoke. He was smart and getting smarter, sounding smarter" (177). In this worker-oriented enactment of the middle-class myth, Mikey's ability to juggle his linguistic eggs signals a supposedly fuller form of masculine self-making than Samuel's literal eggs, enjoyed in the midst of ostensible brotherhood at Dulski's, ever could.

As Mikey begins his willing separation from family, then, he enacts upward mobility by proxy for his parents, Samuel and Mary Kate. But Porter suggests that something else comes with Mikey's ability to juggle language's eggs. Samuel may caution Mikey that "with all you [sic] education you still going to be a black man in a white man's world," but Michael is only half listening. "His attention was focused not on what his father said, but the way he said it. He had dropped all his eggs." As doxic self-making kicks in, Mikey sees in his father an oedipal target, a father who cannot and—in yet another terrible internalization of *doxa*— should not get any higher than the false camaraderie of Dulski's. He has become "a stupid man who did not even know how to speak. He was a man with yolk dripping from his chin" (179).[24] With this painful, negative reprise of the novel's opening dining scene, Porter hammers home an ugly plethora of race-, class-, and gender-based restrictions, victories, and defeats that lie quietly within the dominant rhetoric. What Porter has zeroed in on is that same emotional storm we recognize in Carnegie's infantilization of and intentional separation from his father. Carnegie announces it as a mark of positive advancement, of course, thereby endorsing the underlying oedipal fantasy of defeating the father that is regularly maintained by masculine *doxa* and its myth of success. Porter, however, is more interested in the price charged by the myth than in its reward. Her subversive rhetoric insists that Mikey replace the surface brotherhood of Dulski's diner with a direct enactment of the full fantasy of oedipal betrayal and defeat of the father—and the ugly aggression buried within.

Added to that troubling revelation is the final separation that Mikey fails to hear his father discussing—the separation from race. While Samuel argues that society will not overlook race, his own doxic rhetoric claims that everyone must do so—including Mikey—since the dominant myth of self-making requires race's absence as a restrictive force. In Porter's reprise of racialized self-making, at the age of nine Mikey becomes "an ambassador and an example of what was good and right and white about black people" (180). Whiteness supposedly is not a color, of course, but the neutral norm, the ultimate acquisition for anyone not yet so universalized. Samuel may recognize the falsity of that claim, yet he himself paradoxically speaks the dominant myth's rhetoric by encouraging Mikey in his masculine self-making and upward mobility. He tells Mikey that his blackness will never disappear but also insists on the effort of self-making: "[W]hen you get your ass run ragged, I want you to get some rest, and get on up and try again" (183). As with Big Mat's struggles or Invisible Man's "Keep This Nigger-Boy Running," such effort requires a goal and a sense of reward. In Mikey's world, both are attached directly to the value of whiteness.

Having established this racially valued rhetoric, when Samuel suggests that "I think you forget you black," Porter has Mikey counter with the full logic behind Samuel's myth of middle-class self-making. "Well sometimes I want to forget," he declares. "You want me to dream, and you want me to know my place. That doesn't make sense. It's a contradiction" (184). It is indeed, because the inherently contradictory *doxa* of open-ended, effort-based, masculine self-making refuses to acknowledge any restrictions on the "place" that you can occupy. The rhetoric of self-making not only accommodates but also actively maintains masculine self-making as a degree of separation that ostensibly erases race and class even as it offers them as a gauge of how far one has gone, how large the separations have become.[25] Caught up in these contradictions, Mikey eventually becomes lost in the "nebulous, cold whiteness" of a blizzard. Unable to complete his personal self-making, Mikey is saved by his father, but his salvation is an ambiguous one. In the novel's closing lines, language again enters, as Mikey can no longer hear the words his father says to him. Instead, the wind reaches "into his father's mouth, snatching his words away, sending them flying into oblivion" (224). The novel ends at this point, with Samuel's and Mikey's masculine status unresolved, but with the basic paradox still present; masculine self-making in a racial climate requires a particularly troubling form of masochistic self-erasure.

With self-making and its rhetoric left wide open, it doesn't take much of a stretch of imagination to see many of Wideman's contemporary characters as older versions of Porter's Mikey. All the key appeals or tropes are enacted: separation as a function of advancement out of and away from class and family, the resulting conflicts between individual self-making and communal support and responsibility, the threatening feminization that is coupled to such dependency and support, sadomasochistic tendencies within both the myth and masculinity as a whole, and the attempt to address these concerns through the larger narrative of struggle with the authority of men. But as the opening epigraph of this chapter suggests, Wideman's enactments of these issues all echo his ultimate concern: the paradoxical self-erasure that occurs when the rhetoric of self-making produces "psychological separation from blackness" (Coleman 80). To engage the rhetoric fully, he delves even further into the psychocultural dynamics of masculinity.

Wideman's attempts to pursue the paradox of "unmanning" through masculine self-making are what give rise to figures like Reuben, the title character in a novel from roughly the middle period of Wideman's work (*Reuben* 1987). As a latter-day Paul Van Beaver, Reuben works to solve the legal problems of the poor and working-class members of Homewood. He also does so, like Mikey, with contemporary awareness of the power of language to control, believing as he does that unless he and his clients "started fresh" in the telling of their troubles, "they'd be caught up in one fiction or another, and that fiction would have nothing to do with where they needed to go" (17). Initially, then, Reuben's basic grasp of the phallic symbolic seems to produce power, a reading endorsed by James Coleman, who sees in Reuben "an activist in the black community" whose "fictions allow him to create illusions of progress, change, and movement over time in the black community and thus to help the community" (118).

But Reuben's power, like his status within the masculine myth of chosen separation and return, may not be as dominant as it appears. Wideman also presents Reuben as partially crippled (physically and, by implication, racially and psychologically). More directly, Reuben is himself at the mercy of institutions and their larger storytelling power. He too is arrested when it appears that he has no legal degree and hence no legal right to dispense the advice he provides. Just as the workingman's rhetoric of Tucker was trumped by that of greater economic power, Reuben's individual storytelling is no match for that of institutional rhetoric. With this qualifier to his power in mind, Doreatha Mbalia finds Reuben, Coleman, and Wideman himself to be oddly positive about the extent of Reuben's personal rhetorical strengths: "It is as if Wideman believes the intellectual has the power—an abracadabra power—to create reality. It is puzzling then that Coleman does not see anything awry with this perspective . . ." (93–94).

These varied reactions underscore the conflicted appeal to masculinity that a figure like Reuben enacts whenever the larger doxic structure of masculine self-making is tested, here again by class and racial as well as gender concerns. Key to the *doxa* of masculinity and especially the myth of self-making is the ability to act, and thus control both self and others—whether the ability results from the physical power of a Locke, French, or Tucker, or be it via the verbal prowess of a Carnegie or Van Beaver, a Mikey or Reuben. For his part, Reuben is likely to be read positively if his intellectual approach is itself seen as active and decisive, successful in a world outside—and often represented as hostile to—the frame of his own subjectivity. On the other hand, Reuben will be read negatively if seen as overly intellectual, a college-bred Mikey in opposition to the active, authentic masculinity of a Tommy. In short, Reuben serves as a lightening rod for tensions concerning the necessity for agency in any performance of masculine self-making.[26]

Having raised that ongoing doxic anxiety, Wideman pursues it deep into the realm of the psychocultural, specifically the issue of male sadomasochism. The novel's most specific enactment of these issues occurs in Reuben's complex enactment of another family romance, which mixes preoedipal connection with oedipal aggression and racial domination, all within the rhetoric of masculine self-making. The narrative begins in Philadelphia, where Reuben, while acquiring his legal expertise, has become janitor/mascot/pimp for a group of fraternity boys, leading them on regular sexual excursions to the house of Flora, a black woman who employs her former lover, Dudley Armstrong, as a pianist. Eventually, the frat boys "buy" Flora for a night and present her to Reuben, but only as a ploy. Bursting into Flora and Reuben's room, the frat brothers beat up Reuben for usurping their rights, tie Flora to the bed, and begin a serial rape that only halts when the building burns down around all of them. Reuben escapes by jumping from the second-story window. But unlike James Davis and his consequence-free leap away from his anti-reading buddies, Reuben must be "scraped . . . off the sidewalk" and is hospitalized with the severe injuries that cripple him.

This part of the tale obviously enacts a range of issues for masculinity. But it is the reaction of Reuben's friend Wally that provides a final, key element—the call for action and violence. "Didn't you want revenge?," Wally asks. "Shit, Reuben. The woman was dead. . . . You owed her" (91–92). Reuben, on the other hand, insists that the story he has told is about his love for Flora and notes that the frat house did burn down later. That is enough revenge, were it even the point of the story. Unfortunately for his own masculinity, Reuben is arguing for behavior that is in direct conflict with the dominant rhetoric of masculine action, and action in defense of a woman, no less. Wideman is interested in this dynamic, but he moves beyond it so as to use the tale and reaction to it as a way to engage ongoing, masculine anxieties over agency and dependency, sadism and masochism. He does so, moreover, by again tying these concerns directly to the dominant rhetoric of self-making and identity, doing so through the third male, Dudley Armstrong, in *Reuben*'s primary sexual triangle.[27]

I noted above that Flora's former lover, Armstrong, had been relegated to piano player in her house, a double marker of his failure as a self-made man. "Conservatory trained," a man with "a career, a future," he can no longer finish a piece, because in doing so he would be "reminded of his talents, what he'd dreamed of accomplishing and should be doing now instead of providing musical accompaniment to the humping and grinding going on overhead" (73–74). This linkage of Armstrong's failed self-making to his relegation from Flora's lover to that of musical accompaniment to her sexual use by others completes his masochistic portrait. Having connected these sadomasochistic concerns to the rhetoric of self-making, Wideman adds race, underscoring its presence through the dominance of Reuben and Dudley by the white frat boys, and Flora's current refusal to sleep with any black man.

It is this combination of racial and masculine disempowerment that forms the basis for the family romance that Wideman is about to enact through Flora, her former lover Armstrong, and young Reuben. At this point in the plot, Reuben is still attempting to acquire the same legal skills that his white tormentors are blithely assuming as their right. The hope that drives this ongoing pursuit puts him at odds with the older Armstrong, who must admit to Reuben that "I don't think I'll make it" (76). But what solidifies the oedipal opposition is Reuben's opportunity to make it with Flora, who has altered her rule of not sleeping with black men for Reuben alone, declaring that she would have done so even had the frat boys not paid her. Reuben's role as sexual replacement for Flora's former lover is reinforced, again in connection with self-making, by Flora herself. Telling Armstrong that "he can't do like a man" anymore, even though she has tried to support him in his musical pursuit, she lets him know that that is "precisely why" she takes Reuben upstairs with her. To this rhetoric of oedipal victory, Wideman further adds the preoedipal, as Flora admits to Reuben that "maybe at first I wanted to be your mama" (82). Finally, the full linkage of oedipal victory and self-making appears as Flora again compares Armstrong's failed plans for self-making with those of Reuben. In response, Reuben affirms that he does "have plans. Dreams. Bucketsful. Some days I believe I'll make it" (83). Reuben will not make it with Flora, however. In a last-ditch defense of his authority and agency, Armstrong torches the house. It is a perverse reinscription of his masochistic position, however, resulting only in his and Flora's deaths and Reuben's injuries, while their tormentors escape.

It is through such complex enactments of the rhetoric of masculine self-making that Wideman engages the full sadomasochism of the myth, its general contradictions, and the particular involvement of race. Restrictions on the dominant rhetoric of masculine self-making can lead simply to louder insistence upon one's separation from feminine dependency. But Wideman uses such restraints to consider similarities between forced dependency, racial restriction, and the gender controls and training inherent in the *doxa* of masculinity. It is a dynamic clearly at work in "Picking Up My Father at the Springfield Station," a direct consideration of father/son interaction that significantly begins not with the reunion of the title but with yet another masculine separation: "For some absurd set of reasons my father was left behind. . . . Left behind, the image of powerlessness, alone, broke, stuck in Pittsburgh" ("Picking" 129). The rest of the story, and the book as a whole, mirrors the attempt to heal that separation and, perhaps, to reinstate the father to a position of stature. That reinstatement is uncertain, however, because like Carnegie's tale of meeting his traveling father, these exchanges are deeply colored by oedipal overtones common to the dominant rhetoric of masculine self-making, with college-educated, university-employed, self-made son greeting not a patriarch but a father on the downslide.[28]

That hierarchy is already active as the narrator arrives at the Springfield train station, a "cave in a hillside. Bad light, bad air, the weight of tracks, trains, earth, sky pressing down." It isn't the outside of a canal boat, such as Carnegie's father is forced to ride. It is, in fact, worse, and

Wideman links its economic signals to racial ones. "Train stations," he argues, are like "bus stations, the servants' entrance, where you were supposed to slip in and do your grubby business without disturbing the folks moving about in clean, well-lit rooms of the big house" (157–58). Such scenes reinforce the sense of Wideman's father as impoverished—in terms of race, money, power, and control—and they recast somewhat the narrator's earlier "appropriately" postoedipal sense of "My good home and bed and wife asleep in it. My son's wedding to share with my father. Daddy my guest now" (166). The dominance suggested by "guest" almost seems like overkill, given each man's position.

To complete the full oedipal rhetoric and its tense negotiation of aggression and dominance, Wideman now adds the sexual. With his father's train still to arrive, Wideman decides to go next door to a strip bar, well aware of its overtones of ostensible scopophilic agency. As so often happens, however, Wideman's rhetoric is alert as well to the masochism lurking in such forms of control: "A little thinly disguised self-destruction, descent into the pit, mud-wrestling . . . rubbing your nose in mud because your nose enjoyed rooting around in the briar patch . . ." (160). He is alert as well to the situation's sadism and its regular partner, racism, both "inseparable, finally, from gender politics. How many steps from the stage of the [bar] to the auction block?" (162). With all this in mind, Wideman catches the end of the floor show, as a dancer "crawls on hands and knees to harvest the money in her plexiglass cage":

> Our eyes meet. A smile appears, this time directed at me. She shifts closer to where my hand rests, dangling two dollar bills over the metal-edged wall. I don't know if she intended to brush her skin against my skin or what part of her body she would have allowed to make contact with mine nor how long she might have sustained this intimacy, because the bill-collector bouncer taps me on the shoulder. Huh-uh. That ain't allowed. Stand back, he says. I do. (165–66)

This scene, appearing as it does between Wideman's arrival at the train station and the incipient arrival of the abandoned, failed father finalizes the complex sadomasochistic amalgam that makes up the oedipal rhetoric of masculine self-making; the son has made it, the father has not, there is a reunion of sorts, and it occurs over the sexualized body of a woman desired, met, and then linked to neither, since it "ain't allowed."[29]

It is this scene in the bar that is perhaps most confusing and most important, since it is a blend of connection with and denial of the feminine, followed by nostalgic reunion with the father. Who or what denies the connection (white dominance, personal morality, the woman herself) is left ambiguous. But with the possibilities rhetorically repressed, separation from the father as a key "wound" (in the rhetoric of at least one part of the men's movement) can be reinstated as the focus of the concern.[30] By book's end, the father has missed the wedding yet again, reinforcing a separation and absence that Wideman engages once more through the rhetoric of connection with women. Speaking after the ceremony, the mothers "shared their enormous strength and dignity. Two mothers, mothers of mothers, themselves daughters, they took us backward and forward, connected us to what we once were, might become, would never be again . . ." (172). Wideman reveres this power, granting it special weight in a world of absent fathers. His mother, he has noted earlier, was simply "there." "She was always there. With me. If she had disappeared, no *there* would exist. My world began and ended with her presence" (*Fatheralong* 84).

It is ostensibly the felt wound of the missing father that motivates these visions, but that sense of separation is inextricably connected to—and likewise motivates—the rhetoric of willed separation from the feminine. That connection is clarified as Wideman defines his relationship to his mother through his ability to leave her, noting a feeling of "closeness and intimacy" that he also describes as "the opposite of oppressive, since her presence freed me, helped me grow and expand" (84). Having provided the necessary rhetoric of development through separation from closeness and intimacy, Wideman now supplants that preoedipal loss with a male/male oedipal separation, here taken to the realm of an imagined death: "My father stuck somewhere losing this moment was lost to me. I mourned him. A sudden grief so strong it would have shut out the wonder of my son's wedding if I hadn't been able to call upon my father, retrieve the part of him inside myself that could bow, scatter a handful of dust, turn and walk away from the yawning grave" (84). Wideman's rhetoric thus continues to underscore the trauma/conundrum of masculine self-making—the required/desired separation from the feminine, its replacement by the fantasied oedipal defeat/death of the father, the resulting "success" that paradoxically leaves the performance of correct masculinity with a sense of nonclosure, nostalgia, and guilt.

What Wideman so fully enacts, then, are the processes by which the cultural rhetoric assimilates and overrides anxieties basic to doxic masculinity as it insists on emphasizing oedipal exchanges as the heart of masculinity. It is a dynamic Wideman again makes evident in a vignette reminiscent of the winter storm that ends Porter's *All-Bright Court*. Having come home to visit family in Homewood at Christmas, the narrator of "Welcome" goes out into "this arctic-ass weather" (141) to pick up dinner. As he drives out, he stops at a street light and spots a father and small child on the corner. Like Reuben, the narrator creates a fiction to provide these two—and himself—with a reality. The first fiction enacts a rhetoric of separation and failed self-making with the young, in all likelihood regularly absent father "returning the boy to his mother, or her mother or his and this is the only way, the best he can do and the wind howls the night gets blacker and blacker. . . . [T]hey'll find the two of them, father son man and boy frozen to death . . ." ("Welcome" 141). This is the negative myth, the collapse of the "father son man and boy" rhetoric of masculine separation, agency, and self-making into a nightmare myth of forced separation, loss, and the failure of both fathering and mothering.

But on the return from his trip to buy food, the narrator provides a different rhetoric, as he decides, "Fuck it. They'll make it. Or if they don't somebody else will come along and try. . . . And that's why Homewood's here, because lots of us won't make it but others will try and keep on keeping on" (141). It is a startling reversal. Here the rhetoric of post-oedipal success and paternal lineage is operating fully, as son and father move beyond the failure of the first story, beyond the missing mother, beyond the economic collapse of Pittsburgh's ghettos, beyond even the ambiguity of Porter's closing snowstorm, and into the realm of pure effort and struggle. Were the story to end there, it would not only be a startling reversal but also a startlingly sentimental linkage of the dominant myth of masculine self-making and the African American call to "keep on keeping on." The story is not over yet, however. Something has happened between these two versions, and Wideman fills in that gap in the plot as he provides a third and final paragraph to end the story. In what might be an equally sentimental moment, the narrator describes listening to a young black girl, "a large pretty big-eyed brown girl thirteen or fourteen with black crinkly hair and smooth kind of round chubby cheek babydoll face" singing some Christmas songs "in the sweetest, purest, trilling soprano" (141–42). Hearing this music he begins to cry, and still riding on the emotion of the moment, he passes the father and son a second time and rewrites their story, providing the upbeat second version.

There are a number of ways to read this "explanation." It is, perhaps, another form of sentimentalism, one made a bit more magical by the contrast between the "iron bars . . . on the counter" at the store and the singer's "little riffs in another language of something for this time of year, something old like Bach with Christ's name in it" (142). It is possible to choose, as is often done with Christmas tales, to endorse the sentimentalism as a valid appeal to community, to the feminine, and to the need to strive to succeed, father and son, man and woman. Yet Wideman *still* hasn't ended the story. In the closing lines, the tale uncovers the ultimate motive behind the tears and the embrace of struggle and the myth of self-making, a motive that is deeply masculine in its rhetoric not of community and mutual support but of yet another separation. "I'm no crier, Sis," the narrator declares. "You know me. But I couldn't stop all the way home till I saw those two on the corner again and know how much I was missing Will and then I had to cry some more" (142).

As the story makes clear, Will is the "lost [imprisoned] son" of the narrator's brother (138), named for their father "who shaved every morning and sang, too. Crooned gospel songs and love songs before he deserted us" (138). The second story's endorsement of the rhetoric of self-making is thus a direct function of this last intervening emotional moment, a moment that is finally rooted not in a sense of connection with the larger Homewood community but in a sense of loss and separation. Moreover, *that* emotion is itself not ultimately motivated by the singing of the young girl but by its connection with the singing of the father. What the close of the story does then is perform the necessary rhetorical move required by masculine *doxa*, displacing any preoedipal linkage to the supportive community or the female singer with the pain of a separation firmly rooted in an oedipal distancing of father and son.

This is, of course, the basic whipsaw-tension within the dominant myth of masculine self-making. Preoedipal overtones of mutuality and connection, especially as attached to the feminine, are introduced then quickly replaced with a rhetoric of oedipal loss. That loss is itself sanitized by enacting it not through a separation resulting from direct oedipal struggle between father and son, with victory going to the father, but rather through a more emotionally ambiguous separation. This weakened separation removes the issue of direct oedipal aggression and victory/defeat, thus smoothing the way for the fictional reinscription of a father and son union, however temporary, itself finally colored by the rhetoric of self-making. In short, suggestions of a negative, preoedipal separation from the feminine are finally rewritten as the myth of a positive *masculine* struggle, sometimes between father and son, but mainly in terms of manly performance in the larger world.

It is a sequence that runs through myriad variations on the rhetoric of masculinity and self-making, a sequence further complicated by the contradictions that race introduces in the dominant, ostensibly race-blind myth. As Wideman says in only mock exasperation:

> A motherfucker, ain't it, this Daddy search. Looking for a
> father under every brick or rock or coal pile and me signify-
> ing such a search is the very brick-and-rock foundation of
> various political philosophies, survival strategies from inte-
> gration to separation to burn-baby-burn incineration to self-

> annihilation and starting all over again. Maybe the search for
> father is finally only a trope, a ropa-dope trope containing
> enough rope to hang you up terminally you black bastard.
> (*Fatheralong* 77)

As Wideman's exasperation makes clear, he never writes solely from the
perspective of the privileged, dominant masculine, and full enactment
of the doxic rhetoric is thus always further complicated racially and
psychically—and quite likely already foreclosed—for many of his characters.[31] But his rhetoric also demonstrates that recognition of the myth's
self-contradictory exclusions may only feed the doxic need to prove the
general applicability of its arguments. Stated in terms of the next chapter, masculine self-making—like the steel industry itself—continuously
produces the specter of its own defeat only to initiate its own "resurrection," thus insisting upon the validity of its prophecy of real masculinity for those capable of enacting the myth.

7

Making New Metal from Old: Retooling the Self-Made Man

Big Dave Thompson was six feet four inches tall and he appeared to be several feet wide, but he wasn't fat; he had the marbling of the hot metal man, although the intellectual appearance of his spectacles seemed to contradict the power of his frame. He had been an offensive tackle on his college football team, and he had a master's degree in industrial safety. . . .

"Maybe I have the feeling of the Americans to be a bit . . . what is the word?" The [German] engineer touched his forehead, as if trying to pluck an English word from it. "*Pioneers* is the word," he said. "They are pioneers. You know what I mean. You must look at them. You see? You see these guys with their wagons and their pistols, going to the Wild West."

—Richard Preston, *American Steel: Hot Metal Men and the Resurrection of the Rust Belt*

This is wide, broad-shouldered America, where there is always someplace else for people abandoned by their livelihood. Are you an unemployed steelworker in the Mon Valley? Well, move on, brother! The first hill is the hardest one to cross. After that, the opportunities are limitless . . . Texas, Arizona, or anyplace from here to there where McDonald's needs someone to serve the one-trillionth burger.

—John Hoerr, And the Wolf Finally Came

FOR AFRICAN AMERICAN STEELWORKERS, THE PURSUIT OF self-making in the latter half of the twentieth century is marked by increasing job availability in the mills, and—for many if not most—continuing contradictions between personal experience and the dominant myth of self-making. For many others, most notably ethnic white unionists and management, these years open with multiple successes only to be followed by disaster—the pre– and post–World War II years of a relatively stable industry; the rise, triumph, and later weakening of the AFL-CIO, SWOC, and USW;[1] and, finally, the decline and, in many areas, collapse of both the steel industry and labor's power within it. By the end of the twentieth century, mythic arguments connected with steel have been badly battered, while the shock to a premier industry in the United States reverberates in economic uncertainties that echo throughout the last quarter of the century. Yet the rhetoric of masculine self-making remains strong within *doxa*, maintained mainly by the culture's determined adherence to the myth and some effective retooling of its arguments.

Numerous examples of the myth attest to its effectiveness and popularity, with none as well known—and as lavishly and unabashedly embellished with the contradictions, conflicts, and processes of self-made masculinity—as Lee Iacocca's self-portraits in *Iacocca* and *Talking Straight*—the former so popular that in 1983 it made the top-ten reading list of college students (*Chronicle* April 1998: B7).[2] Not surprisingly, given the uncertainties of the period, one of the key elements of this reworked self-making is its call to anti-institutionalism, to a rejection of the status quo and the flabby, bureaucratic, nonmasculinity embodied in the aging fathers and the corporate powers-that-be. Lately it has even fostered a renewed voice of self-making in a reworked rhetoric of steel. From presidents of upstart steel corporations (like Nucor's Ken Iverson) to self-proclaimed voices of the working man (like former steelworker turned *Chicago Tribune* journalist Michael Lavelle), renewed emphasis on anti-institutionalism revivifies the rhetoric of self-making.

These are not new arguments, of course, and there is real irony in the motif's usage by and about individuals who are deeply a part of, and indeed deeply dependent upon, the very institutional frames that they decry. At the heart of this renewed middle-class rhetoric, then, there is a related renewal of the desire to emphasize the positives of authentic masculinity so as to offset concerns over the negatives of institutional masculinity.[3] Here, once basic masculinity is established through anti-institutionalism, authentic masculinity is regularly enacted through two related motifs that I have discussed before: (1) the unbridled power of verbal self-making and (2) uncontested freedom of workplace craft and creativity, a form of productive power that translates masculine effort into self-making. Both motifs enact a particular agency, a control over acts of making—of self and of one's products.[4]

But the middle-class myth often lacks a sufficient act of creation or production with which to enact the second motif. Symptoms of that lack may be found in bombast, in overvaluation or overreliance upon an authenticity established through the first motif of verbal facility and self-display. Davis's swaggering performances provide an earlier example on the comedic side. But self-parody is not often an intentional component of autobiographical self-making. It is more common to see the dominant myth replace the appeal to direct workplace creativity with the self-maker's taking of risks. Such risks are then presented as the ostensible driving force behind the workplace productivity of others.

Not surprisingly, labor-based visions of workplace productivity and the nature of its driving forces often provide a different rhetoric and a more qualified masculinity—even as they echo various aspects of the dominant rhetoric. Works organized around labor's point of view, such as Michael Frisch and Milton Rogovin's *Portraits in Steel,* readily display conflicts between the middle-class myth and end-of-the-century shop floor experience. The same tensions are visible in Lavelle's *Red, White and Blue-Collar Views: A Steelworker Speaks His Mind about America,* which rejects middle-class self-making even as it speaks the rhetoric of anti-institutionalism and verbal prowess. Ultimately, however, it is Richard Preston's *American Steel: Hot Metal Men and the Resurrection of the Rust Belt* that is most fully committed to, and thus most fully enacts, the complex appeals and anxieties of the dominant myth.

Struggling to unite middle-class and working-class versions of masculine self-making, the ultimate enactment of a renewed rhetoric of steel bursts forth in *American Steel,* with its emphasis on entrepreneurial and physical risk. Economic risk embraces the dangerous making of steel itself, as entrepreneurial self-making is forged in the construction of a continuous-process, steel minimill using technology sought after but unachieved since Bessemer's first blast furnace. Ultimately, masculine self-making unites with the doxic overtones of questing in Preston's text. His hot metal men are out to slay fire-breathing furnaces as well as economic realities. Preston's text thus closes the rhetorical circle begun by nineteenth-century, working-class men who embodied their values in the neoaristocratic code of Knights of Labor.

The rhetoric of Preston's contemporary, middle-class questers renews and embraces rather dated working-class motifs as these self-declared hot metal men attempt to avoid becoming twentieth-century bureaucrats and middle-class middle-managers. Echoing and uniting the traditional elements of masculine self-making, then, is a particular dynamic that colors as a whole the mythic rhetoric—a call for movement into the future that paradoxically is underwritten by nostalgia for the past, a nostalgia enhanced by the need to offset an end-of-the-century threat to U.S. industrial dominance and the masculinity it underpins through a renewed vision of economic power, creativity, and masculine agency. In short, twentieth-century, and especially late-twentieth-century, tensions and concerns over adequate masculinity reinforce the desire and need to go back to the past so as to retool the future of the myth of masculinity and its forms of work.

Anti-institutionalism

Discussing nineteenth-century male writers and their diminishing sense of power and place, Leverenz describes their attempt to enact a viable masculinity within a narrative stance. A general "lurking competitiveness reappears," he tells us, "in the flights of self-refashioning, reinscribing the tensions of manhood" (18). Such an "I/you" rivalry, which extends to writer and reader, is regularly enacted in contemporary rhetoric not only through man-to-man competition but also by projecting the nonmanly or feminine onto the corporation, the boss, or company men and underlings. Sue Miller's patriarch displays the process nicely. For his part, David demonstrates that the degree of corporate presence and power at the end of the twentieth century makes it difficult to maintain an identity outside the corporate frame. It is a difficulty that can be manifested even when the company to be projected as the nonmasculine Other happens to be run by you. Given this situation, and its incipient threat to doxic masculinity's claims to individualism, the rhetoric of masculinity as aggressive separation from and battle with institutions appears constantly—and paradoxically—in middle-class representations of workplace self-making at the close of the century. An increasingly popular version of the motif is the self in opposition to others who are more clearly corporate types, a self in opposition to others and their institutions, which together embody the status quo, the established, the—it need hardly be said—values of the father. The question is not where to find such defensive enactments but where to begin.

In *Iacocca*'s case, for example, the anti-institutional motif is enacted initially as the individual salesman versus the corporate body, the power of "real-world," youthful questing versus the office and its patriarchal domination. "Eventually I got out from behind the telephone," Iacocca declares. "I went from the desk to the field. . . . Finally I was out of school and into the real world. . . . It's the dealers who have always been the guts of the car business in this country. . . . [T]hey're really the quintessential American entrepreneurs" (35).[5] This appeal to individual and "real" versus institutional and false can be sounded from within management as well, where it is possible to define oneself against the corporate status quo in other ways, such as playing the final arbiter in a world of committees and pencil pushers: "To a certain extent," Iacocca repeats, I "always operated by gut feeling. I like to be in the trenches. I was never one of those guys who could just sit around and strategize endlessly" (*Iacocca* 55). As was true with Davis, masculinity equals the "real," and the real is the visceral.

This rhetoric enacts the twentieth-century's typical, self-made individual fighting the trammeling institution, albeit doing so in this case as the president of one of the world's larger corporations. *Iacocca's* appeal to masculinity rests in a blend of aggressiveness and separation or, said differently, in aggressive separation from the anxieties of corporate controls and institutional determinism. Richard Preston has listened to that rhetoric, and his *American Steel: Hot Metal Men and the Resurrection of the Rust Belt* engages it in one of the more intricate representations of steelmaking, steelmakers, and masculine self-making from the postcollapse era of Big Steel. Preston's title provides only a few of the components—nationalism, craft ethos, masculine power, and a form of economic revitalization—that he uses in his appeal to a revised yet still traditional masculinity. These motifs are familiar from any number of texts, although the last aspect, the "Resurrection" of the title, points to a major theme and a major tension to be addressed. As the term implies, Preston appeals heavily in his narrative to the renewal and rebirth of the steel industry, doing so by linking contemporary steelmaking not only to its immediate but also to its long-term past.

While a rising tide may raise all boats, Preston's resurrection is essentially an entrepreneurial rising, and his portraits are of upper- and middle-level managers. From the outset, then, Preston's book emphasizes the dominant, middle-class myth of self-making. At the same time, his narrative also demonstrates a desire to mask any split between laboring and middle-class visions. The key players in this narrative are not institutional managers and working-class drones but individual "hot metal men," "Run-a-Muckers" who embody an All-American desire for playful aggression. Inevitably, appeals to the masculine *doxa* of separation, individuality, and self-formation appear, mixed with backward glances to another, mythic time in U.S. history. Thus, when Preston wishes to characterize the masculine risk taking of his steelworkers (as he does in this chapter's opening epigraph), he brings forward an all-American motif— the Old West—to serve as dramatic background for the risk taking of his self-makers. But the German engineer who voices the connection may not just have trouble translating. Preston's vignette also suggests the engineer's concern with the behavior he sees, and he may be pointing to his head to signal something that Preston chooses to miss—that these pioneers act like crazy boys sometimes, even though they possess college degrees. No matter, the appeal remains—crossing not only class borders or the western plains but national borders as well. Preston's myth of self-making and *Iacocca's* hero are now the visionary base of business schools in the former Soviet Union.[6]

It is precisely this reach of the myth and its desires that make end-of-the-century texts like Preston's so intriguing. Using snapshot anecdotes and vignettes, Preston quickly attempts to establish "Big Steel" as lethargic and incapable of functioning like Nucor, a small, innovative steel company with a board of authentic, entrepreneurial self-makers and hot metal men busily at work building a new steel mill. The ensuing rhetoric of manly difference and noninstitutionality is one of Preston's favorite tropes. Ken Iverson, the chairman and CEO of Nucor, is "something of a cult figure in the international steel industry," Preston argues. "Executives in the American steel industry—at the so-called Big Steel Companies, like the USX Corporation and the Bethlehem Steel Corporation—often asked themselves a similar question—what in hell is Iverson doing now?—and it drove them crazy just to think about it" (*American Steel* 7). David Aycock, who started out as a welder and became Nucor's president and chief operating officer, grows up "on a farm in Anson County, South Carolina, where his father raised cotton on twenty-five acres, plowing the land with mules" (85). Sam Siegel quits his job when Nucor's previous corporate structure ("basically a *schlock* company" [64]) fails. A true self-maker, Siegel agrees to return if the board will hire Iverson to form the new company (68). Renegades all, these three men operate out of rented office space in the Cotswald Building in Charlotte, North Carolina, "a four-story cube of buff bricks, glazed the color of dried vomit" (4). "Most of the company's important decisions," Preston delights in stating, are made at Phil's Deli, in the Cotswald Shopping Center across the street (91). The rhetorical equation is apparent: I/you separation plus rejection of institutional dependency adds up to true, self-made masculinity on a quest to control the power of steel.

Preston furthers this appeal to anti-institutionalism by presenting the men involved in the mill's construction (the heart of the narrative of *American Steel*) as mavericks and renegades, cowboys, hard-drinking "Run-a-Muckers"—only later clarifying them as psychologically tested, carefully selected shop managers. Keith Busse, vice president and manager of the minimill project in Crawfordsville, Indiana, is introduced as "The Marshall and a Few of His Boys" in a chapter of that title (14–22). Mark Millet, twenty-eight years old and the eventual head of the melt shop, is an ex-ski bum and resort cook (18). Will Hawley "had a construction business and a gun shop" in Colorado, until the housing market collapsed and he returned home to Indiana looking for work (46).

To these characterizations of rogue workers Preston adds a note of outsider free play on a grand, and grandly rule-free, scale. "When they weren't pickling their minds in [drinks called] Nucors made of Scotch and gin," Preston declares, "the Run-a-Muckers spent a lot of time reading construction magazines, hoping to learn valuable tips. They were trying to figure out how to build a steel mill" (49). Preston engages such rhetoric to establish a composite myth that blends masculine individuality, youthful aggression, and anticorporate license. He then underscores the argument by making Nucor itself separate from and independent of the confines and mores of Big Steel, the latter firmly personified through-out as a collection of office bound, out of touch suits—clearly nonmas-culine. Big Steel's executives are "on the golf courses in Bermuda and at the private hunting lodges in Canada"; Nucor's men are in bars, gun shops, and on the job site (80).

These last characterizations rely heavily on a negative rhetoric that defines upper class as inherently inside, established, weakly paternal, deeply nonmasculine. Not surprisingly, then, Preston only casually men-tions that many of Nucor's men also have college training—bachelor's and master's degrees in metallurgy, mechanical engineering, industrial safety, business administration. There is good reason to avoid dwelling on that background, of course. For one thing, there is the long-stand-ing tradition of equating higher education with effeminacy. Moreover, the academic world itself provides an institutional frame that is a use-ful target for anti-institutionalism and one not to be wasted.

Iacocca clarifies the argument's usefulness for setting up the correctly masculine role of outside insider. Alert to college experience as a source for class-based attacks on both elitism and institutional dependency, *Iacocca* plays the card well. "In addition to the Whiz Kids," Iacocca notes, "Henry Ford II hired dozens of Harvard Business School gradu-ates. Those of us in sales, product planning, and marketing thought of the financial planners as longhairs—men with M.B.A.s who formed an elitist group within the company" (45). Iacocca's own B.S. in Engineer-ing from Lehigh University is, of course, neatly buried beneath this dual, negative appeal that denounces both excessive theorizing and class elit-ism as embodied in Ivy League schools.[7]

Not all arguments for self-making are so well done, and the failures reinforce tensions that the doxic myth is designed to mask. Where Preston insists upon separation from flabby institutions and CEOs, and Iacocca offers a subtle byplay between institutional insider and outsider, Victor Kiam tends to display no ambiguities at all, bombastically assert-ing an internal-warrior stance. Through his heavy-handed use of com-mon motifs in *Going for It! How to Succeed as an Entrepreneur* (1986)—the entrepreneurial autobiography and self-help guide he published not long after *Iacocca*—Kiam quickly reveals underlying conflicts between working- and middle-class self-making. His self-portrait eagerly char-acterizes corporate life as chest-thumping aggression, a theme readily available in chapter titles such as the nearly parodic "It's a Jungle in There: The Entrepreneur as Corporate Lion" (39).

The rhetoric is reminiscent of Davis's self-absorption and narcissism, but it is intriguing in its failure to sense the tone of privilege that it also expresses throughout. Where Preston and *Iacocca* subtly play the col-lege card, for example, Kiam rather blatantly produces a mixed blend of patrician and entrepreneur. Kiam begins his antieducational/anti-institutional argument adequately, although somewhat dangerously, with an offhand reference to graduation and a need for some time off. As he notes, "When I had gotten out of the navy in 1947, I returned to Yale and put in the final year I needed to graduate." Degree in hand, "I was in no mood to knock my brains out for work that didn't exist. I also needed a vacation" (120–21). More dangerously still, the subsequent discussion carries a tone of privileged insouciance. Kiam blithely hints at the perquisites of the leisure class in his description of some haphazard schooling at the Sorbonne and then Harvard's Business School (itself attacked in *Iacocca* as out of touch with the real world)—training achieved primarily thanks to an application written and mailed by his father (259). Kiam's self-declared separation from institutional strictures thus is rooted not in the rhetoric of hard experience but more in a near-decadent noninterest, a privileged massaging of elite institutions rather than the masculine struggle of opposition that the myth requires.

The impact on the rhetoric of masculinity is evident when anti-institutionalism is approached from the other side of the managerial/labor spectrum. Kiam may overlook or blithely dismiss middle-class insecurities about knowledge and educational institutions, but in *Red, White and Blue-Collar Views: A Steelworker Speaks His Mind about America,* Michael Lavelle uses his oppositional role to engage the rhetoric with a vengeance. As "real" anti-institutional outsider and blue-collar spokesman for steelworkers everywhere, Lavelle skewers intellectuals, college students, faculty, sociologists, and political scientists as isolated in their towers and "justifiably" attacks them on grounds of closed mindedness, ineffectualness, or selling out. Described within this frame, J. K. Galbraith (seen as critiquing affluence under the auspices of a Carnegie grant and trips to Switzerland) is contrasted with guys "at the corner bar." Huey Newton's "call for revolution" drifts down from "the proletarian environs of a penthouse." And college-ensconced faculty are forced by "a strange malaise" to attack Lavelle as "an invader from the boondocks unleashing a barrage of anti-intellectual Bunkerisms" (180–82).

In essence, male intellectuals are class phonies, weak-sister sellouts whose institutional dependency has divorced them from the real masculinity-engaging experiences they address and purportedly perform. To this attack, Lavelle adds a Davis-like note of feminization, arguing that intellectuals display "the frailty of their convictions" by their actions (180). Finally, Lavelle hammers home the ultimate rhetorical nail, noting that intellectuals who formerly were "obliged to look through the pragmatic eyes of the workingman" have since become "ensconced in corporations, universities, and publishing houses" (180). Middle-class intellectuals, and by implication intellectual knowledge and experience, are in thrall to the institutions that offer them a substitute (but ultimately dependent) power.

Yet for all its attacks on middle-class practices, Lavelle's vehemently anti-intellectual, anti-institutional rhetoric also displays ambivalence about both intellectuals and their institutions, especially the institution of higher education. Lavelle does not speak from Kiam's position of privilege, and while universities may have separated from the masculine pragmatism of workingmen, they can still serve as an arena for change. "The American Revolution," Lavelle also argues, "is still going on in bars, campuses, and union halls in spite of the intellectual elite's attempts to abort it" (181). In this quick claim, Lavelle both restates his insistence upon masculine experience ("bars") and reinstates the value of some institutions, notably college campuses and labor unions. But there remains an uneasiness in Lavelle's working-class rhetoric that suggests a doxic concern—that of agency, of who gets to declare what is authentic experience and what is not, who is in charge of one's life and who is not.

The importance of that agency to doxic masculinity is as apparent in its absence as in its endorsement. Nearly all the steelworkers in Michael Frisch and Milton Rogovin's *Portraits in Steel* who are asked about the future for their children make a traditional working-class link between getting an education and having work (97, 146, 264, 312, 315). Getting ahead, getting inside, getting a job speaks something very specific to people who faced the turmoil of Big Steel's collapse, here specifically in the Buffalo-area mills of Porter's *All-Bright Court*. In a culture that valorizes not simply self-control but self-making, job loss has deep identity consequences more powerful in the rhetoric of masculinity than anti-institutionalism. Urging attack in the face of that threat, one steelworker's wife, Lynn Cieslica, offers the full myth of self-making in capsule form:

> I think all of the wives, and the older children, we were all trying to encourage our men to get out there and find something else. This isn't the end of the world, you know, it's not Mr. Gloom and Doom, there are other things that you can do. In the beginning there was a big effort, all of us getting together and saying, "Look," you know, "You live in the United States. That door is open to anything that you want to do. (167)

But actual experience hardly matches the arguments provided by middle-class rhetoric, and Cieslica's next sentence brutally declares that "after a couple of years of pushing this, some of the wives just got tired of it. The husbands were just, 'That's what I wanted to do. I wanted to be a steelworker. I don't want to go back to school, wear a three piece suit . . .'" (167). Invocation of the middle-class myth and its self-making agency has been quickly met with the husband's unhappy denial of its rhetoric, ironically via a working-class enactment of the myth's own anti-institutionalism.

But a seeming conflict between husband and wife, as well as a seeming alignment of working- and middle-class myth, are complicated by the larger context—historical and textual. One page earlier, Lynn Cieslica has declared that the biggest change in their lives is "so many doors being closed in Mark's face. And now we've reached a point after all these years that, you know, you're afraid to take any chances, because you've been shot down so many times. O sure, a steelworker. I mean, how many skills do you really have as a steelworker? All you know is steel . . ." (166). It is a charge she repeats later, specifically linking mythic rhetoric to *doxa* denied: "This country does not really provide for the people and even for those who want to make an effort to better themselves, the doors keep closing in your face" (173). Clearly the rhetorical frame established in one *mythos* as dependency evokes a counterargument in another not so heavily invested in individual agency and masculine self-making. Stated from outside the dominant mythic framework (as differentiated here on both class and gender grounds), the failure described is as likely to be that of group support as of individual effort.

Similar complications of the myth and its calls to personal effort and agency echo in workers' comments on the institution of education. As was true for Porter's Samuel and hesitantly acknowledged by Lavelle, the concept of education and of useful skill go hand-in-hand for many steelworkers, where educational institutions are not just arenas for class separation from working-class origins but are opportunities for achieving masculine agency. Asked if he thinks more troubled times lie ahead, Joseph Kemp says in *Portraits in Steel*, "Well, I'll say they are, [for] the kids if they don't make themselves very educated. . . . As for a kid, make sure he got his head in those books, cramming it all in, and it *got* to be a skilled job, you understand" (315). The skill and the job that goes with it are expressed here as steps toward control over one's situation, with all that means for the concept of masculine agency (and all the damage that its loss entails). These are not simple endorsements of hierarchy and class separation enacted by a middle-class *doxa* of masculine self-making combined with an insider's privileged sense of natural access to institutional power. Here masculine agency is being paired with an institutional outsider's real anxiety over marginalization and its attendant noncontrol and nonmasculinity. Institutions are not to be scorned absolutely. They are to be used to achieve agency. The question is one of how they are to be used—both literally and rhetorically—and at what sacrifice to the still powerful myth of masculine individualism and anti-institutionalism.

The complexity of those competing appeals is clear in the related appeal to institutionally achieved agency suggested by Lavelle's triadic mix of "bars, campuses, and union halls." For Lavelle, still an ardent unionist at the end of the twentieth century, there is no conflict within his larger rhetoric of anti-institutionalism and pro-unionism. Indeed, traditional arguments for worker solidarity and union resistance to corporate control can all be used as counter arguments to institutional nonagency and implied dependency. Unfortunately, those subversive arguments for solidarity are often mitigated by the union's own failure to develop its rhetoric to fit the changing situation. Thus it is with a hint of nostalgia for early and mid-century unionism that Lavelle's and Frisch and Rogovin's workers voice their rhetoric of solidarity and mutual support. In its glory days, "the union would protect you . . . otherwise the plant wouldn't have to pay you no benefits, no retirement, you know, kick you around" (*Portraits* 105). By the 1980s, it's no longer like "back in the thirties when things were forming, you know, it got to be a lot of bureaucracy, I think" (157).

The complex masculinity that supports the rhetoric to which these workers nostalgically refer is readily apparent in the organizational activities of a figure like John ("Dobie") Dobrejcak, the fictional son of Bell's Mike Dobrejcak. In good mythic fashion, Dobie is effectively and then actually orphaned as a teenager by his father's death at the mill and his mother's hospitalization for and eventual death from consumption. Prior to her passing, Dobie helps support the family by collecting junk, by scrounging wood scraps and coal, selling newspapers, working in a glass factory, faking an ID letter, and getting a job in the mills at the age of fifteen. He is, in short, the perfect Alger hero—except these efforts do not produce a Carnegie but a steelworker in the Carnegie (now U.S. Steel) mills. Yet Dobie's masculinity is not reduced by his class status and its noncompliance with the dominant rhetoric of upward mobility. Rather, Dobie enacts his masculinity within a framework of nondominant, but still effectively agentive, masculine self-making. Indeed, Bell presents Dobie's agency and masculinity as resting solidly on a foundation of union organizing and not the anti-institutionalism of doxic self-making. But this rhetoric mutes the full individualization of self-making as argued either in nineteenth- or twentieth-century, dominant or subversive myths of agentive self-making.[8]

The difference between Dobie's institutionally supported masculinity and that of the full myth of individualistic self-making is clear in the contrasting subtleties of Dobie's and Larry Locke's union organizing. Bell does resort to traditional components of masculinity within these frames. Both men struggle for control of their workplace and, by default, their sense of independence and masculinity. But Whittaker emphasizes Locke's individual, nearly mesmerizing powers with the men and only lightly notes his surreptitious techniques for crowd control. From the start, Bell instead emphasizes Dobie's ongoing process of learning how to work within the confines of unions as institutions, chafing somewhat over the half-hearted efforts of the AFL, and manipulating as far as possible the sham company unions they are allowed. Bell, in short, is choosing the mundane over the mythic and criticism of institutions rather than full-blown anti-institutionalism, all the while attempting to provide some arena for Dobie to display his own brand of masculinity.

Perhaps nowhere are the rhetorical similarities and differences more apparent than in the requisite fight scene. As always, the boss (or at least his managerial representative) is to be fought. Dobie's fellow workers certainly castigate their boss: "The trouble with that loud-mouthed son of a bitch," Hagerty declares, "is he don't realize what he's up against. . . . He needs educating" (389). But where Whittaker, Douglass, Davis, and Butler all insist on an actual fight, or where Iacocca, Preston, and Kiam offer a pseudostruggle among corporate behemoths, Bell insists instead on the reality of a fight's unfulfilled threat. Alert to the active presence and power of corporate institutionalism, Dobie is granted the ability to fight, but he does not need to do so for a key reason. He has been trained in how to use SWOC, CIO, and NLRB rules and regulations to get what he wants (387–88). Dobie speaks the rhetoric of solidarity versus singularity, arguing that "working with an organization isn't the same as being on your own" (397).

That doesn't mean a drift into institutional anonymity or nonagency, however. In place of self-making though masculine individuality and personal power, Bell situates Dobie's newfound strength in solidarity and mutuality. "You know, I never realized what this business of feeling you've got a lot of men behind you could do to a man. Or even having them come up and slap you on the back and all" (297). Dobie's masculinity rests on union practices capable of granting agency within institutional dynamics. In short, Bell has completed in Dobie the definition of masculinity that Whittaker was forced to display in two separate characters—Larry Locke and Paul Van Beaver. The gap between individual agency and institutional control, and the resulting masculinity gap that Whittaker could not bridge, has been closed.

To no small degree, the closing of that gap occurs because Van Beaver's ability to use the legal institutions to his own ends is matched in Bell with Dobrejcak's ability to use governmental and union institutional power to his ends. There remains a significant class gap between a Paul Van Beaver and a John Dobrejcak, of course. But Bell is studiously uninterested in addressing the larger complexities of power here, beyond alluding to their possible oppressiveness. In an arena of increasing union strength, masculinity can be adequately argued within a modern form of agency—a representative individualism activated by institutional savvy and union solidarity. This is the heart of the appeal that echoes in the rhetoric of Frisch and Rogovin's steelworkers' comments on 1930s and 1940s union rhetoric. It even appears in reminiscences of their own solidarity. Remembering a wildcat strike staged in support of his unfair firing, Mark Cieslica speaks of their unity almost in wonderment: "Half an hour [after the firing] the whole plant walked out. They had a walkout because they fired me!" (155).

But as unions solidify their strength, the rhetorical appeal available in their masculine opposition to corporate control tends toward stasis. Eventually, when power and control again slip away from unions in the last quarter of the century, the rhetoric shifts from masculine self-making as unified opposition to a rhetoric of aggressive opposition for its own sake.[9] Union rhetoric's potentially subversive power is absorbed into the general rhetoric of masculine self-making. The resulting absence of a subversive rhetoric, coupled with the lack of real union strength, devastates workers sense of workplace control and self-control, as Frisch and Rogovin's steelworkers know only too well, and as is evidenced in the difference between Dobie's and their rhetorical self-enactments. Now only a vague anti-institutionalism is voiced. "The company is the company," the men note cynically. "They're going to do whatever they want" (161). Anti-institutionalism in general becomes the best (because the only) rhetorical game in town.

Talking the Talk

By the end of the century, Preston finds it easy to link the bureaucratic, institutional lethargy of major corporations to unions themselves. For his part, Iacocca is free to reinforce middle-class rhetoric by representing his behavior within the corporation as a particular brand of authentic masculinity enacted through verbal power and corporate risk taking. Like Big Steel, the Chrysler corporation is in danger of imminent collapse and ripe for a self-made savior to remake the company. *Iacocca* and *American Steel* thus enact essentially the same rhetoric. At the same time, *Iacocca* outstrips Preston's arguments on at least one seemingly simple ground, that of genre and its attendant structuring. Preston is writing a narrative in which he provides character portraits and events to dramatize an ongoing and dynamic masculine *doxa*. The process provides immediacy and impact by developing single moments or vignettes into a running argument.[10] The immediacy remains that of observation, however, of third-party viewing in which narrator and reader sit alongside one another to enact the rhetoric.

With his declaration of autobiographical representation, Iacocca moves beyond that frame and introduces himself "directly" as that which he represents. As was true with Carnegie and Davis, the very act of self-representation literally "makes" the figure of Iacocca. The representation becomes an act not of character making or creative nonfiction achieved through anti-institutionalism but an act of self-making twice over, of enacting a self, and of doing so through controlling the verbal/symbolic act of writing. *Iacocca* thus continues the long-standing tradition of displaying masculine self-making by actually painting rather than merely posing for one's own portrait.

This ready blending of subject position and representational agency reinforces contemporary claims about the constructedness of identity. Yet contemporary representations of self-making insist more than ever on precisely the opposite, on their realism and legitimacy, on the self being made as genuine or authentic. The representation is thus not simply immediate, it is offered as unmediated, genuine, the real thing. The long-standing cultural rhetoric of one's self as one's word, exemplified by Ricouer and reinforced by some uses of Lacan, finds full fruition here. The ultimate irony, as many reviewers have taken easy pleasure in noting, is that while *Iacocca* offers the figure of Iacocca in "his own hard-hitting style" (jacket commentary), it does so via the rhetorical action of William Novak, the book's ghostwriter. At the same time, Novak's presence does little to diminish the desired authenticity of the text.[11] Said another way, the audience agrees that figures like Iacocca are really doing precisely what they are not—that is, speaking directly for themselves.

The speech-act dynamics that enact the overall play of *Iacocca*'s rhetoric are fairly straightforward. As George Dillon suggests, "Writers who eschew the role of authority in favor of one of leadership are in a sense the entrepreneurs of authority; their persuasiveness is not based on association with existing institutions but is fashioned out of their own experience, often out of an admittedly impassioned quest" (93).[12] Restated in *Iacocca*, such appeals sound like this: "My years as general manager of the Ford Division were the happiest period of my life. For my colleagues and me, this was fire-in-the-belly time. We were high from smoking our own brand. . . . We were young and cocky. We saw ourselves as artists, about to produce the finest masterpieces the world had ever seen" (65). This declaration is full of masculine verve and a Leverenz-like blending of art and production. But the opening suggests a problem—an institutional affiliation ("general manager") is declared, and declared in the dreaded language of corporate hierarchy. The ultimate persuasiveness, of course, lies in what follows (and in the ability to translate corporate status into an opportunity for masculine rebellion). Anticipating Sam Keen's *Fire in the Belly: On Being a Man* by seven years, *Iacocca* converts the heartburn of managerial labor into a fire-breathing quest, verbally escaping from the banality of Henry Ford's assembly-line autos to the glories of art and nicely transforming his status as auto executive into that of Leverenz's masculine artist. Silently, the automobile industry as institution disappears behind a masculine rhetoric of worker craft and middle-class artistry.

The appeal to creativity and craft is augmented by hints of a supposed honesty and genuineness of self-revelation and brotherhood that contrasts notably with the aggressive, patriarchal opposition of I/you. The I-me-we set now being offered (as opposed to the earlier I/you or I/them rhetoric) is part of an overall self-enactment that appears to provide direct personal revelation and mutuality, Erikson's buddy rather than Miller's patriarch. And for all its staginess, the "fire-in-the-belly" motif adds its effective note of direct, gut-check language needed to offset managerial status. In this way, *Iacocca* rhetorically establishes itself as a personal invitation as well as a personal representation, suggesting that its appeal will be a supposedly "revealing personal tour" (jacket commentary) through Iacocca's life. Yet the work is just as clearly highly impersonal when looked at as gendered self-dramatization, an "*auto*-biography," as one disgruntled reader put it. The proffered authenticity and intimacy of brotherhood notwithstanding, the text actually offers the impersonal posing as the personal, Iacocca the entrepreneurial self-maker posing as Iacocca the man—a more correct (and safer) form of gender construction.

In the introduction, for example, Iacocca nicely enacts masculine self-making and self-revelation while ostensibly downplaying his personal role: "Today I'm a hero. . . . With determination, with luck, and with help from lots of good people, I was able to rise up from the ashes" (xvii). This is an "I" defined neatly according to the dominant rhetoric of masculine growth and self-determination—singularity, struggle, and self-achievement—then modified by acknowledgment that others are present. Mutuality and solidarity are offered but as an obvious cliché—"lots of good people." The personable, direct language thus first establishes Iacocca's bona fides and then allows him to admit to the presence of, if not a full corporate support system, at least those around him. But while *Iacocca* clearly presents itself as direct personal representation, the language of its authenticity actually relies upon well-established and genre-specific stylistic modes.

In reviewing the book, for example, *Time* magazine manages to both enact the style and parody it. "*Iacocca* reads like Iacocca talks," the reviewer declares. "The voice is unmistakable. . . . He is a big guy . . . a driven guy, an earthy, passionate, volatile, funny, and profane guy, a talkative guy who tells it like it is, who grabs for gusto, who damns the torpedoes, and plunges full-speed ahead" (jacket commentary). In short, Iacocca as book and self-made man is a vast number of middle-class clichés and aphorisms about authentic masculinity that are recognizable as such, and that nevertheless validate Iacocca's authentic masculinity for precisely that reason. Paradoxically, and yet very importantly—the rhetoric's formulaic quality reinforces the authenticity of its announced self-making. The argument is persuasive because it is rhetorically accurate.

That rhetorical dynamic is ironically clarified in negative responses to the follow-up book, *Talking Straight,* which provides many of the same motifs. Confessing herself to be "an early Lee Iacocca fan," Patricia O'Toole now complains that in *Talking Straight,* Iacocca needs to "back up his assertions, stick to the point and argue more by logic than anecdote" (11). O'Toole's complaint is not really about the style of *Talking Straight* but about a shift in argument that the famous style no longer fits, the title notwithstanding. For her, the second book is no longer an argument maintaining the dominant masculine myth of self-made success. Rather, it is an apparently serious attempt to analyze particular social and economic difficulties—without providing any particular analysis. The second version only provides the vocabulary of authenticity, of "talking straight," that the first enacts as the full myth of masculine self-making.[13] The stagy, preset language of *Iacocca* as self-made man does not equate with "noneffective," then. In fact, ignoring situational details or contextual complications in favor of an enactment of motifs of direct or forthright speech actually broadens the general mythic quality of the appeal.

The rhetoric of verbal authenticity as a broad, doxic signal of masculinity also enables it to cross class boundaries, doing so precisely because it is regularly validated by *doxa.* Lavelle, for example, readily embraces the symbolic as engendering masculinity—both directly and within his own style. In 1973, Lavelle still believes deeply in unions—and in the idiocy of most corporate bureaucrats (such as the hero of *Iacocca*). Yet Lavelle's own voice pairs nicely with that of Iacocca. "Red, White and Blue" in his views, Lavelle enacts both doxic rhetoric and himself by declaring that "any damn fool or weakling can surrender his mind to a straitjacket of ideology, but a guy who says what's on his mind and then says, 'That's it, that's me; that's where I'm at, like it or not'—that's my kind of man" (22). Just as the rhetoric of verbal authenticity allows Iacocca to escape from the role of corporate manager and send the signal "genuine masculinity sold here," so it overrides divisions between managerial and labor masculinity by enacting the voice of "one of the guys." The language of genuineness and authenticity depends not on assumed ties to objective reality but on faithful maintenance of masculine desires embodied in the myth and its ostensibly authentic rhetoric.

Walking the Walk

Related to masculine authenticity enacted through proper manipulation of the symbolic is authenticity enacted through a broad rhetoric of aggression that is established in motifs of danger and risk taking. Central to the appeal of both motifs is their attachment to a mythically colored battle between individual and established corporate empire. Wideman's Tommy provides a tragic commentary on the pursuit of that aspect of the myth from outside its middle-class frame. Iacocca displays its possibilities from within the heart of the established corporate arena. Preston demonstrates how to fully elaborate the possibilities from both within and ostensibly without the dominant corporate frame.

The larger armature of masculine rhetoric is visible as Preston works hard to establish Nucor's hot metal men as rogues and rebels, an important component to the rhetoric, given their actual managerial and middle-managerial status. But the required separation between proper outsider and corporate power—and the tensions that ensue when crossovers and overlapping become visible—are enacted in an interesting, twentieth-century revision of the time-honored tradition of self-making craftsmen (like Davenport's Paul Scott) who can recognize other self-makers at a glance. Nucor uses a slightly different procedure to find out who has the right stuff. In the case of Will Hawley, Preston admits, Nucor relied not upon recognizing innate masculinity but "had put Hawley through a psychological test devised by a Nucor psychologist, one John Seres, out of Chicago": "Nucor's psychological test, which Nucor gave to all candidates for jobs at the Crawfordsville Project, was supposed to identify goal-oriented people, self-reliant people; Nucor material. The test also weeded out applicants who might sympathize with labor unions. Hawley passed Nucor's head examination and Busse hired him to be a Run-a-Mucker" (*American Steel* 47). As was true with Iacocca's reference to "general managers," the rhetorical success of this surprisingly blatant example of late twentieth-century institutional control depends on a particular dynamic. The appeal to masculine self-making enacted in the rhetoric of "goal-oriented, self-reliant" behavior must override the deeply intrusive, corporate psychological profiling being described. If Preston has enacted the mythic rhetoric well, the rogue corporation (now suddenly revealed by Preston to have all sorts of bureaucratic layers) is not suddenly displayed as a determining force but instead presented as a benign focal point of the search for self-makers (who by force of personality apparently remain separate from the very corporate ethos that is testing them). These men may be identified as psychologically well-formed Nucor material, but their ultimate shaping is cast as self-directed and self-forming, and their authentic masculinity is to be demonstrated through their natural ability for risk taking, which the psychological test merely reveals. In short, the company is not an organization at all but merely a lodestone for risk-taking self-makers. At least that is the gist of the appeal.

It actually is a surprisingly effective claim, thanks both to the significant weight attached to end-of-the-century risk taking in middle-class rhetoric and to Preston's related use of anti-institutionalism in attacks on stodgy, hide-bound corporations (which now conveniently include unions and their no longer subversive rhetoric). The unification of these appeals is clear in Preston's negative portrait of Thomas C. Graham, president of U.S. Steel and thus the latest inheritor of the Carnegie empire—but not the Carnegie mantle. Where Iverson is displayed as a renegade and a contemporary self-made man, Graham is offered up as "a short, balding man in his sixties, with a puckery smile, a physically quiet man who hardly moves," a man who reminds Preston of the ultimate non-risk taker, "a family physician," and who "is said to have the respect of the unionized steelworkers in his company" (*American Steel* 45). The last comment is the kiss of death, and Graham only regains some credibility when he starts to take the same risks as Iverson by considering a minimill, hiring nonunion labor, and eliminating plants.[14]

In the long run, then, unions and corporations remain aligned with images of safety and stasis, of nonmasculine, flabby bureaucracy. In their place is offered a late twentieth-century, rhetorical conjoining of management and labor through a masculinity based on mutual risk taking in service to creativity and craft—these being defined mainly in terms of individual actions rather than high finance or economic power brokering so as to preserve that key aspect of the myth. Corporate risk taking as a form of self-making has its uses, but ultimately the rhetoric must enhance the individual. The Run-a-Muckers, having passed their psychological profiling, are allowed to provide just such an enactment, making themselves by making a steel mill on the fly. Mark Millett demonstrates the blend of youth, risk, and opportunity that Preston relies upon as the basis of the appeal: "In the long glare of a century and a third of burning [casting] machines, F. Kenneth Iverson and Keith Earl Busse had given Mark Millett, an English ex-cook, twenty-eight years old, the assignment to put metal into the machine and to make it work. If something went wrong, the casting machine might literally blow up in Millett's face" (19). The reasons for calling Millett an ex-cook rather than a B.S. in metallurgy (which he is) are obvious. In addition, a ritual passing on of craft is enacted in the full, formal naming of Iverson and Busse. Finally, the possibility of violent death inserts the risk motif with a vengeance.

The centrality of these elements in the doxic ambience of late twentieth-century masculine self-making is hard to underestimate. The joint appeal to individualism and risk taking serves to provide the means for offsetting the rise of institutional stasis and determinism that earlier had marked the loss of craft-based control as the mark of self-making and its replacement by physical effort alone. *American Steel* is replete with appeals to the ensuing rhetoric. Thus Iverson, CEO and millionaire, is enacted mainly as entrepreneur and inventor, physical risk taker and masculine performer nonpareil, his self-made masculinity on display so as to lead his not yet fully masculine workers to their own self-making:

> [The foundry workers] refused to touch Iverson's machine. They were afraid that the first time they poured hot metal into the machine's horn, the machine would explode and spray Illium G around the room, cutting people in half and burning them to death.
>
> Iverson and Illium's president were the only employees of the company who dared to touch Iverson's machine. . . .
>
> "The pipe made a monstrous noise of metal spinning on metal," recalled Iverson. "The president and I talked casually over the sound of the machine, even though we couldn't hear each other's voices." They chatted with smiles on their faces, possibly dying of fright, while they poured hot metal into the horn. The metal ran through the horn and into the spinning pipe. Nothing happened; the machine worked fine. . . . The factory workers were embarrassed and took over the operation of the machine. After that the Illium Corporation did a good business in your sausage nozzles. (57)

The scene is both hilarious and wholly masculine, full of risk and heavy with a message—for both workers and audience. Iverson is a hot metal man, and if you wish to make yourself into him, you must take the risk, while demonstrating all of the aplomb. This is steelmaking, and the danger is real. But as Preston's commentary makes clear, real men note the danger and then grin about it; we're risking our lives to make nozzles for sausage grinders, guys—what a hoot. The violence and risk are all good natured, then, in service to making steel and its attendant masculinity—or to revealing its absence: "The shot-casting machine started to rain liquid steel into the water, and the building began to shake. The guy jumped off the top of the machine and . . . ran out of the building, never to be seen around Cannon Muskegon again. Iverson began to appreciate the fact that some people cannot look hot metal in the eye" (59).

The rhetoric demonstrates how Preston enacts a masculinity cathected to violence and risk in order to rewrite the craft of making steel, nostalgically resurrecting not only the rust belt but also the lost tradition of craft training and its inherent paternalism. "The young people are going to learn about steel," Preston has Iverson envision, and in their learning they will make a steel mill, themselves, and a new-old myth of masculinity. If the men do so as rogues and run-a-muckers, cowboys, and risk takers, so much the better because so much more the masculine:

> "On this kid's first day at work, we got a good cast going," said Iverson. . . .
>
> "Then some hydraulic valves blew off the machine. . . . This kid straddled a hot billet of steel—he stood with his legs apart over a piece of red-hot steel coming out of the cast— and he held the broken hydraulic hoses together with his hands. I was terrified he would burn himself. The hoses blew apart again, and he got hydraulic fluid in his eyes. We took him down to wash his eyes out, and he turned to me and said, 'This is the best job I every had!' He was a hot metal man, only he didn't know it." (78)

It is through such suggestions of baptismal anointing (by hydraulic fluid, in this case) and near circumcision by fire that Preston creates a new brotherhood of self-made men, identifiable to each other (and to the company and its psychological test as well) through a semiritualized revelation of the innate masculine makeup that they share. It is a nostalgic vision that offers great appeal when enacted through the myth of self-making, resting as it does on a reproduction of Davenport's (and the even earlier craftsman's) brotherhood of individuals who recognize each other without ever having to engage in any significant interpersonal exchange. They just know.

To the ritual passing on of the art available in the days of puddling steel, Preston thus adds the ritual behavior that was so attractive to the early Knights of Labor—all without the institutional baggage of a modern union (or the real questions that solidarity, mutuality, and male/male intimacy raise). But as the present nostalgically turns to the past to maintain itself and its vision of the future, other issues appear as well. For one thing, Nucor's minimill does not really make steel the old-fashioned way. It relies heavily on melting down used, scrap steel and reshaping it, a process in which a rhetoric of back to the future must war with images of decay.

The tensions that can erupt when such banal realities enter the rhetoric are equally visible when Preston's ritualized brotherhood of masculinity is contrasted to another, older form of brotherhood, that of the union as seen by Frisch and Rogovin's steelworkers. As the rhetoric of these interviews with laid-off steelworkers is set alongside Preston's narrative, it becomes clear that more than the masculine pleasures of aggressive risk taking and masculine self-making are required to operate a steel mill.

One particularly appropriate example occurs during a discussion of OSHA work rules. Such rules also address issues of risk, but here the rhetoric is not that of self-making but that of workers' missing control over dangerous workplace conditions. As a worker for Crucible Steel notes: "Yeah, a lot of guys were deathly afraid to say anything to OSHA because they were afraid they were going to lose their job. Not that—they couldn't lose their job because they complained to OSHA, but you know, management has ways" (253). Indeed they do, and the risks one faces on the job can be represented as self-making or as doubly self-threatening—complain and lose your job; don't complain and lose your limbs, health, life, and so on.

In comparison, Preston has Iverson argue work rules through the self-making rhetoric of hard work and effort as opposed to some bureaucratic job requirements and descriptions fostered by the unions. "The unions are caught up in a bind over work rules," Iverson declares. "They can't get rid of work rules. If you get rid of work rules, then you reduce the number of people working in a plant, and productivity goes up, and then fewer people can share more of the success of the company" (*American Steel* 83). This characterization works, as Preston knows, to offset issues of risky workloads or shop floor dangers by letting those admittedly "fewer workers" turns risks into "greater productivity," "success," and, best of all, individual effort and masculine self-growth.[15]

Solidarity, Risk Taking, and Hot Metal Men

Enacted within a mythic, nostalgic rhetoric of heavy industry and craft-based self-making, appeals to risk taking as the portal to authentic masculinity maintain the dominant version of late-twentieth-century masculinity. But a rhetoric not so committed to middle-class rhetoric can sometimes enact variant appeals from outside the dominant myth. Frisch and Rogovin's direct interviews with steelworkers continue to raise the possibility of a vaguely subversive, although uncertain and much less celebratory, rhetoric of masculinity. *Portraits in Steel* is more concerned with the banalities of actual steel mills and steel mill life than with the mythic portrayal of either the industry or deeply masculine behavior, and it is through this focus on the day-to-day activities of making steel that the motifs of masculine solidarity, mutuality, and intimacy revisit the rhetoric of masculinity, offering once again a suggestion of alternative masculinities.

There are two kinds of intimacy regularly referred to by Frisch and Rogovin's steelworkers. One is intimacy based on solidarity and group support; the other is a more complex intimacy based on protecting one another from the dangers that Preston uses to establish authentic, risk-taking masculinity. As I described it above, union solidarity engages the first sort as it walks out in support of fired worker Mark Cieslica, or when it asserts a sense of group identity in comments about fellow workers as "standing behind you," "family," and "look[ing] out for each other" (174, 208 and 301, 300). Such comments, which echo those Bell has Dobie state, are based on a general sense of workers helping each other carry the load. But the rhetoric engages a second form of mutuality and intimacy as well—that of Kracha and Dubik's need—and inability—to protect one another from physical (as well as managerial) dangers.

One worker, William Douglass, explains the bond. Asked if he knew his fellow workers well, he agrees and then goes on: "I think it was probably because the type of work that we did in there was dangerous and you depend on the other guy to help you. . . . [Y]ou always depended on somebody else to watch your back while you were pouring [molten steel] or if you were covering up you would watch for the pourer—somebody's always watching for somebody [because people get] killed" in steel mills (250–51). Douglass is discussing not just the danger, which he describes at length, but the reason that "he got to be friends" with the people with whom he worked. The underlying dynamics are reminiscent of Montgomery's long-partnered longshoremen and are emphasized fully in John Krakauer's description of mountaineering and mutual aid: "Ordinarily, one climber is tied to one or two partners . . . making each person directly responsible for the life of the others; roping up in this fashion is a serious and very intimate act" (78).

This form of intimacy is highly complex and, as might be expected, somewhat troubling to a cultural rhetoric that calls for separation and individualism (as well as eschewing the slightest hint of homoeroticism). The intimacy is rooted in an act of caring, of course, but it also provides an admission of danger, so that the intimacy is based partially on pleasure in facing or having risked danger together. That eases masculine anxiety over the intimacy somewhat, making it admittable and admissible—safely masculine in its overtones of violence and death. Nevertheless, this risk-based intimacy differs in subtle but very important ways from Preston's risk taking. Preston emphasizes risk in the service of self-making, of a mysterious brotherhood in which individuation is celebrated and representations of intimacy are muted.

The difference is worth noting at some length, because it demonstrates the complexity of appeal that can attend very similar motifs. I have described this danger/intimacy motif as presented by Bell in *Out of This Furnace* when Dubik is killed in a furnace explosion. In Frisch and Rogovin, William Douglass provides a similar example of workers protecting one another, referring to deaths that are caused by a ladle that falls from a crane with a full load of molten steel (250). The rhetoric engaged to describe the scene is not aligned with self-making but with industrial burns and unpleasant death, and the intimacy it provokes is more than partially attached to anxiety and a resulting belief in the values of mutuality and even dependency.

Preston describes exactly the same type of accident—a ladle drop—in his portrait. But Preston's argument, while concerned somewhat with the sense of intimacy emphasized by Bell and Douglass, is mainly devoted to enacting a masculinity of self-making and heroism. The heroism is undeniable, and Preston's goal clearly is to do justice to the deaths of several workers. Yet the presentation goes beyond the requirements of descriptive accuracy. For one thing, it is not the day-to-day danger of the job and its requisite intimacy that Preston's rhetoric emphasizes. The chapter discussing the accident, for example, is entitled "War Zone," and it draws on that ethos, producing a rhetoric that trends not toward intimacy but toward a violence that is in keeping with his overall appeal to risk, danger, and aggressive self-making. Ultimately, however, Preston himself feels the need to deflate the myth following the accident. As he notes with uncharacteristic reserve, "the heady feeling of playing with gigantic toys had given way to a deepening awareness of the possibility of death inside steel mills" (263). Death on the shop floor finally overrides the risk-taking, masculine rhetoric of battlefield mythology.

There are other tensions and cracks in Preston's attempts to consider manly intimacy (or at least its safer version, solidarity) while sustaining the myth of masculine self-making. As *doxa* encourages, Preston has relied heavily on the rhetoric of individuality and risk taking (along with emphasizing the extra danger of making steel) as a quintessential aspect of masculine self-making. Yet even in the craft-oriented days of puddling, steelmaking was much too complex for it to be truly a lone activity, and the process is by now more nonindividualistic than ever. Responding to the contemporary situation, Preston finds it useful to stress the brotherhood of the team, thus replacing any lingering nostalgia for union solidarity with an analogy to athletics in which the casting foreman (Dave Thompson of the opening epigraph) is coach or quarterback. "Having played football on a college team," Thompson practices a cast by scripting it "like a football play." "It was a matter of moving people through points in space at the right moments in time, slowly at first, then at full speed" (203–4). The analogy is not new, as Rotundo notes in discussing Leonard Ellis's study of sports. Late nineteenth-century football metaphors were often used to provide dramatic analogies with work. There the appeal was not to individual self-making, however, but to orderly corporate labor: "Football . . . emphasized teamwork, an elaborate division of labor, a hierarchy of roles, and intricate strategies in the service of team competition, thus rendering the experience of bureaucratic work—which was just emerging at the end of the century—in dramatic physical form" (244–45).[16]

Ironically, then, Preston's analogy of group solidarity and agency as the teamwork of football enacts a turn-of-the-century, Tayloresque rhetoric of segmented acts subservient to the larger action of a scripted group—and ultimately of a machine. These underlying problems in the analogy become clear as the language shifts from its metaphoric ground to the actual workplace. Using the material of the epigraph, Preston sets up Thompson's football experience to emphasize the "power of [the cast foreman's] frame. . . . Six feet four inches tall . . . he appeared to be several feet wide, but he wasn't fat. . . . He had been an offensive tackle on his college football team . . ." (108). But that individual power must itself be given over to hierarchical organizational skills and a process that smacks of the assembly line. Literally faced with a Tayloresque stopwatch, the workers move through their marionette roles in a dance whose basic nature is not lost on Frisch and Rogovin's steelworkers. They recognize fully the difference between the self-making, craft-oriented masculinity through steelmaking enacted in Preston's opening chapters and the reductive banalities that Nucor's production designs actually offer to Nucor's hot metal men. As one steelworker describes it, continuous casting is "one long assembly from the start of your steel right on out to your rolled product" (Frisch and Rogovin 219).

Preston's narrative eventually admits that assembly-line work rather than creative production is precisely what is being described here. Nucor's steel is to be melted primarily from old scrap, poured into the casting machine, drawn out from the bottom, and a thin strip run continuously into the rolling mills for reduction, while a "thousand feet down the line, along would comes sheets of rich, glistening steel. The steel would be coiled up with a snap, like a roll of paper towels, and from there it would be moved up a conveyor ramp and out into the Midwest" (*American Steel* 11). The mystery of steel has become paper towels, craft mutuality and creativity has become segmented teamwork, and teamwork has become the tending of the production line. The team motif suffers, then, from multiple tensions—it directly reduces the individuality touted in self-making; it clearly establishes a managerial hierarchy; and it replaces the early, craft-based mutualism of making steel with a series of individuated, programmed acts. This sort of labor conflicts heavily with the sort of personal pride in their labor that Frisch and Rogovin's steelworkers demonstrate (86, 103, 117, 134, 151, 182–83, 215, 275, 280, 300, 316), that Lavelle calls for (5–6), or that was part of the early craft tradition of steelmaking.

Preston nevertheless continues to emphasize links to that early tradition in order to maintain a nostalgic sense of steelmaking as creative and thus to maintain an attendant and similarly creative masculine agency and self-making among his hot metal men. The best opportunities for that sort of representation occur not in the mechanized casting process but in the mythic rituals surrounding molten steel itself:

> Lancing a heat, like other aspects of the craft of making steel, is at least as much a black art as a science, requiring more by way of instinct and experience than book learning. There is no school for furnace workers except the river of steel, and no one knows the river except an older furnace worker, a melter with years of experience. The craft is long to learn. . . . Hot metal men have been making heats of liquid steel since at least 3500 B.C. . . . A good melter develops a personal style for lancing down a heat of steel. Lancing has a formal yet individual quality, like a dance. (*American Steel* 184)

Preston is at his best in such characterizations, weaving together threads of traditional/experiential knowledge, craft, ritual, risk, and individuality to form a nostalgic web in which act and actor are both created and creative. It helps, of course, to have a process and product that lend themselves to the representation being offered. Steel provides exactly the power, danger, and mystery that Preston needs to enhance the masculinity he is offering. Analogies abound—sexual, volcanic, literary (even a version of Leverenz's Ahab appears)—and Preston makes use of them all to provide an equivalent masculinity—powerful, individualistic, ritualistic in its brotherhood:

> He might have been a whaleman in a longboat nearing the monster, hefting the lance for the thrust. For a moment time slowed. Then McCaskill raised the lance, profiled the steel, and fell forward and harpooned the whale. . . . The steel protested with shrieks, blow-backs, rumbles, coiling movements and an unbearably bright light. . . . He lanced for a little while and then he passed the lance to another melter, who put the lance into the steel. The melters shared the honor and glory of lancing the first heat of steel. (185–86)

However overwrought this analogy may appear out of context, the making of steel does allow and encourage such vignettes of ritualized masculinity (the sounds, for example, are perfectly described).[17] The making of steel thus provides the real substrate of Preston's text and the masculinity that infuses it. Preston suggests that foundation when he taps into the myth of self-making by representing the building of the steel mill itself as a huge entrepreneurial risk, a David-like attack on the Goliath of Big Steel, a youthful rejection of the lumbering and near-somnambulant fathers. He furthers that myth by portraying his managers as run-a-muckers and cowboys. But making steel, described by Preston as a semi-mysterious, ancient brotherhood requiring an innate "fascination" with steel (8) and mutually shared rites of initiation, underlies the whole appeal. In the end, it is the mystical craft of making steel and its multiple threads of mystery, power, and danger that stitch the narrative together.[18]

The mysterious connection between steel and masculinity eventually exacts its own price from these hot metal men, however. Steelmaking becomes the real myth of the book to which—in a quiet form of masculine masochism—the characters have been sacrificing themselves all along. As the real processes of making Nucor steel come to light in the middle of the book, the myth of steel begins to assert a more banal rhetoric. The whole idea of a minimill is to reduce size, after all, and Nucor's casting machine, although three stories high, is also relatively "miniature," a "funny little thing" (105). Preston can offset to some degree the loss of masculinity associated with reduced size by introducing once again a nostalgic note of craft. The casting machine is small but "built by hand, in the sense that only apprenticed master craftsmen, with years of training, knew how to operate the lathes and machine tools that cut the parts of the CSP" (104). There are also ways in which the very operation of the machine can shift from its assembly-line productivity to a sense of craft, or at least of masculine effort, as individuals perform extraordinary acts demanded by the abnormal workings of the machine. One of the more self-enclosed examples is of the machine's inventor, Manfred Kolakowski, feeding the machine "by hand" for over half an hour until the shaking and heaving "took all his strength" (236).

As this image shows, however, it is ultimately both steel and machines that are used to maintain a rhetoric of power and dominance. If the casting machine won't suffice, the roll housings enact the needed rhetoric: "The machinery was of breathtaking size. . . . The CSP was so massive and complicated that it jammed the factory with machinery. One could hardly find a path to walk among these grandiose monuments of industrial power. . . . Two roll housings made a millstand. The millstands towered halfway to the roof of the factory" (104). But this sort of mystification and mythification can hide its underlying contradictions only for so long. If the machine is supreme, then Kolakowski is not masculinized by his struggles with it but only sacrificed to its needs. The same is true of the plant construction as a whole. The rhetoric of pioneering, risky development, and masculine questing finally must come to an end. References to the past used in service to the future must eventually address that future; the mill must be built, function efficiently, and the narrative closed; nostalgic appeals and vignettes based on the long history of making steel must give way to the eight-to-four shift. The machines may remain monstrously large or devilish, an echo of dangers from out of another mythic past, but ultimately they must be seen in some measure of day-to-day activity or the narrative exhausts itself, burned out by its own aggressive risk taking.

The masculinity that is available at this stage no longer appeals to associations with the dominant rhetoric of authentic masculinity. Nor, at this stage, can other appeals be created out of an alternative rhetoric. Union solidarity, intimacy, the mutualistic craft tradition hearkened back to so thoroughly—all these more or less subversive features of nondoxic masculinity have been set aside in favor of the masculinity of a spectacular self-making. Having been sacrificed, the rhetoric is no longer readily available. In fact, it is as if Preston himself is exhausted by the effort needed to sustain the dominant myth throughout. By the end, his portraits have returned to earth, just as plant manager Busse did following the ladle drop, metal explosion, and worker deaths. The late-twentieth-century nostalgic resurrection of the Rust Belt may or may not have occurred; Nucor steel is being produced at low cost, but it remains plagued by quality issues. Nor are hot metal men apotheosized by the process, as the book's close demonstrates:

> In a pulpit opposite the downcoiler, at the butt end of the hot mill, . . . Will W. Hawley, distinguished former Run-a-Mucker, unguided missile, erstwhile dealer in guns, survivor of a crane drop . . . seems to be dismayed.
> "I'm chomping at the bit," he says. "I'm feeling kind of left out. Eventually I will be replaced by a robot. I like the fast-hitting jobs, where you carry on three conversations at one time. It was much more exciting building this mill than it is actually running it." Hawley had worked at the job site practically since the bulldozers had hit the land, he had logged sixty-hour weeks to restore American steel to its former greatness, and now, somewhat to his surprise, he is a steelworker. (274)

It is difficult to know if Preston appreciates the irony in what he has written. Hawley has become a "steelworker," which means he is bored, dismayed, and faces losing his job to a robot. Hawley is, then, not quite the ultimate "Hot Metal Man." That title would belong to the robot that may replace him (although the importance of plastics in current robotics adds its own note of irony). The pseudoepic catalog of Hawley's deeds thus only weakly sustains masculine self-making. Robotic steelworkers tending machinery that is itself in fealty to steel simply cannot engage the dominant rhetoric of masculine self-making, so Preston shifts his glance away from the man and closes the book with a final, Pisgah vision of "Iverson's machine" and its river of steel.

Noting the same dissonance between a masculine rhetoric of independent, individualistic self-making and the rote behavior demanded by machinery, Erikson had already suggested in 1950 that "the specialization thus developed has led this Western civilization to the mastery of machinery, but also to an undercurrent of boundless discontent and of individual disorientation" (155). "Machines, far from remaining tools and extensions of man's physiological functions, destine whole organizations of people to be extensions of machinery" (237). Erikson even links the pursuit of masculine self-making to near roboticization. The masculinity of John Henry, self-made man of early folktales, is commonly enhanced by giving him "steel ribs, wire intestines, and a barbed wire tail" (Erikson 299). But by mid-twentieth century, the actual usefulness of such assets was questionable. "What will happen to his 'wire guts,'" Erikson wondered, "when he must serve machines . . ." (306).

Alternative versions of the myth have attempted to address that question, or at least portray its implications for and on the rhetoric of masculine self-making. Bell's Dubik is burned to death while pursuing his goals, and Kracha is socially and economically exiled; Attaway's Big Mat sadomasochistically destroys himself; Porter's Mikey faces a lifetime of separation and self-denial. Even in the success stories there are suggestions of concern. Carnegie, after all, was forced to admit defeat, to hand over to institutional minions and subalterns his personal control of the wealth that made him what he was. At least he closed with some sort of a choice. Liquor tycoon Burt Wheeler didn't even maintain that level of agency, becoming in death a good example of what he denied in life. In the end, it is mainly a sense of some form of agency—overemphasized as an individual act of masculine self-making—that undergirds the rhetoric of late-twentieth-century masculine self-making.

As I noted in chapter 2, when agency is aligned with masculine self-destruction in Asimov's "Bicentennial Man," it becomes the central means of taking the ultimate in determined subjectivity and making it the ultimate in manly agency. The tale provides a surprisingly direct enactment of *doxa* that ironically shows no sign of weakening when it appears twenty years later in *Terminator 2: Judgment Day*. In yet another example of hot metal men who shift from determined (literally programmed) to agentive beings, the film enacts the full rhetoric of masculinity with precisely the same choice of an ostensibly masculine end. Technically not a man (he cannot self-terminate and requires the aid of John Connor's own gender-bending mother to kill himself), the full masculinity of Cyberdyne System's Model 101 is nevertheless constantly suggested within the film's rhetoric. From the first, Davis-like display of Schwarzenegger's naked body, his machine-like capacities are continuously masculinized through running contrast to his opposite number's amorphous fluidity and rather slight, feminine features. Literally molten, the more advanced/more childish T1000 fails to embody masculine individuality by being liquid metal only; having no core produces not the ultimate man but the ultimate mimic—finally an even less than adequate sadist.

In contrast, by film's end Schwarzenegger is an increasingly individualized and thus supposedly humanized, cybernetic organism who has adequately defended his somewhat bizarrely constructed but properly postoedipal family. The finest blend of steel and near emotion, Model 101 is the only father who adequately "measures up" to Sarah Connor's requirements, and he is rewarded with the same act of self-making agency as Asimov's earlier robot—a masochistic completion of creation through a chosen self-destruction, in this case in a ladle of molten steel. The film closes, then, with a final, sharp contrast between "Uncle Bob's" chosen end and the destruction forced upon the T1000—both the result of yet one more fight for masculinity upon a steel mill's furnace floor. The T1000 goes to its forced end with multiple shrieks and metamorphoses that further reveal the presence of nonmasculinity. In contrast, Schwarzenegger slips stoically below the surface of the molten steel, thus enacting a heroic agency that revitalizes the rhetoric of separation and sadomasochism that lurks at the heart of the dominant myth of masculine self-making.

Through such varied and reworked arguments, *doxa* continues to maintain and be maintained by the society that enacts it, even as the mythic rhetoric contradicts itself, its own previous arguments, and the wide-ranging personal experience of its enactors. Indeed, through its constant maintenance, the myth of the self-made man exemplifies and underwrites the lurking sense of insufficiency buried within its own rhetoric and the society whose needs and anxieties it enacts. Only by constantly engaging the dynamics of the myth can self-making be sustained. To end the striving is to fall short of the myth—by definition—since there is always more that can be done, achieved, undertaken. Striving thus serves not solely (and in many cases not even primarily) a productive but a masking function, which is why its ultimate enactment yields the paradoxical agency of sadomasochistic self-destruction. The pursuit of self-making is ongoing because its ultimate purpose is finally the denial that one's masculinity is being made and has already been made, forged by a series of separations and defeats enacted and reenacted by and within the designs of the culture's *doxa*.

Since such claims return to arguments with which I began this discussion, let me make clear that no circle has been completed, no closure reached, either in my own arguments or, most assuredly, those of cultural rhetoric. I have argued throughout that the doxic processes at work in the rhetoric of masculinity are too dynamic, too fully a part of the cultural fabric to allow escape from or complete conceptualization of their workings. I don't want to suggest anything less now.

Notes

Works Cited

Index

Notes

Introduction

1. Considered in this way, the workings of myth and *doxa* begin to mesh with or overtake the concept of ideology, "a system (with its own logic and rigour) of representations (images, myths, ideas or concepts, depending on the case) endowed with a historical existence and role within a given society" (Althusser 231) But given my interest in defining gender performance as rhetorical at base, I choose to use terms more specifically rooted in rhetorical discussions. Another primary reason for that choice rests on a growing belief, wryly stated by Fred Inglis, that "a loose and baggy concept like ideology is presently asked to do too much explaining in . . . the humanities" (239). Part of that looseness arises because the initially materialist focus of ideology has come to be more and more tied to issues of desire and subjectivity. In Althusser's words, "In ideology the real relation is inevitably invested in the imaginary relation . . . rather than describing a reality" (233–34). This definition notwithstanding, ideology still carries overtones of that which is produced "out there" and imposed on subjects, as opposed to an ongoing activity of persuasion in which subjects participate—even though their performance actively aids and augments both the myth and its ongoing internalization. These are some of the essential complaints that Raymond Williams uses in supplementing ideology with hegemony, but given my interests, it suits my argument better to replace ideology (and Williams's hegemony) with *doxa* and its specific enactments in dominant and variant myths.

2. "Postoedipal" is not used here as a psychoanalytic term but to indicate the myth's sense of a proper resolution of struggle with the father or, more in line with the rhetoric, the myth's sense of a happy reconfiguration of the basic family scene, with son now occupying the role of a father. As regards psychoanalytic approaches in general, those that emphasize the formation of identity—personal, sexual, social—are often somewhat troubling to general readers. The approaches are the messy end, as it were, of the psychoanalytic stick and the easiest candidates for avoidance. More easily accepted are models that emphasize the discourse frame of the standard analytic situation. There, a schema is offered in which adults (or adult readers of texts) talk things out and over, ostensibly demonstrating a measure of intellectual self-awareness and control in the exchange. Alcorn's *Narcissism and the Literary Libido: Rhetoric, Text, and Subjectivity* is a good example of applied criticism of this form. Yet feminist and

Lacanian reworkings of traditional Freudian dramas of early childhood underwrite a socially active framework for rhetoric at least equal in usefulness to
characterizations based on metaphors of transaction and exchange. In this study,
I draw on traditional Freudian models and their emphasis on the patriarchal;
on feminist object-relations with their counterbalancing concerns with the
preoedipal dynamics of individuation and separation; and on Lacanian meldings
of both in terms of the struggle between self and language, agency and self-
making. Overlap already occurs among these divisions, and my own needs will
eventually muddy this easy separation into categories. I will not draw upon
Jungian and Adlerian models. As R. W. Connell notes, Jungian theory collapses
too readily into a highly essentialist vein (hence its popularity with conservative men's movement groups), while Adlerian thought moves outward so far into
the social as to drift away from close engagement with complexities of psychological makeup (12–17). It is important to reiterate that at bottom I am discussing not the formation of a self but the formation of masculinity, a sociocultural
pattern of behavior that functions independently of individual selves but to
which individuals bear a relation.

3. In defining the mythic Carnegie in this way, I do not mean to suggest that
Carnegie was himself materially middle class nor that the middle class is "in
charge." What I am calling the middle-class myth is not dominant in the sense
of direct manipulation; it is dominant in the sense of most widely distributed,
recognized, and available. In short, the middle-class myth is dominant because
it is the least marginalized and, for that reason, heard above all other voices,
versions, and concerns. In related fashion, when I suggest a working-class version of the myth as possibly subversive, I do not mean to suggest a clearly conscious attempt to override an obviously false rhetoric. Rather, a subversive performance threatens to reveal a doxic myth as merely orthodox, as a construct
serving certain groups or goals in the current social structure.

4. With this progression in mind, those readers more interested in an induc-
tive approach might be best served by reading chapters 3–7 as specific examples
or instances of the cultural myth, and then returning to the theoretical claims
made regarding that "data" in chapters 1 and 2. Readers of a deductive bent
will most likely find it more useful to read the chapters in the given order, with
the theoretical claims made up front and then "proven" through the subsequent examples.

5. These distinctions will be addressed more fully in chapters 1 and 2. For
now, James Berlin's differentiation among rhetorics in terms of the degree of
"subject formation" that each envision summarizes the issue. For Berlin the
question is the degree to which a rhetoric embraces or rejects "the notion of
the individual as finally a sovereign free agent, capable of transcending material and social conditions" (80). Berlin's point of difference is similar to those
separating neo-Aristotelian rhetoricians such as Thomas Farrell from neoso-
phistics such as Susan Jarratt, John and Takis Poulakos, or Victor Vitanza.

6. Those used most here are Butler's *Gender Trouble: Feminism and the
Subversion of Identity* and *Bodies That Matter,* Chancer's *Sadomasochism in
Everyday Life: The Dynamics of Power and Powerlessness,* Connell's *Mascu-
linities,* Massé's *In the Name of Love: Women, Masochism, and the Gothic,*

Savran's *Taking It Like a Man: White Masculinity, Masochism, and Contemporary American Culture,* and Silverman's *Male Subjectivity on the Margins.*

7. Nina Baym's "Melodramas of Beset Manhood" summarizes both the myth and its particular role in U.S. culture:

> The myth narrates a confrontation of the American individual, the pure American self divorced from specific social circumstances, with the promise offered by the idea of America. The promise is the deeply romantic one that in this new land, untrammeled by history and social accident, a person will be able to achieve complete self-definition. . . . [N]owhere on earth do individuals live apart from social groups. But in America, given the original reality of large tracts of wilderness, the idea seems less a fantasy, more possible in reality or at least more believable in literary treatment." (70–71)

8. Cawelti, facing a situation in which "almost everyone—politicians, businessmen, clergymen, writers, and the ordinary citizen—has had something to say about the self-made man, . . . decided that [he] could make a more useful contribution to the study of American attitudes toward success by a more complex treatment of selected sources" (vii–viii). Wyllie, noting that the self-made man "has been active in every field from politics to the arts," chooses to focus on the entrepreneurial, since "nowhere has he been more active, or more acclaimed, than in business" (6). More wide-ranging works study the concept of success in general. Leo Braudy's encyclopedic *The Frenzy of Renown: Fame and Its History,* for example, moves from ancient to modern times, covering a great deal of territory while being unable to pause long at any point. For my part, by limiting range, I hope to engage greater depth. My concern with the nature of the myth's rhetorical appeal and its gendered focus also differs from that of these other studies.

9. As Cawelti (4–6 and throughout), Wyllie (151–52), and Carl Brucker (275) all note, the Jeffersonian vision of a natural aristocracy, whose members establish their rightful social place through personal development, continues through Emerson and is still regularly voiced today in a broad vision of educational purpose as a dual mission of social training and fostering knowledge—the latter seen as producing personal growth by default. As they also note, the desire for a free and open pursuit of individual self-growth too often overlooks the material frameworks and institutional monitoring that actually have a hand in producing—and limiting—personal development.

10. Kimmel also adds class overtones to his version of Leverenz's categories: Genteel Patriarch, Heroic Artisan, Self-Made Man/Entrepreneur. Although the categories are not exclusive, Kimmel's Heroic Artisan is roughly equated with working-class masculinity, and the Self-Made Man with middle-class values. Having noted the range of masculinities and myths, Kimmel emphasizes, as he notes, "only one version of 'Manhood in America'—albeit the dominant version" (*Manhood* 6). See also Anthony E. Rotundo's useful historical overview of American manhood in the nineteenth century, especially his contrasts between "communal," "self-made," and "passionate" manhoods (1–30). Like Kimmel, Rotundo focuses on a single group: "the most influential group of Americans

in the nineteenth century: white, middle-class, Yankee Northerners" (ix). My concerns here will be less singular, since I want to emphasize the process by which dominance is challenged and maintained by variants and tensions within the larger cultural rhetoric of masculinity.

1. Effective Rhetoric/Rhetorical Effects: Maintaining Masculinity

1. The essential design of the oedipal dynamic is well known but worth repeating. The male oedipal period reaches its peak at approximately the ages of three to five. During this period, the boy-child struggles with his role in a traditionally heterosexual triangle, attempting to attain a sexuality characterized primarily by a relation to the mother and against the father. Unable to adequately satisfy his desires within the immediate family frame, the child agrees/is forced to engage in a socially validated, alternatively realized sexual identity and its supposed rewards, again as defined by dominant groups within the society. In the traditional model, this means relinquishing the idea of eliminating the father and repudiating the claim to the mother in favor of identifying with the father (a movement in which defeat is present but partially offset with offers of eventual, masculine social dominance).

2. Few of the materials I look at will completely contain the triangulated framework discussed by Sedgwick in *Between Men: English Literature and Male Homosocial Desire,* since the myth attempts to emphasize masculine exchange in a "pure" state. Male/male mutuality as presented by union solidarity and activity does raise important questions concerning Sedgwick's male homosocial behavior, however. See especially chapter 4 for further discussion.

3. Ultimately I can't agree—on a variety of grounds—with the circumscribing of masculine self-making to workplace enactments of oedipal dramas. Such limitations assume, among other things, that the workplace is itself primarily male and free of "women's influence," or that the types of behavior men display at work are somehow readily separable from the types of behavior they display elsewhere. Such discrete separations just don't hold up to scrutiny, as is clear in Miller's fictional work, Bourdieu's social anthropology, and myriad other representations. Moreover, working and talking about working—on the job, in bars, at home—are intertwined behaviors. The "site" for enacting issues in regard to work thus need not be the workplace alone.

4. Since all theories are subject to current *doxa,* and gender studies more than most, the deep social values attached to gender maintenance cannot be separated from the process of theorizing about gender. The usefulness of psychological theorizing to rhetoric is thus multiple. First, psychoanalytic characterizations of gender are directly applicable to my description of mythic representations and rhetorical maintenance of masculine identity. Second, the ongoing rhetorical impact of masculine *doxa* is exemplified in the internal tensions, arguments, and historical shifts within the models themselves.

5. The modern corporation is often disparaged in masculine self-making. But as is true for all forms of the myth, numerous other variations and emphases exist, sharing mainly an emphasis on oedipal issues. The corporation also can be used to emphasize oedipal power. Michael Douglass, for example, has made a Hollywood career out of playing corporate lions (and sadists). *A Perfect*

Murder is the most recent and among the most virulent. This free-floating, oe-dipal need to de-emphasize not only the feminine but also the maternal is hyperbolized in John Henry, the ultimate steel-driving man who, as Erikson himself tells us, "will not commit himself to any identity as predetermined by the stigmata [*sic*] of birth" (298). Such versions of the myth develop "to its very limits the image of the man without roots, the motherless man, the womanless man" (299). In nineteenth-century working-class versions of the myth the Emersonian virtues of "self-control, . . . temperance, thrift, and hard work" are combined with various oedipalized tests of the hero's masculinity to justify "fistfights, rivalries for women, tests of work skill, courtroom battles, and the climactic strike or election" (Denning, 170–71). Drury Sherrod offers four ap-proaches to this broad question of male/male exchange: psychoanalytic, bio-logical, socialization, and economic-historic. I rely most heavily on the first and last for my arguments, least—if at all—on the second.

6. Various studies raise concerns over workplace masculinity related to Erikson's twentieth-century, dominating "Mom" who usurps the role of genial "Pop." Chodorow notes that "Parsonians and theorists of the Frankfurt Insti-tute for Social Research have drawn on psychoanalysis to show how the rela-tive position of fathers and mothers in the contemporary family helps to create the foundations of men's psychological acquiescence in capitalist domination." For Parsons, the push toward independence by the mother "helps to create in her son a pseudo-independence masking real dependence" (187). For Hork-heimer and the Frankfurt School the "material base for [the fathers'] family authority was . . . eroded" by the rise of capitalism and wage labor (189). Kimmel notes that Parsons suggested the cause of masculine aggression "was father absence and overdominant mothers. Now strong mothers could be blamed for both gay sons and delinquent sons. . . . Pundits, too, went after mom—and with a vengeance. Philip Wylie's *Generation of Vipers* (1942) set the tone for a decade of mom-bashing. . ." (*Manhood* 228–29). Erikson's "Mom," in short, provided a means for reprising an oddly oedipalized struggle over what is seen as the threat of an absent or weak father.

7. Links between psychology and rhetoric are as old as rhetoric itself. Obvi-ous modern examples include Burke, Bormann, Kristeva, Jarratt, Todorov, and Vitanza, among others.

8. Bormann's particular theory develops Robert Bales's work on group fan-tasizing. For Bormann, moments of symbolic convergence or group identifica-tion produce "dramatizations, which catch on and chain out in small groups, are worked into public speeches and into the mass media and, in turn, spread out across larger publics . . . to provide them with a social reality filled with heroes, villains, emotions, and attitudes" ("Fantasy" 398). Ironically, attacks on Bormann's model reinforce arguments for including a psychological com-ponent as much as they dismiss them. If you eliminate Freud and Bales, G. P. Mohrmann argues, "a vacuum exists because an easy dramatism comes to noth-ing" (308–9). But once nonconscious processes, such as *doxa* and myth, are seen as working in cultural rhetoric, Mohrmann's arguments against Bormann are reversed. As for the question of "dramatism," the impact of Burke and Burke's Dramatism on contemporary rhetorical thinking is difficult to overstate. But

Mohrmann's comment is made in regard to an "easy" dramatism, and the complaint really raises the question of the degree to which reference to Burke entails adopting his complex system as a whole. It is a not uncommon problem, as Frank Lentricchia notes (and Mohrmann warns): "Burke cannot be accepted in small, bearable doses; he must be taken all at once or not at all" (Lentricchia 119). This caveat regularly leads to a process that Lentricchia denounces and then follows himself: He notes the impact of several key ideas in lieu of providing the "book-length project" (120) that Burke's work seems to necessitate. It is a process I admittedly follow here as well. Burke's general goals and some of the particulars of his method clearly are applicable to my concerns. Dramatism (his attempt to explain language acts and overall behavior as motivated action or drama) matches well with my own desire to see rhetoric as social action. Likewise, Burke's "third type of identification 'derives from situations in which it goes unnoticed' and the identification is unconscious." As so defined (Foss, Foss, and Trapp 159), this concept is also applicable. But Burke's own use of Freud (and of Dramatism as a whole) is problematic. While William Rueckert argues that Burke's theory should be read as an ongoing process, others such as Henderson see "a perceptible and sometimes disturbing discontinuity" among elements (Henderson 2). Fredric Jameson goes so far as to declare that "Burke's system has no place for the unconscious" (88). The concepts are clearly too complex and vexed to allow ready use here. In addition to Lentricchia's collection, Rueckert's *Critical Responses to Kenneth Burke* provides a now-dated but more mixed range of response to Burke.

9. Lincoln's *Theorizing Myth: Narrative, Ideology, and Scholarship* is a thorough study of the concept and genre from classical antiquity to the modern age. His concerns with modern myth are finally rooted more in revival of the classical and folk myth tradition that grew out of Romanticism and later nationalism than are mine. But his general discussion of the political status of myth, especially during the classical Greek era, is highly useful to the arguments being outlined here. See also Grant.

10. The three-part syllogism is central to Aristotelian proof, and its most commonly cited example is well known: (1) All men are mortal; (2) Socrates is a man; (3) Socrates is mortal. In the case of rhetoric, which must only arrive at probable truth, a full syllogism is not required but only an enthymeme, which allows for unstated assumptions to replace one term. In the case of Miller's grandfather, his use of a full syllogism makes his argument even more irrefutably "logical" within a framework oriented toward seeing logic as masculine and dominant, by default.

11. Differences of opinion concerning historiography and historical usage are worth addressing at the outset. John Poulakos considers historical texts "not as fixed monuments to be consumed cognitively but as elusive documents that can stimulate readers to rethink the constitution of their own lives and to entertain possibilities for their reconstitution" (3). On the other hand, Schiappa uses terms like "voguish" and "self-affirming" to taint interpretive or applied historical reconstructions such as those undertaken by John and Takis Poulakos, Leff, Jarratt, De Romilly, or Vitanza to revisit the Sophists. Schiappa believes that the value of such applications "is measured more on creativity and mod-

ern utility than strictly on historical accuracy." He prefers acts of "historical reconstruction" undertaken in pursuit of an ostensibly achievable accuracy. (*Protagoras* 67–68). I am going to assume from the start that the importance of these concepts and issues lies neither in fixing their meanings nor resolving their clear differences but in discussing them as embodiments of the issues we are pursuing here. That choice is bolstered further by Schiappa's recent easing of his negative characterization of interpretive uses of classical ideas. See his "Isocrates' *philosophia* and contemporary pragmatism" in Mailloux, *Rhetoric, Sophistry, Pragmatism*. For a more negative reading of Schiappa's rejection of Sophistic rhetoric and a corresponding and trenchant rejection of Schiappa himself, see Vitanza's postmodern reading of the Sophists in his *Negation, Subjectivity, and The History of Rhetoric*, especially 27–55. Vitanza also gathers together a useful collection of essays on the traditionalist/revisionist controversy. See his *Writing Histories of Rhetoric*. Sharon Crowley's lead essay, "Let Me Get This Straight," sets up the issues cogently. Finally, although Covino is not directly concerned with reinstating the Sophists, his *Magic, Rhetoric, and Literacy: An Eccentric History of the Composing Imagination* pursues goals similar to mine in revitalizing the idea of magic in relation to rhetoric. Magic, Covino notes "is the *process* of inducing belief and creating community, with reference to the dynamics of a rhetorical situation" (11).

12. Relations among *nomos* and *logos* are themselves complicated by the range of meanings orbiting around each term, meanings further complicated by our own reading of them all through contemporary ideas of the interdependency of language and knowledge. Still, that range of meanings adds not only complexity but richness as well. Rankin notes that *logos* "has a number of meanings in ancient Greek, covering 'word,' 'statement,' 'judgement,' 'argument,' 'reasoning,' 'proposition.' There is an underlying notion of rationality in all its varied shades of significance" (13). Kerferd states:

> In the case of logos there are three main areas of its application or use, all related by an underlying conceptual unity. These are first of all the area of language and linguistic formulation, hence speech, discourse, description, statement, arguments (as expressed in words) and so on; secondly the area of thought and mental processes, hence thinking, reasoning, accounting for, explanation (cf. *orthos logos*) etc.; thirdly the area of the world, that *about* which we are able to speak and to think, hence structural principles, formulae, natural laws and so on, provided that in each case they are regarded as actually present in and exhibited in the world-process. (83)

For its part, *nomos* traditionally has been placed within the general realm of negotiated, social laws, practices, and/or knowledges and contrasted with the more "reasoned" knowledge/truth of *logos* or the more material, measurable, even "fixed" knowledge proper to the realm of *physis*, although the separation varies by idea and context:

> Before there was any discussion of "cultural incommensurability," there was the conflict in fifth-century Greece: *nomos*, the realm of culture and moral truth, and *physis*, the realm of nature and real-

ity. For centuries, Greek philosophers and statesmen had never doubted that the norms and customs of norms were true, by nature. . . . But all this began to change with the increase of contact, sometimes violent, among Greek cities and with other cultures. To the extent that the realms of *nomos* and *physis* are the same, the members of a culture are able to trust in a moral order that is not in question. But this truth is in direct proportion to a foreclosure of cultural alternatives. (Farrell 51–52)

Physis itself shows variations in range, as noted by Kerferd: "The term *physis* is usually translated by 'nature.' It was the term which the Ionian scientists came to use for the whole of reality, or for its most abiding material source or constituents. But it also came early to be used to refer to the constitution or set of characteristics of a particular thing, . . . as in the expression 'the nature of a man'" (Kerferd 111). "The concept of nature 'is thus, following the pattern of the new medical science, transferred from the totality of the universe to the particularity of man, . . .'" (Levi, qtd. in Untersteiner 329; see also De Romilly 113–16, and elsewhere). Nevertheless, the Sophists, among others, separated the laws of *physis* or nature from those of *nomos:* "Most of these Sophists thought *physis* was a more fundamental and genuine entity than the structures of *nomoi* agreed upon by men" (Rankin 85). Ostwald echoes the same separation between naturalized and negotiated knowledges via *thesmos* and *nomos:* "The basic idea of *thesmos* is . . . that of something imposed by an external agency, conceived as standing apart and on a higher plane than the ordinary, upon those for whom it constitutes an obligation. The sense of obligation is also inherent in *nomos,* but it is motivated less by the authority of the agent who imposed it than by the fact that it is regarded and accepted as valid by those who live under it" (55).

13. It isn't just neo-Sophists who are interested in reinstating *nomos.* Reconsideration by rhetorical historians of the place of *nomos* in Greek thinking also is being used to underwrite neo-Aristotelian revaluations of rhetoric. Refusing to consider language as a mere tool in service to pure reasoning, for example, Farrell intentionally restates the Aristotelian solution to Plato's attacks: The practical reasoning of rhetoric produces probable knowledge and with it social structure. Farrell's own goal is to revitalize rhetoric by revitalizing "the concept and elusive practices of reason" (49). Within this realm of practical reason and deliberative rhetoric, language continues to operate as a tool for the negotiation of knowledge and culture rather than either a wholly constitutive force or a solipsistic barrier to communication. In such cases, rhetoric's concern with deliberation and negotiated knowledge is reemphasized through its role in construction of cultural norms. The impetus behind Farrell's revisiting of neo-Aristotelian social knowledge also lies behind reconsideration of both the Sophists and their own conception of *nomos,* or as Ostwald, Kerferd, and others translate it, "norm," "a social construct with ethical dimensions, . . . a belief, opinion, point of view, or intellectual attitude distinguished from transcendent truth" (Ostwald 37–38; Kerferd 112). Ostwald's definition likewise links *nomos* to both naturalized and admittedly negotiated knowledges:

Nomos, in all its senses, signifies an "order" and implies that this order is, or ought to be, generally regarded as valid and binding by the members of the group in which it prevails. This usually means that the members of a given group accept *nomos* without question, and general if not universal acceptance is especially in evidence in the most general senses of the term, when it refers to a way of life, to the normal order of things, to normal procedures, and to normal behaviour, or when it describes the authority on the basis of which or by which norms are issued, or the condition of law-and-order, in which the *nomoi* are obeyed. Acceptance is also implied in the more specific senses, when it designates the mores of a people and its various beliefs and practices in society, religion, and politics. (Ostwald 54)

14. Jarratt's stress on conscious behavior appears to result from her need to clarify her opposition to the traditional progression from the "mythic" consciousness of the presophistic Greeks to the rationalism of post-Aristotelian logos, a progression that Havelock also attempted to complicate, but with mixed results. Jarratt herself notes the connection (and her own stance) by suggesting that "somehow Havelock's attempt to trace the linguistic achievement of a philosophical language came to eclipse his earlier critical approach to the evolution of a political theory," thus unhappily reducing the complexity of sophistic thinking (44–45). For her part, Jarratt's declared goal is to demonstrate the distribution of all these forms of "consciousness" across supposedly discrete texts and historical periods so as "to disrupt the smooth, unidirectional flow from *mythos* to *logos*" (*Rereading* 32). For a more fully traditional, middle-ground approach, see Robert Ivie's work, especially "Metaphor and Mythic Fear: Harry S. Truman's Cold War Legacy" and *Congress Declares War: Rhetoric, Leadership, and Partisanship in the Early Republic.*

15. My use of Rosenfield and later of Roland Barthes here is somewhat perverse, since both critics make their arguments within self-declared autopsies on an ostensibly dead or dying rhetoric. Happily, neither has been proven correct, for reasons given below.

16. Barthes's ultimate goal is to escape from both Platonic idealism and linguistic determinism through ludic, stylistic play. Such a new rhetoric, in Worsham's eyes, would consist of a "new expressive, literary rhetoric [created] from a ludic or black rhetoric of theatrics and hysteria" (153). It would also bear similarities to rhetorical beliefs and practices long used to negatively characterize the rhetoric of the Sophists with its (among other features) intentional playfulness and disruption of linearity.

17. Havelock's definition of *doxa* is similar: "the 'seeming' that goes on in myself, 'the subject,' . . . and the 'seeming' that links me to other people looking at me. . . . It would appear therefore to be the ideal term to describe that fusion or confusion of the subject with the object. . ." (*Preface* 250–51). At the same time, Havelock's use of "confusion" suggests an attendant separation of subject and object echoing the traditional progression from Homeric oral poetry to Platonic rational discourse that he later assumes in his own theorizing.

2. Dominant Myths/Myths of Domination: Masculinity and Agency

1. The question is central to current rhetorical theory as well, as Takis Poulakos makes clear in arguing that rhetoric and the history of rhetoric should be designed as a project "driven by the Marxist commitment to human agency as [well as] by the poststructuralist commitment to the provisional character of subjectivity" ("Human Agency" 78). Lynne Layton argues the same issues in regard to psychoanalysis and identity: "Theory must find some way of including the modern and the postmodern in tension. . . . More attention needs to be paid to the tension between cohesion, which yields a sense of agency, and fragmentation, which does not" (121).

2. Ricoeur also discusses *doxa*. Unfortunately, he does so by setting up the traditional binary opposition by establishing "doxic belief" as secondary to scientific episteme (*Oneself* 21). But the issue is terminological; Ricoeur describes discourse activity similarly to the Sophists.

3. Among the more negative responses to de Man's rhetoric has been that of Brian Vickers, who notes, more than a bit tartly, that "de Man's influence on contemporary criticism, especially in America, has been great, and it may well be beneficial. But as regards rhetoric, his effect can only be harmful" (464). Jonathan Arac's response is more reserved, as Don Bialostosky has noted in discussing both authors (Bialostosky 325). Arac's angle of approach speaks to deep concerns over agency and determinism, noting that much of what guides de Man's *Allegories of Reading* are "Nietzschean concerns" that "complicate the relationship of knowledge and action, of any agent and action" (Arac 246).

4. That question has long been a part of philosophical, rhetorical, and literary critical discussion, but Hayden White gave the question new prominence by foregrounding it in relation to the supposedly factual realm of history. White's own resolution is a blend of rhetoric and Freud, most specifically in his focus on four key tropes: metaphor, metonymy, synechdoche, and irony. White is quite clear in his intentions: to connect the tropes to a general pattern of discourse and of rhetorical representation, and to imply a further connection between those basic elemental structuring patterns and mental behavior. As is true with de Man, reaction to White from traditional rhetorical historians has been mixed. Vicker's "refutative disposition" (Bialostosky 328) allows him to accept "some of White's principles," while claiming he "cannot do much" with White's focus on the master tropes (Vickers 441–42). Vickers is not alone in his complaints, however. White himself notes Gérard Genette's concern over reducing rhetoric to a limited set of figures (121). It is not simply a question of numbers, of course, but of the larger psychodynamics being suggested in regard to the workings of the figures. Tzvetan Todorov expresses a related interest in rhetoric, the figural, and Freud: "The symbolic mechanism that Freud has described lacks specificity; the operations that he identifies [as the dream-work] are simply those of any linguistic symbolism, as they have been inventoried, most notably, by the rhetorical tradition" (*Theories* 248). Interestingly, Todorov's point here is not to dismiss the tropes as conceptual tools but to reject Freud's attempt to link them primarily to unconscious workings of the mind, as he notes more explicitly in the French-language version of the essay (*Théories* 314). As these and

other arguments suggest, the issue of error and validity drives the related question of how to link the figural (and by implication, the rhetorical) to conceptual or psychological processes in particular and sociocultural dynamics and the question of the subject at large. Vickers himself argues that it is important to avoid any clear-cut, modern distinction between "feelings and thoughts," citing "a great pioneer in rhetorical criticism, Rosemond Tuve," for support (277). As for considering psychological categories of mind and rhetorical figures, it bears keeping in mind that the ultimate purpose of psychoanalysis is to describe active social behavior, behavior *describable through* but not *reducible to* Freud's early topography of separable mental structures. Silverman's theorizing exemplifies recent shifts in this direction. Compare, for example, her discussion and use of figural language in *The Subject of Semiotics* to the much wider ranging analyses of general discourse in *Male Subjectivity at the Margins*.

5. The neopragmatist desire for an active agency echoes concerns voiced by Rosenfield twenty-five years earlier, as his own interest in *doxa* paired with a desire to cure a Western tradition "ever more schizoid in its efforts to fragment self and social consciousness" (73). But neopragmatist difficulties are also present in Rosenfield's open-ended references to "human experience" and "public action" (74), where the actual makeup of "public" is quickly replaced by an appeal to successful agency and the action of "doing." This move carries real weight in the United States, with its longstanding tradition of getting on with it. But the argument lacks grounding, and *doxa* threatens to devolve into convenient terms, much like "rhetoric" itself.

6. Raymond Williams notes the impasse as well:

> There is of course that difficulty that domination and subordination, as effective descriptions of cultural formation will, by many, be refused; that the alternative language of co-operative shaping, of common contribution, which the traditional concept of "culture" so notably expressed, will be found preferable. In this fundamental choice there is no alternative, from any socialist position, to recognition and emphasis of the massive historical and immediate experience of class domination and subordination, in all their different forms. (112)

The same issue appears to be at the base of Mailloux's arguments with Paul Armstrong: "Armstrong seems to reject Rorty's attack on epistemology at least partly because it entails a theoretical displacement of the confrontation model of subject and object with a conversation model of disputes among reading subjects" (*Reception* 65).

7. Rosenfield's rhetoric (in both senses) also demonstrates how easily the *doxa* of masculinity finds its way into ostensibly gender-free discussions of agency and masculinity. He urges, for example, reversal of the modern slide toward "an emasculated notion of rhetoric," a failed rhetoric that would be confined to "gestures of impotence" (74).

8. Opposing beliefs do operate in the midst of dominant orthodoxy. As Bourdieu notes, "any language that can command attention is an 'authorized language,'" even if the language of a small group (170–71). Such a language

legitimates its self-image by offering a coherent discourse outside that of the dominant power structure. Yet heterodox visions regularly substitute one dominant—*doxa*—for another. Cults are a good example.

9. Many of Pleck's SRS propositions emphasize such an active dynamic.

> PROPOSITION 2.* *Sex roles are contradictory and inconsistent* . . . mak[ing] it difficult, if not impossible, to conform to sex roles. . . . PROPOSITION 3.* *The proportion of individuals who violate sex roles is high.* . . . PROPOSITION 8.* *Certain characteristics prescribed by sex roles are psychologically dysfunctional.* This proposition . . . holds that even if [men] successfully live up to the male role, they suffer adverse consequences. . . . PROPOSITION 10.* *Historical change causes sex role strain.* (142–52)

10. Connell states his similar attitude in discussing a "dramaturgical metaphor of role." Such a concept is not "entirely useless in understanding social situations," he admits (26). But masculinity as a role is quickly introduced and then removed, reduced to stylized dramaturgical behaviors outside of any sophisticated science or ethnography of masculinity or, even more importantly, outside of any complex or deep-rooted internalization of masculinity by the role player.

11. Mitchell and Rose argue that much of Lacan's theorizing (and much of the negative reaction to him) comes from his direct attacks on what he saw as an attempt to meliorate the necessary division of subjectivity through a shift from the oedipal paternal to a more satisfactory preoedipal maternal (22–26). These arguments are very specific to the discipline and rest on particulars of psychoanalytic theory I am not developing here, although Mitchell and Rose provide a full discussion of them. Some broad points of disagreement with Lacan can be noted, however. The well-known slippage between the supposedly discrete meanings of phallus/penis is one obvious difficulty, but there are others. As Schapiro notes in regard to language acquisition, much clinical research, "particularly empirical work such as Stern's on the early interactions and response of infants," doesn't match well with Lacan's arguments, especially as regards "Lacan's view of the primacy of language in the construction of subjectivity. Affective attunement precedes linguistic development and creates its own idiom" (22). Kristeva likewise argues for the presence of signifying practices that are linked more readily to preoedipal issues and precede full formal language acquisition (19–37). These arguments suggest difficulties with correlating the onset of language acquisition, the symbolic, and the oedipal period itself.

12. As Jacqueline Rose notes, feminist projects in general (and Juliet Mitchell's work in particular) have a long tradition of insisting on linkages between sexuality, psychoanalysis, and cultural training. "By presenting [her] case through psychoanalysis," Rose argues, "Juliet Mitchell was not, however, only arguing for the importance of psychoanalysis for feminism. She was equally inserting the question of femininity back into a project which, as long ago as the 1930s, had seen psychoanalysis as the only means of explaining the exact mechanisms whereby ideological processes are transformed, via individual subjects, into human actions and beliefs" (*Vision* 7).

13. Butler makes essentially the same point in regard to the disjunction between the performance of Lacanian masculinity as scripted by society and the anxieties of personal experience: "There is then *presupposed* in the imaginary masculine effort to identify with this position of having the phallus, a certain inevitable failure. . . . In this sense, the phallus is always already lost, and the fear of castration is a fear that phantasmatic identification will collide with and dissolve against the symbolic, a fear of the recognition that there can be no final obedience to that symbolic power, and this must be a recognition that, in some already operative way, one already has made" (*Bodies* 101–2).

14. The recent film version of "The Bicentennial Man" underscores the deep threat to the myth's rhetoric that is posed by Martin's unintended admission of failure. In typical Hollywood fashion, the film simply erases that insight, doing so over the course of the whole movie. To begin, Andrew Martin's pursuit of manhood is subtly conflated with his pursuit of a family. Indeed, the first words Andrew Martin speaks after naming himself to his owners are "Hello. . . . Is this one's family?" Such a question only establishes how outside the "properly" postoedipal, familial frame he is, and it sets the tone for the rest of his pursuit—family and the ostensible masculine wholeness it represents. Supposedly attempting to become human, what Andrew actually pursues is union with/ via Little Miss. But while that glance might hint at a fantasy of return to a previous wholeness that self-making typically denies, it actually only introduces it so as to allow Martin to succeed spectacularly in his self-making. Martin acquires language, a penis (an easy solution to Lacan's phallus/penis controversy), and a ready substitute for Little Miss: her nearly identical granddaughter (Portia, no less). The myth of self-making and its denial of a fantasied wholeness achieved through return to the female is thus conflated with a myth of "properly" postoedipal, masculine self-making in which struggle and effort produce union with the female. Having bedded Portia, Martin provides the ultimate declaration of masculinity: He farts. The World Congress's official declaration of his manhood (itself achieved through validation of his marriage to Portia) is hardly needed after such a performance, a fact underlined in the film by having Martin die before the declaration is announced. Even the sting of death is reduced, however, since Martin dies in bed with Portia at his side. She, on the other hand, must now also kill *herself* as a mark of her love—an issue worth investigating in itself.

15. Savran suggests the possibility in discussing contemporary, white male narratives of cultural victimization. He couples that discussion with reference to Judith Butler's question of whether "the strategies of male masochism and 'feminization' . . . couldn't also be construed as a subtle strategy of the phallus, a ruse of power—that's to say that 'divestiture' could be a strategy of phallic self-aggrandizement'" (Butler, "Body You Want"; also qtd. in Savran 205). Rephrased by Savran, the masochist "gains a certain authority by proving that he or she can take whatever is being dished out" (205). At base, however, power is retained by those claiming to have none, which clearly qualifies the claimed victimization and its possible masochism.

16. Savran draws on Freud's discussion of "reflexive sadomasochism, a condition in which the ego is ingeniously split between a sadistic (or masculinized)

half and a masochistic (or feminized) half" (Freud, "Instincts" 14: 111–40). It should also be noted that Savran refers regularly to Silverman but sets himself apart from what he sees as an extensive a-historicity in her work. He finds in her work "unremittingly universalizing tendencies of psychoanalysis—at least as she uses it" and a "disdain for 'economic determinism.'" Savran even argues that Silverman's "historical trauma" ignores any "consideration that the crisis might have material as well as psychological causes" (9–10). Savran is arguing that Silverman's universalizing of the ongoing oedipal myth as the basis of masculinity differs from his stress on a more fundamental role for historical materiality in its production of particular masculinities. I can't resolve their arguments here, but I will note that the historical range that Savran covers with his model (the seventeenth to twentieth centuries) doubles the historical range of my materials.

17. In citing Massé, I have no desire to argue that masochism is the same across gender lines. Nor am I suggesting that myths exist primarily to allow insight into the practice of engendering. Like Gothic fictions, mythic representations of masculine self-making are components of ongoing cultural rhetoric that constitutes not only gender training but also "regular" gender behavior, painful or not, understood or not.

3. A Father Is Being Beaten: History-Making Selves and Self-Making Histories

1. Ralph Ellison's protagonist in *Invisible Man* may quote Popeye directly, but Ellison tends to agree more with Bert Wheeler, as a scene punning on Popeye's diction makes clear. Seeing the actual cooked tuber for sale by a street vendor in New York, Invisible Man is reminded of his childhood and fantasizes an essential self. Caught up in his fantasy, he buys one, begins eating it, and punningly declares his inalienable essence: "I yam what I am." But that fantasied "essence" serves mainly as a social marker. As a black man, Invisible Man is indelibly marked by the social frame that surrounds him. His self-making declaration of identity is easily usurped, and his semirebellious act of eating yams to get back to his roots is met with "an unpleasant taste" (267). The yam has literally gone bad and turns bitter in Invisible Man's mouth, as does the prospect of a self-declared identity.

2. George Lipsitz, in particular, argues that popular fictions belong to "a realm between myth and history. . . . It is literature that brings out the hidden resources of collective historical memory" (229–30). Lipsitz combines myth, history, and Foucault's "counter-memory" in ways clearly applicable to my arguments, although his generic concerns are not mine.

3. A count of Carnegie's essays produces "sixty-eight articles, forty-six in American and twenty-two in British publications. . . . Of this total, twenty-five— a little more than one-third—were later printed in book form in his lifetime, thirteen in *The Gospel of Wealth*, eleven in *The Empire of Business*, and one in *Problems of Today* (Swetnam 58–59). The *Autobiography* itself was an on-going project for Carnegie (1835–1919). It covers the entire life of Carnegie, from his childhood in Scotland to his eightieth year as a U.S. citizen, albeit in an obviously selective way. According to the preface, written by Carnegie's wife,

Louise, he began jotting down materials after his retirement but stopped doing so in July 1914, because of the impact of World War I. It was, however, "substantially completed" by that time (Tichi, Foreword xi). The editor of the materials, John C. Van Dyke, claims to have done little with the materials, other than arrange them chronologically, prior to their publication in 1920 (Editor's Note ix).

4. For a discussion of Whittaker, see the sections in chapter 4 devoted to *Larry Locke*.

5. The project most readily available for such mythic self-making would be one noted by Tichi: the 1868–1874 construction of James Eads's St. Louis bridge, which united West and East across the Mississippi as never before possible. Carnegie's Keystone Bridge Company and his Carnegie, Kloman, and Company steel mills produced the bridge's structural components.

6. Carnegie obviously wrote the *Autobiography* from this latter position, and it certainly affected portraits of the earlier life. But the differing rhetorical stances remain visible throughout.

7. My use of the specific psychoanalytic term *family romance* relies on its traditional definition while extending it somewhat: "fantasies whereby the subject imagines that his relationship to his parents has been modified (as when he imagines, for example, that he is really a foundling). Such fantasies are grounded in the Oedipus complex" (LaPlanche and Pontalis, 160). As the parenthetical statement makes clear, the fantasies traditionally attached to the complex are fairly specific and particular. My use of the term assumes a more general narrative of development, a sequential progression marked by a series of fantasies of parental replacement or reorientation that do effectively alter the child's relation to the parent, but not in so radical a fashion as the typical romances suggest. Although I include preoedipal as well as oedipal concerns as the frame and motivation for the fantasies, the rhetoric of self-making does emphasize the latter in order to stress "proper" manly exchange (and to reverse masculinity's primary defeats).

8. This passage certainly provides a more than adequate representation of a mother "won" by the dominant male. Whether it is an accurate portrait of Carnegie's psyche is another question. Wall, for example, raises and then drops such questions about Carnegie's family dynamics:

> All of the psychological explanations so dear to the amateur Freudian could be brought forth in way of explanation: a weak, ineffectual father who had been unable to provide for his sons; a domineering, ambitious mother who *had* provided; an unduly prolonged childhood innocence of sexual knowledge; a sense of competition with a younger brother for his mother's affection; a personal vanity so strong as to indicate latent narcissism. . . . But the historian lacks the competence to probe so deeply into Carnegie's psyche as to offer an explanation for Carnegie's attitudes toward his mother and marriage. (416–17)

Wall's demurral is more than a bit disingenuous, although he does tend to hold to his word. I'm not looking for closeted details of a personal life, either, but for revealed tensions in cultural *doxa* and myth. Carnegie's essential declaration that his mother is for him alone certainly raises eyebrows, but his more direct exchanges with his father are more useful still. See this chapter's following discussions of Carnegie's telegraph position and his meeting with his father on a boat.

9. It is possible that Carnegie is referring to himself as "the Scot." Whichever reference is assumed, it remains clear that Carnegie ignores possible readings of his father's silence that would reflect badly on himself.

10. Carnegie made no concerted use of the social mobility often available through marriage. He did not marry until he was fifty-one and already phenomenally successful economically. Nor did he marry into Pittsburgh social circles, choosing instead to marry Louise Whitfield, "the daughter of a fairly well-to-do [New York City] merchant" (Wall 400). This material provides no opportunity for mythmaking, but it does give Wall an opportunity to reinforce the mother/son dynamics he claims to be unable to fully develop. He notes that Carnegie's mother "apparently had no fear that Andrew would ever revolt and declare his personal independence from her matriarchal control. His sense of indebtedness to her was too great" (400). Carnegie himself does not speak to that issue.

11. Ingham's discussion relies on Ralph Turner's concepts of contest and sponsored mobility, which are designed to describe educational opportunities in England: "*Contest* mobility is a system in which elite status is the prize in an open contest and is taken by the aspirants own efforts. . . . Under *sponsored* mobility elite recruits are chosen by the established elite or their agents, and elite status is *given* on the basis of some criterion of supposed merit and cannot be *taken* by any amount of effort or strategy" (856). Sponsored mobility obviously dampens the rhetoric of independent self-making.

12. Again countering the rhetoric of decisive agency, Wall claims that "some of Carnegie's fellow operators would later be convinced in their own minds that Carnegie was curiously reluctant to accept Scott's offer when it was formally made, and that they had persuaded him his prospects would be better with the railroad" (116).

13. The desire to escape from institutional dependence was ironically reinforced by other issues than a desire for self-making in the later nineteenth century, when the increasing power and growing complexity of corporate institutions was less a direct concern to most workers than job security. Such a labor market did not erase and could actually increase hopes in the validity of "persisting popular images of business success through self-help, luck and pluck, and venturesome risk taking" (Trachtenberg 65).

14. Carnegie's business dealings are rife with opportunities for contradicting his mythic rhetoric. Another famous example is redolent less of self-making and more of fraud: "Before the first rail was even rolled at [the rival mill,] Duquesne, Carnegie sent a circular to the railroads, warning them that rails made by the continuous process . . . would be defective. . . . Carnegie, of course, knew that this claim was false, and after he took over the Duquesne works he retained the continuous process with never another word said about its defects. . . . The duplicity of Carnegie at this juncture was stupendous. . . ." Such busi-

ness behavior offers another reason, besides class snobbery, why "Carnegie and his mills were so despised by the older Pittsburgh steel men" (Ingham, *Making Iron and Steel* 70–71).

15. Misa, for example, suggests a rather different workplace from that of the dominant myth, one in which "Carnegie's personal friends in government, such as Secretary of State James G. Blaine (1889–1892) and the ambassador to Russia, Andrew D. White (1892–1894), intervened periodically on his company's behalf. Less exalted persons were no less useful. . . . [N]aval technocrats proved invaluable for the steel companies, securing contracts, negotiating the maze of naval bureaucracy, and forestalling the entry of rivals into the armor market" (104).

16. The tensions between mutualism and individual agency are exacerbated at all economic levels in the United States by doxic arguments for individuality as prime criterion for masculinity. The resulting implications for mutualism are noted in Denning's *Mechanic Accents: Dime Novels and Working-Class Culture in America,* Ingham's *Making Iron and Steel,* Brody's *Steelworkers in America: The Nonunion Era,* and Montgomery's *The Fall of the House of Labor: The Workplace, the State, and American Labor Activism, 1865–1925,* among others. I discuss the impact of these tensions on working-class and, particularly, union-based myths of masculinity at length in the upcoming chapters, most thoroughly in chapters 4 and 5.

17. Wall cites the passage in stony silence. Meanwhile, Carnegie's "It counts many times more to do a kindness to a poor working man than to a millionaire" is matched for sheer smarminess only by "reward is sweet in proportion to the humbleness of the individual" (*Autobiography* 82). This paternalistic claptrap also contains the seed arguments for dependent welfare capitalism versus self-controlled unionism.

18. These labor disputes have been studied in great detail for over one hundred years, and the discussions are a combination of specific detail and labor/management orientation. Briefly stated, a wide variety of labor issues arose at various Carnegie mills. Chief among them were the so-called sliding scale (adjustments to the amount paid per ton of steel produced) and the eight- versus twelve-hour workday (also known as the three- or two-turn workday). Behind these issues was the larger management desire to co-opt or destroy the unions. It is worth noting that many mills in Pittsburgh were partially unionized, although unionization was often limited to the skilled workmen. Even when limited in membership, trying to destroy the unions or remove them from a mill "still appeared to be folly to most of the iron masters in 1882" (Ingham, *Making Iron and Steel* 125). Carnegie Steel's antiunion actions thus signal a shift in both industrial attitude and practice.

19. The importance to cultural rhetoric of individualism is made apparent in its use by the Amalgamated Union's lawyer, W. W. Erwin, in his defense of Sylvester Critchlow in the Homestead trials following on the heels of the job action. To appeal to the jury, Erwin describes Critchlow as a lone union man battling a corporate head who possesses the unlimited institutional power granted by controlling mindless minions—a reversal of the claim normally lodged against union leaders: "And [the Pinkertons] were under captains and

had waived their right to think for themselves; had sworn to obey their captain when he told them to kill the people at Homestead. This shows you the abandonment of individuality and concentration of power under one executive head; and that is the primary principle that constitutes war" (Burgoyne 255). The appeal was not successful.

20. Gilligan summarizes the dynamic, and along with it the rhetorical appeal for the male reader of Carnegie's behavior: "Transposing a hierarchy of power into a hierarchy of values, [the male] defuses a potentially explosive conflict between people by casting it as an impersonal conflict of claims. In this way, he abstracts the moral problem from the interpersonal situation, finding in the logic of fairness an objective way to decide who will win the dispute" (32).

21. He also can portray the craft-based (and therefore closed) Amalgamated Association of Iron and Steel Workers as an antidemocratic, elitist club, since most craft-based unions did not admit regular laborers as members. This membership rule, and its clear links to ethnocentrism and racism, reinforced the dominant myth's appeal to individualism. See chapters 4 and 6.

22. Michael Lavelle notes the explicit antiunion goals behind most "Right to Work" laws in his *Red, White and Blue-Collar Views: A Steelworker Speaks His Mind about America.* He uses his own rhetoric to clarify the laws: "I'd like to call 'right to work' what it should be correctly labeled: right to scab" (47). See chapter 7 for a fuller discussion of Lavelle.

23. Moving between them is like moving between eras and their accompanying arguments. The individual entrepreneur is portrayed as a blend of cheerful action and aggressive response: Where direct opposition does not work, shrewd manipulation of the symbolic takes over. The second portrait offers only broad generalizations about Homestead and labor at large. It is as if the damage to the myth that Homestead wrought needed to be offset by glancing even further backward historically in order to find the good old days of self-making and labor control.

24. Burgoyne describes the full range of the impact:

> [The Homestead lockout] was watched with anxiety by both friends and foes of organized labor on both sides of the Atlantic; it claimed the attention of leaders of thought in all departments of human activity; it stirred up the British House of Parliament and the United States Congress, agitated the newspaper press of both continents, became an issue in the election for President and is said to have contributed more largely to the defeat of Benjamin Harrison by Grover Cleveland than any other influence. (iii–iv)

25. In a further irony, Carnegie's public portrait was drawn using the same cultural rhetoric that he earlier had enacted for his own self-made portraits. The *Pall Mall Gazette*, for example, printed a double-column discussion. "On one side appeared a report of Mr. Carnegie's philanthropic talk at the opening of the free library at Aberdeen . . . and on the other a tell-tale table of reduced wages at Homestead" (Burgoyne 108). Carnegie is clearly not in control of the symbolic at this point.

26. It is worth noting that nonunion workers often directly supported union actions by voting to endorse them, even if they did vote as actual members of the union. This was true at Homestead in 1892: "Homestead was in fact exceptional; for the eight lodges in the plant, despite a membership limited to 800 of the 3,800 workmen, were able to bring out almost the entire labor force. But for the battle, the union might well have won the strike" (Brody 59).

27. The most notorious example of that failure rests in a cable supposedly sent to Carnegie by the workers asking for direction from the "Kind master." No evidence for the cable's existence could ever be found, much as Carnegie sought after it. Carnegie leaves the claim in the *Autobiography* anyway (223) and, in doing so, displays a singular talent for misreading his relationship with his workers (Wall 575–76). He likewise fails to hear any sarcasm in the comment by former mayor, now exiled-to-Mexico mill-worker John McLuckie. Told that Carnegie made an offer of money to get him back on his feet, McLuckie is reported to have said: "Well, that was damned white of Andy, wasn't it?" (*Autobiography* 228). In all these portraits, Carnegie shape shifts from self-made man, to decisive mill owner, and on down to paternalistic, corporate manager. The rhetoric of the self-made man barely survives in such conditions.

28. "*Triumphant Democracy* was a highly successful book in the United States, where it went through four printings and sold more than 30,000 copies. In Britain it did almost equally well, besides having a cheap addition in paperback which sold an additional 40,000. It was translated into several languages and sold all over Europe" (Swetnam 80).

29. There were direct rejections of Carnegie's gospel, among them that of William Tucker, an Andover theologian, "who with cold logic pointed out the deep cracks in the very foundations of Carnegie's refuge" (Wall 813–14). But in general, *doxa* simply accommodated the particulars or overrode them. The *Autobiography*, with its varied but largely unchanged version of the myth, is evidence of that, as are its discussions of labor.

30. In a famous 1868 note to himself, Carnegie declared that his goal was to stop pursuing wealth as a form of self-making and instead pursue knowledge (albeit a knowledge that could be attained in three years of "active work" and that was geared toward "speaking in public" [Wall 225]). Carnegie's willing support of higher education (mostly technical) and his role in its retirement package (eventually TIAA), his longstanding personal interest in literature, and his dedication to libraries undercut his own antieducational rhetoric.

4. Beyond the Buddy Principle:
Individual Struggle and Masculine Solidarity

1. Gompers replicates the conflict in a speech delivered at the height of the Homestead lockout of 1892. "We want," Gompers declares, "to maintain the rights of the people and their manhood and we can only do this by organization" (qtd. in Burgoyne 217–18). Here the needed rhetoric of "manhood" is linked to that of union "organization," introducing a tension between individualism and "organization" that operates constantly in the masculine ethos of the workplace. Mutuality versus individualism is also visible in popular songs from the heyday of the Knights of Labor, an open-membership union that declared:

"Knights of Labor, all fraternal, / Meet we here for mutual help; / Guarded each by truth and justice, / All our thoughts are not on self" (C. S. White, qtd. in Foner, *American Labor Songs* 146). That very mutuality was troubled, however, by anti-Semitic reference to "Old Shylock's greed," as well as policies intended to keep Chinese laborers out of the country and out of the union. The appeal to mutuality clearly is complicated by a variety of tensions and limits.

2. Robert Carlyle ("Gaz") directly states the masculine/feminine tension in an interview: "Suddenly, these guys were forced to look at themselves the way they had always looked at women. They had to re-reevaluate their place in society because the women now had jobs and they didn't" (Riding). The movie's concern is laudable, but it tends to resolve more subtle questions via an ambiguous masculine agency rooted in self-display—full nudity before an admiring female audience. The relatively large, positive popular reception given to *Full Monty* compares interestingly with the much quieter reaction to a film released one year earlier entitled *Brassed Off*, which deals with the closing of Britain's coal mines. Although sentimental, the latter provides little sexual humor and little affirmation of individual masculinity, instead offering the group as support mechanism. Both considerations were probably factors in the film's thin marketing and subsequent quiet reception. Its bitter denunciation of Thatcher's antilabor policies was probably another, not minor, factor.

3. The major texts to be addressed here are Captain Whittaker's novel *Larry Locke: Man of Iron; or, A Fight for Fortune: A Story of Labor and Capital,* James Davis's autobiography *The Iron Puddler: My Life in the Rolling Mills and What Came of It,* Robert Olen Butler's fictional *Wabash,* and Edward Bellamy's futuristic novel *Looking Backward: 2000–1887.*

4. Puddling consisted of "kneading" small batches (approximately two hundred pounds) of iron in a furnace until it reached the right consistency. The ball then was removed and passed on to the heaters, reheated, and passed on to rollers. They formed the ball to the necessary size and shape—rails, sheets, and so on. These activities were performed by relatively independent crews. The puddler was usually the head of each crew and, traditionally, the most knowledgeable craftsman.

5. Davis engages heavily paternalistic rhetoric throughout his workplace narrative. It is an argument cemented by his position as U.S. secretary of labor and his deep personal investment in the myth of individual self-making as the perfect model for the worker in capitalist America.

6. Ultimately, the blend of individual and group identity is reinforced through external performance, such as negotiating the value of the group's work with other authority figures. Montgomery offers one example of the process. As late as 1874, a group of rollers employed by the Columbus Rolling Mill Company was still in a position to negotiate amongst themselves the distribution of the company's wage offer of $1.13 per ton. Meeting "as a group, not as individuals . . . [they] decided collectively on the terms of the arrangement." The crews basically "subcontracted the entire job from their employers" (*Fall* 9–11), thus blending mutualism with opposition to power.

7. Noteworthy formation dates include April 17, 1858 (Iron City Forge); August 1872 (Associated Brotherhood of Iron and Steel Heaters, Rollers, and

Roughers); September 8, 1862 (United Sons of Vulcan); and June 2, 1873 (Iron and Steel Roll Hands Union) (Wright 409–18).

8. Ingham's work provides three major emphases among historians of labor: Brody's "image of labor relations in the industry keyed to the psychology of steel making" in which "whole armies of skilled workers" were replaced by "continuous processing machines manned by unskilled immigrants" (96); Montgomery's "graphic portrayals of the persistence of craftsman empires in the iron and steel mills" (*Making* 96–97); and Ingham's own position, described by Misa as "de-emphasiz[ing] the class-conscious battles, stressing instead the mutual accommodation of workers and managers" (Misa 266). Whatever the degree of worker control remaining, all the arguments underscore a significant loss of worker agency in steelmaking as a whole.

9. The first wave of primarily nonskilled immigrants came from eastern and southern Europe. The second arrived via the migration of black workers (initially skilled but later primarily unskilled) from the South. Most labor historians note craft and racial exclusions as fatal mistakes in unionization (see Brody 58; Couvares 22; and Montgomery, *Fall* 24–27). Effects of immigration and racism on unionization and the myth of self-making are discussed further in chapters 5 and 6.

10. Rodgers's *The Work Ethic in Industrial America* surveys the fiction of this period in terms of shifts in traditional ethical and moral values. The situation clearly fits Silverman's "historical trauma": A historical event "brings a large group of male subjects" into intimate contact with a loss of generally assumed power and status, and that event threatens "to *interrupt* or even *deconstitute* what a society assumes to be its master narratives" (*Male Subjectivity* 54–55).

11. Whittaker's labor novels include *John Armstrong, Mechanic; Jaspar Ray, the Journeyman Carpenter; Norman Case, Printer; Larry Locke; Job Manly; Jack Corwin, Boatbuilder;* and *Joe Downes, Truckman.* These stories "constituted only one-tenth of the 70 novels Whittaker churned out; the others dealt with the standard characters such as cowboys, detectives, pirates, and Russian spies" (Grimes 25n). However standard, *Larry Locke* is much less melodramatic than other available fiction about workers, such as Rebecca Harding Davis's *Life in the Iron Mills; or, The Korl Woman.* Whittaker is not necessarily less sentimental in his fiction, but he does work more from the point of view of the laborers and more fully addresses the inculcation and maintenance of popular manly attributes. See Fay Blake's *The Strike in the American Novel* for a helpful bibliography of strikes, strikers, strikebreakers, and mill owners in fiction.

12. Denning's claim that luck plays little part in Whittaker's stories deserves a bit more discussion. Larry Locke's fortunes don't have the blatant *deus ex machina* quality of a Ragged Dick who, as savior of a merchant's drowning son, is launched upward into his career. Locke benefits from chance encounters, but they are truer to the institutional patronage found in modern industrial America. I should also note that Denning basically is arguing that all narratives of self-making use the same language, but their accents are decidedly different (167). Alternatively, Rodgers argues for a greater separation between forms and social classes (39). But Denning's language image is apt, more useful than the image

of the "line" he later draws between Alger and Whittaker (171). None of the stories are completely sundered from the broad appeals and anxieties of the dominant, middle-class myth of masculine self-making.

13. Davis's nighttime reading may seem to suggest intellectualism or even higher education. But Davis has already established himself as different from both pseudointellectuals like "Comrade Bannerman" and effete college-types who know nothing of the real world. Reading in Davis's case is not a dangerous road toward feminine softening but rather an Algeresque road to self-making that is already masculinized by the reader's knowledge of his eventual economic rise and dominance of lesser males. For an African American take on "Bucket of Blood," see Wideman's representation in chapter 6.

14. Race and ethnicity deeply complicate self-making and its sadomasochism, of course. See chapter 5 and especially chapter 6's discussion of William Attaway's *Blood on the Forge* for a further discussion of this aspect of both scenes. See also Robyn Wiegman's discussion of the battle royal scene, in which she likewise discusses masculinity as a component of dominance and threatened feminization (105–6). Wiegman's work overall provides useful critiques of the cultural maintenance of masculine *doxa*. While she emphasizes the "how" of that process, I am suggesting that how and "why" are joined and jointly describable (2).

15. Not all hierarchical relations are sadomasochistic, although all have that possibility. For Chancer and other psychoanalytic theorists, the dividing line is not the sexual nature of the dominance but the degree of danger, physical or otherwise. The "most central criterion for determining the presence or absence of the sadomasochistic dynamic is whether individuals (or groups) positioned masochistically face severe consequences should they question, talk about, or challenge the power of those individuals (or groups) who are structurally more powerful" (3–5).

16. John E. Barrett's *A Knight of Labor; or, The Master Workman's Vow* uses an impending strike to stage a similar struggle over workplace control and its resulting dependence on or independence of a boss who is insisting upon a wage reduction. In this exchange, Tom Wilbur first hears the owner infantilize the workers by calling them dependents:

> "[Tell the workers] that the reduction must take place. We don't propose to be dictated to by our dependents—men whom we feed and clothe, and to whom our works give shelter."
>
> "I beg your pardon, Mr. Brandon," said Tom Wilbur, his face reddening with anger, "but the men are not your dependents. They earn every dollar you pay them, and the food and clothing of which you speak is the result of hard work. It is the men who feed and clothe their employers so handsomely, but for my part I'd rather leave out that phase of the discussion." (2)

17. It perhaps goes without saying that hats, manhood, and male genitalia are regularly linked in dreams, for obvious physical and social reasons. See Freud, "A Hat as a Symbol of a Man (or of Male Genitals)."

18. Moral masochism, as defined by Laplanche and Pontalis, is "seek[ing] out the position of victim" (244), a description that aligns it with some aspects of Christian martyrdom. But martyrdom is rarely seen as masochistic by those who praise it. Key to these differing opinions (as regards my interest in their implications for masculinity) are the issues of nonagency (although its degree and even presence are variable and debatable within and between both forms) and feminization (or emasculation). Suffice it to say that for many analysts and critics, martyrdom—at the least—shares some definite connections with the pleasures of masochism. For a fuller discussion of martyrdom and "Christian masochism," see especially Silverman's *Male Subjectivity at the Margins* and Savran's *Taking It Like a Man: White Masculinity, Masochism, and Contemporary American Culture.* See also chapter 2.

19. Other worker-oriented resolutions enact one of two common plot moves. The first simply promotes the Master Workman to manager, thus collapsing the figures of Larry and Paul into one seamlessly self-made man. Laboring mutuality is replaced by "rightfully earned" individual self-making. In Whittaker's *A Knight of Labor* for example, Job Manly maintains his manliness not only by rising from employee to employer but also by remaining a member of the union. That resolution sets aside all tensions even as it strains all credulity. The second common move resembles the Cinderella plot (also present in differing form in *Job Manly*). Here, the good workman is revealed as a part of management all along. Barrett's *A Knight of Labor* offers an example of this structure along with the requisite declaration of proper masculinity. Tom Wilbur tries to convince Dick Russell (in reality the owner's son, Basil Brandon) to join the Knights of Labor. "Stand with us" Wilber implores. "You will find that the honorable, manly course to pursue." Russell/Brandon agrees and Tom affirms the choice by noting that "I think your decision shows that you are every inch a man." (3). While worker Russell's choice of solidarity supposedly displays his manly inches, what actually is being portrayed is aristocratic Brandon's inherent manliness. The psychological appeal is not really to achieving manliness so much as to having its presence unveiled in one of the traditional story lines of the family romance. Whichever plot version is used, the blended appeal to craft labor and necessary rise offers a too-easy erasure of class issues, as Sedgwick's discussion of Adam Bede notes. She suggests that Bede's appeal not only engages "the values of an individualized, pre-industrial artisanry" but erases Bede's own status: "Adam is speaking from the position of heir-apparent to Jonathan Burge who owns the workshop. . . . It makes sense for *him* to want to reimpose the now emptied-out values of 'pride and delight' in work" since he is engaged in a "quiet slippage upward from worker to owner" (144–45).

20. It is possible that Whittaker's own middle-class status prevents him from incorporating working-class ethos, and so he necessarily reinscribes the value of middle- over working-class masculinity. That claim has several problems. First, one need not be of the class portrayed, as we noted in the reverse in regard to Carnegie, to enact the myth. Moreover, mythic rhetoric and *doxa* readily cross class boundaries. Finally, while Whittaker may engage in some romantic glances back to the days of craft labor, his concerns with modern industrial

laboring and the degree of masculine independence that can be wrung from it are rooted in explicit labor concerns not unlike those of the Frankfurt School and its characterization of working-class masculinity (see chapter 1, note 6). The degree of Whittaker's success in resolving working-class issues may be questioned, but not simply on the basis of class awareness.

21. John L. Thomas describes the novel's reception:

> *Looking Backward,* in 1888, propelled [Bellamy] from the literary wings into the middle of the American political scene. Sales of the book, sixty thousand the first year, soared over a hundred thousand the next as editions appeared in England, France, and Germany. . . . If the young John Dewey read the novel as a plea for an untried scheme of social engineering, the compilers of the Sweet Home Family Soap Album considered themselves warranted in including Bellamy along with Louisa May Alcott and James Whitcomb Riley as celebrants of traditional American values. (1)

22. This vision of upward mobility demonstrates cultural rhetoric's drive to essentialize agency as native ability. Rodgers suggests how the nineteenth-century doxic rhetoric brings together the myth's "disparate strands" of working and rising "to reaffirm the central premise of the work ethic: that work was the core of the moral life." (14). Within that doxic framework, nonrisers were simply "deficient," in Bellamy's words. An ostensibly more scientific article of faith was expressed by Frederick Taylor in testimony to the U.S. Congress. For Taylor, nonmovement up the industrial ladder equated with nonmovement up the evolutionary ladder. "I can say, without the slightest hesitation," Taylor told a congressional committee, "that the science of handling pig-iron is so great that the man who is . . . physically able to handle pig-iron and is sufficiently phlegmatic and stupid to choose this for his occupation is rarely able to comprehend the science of handling pig-iron" (qtd. in Montgomery, *Fall* 251).

23. Montgomery's own reading of Thomas Bell's *Out of This Furnace* leads him to consideration of the relationship Bell describes between fellow steelworkers Kracha and Dubik: "Chance had made them buddies, sharing the same room, the same bed; time made them good friends. They never had to learn about each other, feeling their way; as Kracha once said, they spoke the same language. They had honestly liked each other almost from the hour they met" (Montgomery, *Fall* 89; Bell 13; see chapter 5 for a discussion of Bell). Rotundo also extensively discusses such forms of male/male exchange (75–91). Interestingly, Rotundo moves to the other side, arguing at length that middle-class, male/male intimacy was highly common, while always insisting that it must be seen as "innocent": "In other words, a man who kissed or embraced an intimate male friend in bed did not worry about homosexual impulses because he did not assume that he had them. In the Victorian language of touch, a kiss or an embrace was a pure gesture of deep affection at least as much as it was an act of sexual expression" (84). But such full erasure of homosexuality tends to flatten the complexity of male/male intimacy even as it endorses the behavior. Peter Gay's reading of these complexities, specifically in relation to his and Rotundo's shared interest in Albert Dodd and Victorian sexual mores, seems a bit different to me (*Tender*

Passion 201–19). The section in which Gay discusses Dodd (and to which Rotundo refers) is entitled "Dividends of *Denial*" (emphasis added), for example. Gay also lists a wide number of mid-nineteenth-century laws punishing homosexuality and refers to such laws and such denials as a "convoluted ballet of social anxieties and unintended consequences" (220). This language paints a somewhat different picture than that of an anxiety-free innocence.

24. The range of contradictions and conflicts in the Promise Keepers and the mythopoetic men's movement as a whole—often exemplified in the *Iron John* motifs of Robert Bly—is discussed at length in Michael Kimmel's collection *The Politics of Manhood: Profeminist Men Respond to the Mythopoetic Men's Movement (And the Mythopoetic Leaders Answer)*. In discussing Catherine Stimpson, Savran also provides some useful connections: "The neoprimordial young man, victorious in the Oedipal struggle against his bureaucratized father, will, in other words, mark the fantasmatic return of an earlier stage of capitalism and the entrepreneurial masculinity to which it was historically linked" (126–27). A similar nostalgia for old-school self-making and masculinity is visible in Erikson's description of the twentieth-century's inadequate father, "Pop," who is inadequate in his ability to effect a properly oedipal separation and inadequate in his subsequent forcing of "American mothers [to step] into the role of the grandfathers as the fathers abdicated their dominant place in the family, the field of education, and in cultural life" (295). The guilt of separation from the mother noted in Erikson's earlier discussion of self-made men is rewritten significantly here. Mom separates from son, but does so by enacting what amounts to a "positively" cross-gendered, neo-oedipal booting of the son out into the real world. The family narrative closes with the usual ending, only the sex of the players has changed.

25. Erikson's description of the "American Identity" draws heavily on the motifs of the myth of self-making as a whole, while stressing its emphasis on the child who chooses to separate from the mother in order to pursue personal self-making. Such large-scale generalization of national identities is not without problems. But if Erikson's characterizations are seen as descriptions not of an American identity but of narratives about gender that society tells itself, as Erikson himself suggests, then his descriptions can be seen as usefully representing the dominant, middle-class myth of American masculinity. The difficulties occur when these narratives are set up as all inclusive, by society or social critic.

26. The cooperative (or co-op) movement provided an alternate opportunity for considering mutualism and interdependency within the larger frame of competitive capitalism. Organized primarily by skilled laborers, the movement achieved some success, especially through support by the Knights of Labor, but the fading of the Knights by the late 1880s pairs with that of co-op movements in the United States (see Rodgers 40–45). However interesting as a movement, co-operatives appear to lack the necessary motifs of individualism and struggle needed to become material for fiction that would be attractive to men.

5. Moving Up or Moving Out: Separation, Mobility, Agency

1. Boundaries between ethnicity and race are in constant flux, even as it is argued that they are clear and clearly valid markers of difference. As regards

the rhetoric of self-making, ethnicity is often seen as more easily "overcome" than race. My purpose here is not to endorse either the categories or social theories and cultural beliefs that assume such categories are not only apparent but natural. With that in mind, I often will refer to issues of ethnicity and race conjointly, seeing their ostensible borders as highly fluid within ongoing cultural rhetoric, while treating "standard" rhetorical enactments of them in separate chapters.

2. Kimmel's "Born to Run: Self-Control and Fantasies of Escape" in *Manhood in America: A Cultural History* offers a useful historical overview of the essential theme and its place in westward expansion. In Kimmel's words, "American men try to *control themselves;* they project their fears onto *others;* and when feeling too pressured, they attempt an *escape.* These three themes recur frequently in the following pages, as men return to self-control, exclusion, and escape in their efforts to ground a secure sense of themselves as men" (9). At the same time, Kimmel notes late in the book that such agency is suspect. "As feminist psychoanalysts have argued," Kimmel tells us, "the problem with men isn't that they have not separated enough from mother, but that they have separated *too much.* The project of Self-Made Masculinity, of a manhood constantly tested and proved, becomes equated with a relentless effort to repudiate femininity, a frantic effort to dissociate from women" (318). This need to replace the anxiety of separation from the feminine with the positive, ostensible self-making of mobility is the viewpoint I am emphasizing.

3. Terence V. Powderly, eventual head of the Knights of Labor, conveys the connection between journeyman freedom, identity, and economic issues: "It used to be the custom in those days for machinists, not held back by home ties, to lend an attentive ear to the call of the wanderlust when the blue birds ventured north in the spring. In our shop were quite a few who had intimated to me that they would like to 'go west' or somewhere with the opening of warm weather" (28).

4. Powderly himself was forced into tramping after being fired for union activities, and he found the experience devastating: "Only the man who stands utterly alone, friendless, moneyless, ill clad, shelterless and hungry, looking at the sun sinking in a mid-winter snow, can know what it is to be a real tramp. . . . I have sampled in all its awful reality the desolation and misery of tramp life that at times, during blinding storms of sleet and snow, seemed to shut out all sight and sound and hope of God" (27). Michael Lavelle offers a contemporary version: "I can remember a time when I was unemployed that I seriously considered going to Alaska or Australia. I would have thumbed to one or worked my passage to the other. . . . But when you sell the furniture and take off with the wife and kids, at some low point, it's not a high adventure, but a belly-to-backbone need for survival" (48). This is certainly not the mythic rhetoric of unbridled opportunity. Chapter 7 discusses Lavelle's modern self-making rhetoric more fully.

5. For Whittaker, it was enough for Locke to be metaphorically a man of iron, capable of physical feats evoking masculine struggle in general, For Davis, writing amidst growing interest in the well-tuned male physique, there was a desire to move closer and linger over the body itself. Bodily worship as part of a late nineteenth- and early twentieth-century cult of manhood has recently been

discussed by several authors. Kimmel for example, notes, that "by the turn of the century, a massive, nationwide health and athletics craze was in full swing as men compulsively attempted to develop manly physiques as a way of demonstrating that they possessed the interior virtues of manhood" (*Manhood* 120). See also Kim Townsend's *Manhood at Harvard: William James and Others* and Rotundo's "Passionate Manhood" in *American Manhood: Transformation in Masculinity from the Revolution to the Modern Era* (222–46). The argument has proven very useful to later periods and places as well. Suzanne Clark's *Cold Warriors: Manliness on Trial in the Rhetoric of the West* offers a detailed analysis of the Cold War period in the United States. Her study elucidates how the era's "hypermasculine national mythology" drew on the ethic embodied in Theodore Roosevelt and discussed by both Kimmel and Townsend. More importantly, she also makes clear that the myth was "threatened at every moment" by the evident unreality of the surrounding cultural spectacle that it supposedly supported (5). Richard Dyer's "White Man's Muscles" also provides an interesting discussion of bodybuilding, race, and imperialism in Italian *peplum* films that reflects in useful cross-cultural ways on Davis's blend of physical prowess and racial dominance.

6. Davenport's contrast relies on historical issues noted by Ingham *(Making Iron and Steel)*: The broad, nineteenth-century shift to large-scale, mass-production steelmaking has overshadowed the continuing presence of smaller but equally important specialty and alloy steel manufacturers. But Davenport's purposes are not only historical. Mass production of steel has an air of crudity and excess. Like his production techniques, Carnegie is refigured as corporately and personally unrefined and *nouveau riche*—Jay Gatsby in the foundry. Specialty steels connote craft-based, artisan processes—and by implication Paul Scott's more refined manliness. At the same time, Carnegie also lacks the craftsman's sense of manly creativity and hot metal mystery, as the film version has Paul note in urging his father not to sell their mill to Carnegie: "What does a blazing flame of molten iron mean to an owner who's a thousand miles away?"

7. To reinforce the difference between producing and manipulating, between true self-making and unnatural increasing, Davenport provides a wealth of East Coast money managers and stock manipulators throughout the novel. William Scott Jr., never able to love the mill and its labor, marries Boston money and is controlled by it from that point on. Thus unmanned, he further reduces his masculinity in a foiled plot to sell the Works to U.S. Steel. But the ultimate model of corporate indirection and nonmasculinity must be Ben Nicholas. A "stock manipulator of genius" (493), Ben is also an adulterer and (even more significant in a novel appearing in 1945) a Nazi sympathizer. A child born late into a weak marriage that is itself founded on old Boston money, he is presented by Davenport as a superior sadist, "super-skilled in the technique of unscrupulous business warfare" (588). As a negative vision of masculinity gone awry, Ben Nicholas himself embodies a multinational corporation—self-serving and soulless—so that Davenport can condemn fascism via a pseudoepic battle between Paul's offspring and Ben. There is a terrible irony in all these personifications. Their rhetoric of individual, manly battle sentimentalizes and erases the very institutionalizing powers and processes that allowed corporate support of

fascism. See Raul Hilberg's *The Destruction of the European Jews* for a less sim-plified view of the governmental/corporate nexus in Nazi Germany.

8. Further changes in the film version are also worth noting. As regards Mary and Paul, Pat Rafferty's most perverse enactment of twisted patriarchy is his cursing of her proposed marriage and any children that may issue from it. As regards the labor union, in the film it is the older Rafferty who murders Wil-liam Scott Sr. in a rage, leading to his own death and that of the film's appalled union leader, Jim Brennan. In the novel, it is the brother James who both leads the union and kills William Scott. All these changes serve to emphasize the role of the false father, and the need to oppose versions of his, but not all, law.

9. Davenport continually works to make corporations disappear into in-dividuals, reversing the direction but not the motive behind Carnegie's morphing of real workers into the image of the true American workman. In one example, Davenport uses wartime rhetoric to establish the mill as an extension of Paul's masculinity and his ability to "[make] death for anybody that bothers the U.S.A." Lest anyone miss the engendering rhetoric, Mary specifically declares its importance: "Oh, Paul, I—I love to hear you talk that way," she declares, her eyes becoming "moist and shiny" (322). These rather mawkish frameworks set a stage in which unions likewise disappear into individual political speeches. Paul's son Ted and niece Claire resolve the merits of the CIO, for example, when Claire opines: "All I know is that organized labor is the single strongest force opposed to Fascism in the world and that's the best reason for supporting or-ganized labor" (567). The tensions between unionism, owner control, and masculine ethos are swept away as World War I and World War II propaganda is put in the mouths of single speakers.

10. It cannot and should not be argued that upward mobility is simply a cynical corporate argument, nor that such mobility was never experienced. For skilled workers especially, the appeal of an upward move was an ongoing and regularly maintained component of mythic rhetoric and, as such, an undeniable aspect of workers' lives: "As a group, intelligent steelworkers had always been eager to rise. Horatio-Alger-type stories were popular in the columns of union periodicals. Superintendents were customarily recruited from the ranks. The lodge correspondence of the *Amalgamated Journal* carried frequent congratu-latory notices of brothers who had taken managerial positions" (Brody 86). "The crucial fact," Brody continues later, "was that in the steel mills immigrants did rise" (107)—desire is never untutored, nor is *doxa* enacted in myths that are completely inoperative in society. At the same time, the myth's instructions for masculinity are provided by a rhetoric never adequate to the complexity of the situation. Part of the myth's appeal, of course, lies precisely in its ability to reduce that very complexity to individual examples and individual models, what-ever the general experience of most.

11. Homes served to provide other forms of corporate control as well. For example, injured workers could easily be induced to sign inadequate compen-sation waivers if they feared having their mortgages foreclosed if they did not (Powderly 36–37).

12. The same mixed rhetoric is at work in profit sharing, the ostensible con-version of workers into capitalist owners of their own company. As early as

1900, organized labor concluded that "in essence profit sharing was a bribe for docility and substandard wages" (Rodgers 48–49).

13. Davenport reinforces Rafferty's manliness by granting him the mobility of the craftsman and then trumping that positive argument with one of even greater masculinity—that is, refusal of separation from his fellow union members at the mill. At the same time, Davenport will eventually turn on such solidarity, seeing in it a misplaced sense of brotherhood. Ultimately, in Davenport's masculine rhetoric, Rafferty should have placed his loyalty in Paul Scott as owner/craftsman, thus endorsing class separation and upward mobility as the ultimate form of separation and agency in masculine self-making.

14. Montgomery notes how such essentializing rhetoric can be used to blame nonachievers for their own exclusion: "In one sense, American culture at the turn of the century categorized all the strangers who filled the laborers' ranks as 'lesser breeds,' except those who were native white Americans, and they were 'bums'" (Fall 81) On the other hand, the rhetoric can be used to maintain the myth by emphasizing individual exceptions (such as Karel Hrdlička) who prove the rule. Upward mobility tainted by ethnic exclusion is paradoxically that; it is tainted by lesser types who can't follow the rules of real masculinity and succeed on their own.

15. It is a mark of Davenport's commitment to individualism and masculinity that she risks portraying Hrdlička's deep dependency in these tears. But she does so to further Paul's paternal masculinity. Likewise, although Davenport's portrait of Anglo-Irish opposition to "lesser" eastern European immigrants is historically correct, she also displays her own collusion in it. Davenport has Mary "gently" scold Paul for indiscriminately referring to all his eastern European employees as "Hunkies" (318). But Mary's categorical discriminations are followed up with a vengeance by Charlie's wife Julka, one of the book's heroines who chooses to separate herself from Slovaks on specific grounds. Julka insists upon "making distinctions between herself and Charlie as Czechs, and the other Hunkies who, she shrugged, are 'doity Slovaks,'" "poor doity Slovaks starving in hills" (315, 370).

16. Kracha is twenty-one years old when he leaves Hungary not as the stereotypical orphan but as a husband with a pregnant wife, a sister, a widowed mother, and another sister and a brother-in-law in America who will help him find a job. On the trip over, he befriends fellow countrymen and spends all his money trying to impress Zuska, whom he considers "unluckily married" (4). Thanks to this fantasy—and not because he is on a quest for self-growth and development—Kracha has no train fare when he docks and so must walk to Pennsylvania. Once there, Kracha gets a job through the help of his brother-in-law, meets his best friend Dubik, and after a year of saving, sends for his wife Elena. Shortly thereafter, all these people begin their movement into Pittsburgh-area steel mills.

6. Tapping the Heat: Race, Racism, and Erasure

1. In Toni Morrison's words, "There is still much solace in continuing dreams of democratic egalitarianism available by hiding class conflict, rage, and impotence in figurations of race. . . . [I]ndividualism is foregrounded (and believed in) when its background is stereotypified, enforced dependency" (64).

2. The comparison to Carnegie is common: "[Douglass] gave accounts of his standard speech on 'Self-Made Men' often . . . , [and] Andrew Carnegie's *Autobiography* exemplified this myth. Douglass's standard speech on 'Self-Made Men,' however, accentuated the morality of success rather than its economics" (Martin 256). Linkage to the general myth is even more prevalent. Valerie Smith suggests that "the plot of the [*Narrative*] offers a profound endorsement of the fundamental American plot, the myth of the self-made man" (27). Deborah McDowell argues that "Douglass's *Narrative* not only partakes of these [cultural] definitions of masculinity, but is also plotted according to the myth of the self-made man to which these definitions correspond" (198).

3. Other comments abound. Speaking directly of both the myth and Douglass's version of it, David Van Leer suggests that "the success of [the] narrative as literary statement . . . inevitably distances Douglass from the self he authenticates" (128). In Wilson J. Moses's words, "Douglass . . . was both a product and a casualty of his own self-promotion. . . . Frederick Douglass's rags-to-riches success story was typically American. . . . [But] Douglass became a stereotype, limited by the constraints of the myth to which he so successfully contributed" (68–69). Richard Yarborough notes that "like the majority of nineteenth-century black spokespersons, Douglass was unable or unwilling to call into question the white bourgeois paradigm of manhood itself. . . . [H]e sought validation in the most conventional, gender-specific terms for himself in particular and for black men in general from a white society unwilling to acknowledge the complex humanity of blacks in any unqualified way" ("Race, Violence, and Manhood" 182).

4. Ultimately, Baker's claim seemed to replace a romantic notion of individual speech with that of complete control by the dominant. More recent discussions have tended to see the question as one more of negotiation between the two poles. See, for example, Ziolkowski (151); Andrews (10–11); and Kibbey and Stepto (167), among others. For a broader discussion of the issues of life writing and African American autobiography in particular, see the work of James Olney. His "'I was born': Slave Narratives, Their Status as Autobiography, and as Literature" and "The Founding Fathers—Frederick Douglass and Booker T. Washington" are specifically concerned with Douglass. V. P. Franklin's *Living Our Stories, Telling Our Truths: Autobiography and the Making of the African-American Intellectual Tradition* provides overviews of many major African American autobiographers.

5. The appeal to rationality is reminiscent both of Barrett's sense of solidarity and of antisophistic visions of a rational society and rhetoric. Hartman's own approach matches my own regarding cultural rhetoric fairly well. As she notes in her introduction, her goal is "to critically interrogate terms like 'will,' 'agency,' 'individuality,' and 'responsibility' . . . [through] examining the constitution of the subject by dominant discourses as well as the ways in which the enslaved and the emancipated grappled with these terms and strived to reelaborate them in fashioning themselves as agents" (6). An interesting cross comparison to Hartman's sense of performing correct behaviors is visible in David Roediger's discussion of Irish development of a similar social correctness with the added fea-

ture of "whiteness," thus differentiating Irish from that of incorrect—read black—masculinity (*Wages of Whiteness*).

6. Peter Dorsey agrees that Douglass may frequently invoke patriarchal sources of manhood but notes that "major elements of his manly performance are attributed to his imitation of women" (442) Dorsey uses such examples to suggest the importance of noting an "ambivalence about manhood" (443) in Douglass, and his argument is most convincing in its discussion of Douglass's attempts to address issues regarding the feminine rather than seeing his rhetoric as enacting manhood through feminine mimesis. Douglass's mimesis does not exclude rich and powerful white males, for example. Likewise, Hartman notes that much of the discourse concerning self-making was notable for "effacing the presence of women with the discourse of freedom, thereby restricting the act of making to masculinity" (152). As for Douglass himself, Leverenz acknowledges Douglass's commitment to feminism, but still notes that "Douglass's preoccupation with manhood and power all but erases any self-representation linking him to women, family, and intimacy or to lower-class black people" (109). It is a masculinity defined "through increasingly heroic separations" (131) or, stated in Yarborough's terms, Douglass's "celebration of solitary male heroism leaves little room for women" ("Race, Violence, and Manhood" 176) even as it extols the importance of their role.

7. It is a struggle further validated by its overcoming of race, as Douglass's closing reference to "tendencies of circumstance" quietly notes.

8. Hartman develops this oppositional rhetoric further:

> "Burdened individuality" designates the double bind of emancipation—the onerous responsibilities of freedom with the enjoyment of few of its entitlements, the collusion of the disembodied equality of liberal individuality with the dominated, regulated, and disciplined embodiment of blackness, the entanglements of sovereignty and subjection, and the transformation of involuntary servitude effected under the aegis of free labor. . . . The power generative of this condition of burdened individuality encompassed repression, domination, techniques of discipline, strategies of self-improvement, and the regulatory interventions of the state. (121)

9. The degree to which Douglass manipulated voice in his writing and oratory with attention to his audiences is suggested by Fishkin and Peterson. See their "'We Hold These Truths to Be Self-Evident': The Rhetoric of Frederick Douglass's Journalism," in Sundquist.

10. Most scholars note that black unskilled laborers broke few strikes, and the majority did not enter the mills as strikebreakers (Epstein 36; Dickerson 15; Spero and Harris 131).

11. Hamilton points to this dynamic but sees the collusion as more complex. "While urban society emphasizes individualism," she notes, "the older tradition of rural migrants was one of group identification. . . . Therefore group formations, whether family, church, union, or community, would be critical political tools, and it is precisely this fact which determined industrialists to try

to thwart the development of such formations" (158–59). One way to gain control, of course, was to encourage churches to adopt the corporate myth rather than speaking a subversive rhetoric.

12. Once again, to discuss limits on African American self-making is not to argue that there was no upward mobility and no actual success story to be pointed to as proof. I've already noted that cultural rhetoric regularly co-opts particular examples for a dominant myth. Likewise, upward mobility itself could be qualified somewhat to fit the myth. John Butler suggests that "within the realities of racism, prejudice, and discrimination" (34), black entrepreneurship was not open ended but consisted in finding a niche role between dominant and marginalized groups: "Those of today who can trace their roots back to entrepreneurship and the self-help experience possess a set of values which are similar—if not identical—to middleman ethnic groups" (314). A similar sense of limited success is evident in Trey Ellis's sarcastic revision of the myth: "If we play by [Shelby] Steele's rules—work hard, scrimp, save, and study—then one day one of us just might become Vice-President of the United States" (10).

13. There is a long history of associating jobs with race or ethnicity. "Laborers of the early twentieth century seldom quizzed a native white American who joined them about his origins. They took it for granted that he was either a drunkard or someone on the run from the law or his family. A 'normal' laborer was a foreign-born or black farm youth" (Montgomery, *Fall* 65).

14. Spero and Harris argue that corporate manipulation of class tensions among workers and the inherent individualism of craft unions had an effect equal to that of worker racism (56, 462). There is merit in their emphasis on class manipulations as the source of tensions, but it does not eliminate the presence of racial discrimination. For his part, Dickerson wants no complications of the issue. He simply declares that "race, not class, has fixed the status of contemporary Black workers" (1). It is certain that corporate and union executives together agreed in a 1974 consent decree that they had "systematically" discriminated against blacks, Hispanics, and women (Dickerson 244). This decree adds its own note of irony. As was true in *Larry Locke,* greater access to the myth by black workers was achieved not via individual effort but through the institutional power of the legal system.

15. In a stereotype of rational rhetoric itself, Thanet declares that such men "were past argument. They needed a demonstration" (458)—or perhaps a Sophist as orator.

16. Attaway's labor concerns run deep. See Yarborough's discussion of his work as a labor organizer and his further connections with left politics and other concerned writers such as Wright and Ellison (Afterword). V. P. Franklin adds further context by discussing Harry Haywood's *Black Bolshevik: Autobiography of an Afro-American Communist* and his role in the Communist Party in the United States during the 1930s and 1940s. Murray Kempton's sense of "myth" is more traditional than mine, but he provides a useful historical discussion of writer/worker connections during the 1930s and 1940s in his *Part of Our Time;* see especially "The Social Muse" and "George" for a quick sense of the tenor of the times. These materials provide a quick introduction to a large, fertile, and deeply complex body of work that I can only suggest here.

17. Phillip Harper notes not only the linkage of verbal prowess and masculinity but also its implications within black culture: "Verbal facility becomes proof of one's conventional masculinity and thus silences discussion of one's possible homosexuality, in a pattern that has been extended—to wide notice—in much contemporary rap music." At the same time, "a too-evident facility in the standard white idiom can quickly identify one not as a strong black man, but rather as a white-identified Uncle Tom, who must, therefore, also be weak, effeminate, and probably a 'fag'" (11). See below for discussions of Mikey's and Wideman's speech patterns.

18. As Hamilton notes, following bell hooks, putting black and white men "in a work situation in which neither had permanent female and family attachments [produced an] illusion of 'equality,' whereas when women, black or white, entered the picture, the behavioral codes of the color bar became more overt. . . . The illusion of male equality in industrial cities with the absence of 'attached women' provided a major service to employers" (149).

19. The young Zanski, Big Mat's fellow steelworker, provides the subversion of individualistic self-making through union solidarity that Attaway desires but cannot fulfill in Big Mat. That missed connection is also elaborated through the elder Zanski, whom Melody has befriended. All these men fail to unite, in Attaway's eyes, because of the cruelty of racism and the manipulative forces of big business.

20. This bleak conclusion led to negative reactions when Attaway's novel first appeared. As Yarborough notes, reviews were generally positive, but "two of the harshest judgments were rendered by critics most sensitive to the political implications of Attaway's novel—Ralph Warner of the *Daily Worker* and Ralph Ellison in *Negro Quarterly*. . . . Ultimately, what Warner and Ellison found most objectionable was the tragic nature of Attaway's vision" (Afterword 308).

21. Wideman's work at the time of this writing consists of eleven novels, a short story collection (depending on how *Damballah* and *Fever* are categorized), two book-length nonfiction pieces, and various articles. Given that large body of work, I am discussing a variety of texts, while concentrating my discussion on the well-known Homewood trilogy, the novel *Reuben,* and the autobiographical *Brothers and Keepers* and *Fatheralong: A Meditation on Fathers and Sons, Race and Society.* These works are representative of various periods and enact key tensions in Wideman's work related to masculinity and self-making. For ease of presentation, I simply refer to figures as characters within all writings. My discussions of "Wideman," for example, will be discussions of the figure that appears in the writing, whatever the assumed link of that figure to the author. Finally, I will not discuss to any extent the formal qualities of Wideman's work. Byerman sums up Wideman's style in ways useful to my ideas of cultural rhetoric: "In [Wideman's] hands, versions of folk narration accommodate postmodern issues, and postmodern techniques . . . are made to resemble traditional storytelling" (56). In short, linearity and single-voiced narration are rejected in favor of a fluid, active mode of storytelling committed to language as at least partially constitutive of subjectivity.

22. Wideman's Homewood is due north of the original site of the Carnegie

works in Homestead, across the Monongahela. In between lie Frick Park and Homewood Cemetery, a geographical irony with its own significance.

23. George Will, no enemy of the myth, also provides a specific example of ghetto entrepreneurship. In reviewing William Adler's *Land of Opportunity,* Will begins by declaring that Adler's book is about "the remarkable Chamber brothers [who] rose from grinding poverty in the Arkansas delta to running a retail trade earning $1 million a week in Detroit." This article's opening sentence signals the rhetoric of self-making and primes readers for the links that follow, albeit with a twist. The self-made Chambers brothers are "Lee Iacoccas," Adler declares, "of the crack business." That statement, quoted by Will, more than hints at the impending mythic tensions, such as the Chambers brothers' belief that doing it all on one's own includes brutally beating your business opponents with hammers. Not surprisingly, given Will's commitment to the dominant myth, he solves the difficulty by attacking not the appeal and validity of the myth but the morality of the Chambers's techniques. The same sort of ready differentiation occurs when Will describes Adler's book as "a virtuoso performance" while attacking his anti-Reagan views and, more importantly, Adler's supposedly leftist desire to blame "social imperatives or cultural promptings" for the sadistic business practices behind the Chambers's self-made success. In a fine example of the rhetorical gyrations required by *doxa,* social practices and cultural rhetoric (or at least Reaganesque visions of them) cannot be blamed for the Chambers's behavior because that would vitiate the whole argument for self-making as real (and the conservative imperatives in its call to individuality). The Chambers brothers thus remain exemplars not of a myth but of the real—with necessary qualifiers added.

24. Wideman enacts the same paradox as his own child-narrator eats eggs, a food he hates, at the table of a family for which his grandmother cooks. Determined to show he belongs, he is surprised to see his "eggs were gone. Clean plate. Another sign of good breeding, of what a nice little gentleman I was. Except everybody else left lots of stuff on their plates" (33–35). Having followed one set of rules for proper behavior, the narrator finds that different rules only prove him to be Other anyway.

25. The same doxic logic is repeated by Wideman via Freeda French, the grandmother of many of the later novels and the wife of John French—two figures who are, in Mbalia's words, "perhaps the two people whom Wideman most respected as a child" (55). It is Freeda, a direct descendant of the biracial couple who established Homewood in the 1860s, who is unhappy with "the black tide of immigrants from the South [that] changed Homewood forever," referring to them as behaving like "roaches" and "people in the jungle" (*Sent* 368–69). This is devastating language, complicated by the positive role Freeda plays in Wideman's work as a whole. What it represents, however, is Wideman's argument that such racism is an ugly by-blow of internalization of the myth and the resulting felt need to establish separation and class distance from those now just arriving. As Wideman himself states in a later work, "When hordes of dark southern folks emigrated during the early 1900s to find work in Pittsburgh's mills, Freeda saw them as a threat to the live-and-let-live, mellow détente the Frenches and other early, predominantly light-skinned Homewood residents had

achieved with their Italian neighbors" (*Fatheralong* 122). Freeda's comments are a clear commentary not on Freeda alone but on the capacity of the myth to maintain itself under the pressure of racial contradictions.

26. Reinforcing that opposition, Mbalia rejects *Reuben,* preferring instead the political activism she finds in Wideman's subsequent novel, *Philadelphia Fire,* which teaches that "theory without practice is empty. Action is needed" (Mbalia 66). The appeal of political activism is reinforced by "Tommy" as well. He considers leading a high school strike among his best memories: "I was proud of that. . . . Didn't know exactly what I was doing, but I was steady doing it" (*Brothers* 117). Once again, however, individualistic activism is met by the power of established institutions, here the school board. Over the summer, the students' strike collapses, and its successes are simply set aside.

27. Wideman is aware of the dynamics of homosocial exchange within masculinity as well. In *Brothers and Keepers,* for example, he has noted the importance of presenting himself as a strong black man whenever he visits his brother in prison. To do so, he walks "separate from the women and separate from the children. I need to say to whoever's watching . . . [t]hese are my people. They're with me" (44). Wideman also complicates the issue of masculinity by refusing to let race disappear from male/male exchanges, thus reversing a rhetorical process that Wiegman cogently describes in her discussion of black/white "buddy" films such as the *Lethal Weapon* series. In those movies, "the ideological investments of regenerating the masculine are done to rearticulate dominant relations not just between men and women but, significantly, among men themselves. In such a process, the African-American male's inclusion in the separate world of the masculine is accomplished by detaching him from the historical context of race and installing him instead within the framework of gender" (124–25). Wideman clearly refuses any such easy representation of male homosocial exchange as a means to racial innocence.

28. As Wiegman notes, if general use of a positive father-figure allows "reestablishment of the masculine as the site for healing and wholeness," then presentation of a strong, black father-figure allows "dominant discourses [to] provide images of individual African-American males that offer the appearance of a reconfigured U.S. culture" (138). The dynamics of oedipal struggle complicate such an easy reinstatement of black masculinity, however, as Byerman suggests:

> If the father conventionally represents a figure of authority and thus both threat and model for the son, then the position of the black father in a racist society is highly problematic. Such a man lacks economic, political, and social power and thus can be seen as impotent by his son; moreover, if . . . the father symbolizes the law, then the black man, stereotyped as criminal, can never embody legitimate authority. The real power, the true father, in this sense must always be the white man. (13–14)

The oedipal frame, with its clear issues of dominance, thus further complicates popular attempts to meliorate issues of race within the *doxa* of masculinity.

29. The discussion of the station includes other scopophilic vignettes and their mixed agencies. For example, a young prostitute enters to buy coffee, is freely

eyed by the men in the building, but still suggests that "she's in charge of what's free and what ain't" (156–57).

30. In becoming sexual, Wideman says, he learned "boundaries, places I could touch and not touch, places where the women's bodies changed, attracting me, scaring me." Facing that threat, he births his own father, oddly enough as a helpful "absence": "In the room full of women's secrets I birthed him" (56). This is a highly complex blending of masculine and feminine, self-making and dependency that once again is underwritten by a rhetoric of necessary separation.

31. It is present as well in Wideman's most recent work, *Two Cities* (1998). In this novel, Robert Jones returns to his old neighborhood but as a middle-aged man separated from the Homewood community as a whole. In that separation, he is like Martin Mallory, an old man living in a house on Cassina Way that may well be Robert's own childhood home. The connection between these two men, beyond their shared sense of separation, is once again a woman who lives in the same building as Mallory and with whom Jones begins an affair.

7. Making New Metal from Old: Retooling the Self-Made Man

1. The acronyms stand for American Federation of Labor-Congress of Industrial Organizations, Steel Workers Organizing Committee, and United Steel Workers, respectively.

2. Because "Iacocca" is discussed here as a rhetorical and historical construct and not the man, I will tend to refer to the book as *Iacocca* and the figure it enacts as Iacocca. In almost no cases, however, am I referring to the Iacocca who gets up in the morning, scratches (or doesn't), and may well attempt to live a life similar to that of the figure that appears in the book. The same holds true for "Michael Lavelle" and, indeed, for almost all figures who lay claim to authenticity through verbal construction.

3. In an increasingly service-oriented, deindustrialized workplace, authenticity signals a particular concern with escaping the trammeling ties of institutional nonagency. The late-nineteenth century had similar anxieties. See Leverenz and also Kimmel, "The Contemporary 'Crisis' of Masculinity." See also my discussion in "The Rhetoric of Masculinity: Origins, Institutions, and the Myth of the Self-Made Man."

4. Tichi's (and Carnegie's) iron bridges are one early example. Preston's steel allows a similar alliance of entrepreneurial risk, dangerous product, and authentic masculinity. *Iacocca*'s automobiles work but are a little less immediate in their sense of mystery and danger. Victor Kiam, on the other hand, faces the more difficult task of how to align authentic masculinity with such products as a vacuum cleaner. His attempts demonstrate rather clearly the gap between modern entrepreneurial manipulator and traditional creator or worker.

5. As Kimmel notes in discussing another "crisis" in masculinity at the opening of the twentieth century, "With office work increasingly feminized, aspiring white-collar men were counseled to enter the newly expanding field of sales. Salesmen were hailed as the self-made men of the new century. Sales reinforced 'independence and individuality,' wrote one salesman" (103). Arthur Miller's Willy Loman, the quintessential, downtrodden salesman, stands historically

between these two enactments of self-making, but the myth prefers to ignore his version of masculinity in stress.

6. The application does not transfer perfectly:

> This is a business school, Russian style. . . . New Business Technologies, which opened in November, preaches hard work and discipline around the clock. The 101 students, all men ages 17 to 22, live in tightly supervised dorms, adhere to a strict schedule and are in coat and tie by the time they hit the cafeteria for breakfast. There are no women because school officials contend the physical aspects like jogging are too difficult for them. In the five-year program, the essential reading includes the autobiography of Lee Iacocca. (Myre 16A)

Unfortunately, in the current economic climate of Russia, Preston's pioneers have become not just "well-connected, steel-nerved businessmen" but also decidedly negative embodiments of "Wild Western-style entrepreneur[s]" and "Cowboy bankers" whose personal self-making has "put an economy on its knees" (*New York Times* 3, 1).

7. There is another aspect to Ivy League schools not necessarily prevalent in all college training. In addition to reducing the arguments for "real-world" experience, college training at the Ivies suggests insider contacts and male clubbishness.

8. By Dobie's time, individual self-making as a function of craft-based separation and mobility would be even more obviously a nostalgic enactment of a traditional rhetorical appeal. Dobie does have "a trade," but he admits it "wouldn't be much good outside of a steel mill. And I've got nearly fifteen years' service in that mill. Fifteen more and I might get a pension, if you want to look at it that way" (370).

9. John Hoerr argues a similar point when he notes the inability of either union or management to change its basic oppositional stance even during the collapse of the industry in the 1980s. Following the collapse, all that remained for many workers was oppositional rhetoric, and two targets for it instead of one. See especially pages 20–23 in Hoerr's *And the Wolf Finally Came*.

10. Preston's technique of stitching together technical language and dramatic events is likewise visible in his yoking of biology, human symptomology, and the Ebola virus. See his *The Hot Zone*. In reviewing Sebastian Junger's *The Perfect Storm*, David Gates a bit snidely but not altogether inaccurately describes the genre in general as a "classic high-end journalistic mix: history, techie arcana, gee-whiz factoids and memorable characters" (55).

11. Novak himself has become a minor celebrity, "The King of the Ghosts" (Starr 67), precisely on the strength of his ostensible ability to let his high profile clients "speak in their own voices" in the texts he produces for them (67). This willful insistence on the genuine article, the authenticity of the self-made/represented, is not uncommon. The call for straight talk as an aspect of self-making is a well-worn motif available as early as Benjamin Franklin.

12. Dillon's *Rhetoric as Social Imagination* uses a blend of speech-act and rhetorical theory to analyze the discourse structure of self-help and entrepre-

neurial manuals. He describes social exchanges in terms of Erving Goffman's footings (*Forms of Talk*)—established roles for exchange—that also imply the gendered identity roles enacted in the myth. Dillon's own footings are established as a series of binary oppositions or opposing appeals—impersonal/personal, distant/solidary, superior, authoritative/equal, limited/direct, confrontive/oblique, formal/informal (14–42)—and analyses of behavior. Such terms match readily with stereotypical gender-behavior, although they also risk falling into a simplifying binarism.

In addition to Dillon's study, there has been a great deal of recent work that is of interest to those wishing to pursue a more language-oriented study than is attempted here. Sociological analyses of language as rhetorical activity (in particular, ostensibly factual languages such as those of science) have proved a fruitful ground for studying the constructedness of social "reality" and its members. Jonathan Potter's recent *Representing Reality: Discourse, Rhetoric, and Social Construction* is a good example, especially in terms of his melding of formal language theory, description, and social construction. The work also provides a survey of related materials in various disciplines. Donna Jeane Haraway works in the same area, but her *Primate Visions* also considers the whole question of gender production. Teun A. Van Dijk's two-volume *Discourse Studies: A Multidisciplinary Introduction* provides more formal language and communication analyses.

13. The difference in the two is reinforced by O'Toole's further reactions. She dislikes the sections dealing with Wall Street (pseudoanalysis) but likes the sections dealing with family (implied self-making).

14. Where previously a Carnegie opposed individuality to union self-erasure, Preston now opposes individuality to institutional culture in general; the twentieth-century success of unions leads to their easy portrayal as stuffy bureaucracies. Faced with this common attitude, Lavelle is himself forced to base his pro-union arguments very heavily on individualized portraits of his experience as an honest steelworker. In a battle of anecdotal arguments, Preston's full-blown use of the myth of masculine self-making thus is ultimately more effective than Lavelle's "union-tainted" rhetoric because both appeals are rooted not only in doxically validated cultural desires for individualism and agency but also in a related antipathy to corporate bureaucracy and facelessness, which now can be attached to unions as well.

15. There are brief moments in which Preston allows unions to appear in a differing light. "There is another way to look at this story," he admits. "It was pretty clear that if a Nucor plant voted to join a labor union, Iverson might decide to sell off the plant or even close it down" (*American Steel* 82). Here, as individual worker agency is forced to take a backseat to corporate power, another form of risk taking appears, and it is one that decidedly complicates the dominant myth of self-making. Nevertheless, the appeal of identifying with Iverson's power and dominance is assumed to outweigh the danger of acknowledging his threat to worker agency.

16. Nostalgia regularly leads to reenactments and rewritings of earlier rhetorics of masculinity and their motifs. See Clark's *Cold Warriors: Manliness on Trial in the Rhetoric of the West,* for example, for insight into the "markedly

new use for the old narratives" of Theodore Roosevelt and his rhetoric of masculinity during the Cold War era (70).

17. Direct ties to Leverenz and his discussion of Ahab, homoeroticism, and homosexuality spring readily to mind at this point. Unfortunately, the complex issues that lurk elsewhere in Preston (or Davis and others) are not really present in this particular vignette, devoted as it is to individual acts of manly power rather than manly exchange. Not surprisingly, Preston shows no real desire to dig down into such questions. His attentions are already fully engaged by his need to offset the tensions between ritual craft and the actualities of steelmaking at the end of the century.

18. The appeal to masculinity and self-making is harder to achieve with other production methods and products. Iacocca risks losing some degree (or classbased component) of masculine appeal when he appears in advertisements wearing a three-piece suit. But he regularly does so while providing a backdrop of another truly American fantasy—the car—or a shot of the line with some extraspectacular heli-arc welding or, if all else fails, the man and a Jeep. Any of these products carries sufficient masculinity to trigger the sense of an intimate brotherhood of risk takers and craftsmen. The importance of that linkage is particularly visible in its absence, as Kiam again demonstrates. His early commercials show him in a bathrobe, risking mainly domesticity. Nor is his producing of vacuum cleaners and electric razors of much help in enacting masculine *doxa*. It is possible that these commercials are their own form of ironic gender argument, a reversal or refusal, even a parody of Preston's and Iacocca's product-based masculinity. But Kiam tends to rely on other, less savory representations that offset such readings. A man who began his career selling women's cosmetics and underwear, Kiam chattily presents himself playing the misogynistic "Mr. Omar," who happily urges any woman to buy face cream so that "if she happened to walk under a neon light, she would glow" (28). Nor does Kiam evidence any alertness to the overtones of his self-portrait when he presents the general roguery of "Dave the Rave," a salesman who regularly auditioned women to model bras and underwear in his motel room (56). Kiam facetiously asks whether he could fire Dave—after all, Dave always produced. In the end, this not-so-quiet misogyny only underlines the near-parodic excesses in Kiam's end-of-the-century portraits of masculinity:

> As an entrepreneur, I consider selling to be one of the noblest of professions. . . . You have no help in this endeavor. You are very much in the same situation as the boxer, standing alone in the naked, questioning glare of the klieg lights as he waits to face the vindication or repudiation of the career he's chosen. Joe Louis . . . once said of the elusive Billy Conn, "He can run, but he can't hide." Neither can the salesperson. (117)

It is an analogy that enacts none of the intimate brotherhood of craft, and it collapses under the weight of its own strained comparisons.

Works Cited

Alger, Horatio. *Fame and Fortune.* Philadelphia: Porter and Coates; copyright A. K. Loring, 1868.

Althusser, Louis. *For Marx.* 1965. Trans. Ben Brewster. London: Verso, 1982.

Andrews, William L., ed. *Critical Essays on Frederick Douglass.* Boston: Hall, 1991.

Arac, Jonathan. *Critical Genealogies: Historical Situations for Postmodern Literary Studies.* New York: Columbia UP, 1987.

Asimov, Isaac. "The Bicentennial Man." 1976. *The Bicentennial Man and Other Stories.* New York: Doubleday, 1976.

Atkinson, Edward. Letter to Andrew Carnegie. 3 February 1892. *Andrew Carnegie Papers.* Library of Congress.

Attaway, William. *Blood on the Forge.* New York: Doubleday, Doran, 1941. Rpt. New York: Monthly Review P, 1987.

Baker, Houston A., Jr. *The Journey Back: Issues in Black Literature and Criticism.* Chicago: U of Chicago P, 1980.

Barrett, John E. *A Knight of Labor; or, The Master Workman's Vow.* Street and Smith's *New York Weekly* 40 #4–15 (1 December 1884–16 February 1885). Rpt. Log Cabin Library #85 (30 October 1890).

Barthes, Roland. *Image—Music—Text.* Trans./Ed. Stephen Heath. New York: Hill and Wang, 1977.

———. *Mythologies.* Trans. Annette Lavers. New York: Hill and Wang, 1972.

———. "The Old Rhetoric: An aide-mémoire." *Communications* 16 (December 1970). Rpt. in Barthes, *The Semiotic Challenge* 11–94.

———. *The Semiotic Challenge.* Trans. Richard Howard. New York: Hill and Wang, 1988.

Battaglia, Debbora. *Rhetorics of Self-Making.* Berkeley: U of California P, 1995.

Baym, Nina. "Melodramas of Beset Manhood: How Theories of American Fiction Exclude Women Authors." Showalter 63–80.

Bell, Thomas. *Out of This Furnace.* 1941. Pittsburgh: U of Pittsburgh P, 1976.

Bellamy, Edward. *Looking Backward: 2000–1887.* 1888. Ed. John L. Thomas. Cambridge: Harvard UP, 1978.

Belton, Don, ed. *Speak My Name: Black Men on Masculinity and the American Dream.* Boston: Beacon, 1995.

Berlin, James A. *Rhetorics, Poetics, and Cultures.* Urbana, IL: NCTE, 1996.

Bialostosky, Don. "The Rhetorical Tradition and Recent Literary Theory." *College English* 51 (1989): 325–29.

Bicentennial Man. Screenplay by Nicholas Kazan. Dir. Chris Columbus. Perf. Robin Williams, Embeth Davidtz, and Sam Neill. Columbia Pictures, 1999.

Bitzer, Lloyd, and Edwin Black, eds. *The Prospect of Rhetoric.* Englewood Cliffs, NJ: Prentice Hall, 1971.

Black, Edwin. *Rhetorical Questions: Studies of Public Discourse.* Chicago: U of Chicago P, 1992.

Blake, Fay. *The Strike in the American Novel.* Metuchen, NJ: Scarecrow, 1972.

Blassingame, John W., and John R. McGiven, eds. *The Frederick Douglass Papers. Series One: Debates and Interviews. Volume Five: 1881–1895.* New Haven, CT: Yale UP, 1992.

Bormann, Ernest G. "Fantasy and Rhetorical Vision: The Rhetorical Criticism of Social Reality." *Quarterly Journal of Speech* 58 (1972): 396–407.

———. "Fantasy and Rhetorical Vision: Ten Years Later." *Quarterly Journal of Speech* 68 (1982): 288–305. (See Mohrmann for rebuttal.)

Bourdieu, Pierre. *Outline of a Theory of Practice.* 1972. Trans. Richard Nice. Cambridge: Cambridge UP, 1977.

Brassed Off! Dir. Mark Herman. Perf. Ewan McGregor and Tara Fitzgerald. Miramax, 1996.

Braudy, Leo. *The Frenzy of Renown: Fame and Its History.* New York: Oxford UP, 1986.

Bridge, James Howard. *The Inside History of the Carnegie Steel Company: A Romance of Millions.* New York: Aldine, 1903.

Brod, Harry, ed. *The Making of Masculinities: The New Men's Studies.* Winchester, MA: Allen and Unwin, 1987.

Brod, Harry, and Michael Kaufman, eds. *Theorizing Masculinities.* Thousand Oaks, CA: SAGE, 1994.

Brody, David. *Steelworkers in America: The Nonunion Era.* Cambridge: Harvard UP, 1960.

Brucker, Carl W. "Virtue Rewarded: The Contemporary Student and Horatio Alger." *Journal of General Education* 35.4 (1984): 270–75.

Burgoyne, Arthur G. *Homestead: A Complete History of the Struggle of July 1892 Between the Carnegie Steel Company and the Amalgamated Association of Iron and Steel Workers.* 1893 (privately printed). Rpt. New York: Kelley, 1971.

Butler, John Sibley. *Entrepreneurship and Self-Help among Black Americans: A Reconsideration of Race and Economics.* Albany: State U of New York P, 1991.

Butler, Judith. *Bodies That Matter: On the Discursive Limits of "Sex."* New York: Routledge, 1993.

———. "The Body You Want: Liz Kotz Interviews Judith Butler." *Artforum* 1992: 88.

———. *Gender Trouble: Feminism and the Subversion of Identity.* New York: Routledge, 1990.

Butler, Robert Olen. *Wabash.* New York: Ballantine, 1987.

Byerman, Keith E. *John Edgar Wideman: A Study of the Short Fiction.* Boston: Twayne, 1998.

Carnegie, Andrew. *The Autobiography of Andrew Carnegie*. 1920. Boston: Northeastern UP, 1986.

———. *The Empire of Business*. 1900. New York: Doubleday, 1902.

———. "The Gospel of Wealth." *North American Review* (June, December 1889): 653–64, 682–98.

———. *The Gospel of Wealth and Other Timely Essays*. Cambridge: Harvard UP, 1965.

———. *Problems of Today, Wealth, Labor, Socialism*. New York: Doubleday, Page, 1908.

———. *Triumphant Democracy; or, Fifty Years' March of the Republic*. 1886. 2 Vols. Port Washington, NY: Kennikat, 1971.

Cashman, Sean Dennis. *America in the Gilded Age: From the Death of Lincoln to the Rise of Theodore Roosevelt*. 1984. 3rd ed. New York: New York UP, 1993.

Catano, James V. "The Rhetoric of Masculinity: Origins, Institutions, and the Myth of the Self-Made Man." *College English* 52 (1990): 421–36.

Cawelti, John. *Apostles of the Self-Made Man*. Chicago: U of Chicago P, 1965.

Chancer, Lynn S. *Sadomasochism in Everyday Life: The Dynamics of Power and Powerlessness*. New Brunswick, NJ: Rutgers UP, 1992.

Chodorow, Nancy. *The Reproduction of Mothering: Psychoanalysis and the Sociology of Gender*. Berkeley: U of California P, 1978.

Chronicle of Higher Education. 31 January 1997: A15; 3 April 1998: B7.

Clark, Suzanne. *Cold Warriors: Manliness on Trial in the Rhetoric of the West*. Carbondale: Southern Illinois UP, 2000.

Cohen, Tom. "Diary of a Deconstructor Manque: Reflections on Post PostMortem de Man." *Minnesota-Review*. (Fall 1993–Spring 1994): 41–42, 157–74.

———. "The 'Genealogies' of Pragmatism." Mailloux, *Rhetoric, Sophistry, Pragmatism* 94–108.

Coleman, James William. *Blackness and Modernism: The Literary Career of John Edgar Wideman*. Jackson: UP of Mississippi, 1989.

Connell, R. W. *Masculinities*. Los Angeles: U of California P, 1995.

Conway-Long, Don. "Ethnographies of Masculinity." Brod and Kaufman 61–81.

Couvares, Francis G. *The Remaking of Pittsburgh: Class and Culture in an Industrializing City, 1877–1919*. Albany: State U of New York P, 1984.

Covino, William. *Magic, Rhetoric, and Literacy: An Eccentric History of the Composing Imagination*. Albany: State U of New York P, 1994.

Crowley, Sharon. "Let Me Get This Straight." Vitanza, *Writing Histories of Rhetoric* 1–19.

Davenport, Marcia. *The Valley of Decision*. New York: Scribner's, 1945.

Davis, Charles T., and Henry Louis Gates Jr., eds. *The Slave's Narrative*. New York: Oxford UP, 1985.

Davis, James J. *The Iron Puddler: My Life in the Rolling Mills and What Came of It*. New York: Bobbs-Merrill, 1922.

de Man, Paul. *Allegories of Reading: Figural Language in Rousseau, Nietzsche, Rilke, and Proust*. New Haven: Yale UP, 1979.

Denning, Michael. *Mechanic Accents: Dime Novels and Working-Class Culture in America*. New York: Verso, 1987.

De Romilly, Jacqueline. Trans. Janet Lloyd. *The Great Sophists in Periclean Athens*. Oxford: Oxford UP, 1992.

Dickerson, Dennis C. *Out of the Crucible: Black Steelworkers in Western Pennsylvania, 1875–1980*. New York: State U of New York P, 1986.

Dillon, George. *Rhetoric as Social Imagination*. Bloomington: Indiana UP, 1986.

Dorsey, Peter A. "Becoming the Other: The Mimesis of Metaphor in Douglass's *My Bondage and My Freedom*." *PMLA* 111.3 (May 1996): 433–50.

Douglass, Frederick. *My Bondage and My Freedom*. 1855. New York: Dover Publications, 1969.

———. *Narrative of the Life of Frederick Douglass, an American Slave*. 1845. New York: Penguin, 1982.

———. "Self-Made Men: An Address Delivered in Carlisle, Pennsylvania, March 1893." Blassingame and McGiven 545–75.

Dubofsky, Melvyn. *Industrialism and the American Worker, 1865–1920*. New York: Crowell, 1975.

Dyer, Richard. "White Man's Muscles." Stecopolous and Uebel 286–314.

Eisner, Robert. "Fantasy Islands." Rev. of *Imagining Atlantis*, by Richard Ellis. *New York Times Book Review* 2 June 1998: 13–14.

Ellis, Leonard. "Men among Men." Ph.D. diss. Columbia U, 1982.

Ellis, Trey. "How Does It Feel to Be a Problem?" Belton 9–11.

Ellison, Ralph. *Invisible Man*. 1947. New York: Vintage Books, 1989.

Enos, Richard Leo. *Greek Rhetoric Before Aristotle*. Prospect Heights, IL: Waveland Heights, 1993.

Epstein, Abraham. *The Negro Migrant in Pittsburgh*. 1918. New York: Arno, 1969.

Erikson, Erik. *Childhood and Society*. 1950. 2nd ed. New York: Norton, 1963.

Farrell, Thomas B. *Norms of Rhetorical Culture*. New Haven, CT: Yale UP, 1993.

Fishkin, Shelley Fisher, and Carla L. Peterson. "'We Hold These Truths to Be Self-Evident': The Rhetoric of Frederick Douglass's Journalism." Sundquist 189–204.

Foner, Philip S. *American Labor Songs of the Nineteenth Century*. Urbana: U of Illinois P, 1975.

———. *Frederick Douglass: A Biography*. New York: Citadel, 1964.

Foss, Sonja K., Karen A. Foss, and Robert Trapp. *Contemporary Perspectives on Rhetoric*. Prospect Heights, IL: Waveland, 1985.

Franchot, Jenny. "The Punishment of Esther: Frederick Douglass and the Construction of the Feminine." Sundquist 141–65.

Franklin, V. P. *Living Our Stories, Telling Our Truths: Autobiography and the Making of the African-American Intellectual Tradition*. New York: Oxford UP, 1995.

Freifeld, Mary. "The Emergence of the American Working Classes: The Roots of Division, 1865–1885." Ph.D. diss. New York U, 1980.

Freud, Sigmund. "The Economic Problem of Masochism." Vol. 19. *The Standard Edition* 157–70.

———. "A Hat as a Symbol of a Man (or of Male Genitals)." *Interpretation of Dreams*. Vol. 5. *The Standard Edition* 360–62.

———. "Instincts and Their Vicissitudes." Vol. 14. *The Standard Edition* 111–40.

———. *Jokes and Their Relation to the Unconscious.* Vol. 8. *The Standard Edition.*

———. *The Standard Edition of the Complete Works of Sigmund Freud.* Trans. James Strachey. London: Hogarth, 1953.

Frisch, Michael, and Milton Rogovin. *Portraits in Steel.* Ithaca, NY: Cornell UP, 1993.

The Full Monty. Dir. Peter Cattaneo. Written by Simon Beaufoy. Perf. Mark Addy, Paul Barber, Robert Carlyle, Steve Huison, Hugo Speer, and Tom Wilkinson. Fox/Searchlight Pictures/Redway Films, 1997.

Gates, David. *Newsweek* 16 January 1997: 55.

Gay, Peter. *The Tender Passion.* Vol. 2. *The Bourgeois Experience: Victoria to Freud.* New York: Oxford UP, 1986.

Genette, Gérard. *Figures of Literary Discourse.* Trans. Alan Sheridan. New York: Columbia UP, 1982.

Gilbert, Sandra, and Susan Gubar, eds. *The Norton Anthology of Writing by Women: The Traditions in English.* 2nd ed. New York: Norton, 1996.

Gilligan, Carol. *In a Different Voice: Psychological Theory and Women's Development.* Cambridge: Harvard UP, 1982.

Goffman, Erving. *Forms of Talk.* Oxford: Blackwell, 1981.

Grant, A. J. "Vico and Bultmann on Myth: The Problem with Demythologizing." *Rhetoric Society Quarterly* 30 (2000): 49–82.

Grimes, Mary C. Introduction. *The Knights in Fiction: Two Labor Novels of the 1880s.* Urbana: U of Illinois P, 1986. 1–26.

Hamilton, Cynthia. "Work and Culture: The Evolution of Consciousness in Urban Industrial Society in the Fiction of William Attaway and Peter Abrahams." *Black American Literature Forum* 21.1 (Spring 1987): 147–63.

Haraway, Donna Jeane. *Primate Visions.* New York: Routledge, 1991.

"Hard Work Can't Stop Hard Times." *New York Times* 25 November 1990: A1.

Harper, Phillip Brian. *Are We Not Men? Masculine Anxiety and the Problem of African-American Identity.* New York: Oxford UP, 1996.

Hartman, Saidiya. *Scenes of Subjection: Terror, Slavery, and Self-Making in Nineteenth-Century America.* New York: Oxford UP, 1997.

Havelock, Eric. *Preface to Plato.* Cambridge: Harvard UP, 1963.

Haywood, Harry. *Black Bolshevik: Autobiography of an Afro-American Communist.* Chicago: Liberator, 1978.

Heidegger, Martin. *An Introduction to Metaphysics.* New Haven, CT: Yale UP, 1959.

Henderson, Greig E. *Kenneth Burke: Literature and Language as Symbolic Action.* Athens: U of Georgia P, 1988.

Hendrick, Burton J. *The Life of Andrew Carnegie.* New York: Doubleday, 1932.

Hilberg, Raul. *The Destruction of the European Jews.* Chicago: Quadrangle Books, 1961.

Hoerr, John P. *And the Wolf Finally Came: The Decline of the American Steel Industry.* Pittsburgh: U of Pittsburgh P, 1988.

"Homer's Phobia." *The Simpsons.* With John Waters. 16 February 1997.

Hutcheon, Linda. *The Politics of Postmodernism.* London: Routledge, 1989.

Iacocca, Lee. *Iacocca: An Autobiography.* New York: Bantam, 1984.

———. *Talking Straight.* New York: Bantam, 1988.

Ingham, John N. *The Iron Barons: A Social Analysis of an American Urban Elite, 1874–1965.* Westport, CT: Greenwood, 1978.

———. *Making Iron and Steel: Independent Mills in Pittsburgh, 1820–1920.* Columbus, OH: Ohio State UP, 1991.

Inglis, Fred. *Cultural Studies.* Oxford: Blackwell, 1993.

Ivie, Robert. *Congress Declares War: Rhetoric, Leadership, and Partisanship in the Early Republic.* Kent, OH: Kent State UP, 1983.

———. "Metaphor and Mythic Fear: Harry S. Truman's Cold War Legacy." 1994 Giles Wilkeson Gray Lectures. Louisiana State U. 9 March 1994.

Jameson, Frederic. "The Symbolic Inference; or, Kenneth Burke and Ideological Analysis." White and Bros 68–91.

Jarratt, Susan C. "In Excess: Radical Extensions of Neopragmatism." Mailloux, *Rhetoric, Sophistry, Pragmatism* 206–27.

———. *Rereading the Sophists: Classical Rhetoric Refigured.* Carbondale: Southern Illinois UP, 1991.

Johnson, Daniel M., and Rex R. Campbell. *Black Migration in America: A Social Demographic History.* Durham, NC: Duke UP, 1981.

Josephson, Matthew. *The Robber Barons.* New York: Harcourt, 1934.

Junger, Sebastian. *The Perfect Storm: A True Story of Men Against the Sea.* New York: Norton, 1997.

Kelland, Clarence Budington. *Dynasty.* New York: Harper, 1929.

Kempton, Murray. *Part of Our Time: Some Ruins and Monuments of the Thirties.* New York: Simon, 1955.

Kerferd, G. B. *The Sophistic Movement.* Cambridge: Cambridge UP, 1981.

Kiam, Victor. *Going for It!: How to Succeed as an Entrepreneur.* New York: William Morrow, 1986.

Kibbey, Ann, and Michele Stepto. "The Antilanguage of Slavery: Frederick Douglass's 1845 *Narrative.*" Andrews 166–91.

Kimmel, Michael S., ed. *Changing Men: New Directions in Research and Masculinity.* 5th ed. Newbury Park, CA: Sage, 1987.

———. "The Contemporary 'Crisis' of Masculinity." Brod, *The Making of Masculinities* 121–53.

———. *Manhood in America: A Cultural History.* New York: The Free Press, 1995.

———, ed. *The Politics of Manhood: Profeminist Men Respond to the Mythopoetic Men's Movement (And the Mythopoetic Leaders Answer).* Philadelphia: Temple UP, 1995.

Krakauer, Jon. *Into Thin Air: A Personal Account of the Mount Everest Disaster.* New York: Villard, 1997.

Kristeva, Julia. *Revolution in Poetic Language.* Trans. Margaret Waller. New York: Columbia UP, 1984.

Lacan, Jacques. *Feminine Sexuality: Jacques Lacan and the école freudienne.* 1982. Ed. Juliet Mitchell and Jacqueline Rose. Trans. Jacqueline Rose. New York: Norton, 1985.

LaPlanche, J., and J. B. Pontalis. *The Language of Psycho-Analysis*. Trans. Donald Nicholson-Smith. New York: Norton, 1973.

Lavelle, Michael. *Red, White and Blue-Collar Views: A Steelworker Speaks His Mind about America*. New York: Saturday Review, 1975.

Layton, Lynne. "Trauma, Gender Identity, and Sexuality: Discourses of Fragmentation." *American Imago* 52.1 (Spring 1995): 107–25.

Leff, Michael C. "Modern Sophistic and the Unity of Rhetoric." Nelson, Megill, and McCloskey 18–37.

Lentricchia, Frank. "Reading History with Kenneth Burke." White and Bros 119–49.

Leverenz, David. *Manhood and the American Renaissance*. Ithaca, NY: Cornell UP, 1989.

Lincoln, Bruce. *Theorizing Myth: Narrative, Ideology, and Scholarship*. Chicago: U of Chicago P, 1999.

Lipsitz, George. *Time Passages: Collective Memory and American Popular Culture*. Minneapolis: U of Minnesota P, 1990.

"Liquor Giant Bert Wheeler Dies in Texas." *Baton Rouge Morning Advocate* 30 July 1996: B8.

Livesay, Harold C. *Andrew Carnegie and the Rise of Big Business*. Boston: Little, 1975.

Lyman, Peter. "The Fraternal Bond as a Joking Relationship: A Case Study of the Role of Sexist Jokes in Male Group Bonding." Kimmel, *Changing Men* 148–63.

Lyotard, Jean-François. *The Postmodern Condition: A Report on Knowledge*. Trans. Geoff Bennington and Brian Massumi. Minneapolis: U of Minnesota P, 1984.

Mailloux, Steven. *Reception Histories: Rhetoric, Pragmatism, and American Cultural Politics*. Ithaca, NY: Cornell UP, 1998.

———, ed. *Rhetoric, Sophistry, Pragmatism*. Cambridge: Cambridge UP, 1995.

Martin, Waldo E., Jr. *The Mind of Frederick Douglass*. Chapel Hill: U of North Carolina P, 1984.

Massé, Michelle. *In the Name of Love: Women, Masochism, and the Gothic*. Ithaca, NY: Cornell UP, 1992.

Mbalia, Doreatha D. *John Edgar Wideman: Reclaiming the African Personality*. Selinsgrove, PA: Susquehanna UP, 1995.

McDowell, Deborah E. "In the First Place: Making Frederick Douglass and the Afro-American Narrative Tradition." Andrews 192–214.

McDowell, Deborah, and Arnold Rampersad, eds. *Slavery and the Literary Imagination*. Baltimore: Johns Hopkins UP, 1989.

Miller, Susan. *The Good Mother*. New York: Harper, 1986.

Misa, Thomas J. *A Nation of Steel: The Making of Modern America, 1865–1925*. Baltimore: Johns Hopkins UP, 1995.

Mitchell, Juliet. "Introduction—I." Mitchell and Rose 1–26.

———. *Woman's Estate*. New York: Random, 1971.

Mitchell, Juliet, and Jacqueline Rose, eds. *Feminine Sexuality: Jacques Lacan and the* école freudienne. 1982. New York: Norton, 1985.

Mohrmann, G. P. "An Essay on Fantasy Theme Criticism." *Quarterly Journal of Speech* 68 (1982): 109–32.

Montgomery, David. Afterword. Whittaker, *Larry Locke* 327–30.

———. *Beyond Equality: Labor and the Radical Republicans, 1862–1872*. New York: Vintage, 1967.

———. *Citizen Worker: The Experience of Workers in the United States with Democracy and the Free Market During the Nineteenth Century*. New York: Cambridge UP, 1993.

———. *The Fall of the House of Labor: The Workplace, the State, and American Labor Activism, 1865–1925*. New York: Cambridge UP, 1987.

Morrison, Toni. *Playing in the Dark: Whiteness and the Literary Imagination*. New York: Vintage, 1992.

Moses, Wilson J. "Writing Freely?: Frederick Douglass and the Constraints of Racialized Writing." Sundquist 66–83.

Mulvey, Laura. *Visual and Other Pleasures*. Bloomington: Indiana UP, 1989.

Myre, Greg. "Business School Touts Capitalism in Russia." Associated Press. *Baton Rouge Morning Advocate* 8 March 1998: A16.

Nackenoff, Carol. *The Fictional Republic: Horatio Alger and American Political Discourse*. New York: Oxford UP, 1994.

Nelson, John S., Allen Megill, and Donald N. McCloskey, eds. *The Rhetoric of the Human Sciences*. Madison: U of Wisconsin P, 1987.

Newsweek 28 October 1991: 23.

New York Times 27 September 1998: 3, 1.

Nietzsche, Friedrich. "Lecture Notes on Rhetoric." Trans. Carole Blair. *Philosophy and Rhetoric* 16 (1983): 94–129.

Olney, James. "The Founding Fathers—Frederick Douglass and Booker T. Washington." McDowell and Rampersad 1–24.

———. "'I was born': Slave Narratives, Their Status as Autobiography, and as Literature." Davis and Gates 148–75.

Ostwald, Martin. *Nomos and the Beginnings of the Athenian Democracy*. Oxford: Clarendon, 1969.

O'Toole, Patricia. "Son of 'Iacocca.'" *New York Times Book Review* 17 July 1988: 11.

Pleck, Joseph. *The Myth of Masculinity*. Cambridge: MIT P, 1981.

Porter, Connie. *All-Bright Court*. Boston: Houghton, 1991.

Potter, Jonathan. *Representing Reality: Discourse, Rhetoric, and Social Construction*. Thousand Oaks, CA: Sage, 1996.

Poulakos, John. *Sophistical Rhetoric in Classical Greece*. Columbia: U of South Carolina P, 1995.

Poulakos, Takis. "Human Agency in the History of Rhetoric." Vitanza, *Writing Histories of Rhetoric* 59–80.

———. "Recovering the Voices of the Text: Rhetorical Critique as Ideological Critique." Wenzel 39–44.

Powderly, Terence V. *The Path I Trod: The Autobiography of Terence V. Powderly*. Ed. Harry J. Carman, Henry David, and Paul N. Guthrie. New York: Columbia UP, 1940.

Preston, Richard. *American Steel: Hot Metal Men and the Resurrection of the Rust Belt.* New York: Prentice Hall, 1991.

———. *The Hot Zone.* 1994. New York: Random, 1996.

Quarles, Benjamin. *Frederick Douglass.* Washington: Associated Publishers, 1948.

Rankin, H. D. *Sophists, Socratics, and Cynics.* Totowa, NJ: Barnes and Noble, 1983.

Ricoeur, Paul. *Hermeneutics and the Human Sciences: Essays on Language, Action, and Interpretation.* Ed./Trans. John B. Thompson. Cambridge: Cambridge UP, 1981.

———. *Oneself as Another.* Trans. Kathleen Blamey. Chicago: U of Chicago P, 1992.

Riding, Allen. "A Man Who's True to His Convictions." Arts and Leisure. *New York Times on the Web.* 6 August 1997. <http://www.nytimes.com>.

Rodgers, Daniel T. *The Work Ethic in Industrial America, 1850–1920.* Chicago: U of Chicago P, 1974.

Roediger, David R. *The Wages of Whiteness: Race and the Making of the American Working Class.* New York: Verso, 1991.

Roman, Camille. "Female Sexual Drives, Subjectivity, and Language: The Dialogue with/beyond Freud and Lacan." Roman, Juhasz, and Miller 7–19.

Roman, Camille, Suzanne Juhasz, and Cristanne Miller, eds. *The Women and Language Debate: A Sourcebook.* New Brunswick, NJ: Rutgers UP, 1994.

Rose, Jacqueline. "Introduction—II." Mitchell and Rose 27–57.

———. *Sexuality in the Field of Vision.* London: Verso, 1986.

Rosenfield, Lawrence. "An Autopsy of the Rhetorical Tradition." *The Prospect of Rhetoric.* Bitzer and Black 64–77.

Rotundo, Anthony E. *American Manhood: Transformations in Masculinity from the Revolution to the Modern Era.* New York: Basic, 1993.

Rueckert, William. *Critical Responses to Kenneth Burke: 1924–1966.* Minneapolis: U of Minnesota P, 1969.

———. *Kenneth Burke and the Drama of Human Relations.* 1963. 2nd ed. Berkeley: U of California P, 1982.

Savran, David. *Taking It Like a Man: White Masculinity, Masochism, and Contemporary American Culture.* Princeton: Princeton UP, 1998.

Schapiro, Barbara Ann. *Literature and the Relational Self.* New York: New York UP, 1994.

Scharnhorst, Gary, and Jack Bales. *The Lost Life of Horatio Alger, Jr.* Bloomington: Indiana UP, 1985.

Schiappa, Edward. "Isocrates' *Philosophia* and Contemporary Pragmatism." Mailloux, *Rhetoric, Sophistry, Pragmatism* 33–60.

———. *Protagoras and Logos: A Study in Greek Philosophy and Rhetoric.* Columbia: U of South Carolina P, 1991.

Schneider, Linda. "The Citizen Striker: Workers' Ideology in the Homestead Strike of 1892." *Labor History* 23 (1982): 47–66.

Sedgwick, Eve Kosofsky. *Between Men: English Literature and Male Homosocial Desire.* New York: Columbia UP, 1985.

Sherrod, Drury. "The Bonds of Men: Problems and Possibilities in Close Male Relationships." Brod, *The Making of Masculinities* 213–39.

Showalter, Elaine, ed. *The New Feminist Criticism: Essays on Women, Literature, and Theory.* New York: Pantheon, 1985.

Silverman, Kaja. *Male Subjectivity at the Margins.* New York: Routledge, 1992.

———. *The Subject of Semiotics.* Oxford: Oxford UP, 1983.

Smith, Valerie. *Self-Discovery and Authority in Afro-American Narrative.* Cambridge: Harvard UP, 1987.

Spero, Sterling D., and Abram L. Harris. *The Black Worker: The Negro and the Labor Movement.* New York: Columbia UP, 1931. Rpt. Port Washington, NY: Kennikat, 1966.

Starr, Mark. "The King of the Ghosts." *Newsweek* 25 January 1988: 67.

Stecopolous, Harry, and Michael Uebel, eds. *Race and the Subject of Masculinity.* Durham, NC: Duke UP, 1998.

Sundquist, Eric J., ed. *Frederick Douglass: New Literary and Historical Essays.* Cambridge: Cambridge UP, 1990.

Swetnam, George. *Andrew Carnegie.* Boston: Twayne, 1980.

Terminator 2: Judgment Day. Dir. James Cameron. Perf. Arnold Schwarzenegger, Linda Hamilton, Robert Patrick, and Brad Fiedel. Cameron Pictures, 1991.

Thanet, Octave [Alice French]. *The Man of the Hour.* Indianapolis: Bobbs Merrill, 1905.

Thomas, John L. Introduction. Bellamy 1–89.

Tichi, Cecelia. Foreword. Carnegie, *Autobiography* xi–xvi.

———. *Shifting Gears.* Chapel Hill: U of North Carolina P, 1987.

Todorov, Tzvetan. *Théories du Symbole.* Paris: Éditions du Seuil, 1977.

———. *Theories of the Symbol.* 1977. Trans. Catherine Porter. Ithaca, NY: Cornell UP, 1982.

Townsend, Kim. *Manhood at Harvard: William James and Others.* New York: Norton, 1996.

Trachtenberg, Alan. *The Incorporation of America: Culture and Society in the Gilded Age.* New York: Hill and Wang, 1982.

Truth, Sojourner. "Ain't I a Woman?" Gilbert and Gubar 370.

Turner, Ralph H. "Sponsored and Contest Mobility and the School System." *American Sociological Review* 25 (1960): 855–67.

Untersteiner, Mario. *The Sophists.* 1948. Trans. Kathleen Freeman. Oxford: Basil Blackwell, 1954.

The Valley of Decision. Dir. Tay Garnett. Perf. Greer Garson and Gregory Peck. MGM, 1945.

Van Dijk, Teun A., ed. *Discourse Studies: A Multidisciplinary Introduction.* 2 Vols. Thousand Oaks, CA: Sage, 1997.

Van Dyke, John C. Editor's Note. Carnegie, *Autobiography* ix–x.

Van Leer, David. "Reading Slavery: The Anxiety of Ethnicity in Douglass's *Narrative.*" Sundquist 118–40.

Vickers, Brian. *In Defense of Rhetoric.* Oxford: Clarendon, 1988.

Vitanza, Victor. *Negation, Subjectivity, and the History of Rhetoric.* Albany: State U of New York P, 1997.

———, ed. *Writing Histories of Rhetoric*. Carbondale: Southern Illinois UP, 1994.

Walker, Peter F. *Moral Choices: Memory, Desire, and Imagination in Nineteenth-Century American Abolition*. Baton Rouge: Louisiana State UP, 1978.

Wall, Joseph Frazier. *Andrew Carnegie*. New York: Oxford UP, 1970.

Wenzel, Joseph W., ed. *Argument and Critical Practices: Proceedings of the Fifth SCA/AFA Conference on Argumentation*. Annandale, VA: SCA, 1987.

West, Cornel. *The American Evasion of Philosophy: A Genealogy of Pragmatism*. Madison: U of Wisconsin P, 1989.

White, C. S. "Opening Ode for Knights of Labor." 1881. Rpt. in Foner, *American Labor Songs* 146.

White, Hayden. *Tropics of Discourse: Essays in Cultural Criticism*. Baltimore: Johns Hopkins UP, 1985.

White, Hayden, and Margaret Bros, eds. *Representing Kenneth Burke*. Baltimore: Johns Hopkins UP, 1982.

Whittaker, Captain Frederick. *John Armstrong, Mechanic; or, From the Bottom to the Top of the Ladder: A Story of How a Man Can Rise in America*. *Beadle's Weekly* #1–12 (18 November 1882–3 February 1883).

———. *A Knight of Labor; or, Job Manly's Rise in Life: A Story of a Young Man from the Country*. *Beadle's Weekly* #74–85 (12 April 1884–28 June 1884).

———. *Larry Locke: Man of Iron; or, A Fight for Fortune: A Story of Labor and Capital*. *Beadle's Weekly* #50–61 (27 October 1883–12 January 1884). Rpt. in *The Knights in Fiction: Two Labor Novels of the 1880s*. Ed. Mary C. Grimes. Urbana: U of Illinois P, 1986.

Wideman, John Edgar. *Brothers and Keepers*. New York: Holt, Rinehart and Winston, 1984.

———. *Damballah*. 1981. *Homewood Books*. U of Pittsburgh P, 1992.

———. *Fatheralong: A Meditation on Fathers and Sons, Race and Society*. New York: Pantheon, 1994.

———. *Fever*. New York: Penguin, 1989. Rpt. Wideman, *Stories* 145–266.

———. *Hiding Place*. 1981. *Homewood Books*. U of Pittsburgh P, 1992.

———. *Homewood Books*. U of Pittsburgh P, 1992.

———. "Picking Up My Father at the Springfield Station." *Fatheralong* 129–76.

———. *Reuben*. New York: Henry Holt, 1987.

———. *Sent for You Yesterday*. 1983. *Homewood Books*. U of Pittsburgh P, 1992.

———. *The Stories of John Edgar Wideman*. New York: Pantheon, 1992.

———. *Two Cities*. Boston: Houghton, 1998.

———. "Welcome." *Stories of John Edgar Wideman*. New York: Pantheon, 1992.

Wiegman, Robyn. *American Anatomies: Theorizing Race and Gender*. Durham, NC: Duke UP, 1995.

Will, George. "They Weren't Obeying Social Imperatives." *Baton Rouge Advocate* 18 May 1995: B17.

Williams, Raymond. *Marxism and Literature*. New York: Oxford UP, 1977.

Wolff, Leon. *Lockout: The Study of the Homestead Strike of 1892: A Study of Violence, Unionism, and the Carnegie Steel Empire*. New York: Harper, 1965.

Worsham, Lynn. "Eating History, Purging Memory, Killing Rhetoric." Vitanza, *Writing Histories of Rhetoric* 139–55.

Wright, Carroll D. "The Amalgamated Association of Iron and Steel Workers." *Quarterly Journal of Economics* 7 (July 1893): 400–432.

Wylie, Philip. *Generation of Vipers*. New York: Farrar and Rinehart, 1942.

Wyllie, Irvin G. *The Self-Made Man in America: The Myth of Rags to Riches*. New Brunswick, NJ: Rutgers UP, 1954.

Yarborough, Richard. Afterword. Attaway 295–315.

———. "Race, Violence, and Manhood: The Masculine Ideal in Frederick Douglass's 'The Heroic Slave.'" Sundquist 166–88.

Ziolkowski, Thad. "Antithesis: The Dialectic of Violence and Literacy in Frederick Douglass's *Narrative* of 1845." Andrews 148–65.

Index

James V. Catano is a professor of English and a member of the Women's and Gender Studies Program at Louisiana State University, Baton Rouge. He is the author of *Language, History, Style: Leo Spitzer and the Critical Tradition.*